McGraw Hill

New York City

SHSAT

McGraw Hill
New York City
SHSAT

Fourth Edition

Drew D. Johnson

New York Chicago San Francisco Athens London Madrid
Mexico City Milan New Delhi Singapore Sydney Toronto

1 2 3 4 5 6 7 8 9 LOV 27 26 25 24 23 22

ISBN 978-1-264-28575-4
MHID 1-264-28575-2

e-ISBN 978-1-264-28576-1
e-MHID 1-264-28576-0

CONTENTS

PART 1

Getting Started

PART 2

SHSAT Diagnostic Test

PART 3

SHSAT Topic Reviews

ABOUT THE AUTHOR

Drew Johnson is cofounder of Anaxos Inc., an Austin-based company specializing in test-preparation material for all major standardized tests.

McGraw Hill
New York City
SHSAT

PART 1

Getting Started

CHAPTER 1

All About the Specialized High School Admissions Test

Before you know it, you'll be walking the halls of high school. The four years you spend there will undoubtedly be exciting and memorable. Although there are more than 400 high schools in New York City, there are only nine New York City Specialized High Schools. Entrance into these elite, free schools is extremely competitive. In order to be admitted into eight of these programs, students must pass the Specialized High Schools Admissions Test (SHSAT). In fact, this test is the only factor considered in whether or not students are accepted into these schools.

Schools that require students to take the SHSAT are:

- The Bronx High School of Science
- The Brooklyn Latin School
- Brooklyn Technical High School
- High School of Mathematics, Science and Engineering at City College of New York
- High School of American Studies at Lehman College
- Queens High School for the Sciences at York College
- Staten Island Technical High School
- Stuyvesant High School

These schools are run by the New York City Department of Education and were created in order to better meet the needs of gifted students in New York City. Each of the schools has its own unique characteristics. Several offer programs focusing on math and science in addition to the courses that are required by the state. Each of these schools has an outstanding reputation and offers students a competitive advantage when applying for college. Many college credit and advanced placement (AP) courses are offered. Also, the Specialized High Schools allow students to focus on the fields that interest them.

New York City's Specialized High Schools have been attended by a number of people who have gone on to make extraordinary achievements in many fields. These graduates include Nobel Laureates, politicians, award-winning actors and actresses, musicians, sports figures, and even an astronaut. Students earning the opportunity to graduate from one of these schools are definitely in good company and are taking steps toward a promising future.

Taking the Test

The SHSAT is generally given in late October for eighth grade students, and in November for ninth grade students who have taken the test in the past and not been accepted into one of the programs. Actual test dates are not released until late in the previous school year. If you plan to take the test, you must register for it through the guidance counselor at your current middle school.

In order to take the SHSAT and be considered for one of the Specialized High Schools, you must live in the Bronx, Brooklyn, Manhattan, Queens, or Staten Island. Because admission into these schools is extremely competitive, being prepared for the SHSAT is a must. Test scores are ranked highest to lowest, with students receiving the highest scores being placed into their first choice school. So, the higher your score, the better your chances of being invited to attend the school you are most interested in. Generally, only about 15 to 20 percent of the students who take the SHSAT are placed into one of the Specialized High Schools each year. That's less than one in five students who take the test. The best way to make sure that your score is near the top of the list is to be prepared.

About 29,000 students took the SHSAT for the September 2019 admission and approximately 5,000 students received an offer. Of those, fewer than 20 percent were accepted into one of the Specialized High Schools. You will only have one chance to take the test during eighth grade and possibly one chance during ninth grade. Since there are fewer open spots in tenth grade, the competition for ninth graders taking the test is even tougher. Knowing as much as possible about what to expect and preparing early for the test will help to increase your chances of doing your very best.

What to Expect on the SHSAT

Although the SHSAT consists of English Language Arts (ELA) and math questions, these questions are different from what you would generally expect to see on a test. Many of the questions require you to use reasoning skills and logic in a way that you usually do not have to in school. This helps determine which students will perform best in a rigorous academic program.

The skills covered on the test are usually part of the eighth grade curriculum. However, since the test is taken early in the school year, they may not have been taught by the time you take the test. Although many of the Specialized High Schools focus on science, there are no science questions on the test. Some of the reading passages may address science topics, but the test will not assess your knowledge of science.

On test day, you will have three hours to complete the SHSAT. The test is divided into two sections, ELA and Mathematics, but there is no break between the two sessions. You may start with either section and divide your time between the tests in any way you choose. You may move on to the next section whenever you are ready, and you may go back to check your work on the first section after you have completed the second, if time allows.

The following table will give you an idea of how the test is set up:

NUMBER OF QUESTIONS	
ELA: Two revising/editing passages	12–16
ELA: Standalone revising/editing	5–8
ELA: Reading Comprehension	30–35
Mathematics	57

English Language Arts (ELA) Section

There are 57 questions in the ELA section of the test. These are divided into two categories: revising/editing and reading comprehension. The revising/editing category will consist of 20 questions. There will be two passages with 6–8 questions relating to each passage as well as 5–8 stand-alone questions. All the questions will be multiple choice questions. These questions will test your writing skills and your analytical skills. You will be expected to improve the writing quality of paragraphs and to correct errors so that the paragraphs follow the conventions of standard written English.

The second part of the ELA section will assess your reading comprehension. There will be six passages with five to seven comprehension questions after each. These 30–40 items measure how well you are able to understand and interpret information you have read. All of the passages you read in this section will be nonfiction.

Math Section

The Math section includes 57 multiple choice problems that assess your understanding of the New York City math curriculum. There will be 52 multiple choice questions as well as 5 "grid-in" questions. Instead of choosing from a list of possible options, for the 5 grid-in questions you will be expected to solve a problem and provide the answer by filling in a grid with the correct numerical solution. Students taking the Grade 8 SHSAT are tested on NYC mathematics curriculum through Grade 7. Students taking the Grade 9 SHSAT are responsible for mathematics material covered through the eighth grade New York City Mathematics Curriculum.

The diagnostic test and the two practice tests in this book are designed to cover only Grade 8 SHSAT mathematics. The last chapter of this book has 30 questions that test your understanding of the additional mathematics content that is tested in the Grade 9 SHSAT.

Ranking Schools

On the day of the test, you will rank the Specialized High Schools of your choice on the back of your Admissions Ticket according to which you are most interested in attending. This list must be signed by your parent or guardian. Make sure you know ahead of time which school or schools you would like to apply for, and prioritize your choices. You may choose to select only one, or as many as eight of the schools. You may not change your choices after testing day.

Ranking the schools is extremely important because you will only be assigned to one particular school. Acceptance into the schools is based first on the score you earn on the SHSAT and second on the ranking you have given to the school. Before you rank the schools, there are several things you should take into consideration. Think about:

- Your interests and goals
- Which programs are offered at each school
- The schools' locations
- Commuting options available to each school
- Extracurricular activities
- Sports and other programs available

Make sure you have researched each school's website to make the best choice. Call the school or schools you are interested in and try to arrange to visit them ahead of time.

> Be sure to rank as many of the schools as you are interested in attending to increase your chances of being accepted into one of the programs. If you only rank one school and there are no seats available by the time you are placed, you will not be able to attend any of the specialized schools.

Once the test is completed, you will not have the opportunity to change the rankings. Keep in mind that even if you are assigned to a school that was not your first choice, all of these schools are very competitive and offer excellent programs and an outstanding educational experience.

Test Day

On the day of the test, be sure to bring your signed Admission Ticket, with your school choices marked. You will also need several sharpened number 2 pencils, an eraser, and a watch that does not have a calculator. Calculators, cell phones, beepers, and pagers will not be allowed to be brought into the test. NYC public school students will also need to provide their student ID number. In addition to the test booklet and answer sheet, the testing center will provide scratch paper that will be collected after the test.

Test Scores

SHSAT scores are reported as *scaled scores*. These scores are based on how many correct answers you had on the test. All questions are worth one point. These points, known as the *raw score*, are combined with the questions' level of difficulty. (There is no penalty for wrong answers.) A formula is used to assign a scaled score based on these factors. The scaled scores for the ELA and math sections are then added together, giving a composite score of up to 800 points.

> You are likely to have a different test with different questions than the people sitting near you. There are several versions of the test. Scaled scores account for these different versions of the test.

You are probably wondering what score you have to earn to get into one of the specialized high schools. Actually, there is not a specific score that guarantees the opportunity to attend one of these schools. Placement is based on how well each student scores on the test.

As you know, student scores are ranked highest to lowest. The student with the highest score is placed into a school first, followed by the student with the second highest score, and so on. Students are placed into their first choice school if there is a spot available. If not, they will be placed into their second choice school. If that school is also full, they will be placed into their third choice, and so on, until all of the spots in all of the schools have been filled. The number of students accepted into each school varies by year. In the fall of 2019, some of the schools accepted approximately 120 freshmen, while others accepted as many as 1,800.

In the February following the test, results will be sent to your current school. Students whose scores earn placement in one of the Specialized High Schools will be offered a seat in a particular school. The offer must be accepted or declined. Students who choose to decline the offer will *not* be offered a chance to attend another of the Specialized High Schools. Once you accept a seat in one of the Specialized High Schools, you must stay at that school for at least one year.

Preparing for the Test

Now that you know what to expect on the SHSAT, you are ready to prepare yourself. Each type of question on the test will be discussed in its own chapter of this book. You will find practice questions, strategies for answering the items, and tips for doing your best on the test. Carefully read through each chapter, become familiar with the format of the assessment, take the practice tests, and discover your areas of strength, as well as what skills you need to review before test day. Being well prepared will make you more comfortable, increase your confidence, and improve your chances of earning the best possible score on the SHSAT. Now, let's get started!

CHAPTER 2

SHSAT Test-Taking Strategies

Throughout this book, you will learn many skills, definitions, and formulas that you need to know in order to do your best on the SHSAT. You will learn what material will be tested and the types of questions to expect. You are off to a great start in preparing for the test!

In this chapter, we'll talk about a few test-taking strategies that can help you be successful as you prepare for and take the SHSAT. As you read, think about which of these strategies will be most beneficial to you. Everyone is different. Everyone learns differently. And everyone tests differently. Find tips that you think can help you do your best on the SHSAT.

Preparing for the Test

Doing well on a test does not begin on test day. Doing well begins in the weeks and months prior to the test as you study and prepare. This is probably not news to you, since you have already begun to prepare by working through the chapters and practice items in this book. So give yourself a pat on the back, because you are already off to a great start! Now let's talk about a few other things you can do to make sure you are ready for the big day.

Look Ahead

The arithmetic, algebra, geometry, and probability and statistics questions you will find on the SHSAT involve skills that are generally a part of the eighth grade math curriculum, which means that these are all skills you will learn by the end of eighth grade. However, you will be taking the SHSAT toward the beginning of eighth grade, before many of these skills are covered in class. So, what should you do? Look ahead in your math textbook. Find out what you will be learning throughout the year, and determine which skills you are already comfortable with and which you should practice before test day. If you are not yet in eighth grade, borrow a textbook from your school, a friend, or the library. Be sure to look through the glossary as well as the chapters.

Keep in mind that it usually takes a year to learn a whole textbook full of material. You may or may not have that long between now and the time you take the SHSAT. Pace yourself accordingly. There are probably a lot of things you know well already, so a quick review will be sufficient. There may be other things that you will need to spend a little more time learning.

In addition to looking ahead in a textbook, check out the state math standards online. Find out what eighth grade students are expected to know, and make notes of the areas you need to learn more about.

Know the Terms

As you will read repeatedly throughout the practice tests in this book, mathematical terms and formulas will not be provided on the SHSAT. Review these ahead of time. Look at the glossary in your math textbook or find the definitions in this book. Write down terms, definitions, symbols, and formulas on a chart or on flash cards, and then memorize them. Quiz yourself or ask your parents or friends to quiz you.

Remember That Practice Makes Perfect

Practice solving different types of math problems each day. Do some fairly simple questions and some that are more difficult. Do not just practice skills with which you are already comfortable. Try some new things to stretch your knowledge. The more you practice, the more comfortable you will become with the skills.

Read, Read, Read!

Read a variety of materials, such as books, magazines, fiction, and nonfiction. This is a great way to expose yourself to new vocabulary words. If you find unfamiliar words, use context clues to determine their meaning, then look the words up in a dictionary to be sure you are correct. Even though you will not be expected to read fiction on the SHSAT, reading good fiction is still a terrific way to expand your vocabulary.

Ask Yourself Questions

As you read, ask yourself questions to monitor your own comprehension. Ask yourself what the main idea of a passage is, what facts and details help support the main idea, what the author's purpose might have been for writing the piece, and so on. Do this as you read self-selected materials, as well as when doing required reading for class. Your science and history textbooks offer excellent opportunities for checking your reading comprehension, as well as learning new words and information.

Pretend It Is Test Day

Set aside three hours to do a practice run of the test. Find a quiet place where you will not be disturbed, set the timer, and begin taking one of the practice tests in this book. Not only will you find out how well you know the material, you will also see which parts of the test take the most time for you to complete. Did you finish the ELA questions quickly? Awesome! Did you find that you needed a little bit more time for math? Great information to have! Did you finish the test with enough time left to check your work? Super! All of this information will help you know how to pace yourself on the day of the actual test.

Study Your Mistakes

Everyone makes mistakes. Take the practice tests in this book, and then check your work. If you made a mistake, don't sweat it! This can be an awesome learning tool. Take every opportunity to learn from your mistakes. Reread each question and the correct answer. Notice which types of questions you answered correctly, and which types were incorrect. This will help you find areas in which you need practice. For example, if you missed several algebra questions, you know that a review of algebra skills would be helpful.

Use your tests, quizzes, and assignments in school to learn from your mistakes as well. Pay close attention to the types of skills that trip you up, and spend some time learning how to answer these questions correctly in the future.

Get Some Rest

Make sure you get plenty of sleep the night before the test. It may be tempting to stay up all night to study, but in actuality, it is probably best not to study too much the day before the test. Study, study, study in the weeks and months ahead of time. Then, take it easy the day before the big day. Look over your notes, do a quick review, glance over the vocabulary and formulas, but only spend an hour or so doing this. Then give your brain a break. Take a walk, call a friend, or shoot some hoops.

If you are concerned that you won't be able to sleep if you go to bed early the night before the SHSAT, try getting up extra early the previous morning. That way, you'll be tired before your usual bedtime and have a better chance of catching some extra z's.

Things to Remember on Test Day

You know how to prepare for the test, and you're ready to answer the questions carefully and accurately. Here are a few more things to keep in mind on the day you take the SHSAT.

Before You Leave Home

Making sure you are ready for the test can be as easy as A, B, C!

- **Admission Ticket.** Check your Admission Ticket to find out which test site you have been assigned to and what time you are expected to arrive. Bring the ticket with you to the test. Make sure you have ranked the Specialized High Schools of your choice on the back of the ticket and the list has been signed by your parent or guardian.
- **Breakfast.** Having a nutritious breakfast before the test is important. You need the energy to focus on doing your best, and you don't want a growling stomach to take any of your attention. Even if you don't feel like having a huge meal, at least grab some fruit and trail mix, yogurt and granola, or a smoothie.
- **Clothes.** Wear something that makes you feel good and gives you confidence. You certainly don't want to wear something that is too tight or leaves you feeling too warm or too cold. Consider dressing in layers and bringing a lightweight sweater or jacket. Also, wear a watch if you have one. That way, you will be able to easily keep track of how much time is left during the test.

At the Test Center

Once you get to the test center, there are a few things to keep in mind before you begin taking the test.

- If you get to the test center and do not feel well enough to take the test, be sure to tell the proctor right away. You may not request a makeup test due to illness if you have already begun the test. If you are not feeling well, immediately let the proctor know so your test can be rescheduled. If you start taking the test, no matter how few questions you have answered, you will not be able to reschedule it.
- When instructed to "bubble in" your name, be sure to fill it in as it appears in your school records. Do not use your nickname. For example, if school records indicate that your name is Christopher, fill in *Christopher* on your test, even though your friends and family may call you Chris, CJ, or Junior.
- Make sure you only fill in one answer for each question. If you change an answer, completely erase the first answer before filling in the correct response.
- When filling in answers, make sure the number of the question corresponds to the answer on the answer sheet. Be especially careful if you choose to skip any questions. If you skip a question in the test book, make sure you also skip the corresponding answer space on the answer sheet and fill in the answer on the correct line.
- If you start to feel nervous or anxious at any time, take a few seconds to calm down. A couple of deep breaths can help you calm yourself and refocus. Don't worry that this is a waste of time. You'll probably be able to work better if you are feeling calmer.

Tips for Taking the Test

As you know, there are two sections on the SHSAT: ELA and Mathematics. The ELA section is first, then the Math section. Let's talk about a few strategies to help you do your best on each of these, as well as some tips that can be used on either part of the test.

Keep Your Eye on the Time

You will have three hours to complete the entire test. The test itself is divided into two parts; however, there will not be a break between the two sections. So, you will need to pace yourself. Since the ELA section is first, try to spend about half your time, approximately one hour and fifteen minutes, completing these questions. This will leave you an equal amount of time to complete the mathematics questions.

Since there are 57 questions on the ELA section of the test, you will have an average of a little more than a minute and a half to answer each of these questions. Try to answer the questions as quickly as possible without rushing. If you think that the reading comprehension questions are a breeze, you might try to answer these a little more quickly. That way, if you feel like you could benefit from a little extra time to answer the revising/editing questions, for example, the time will be available for you.

The Math section of the test has a total of 57 problems, which, again, gives you an average of one and a half minutes per question. Try not to spend too much time on any single question. If you complete this section of the test before time is called, you can go back and check your work on either section of the test.

Here are a few other tips for pacing yourself for the test:

- If you feel that the ELA section of the test will be your strong point, consider allowing yourself only an hour for this section, which will give you additional time on the math.
- If you feel that the Math section will be your strong point, stop working on the ELA questions after half of your time has passed, and move on to math. Work through these items at a faster pace, and then use the extra time to go back to the ELA questions.
- Since there are a total of 114 questions on the SHSAT, and you have 180 minutes to complete the entire test, aim for answering about 10 questions every 15 minutes. That means you will have answered 20 questions in the first half hour, and 40 in the first hour. At this pace, you will complete the test with a few minutes to spare. If you can occasionally answer 11 questions in a 15 minute segment, you will have enough time at the end to check your work or go back to answer questions that you may have skipped.

Remember That This Is a Test, Not a Race

Didn't we just discuss the importance of working quickly? Yes. However, working *too* quickly can lead to careless mistakes. Find a pace that is comfortable for you. There is no prize for being the first one finished. There are no bonus points awarded for completing the test in less time. Working too fast and making mistakes could be more detrimental to your score than running out of time to complete the last couple of questions. You definitely need to work quickly, but it is just as important, if not more important, to work carefully. Be aware of the time, but keep your attention on doing your very best.

Use the Time Wisely

With only about a minute and a half to answer each question, you will not be able to spend a lot of time deciding which answer to select. If you come across a question that has you baffled, take your best guess, and then move on. Spending too much time on one tricky question could cause you to run out of time to answer a really simple question later on. Some questions may only take 15 seconds to answer while others may take upwards of two minutes to answer.

Any time you find a question that you want to take another look at later, be sure to circle the item number in your test book so you can come back to it if time allows. Who knows? You may find that the answer is very clear once you have had some time to think about it.

Read the Questions First

On the reading comprehension questions, read the questions first. This will alert you to what information you should be looking for as you read. Then, completely read the passage; do not try to skim the text to find the information. Read the entire passage completely and carefully, and then select the best answer choice for each question.

Remember, all of the correct answers are based solely on information given in the passage. Even though you may be reading the questions ahead of time, it is important that you do not try to select an answer before reading the text.

Read Everything Carefully

Despite the fact that the clock will be ticking, make sure you take the time to read slowly and carefully enough to catch every fact and detail. Quickly scanning a passage to get the main idea is fine, but then go back and read carefully enough to be able to focus on each and every word.

The importance of reading carefully does not just apply to comprehension passages; this goes for questions and answer choices as well, on both the ELA and math sections of the test. Overlooking a simple word such as *not* or *except* can completely change the meaning of the question and cause you to select the wrong answer. Be careful!

Cover the Negatives

Negative words such as *not* and *except* in a question can cause confusion. When you come across one of these words, try covering it up and reading the question without the negative. Then, see which of the answer choices does not belong. For example:

Which of these is not a planet?

A. Earth
B. Mars
C. Mercury
D. Mexico

Now, that's a pretty simple question, but reread it, eliminating the word *not*: *Which of these is a planet?*

As you can see, Mexico is clearly the answer choice that does not belong. Negative words in a question cause your brain to have to think backward in a way. If you get stuck on a question that contains a negative, try this trick and see if it helps!

Make Your Mark

As you read, underline or circle important information that you will need in order to answer the questions. Consider marking:

- Names
- Dates
- Specific details
- Clues about mood, tone, and theme
- Facts
- Figures
- Numbers
- Percents
- Clue words indicating mathematical operations

This can be helpful when it comes to answering the questions. If the important information has been underlined, you can locate it quickly without having to reread the entire passage each time you need to answer a question.

Try to Answer the Questions Yourself

Try to answer the reading comprehension questions before reading the answer choices. Then, see which answer choice is closest to your response. If none of the choices match your answer, reread the passage and try again.

Make sure your answer is based only on the information in the passage. You may know a lot about a topic, but the test is not intended to measure how much you already knew about a given subject. It is intended to measure how well you comprehended the information in the passage.

Choose the Best Answer

You will see a number of questions that ask you to choose the **best** answer. The best answer is the one that most completely answers the question. More than one choice may be partially correct, or look tempting. Avoid answers that are partially correct but too broad, general, or vague. Read every answer choice carefully before making a selection. Be sure to choose the **best** answer choice, not the first one that looks good. Answer choice A might look good, but answer choice D could be better!

Think About Each Answer

You may find that the answers to some questions seem completely obvious right away. Be careful to take your time selecting the answer choice, no matter how easy you think the question is. Take the time to read the question and every answer choice carefully, just to be sure the answer you select is truly the best one. It would be a shame to lose points over a careless mistake.

Use Scratch Paper

You will have scratch paper, so make sure to use it. Draw diagrams, charts, tables, pictures, or anything else that will help you solve the logical reasoning or math problems on the test.

You may write in the test book or on scratch paper. However, these will not be scored. Solve problems, draw diagrams, and complete calculations in one of these places, and then mark your final answer on the answer sheet. Make sure there are no extra or stray marks on the answer sheet. Doing work or making marks on the answer sheet could cause answers to be scored incorrectly.

Make a Drawing

Try drawing figures, diagrams, or models to help you solve problems. For example, if you are asked to find the area of a rectangle that is 2 inches longer than a given shape, draw and label the new figure. Being able to visualize the problem can be helpful in solving it.

Check Your Work

Work carefully when solving the math problems. The incorrect answer choices are the result of mistakes that students commonly make. That means, just because your first answer is one of the choices listed, it may not be correct. Work the problems, double-check your work to find any errors, and then read the answer choices.

If you are confident that your answer is correct, but it is not one of the choices, try converting your answer to a different form. For example, if your answer is a fraction, try converting it to a decimal or percent, or try simplifying the fraction. Then, see if your answer is among the choices.

Reread the Question

After selecting the best answer choice, go back and read the question one last time. Make sure that you understood what it was asking and that the answer you chose completely answers the question. If you determine that your answer does not make sense or is not the best choice for any reason, change your answer and mark your new selection.

Change Things Up

Know which types of questions you do best on, and do these at the start of the test. This can help you build your confidence and get a few correct answers under your belt right away. Just be careful that you do not end up skipping any of the questions by working out of order. Make sure you answer every question during the given time.

Answer Every Question

Make sure you answer every single question, even if it means you have to take your best guess. Your score is calculated by the number of correct answers. On the SHSAT, a question that is left blank is the same as a wrong answer. So, you might as well take a stab at every question, even if you honestly have no idea which is the correct answer. Think back to what you learned about probability; it is impossible to get an answer correct if it is left blank. You are more likely to get it right if you at least fill in something.

If you see that there are only a couple of minutes left, and there is no way you are going to finish all of the questions, just start filling in bubbles. Sounds crazy, right? Wrong! If time is called and the answers are blank, they are wrong. Spend the final minute or so quickly filling in something. That way, at least there is some chance of getting a couple of the answers right. When the competition is as stiff as it is on the SHSAT, every single point helps!

Take Your Best Guess

Obviously, guessing is not the best way to answer any test question, but let's face it: there are times when guessing is necessary. So, if you're going to take a guess, make the most of it.

The key to guessing is to first eliminate as many of the incorrect answer choices as possible. This will increase the likelihood of selecting the correct answer. Since there are 4 answer choices for each question, a random guess has a 1/4 probability of being correct. That's 25 percent.

Not great, but better than a 0 percent chance of getting it right if you leave it blank.

If you are able to eliminate one of the incorrect answers, then guess between the remaining three choices, the probability of getting the right answer increases to 1/3, or 33 percent. Finally, if you can eliminate two incorrect answers, you will be able to guess between two answer choices: one is correct and one is incorrect. You have increased the probability of selecting the correct answer to 1/2, or 50 percent. That is much better than the 25 percent we started with!

So, how do you eliminate incorrect answer choices?

- Think about what type of answer would make sense, then eliminate answer choices that are not logical. For example, if the question asks about the mean of a set of data, you know that the answer must be between the lowest and highest values in the set. So, you can eliminate any answer choices that do not fit the criteria.
- Estimate the correct answer to math problems. Any choices that are too far off from the estimate can be eliminated.
- Look for an answer choice that sticks out from the rest for some reason. It may be significantly longer or shorter than the other choices. It may be the only negative number listed, or the only decimal number among a set of whole numbers. It might be much higher or lower than the other values.
- Look for answers that are very similar. If there are two answer choices that are nearly the same, other than a few words, consider eliminating the other answer choices and selecting between these two.
- Look for answers that are opposites. Since there is no way for both of the choices to be correct, try to eliminate one of them. Be careful, though, because they may both be incorrect.
- Check for any grammatical hints. This may be especially helpful when answering reading comprehension questions. If an answer choice does not fit grammatically, if the part of speech is incorrect, or if the tense does not match, the answer choice may not be correct, and can be eliminated.
- Watch out for absolutes such as *always*, *never*, and *every*. There are very few things that *always* happen, are *never* true, or occur *every* time. These words could indicate that the answer is not correct, and that it can be eliminated.

Go with Your Gut

Believe it or not, your first instinct regarding the correct answer choice is often correct! If you are confident that you have read the passage carefully or worked the problem accurately, the answer choice that you are leaning toward at the beginning is probably a great choice!

If you go back to check your work at the end of the test and are considering making a change to one of the answers, think carefully. Ask yourself, *Did I make a mistake in the calculations? Did I misunderstand the question or the passage? Is there a valid reason for thinking that this answer choice might not be the best one?* Unless there is a strong reason for changing an answer, it might be a good idea to leave it alone.

Let's Review!

In this chapter, you've learned some tips and strategies that will help you do your best on the SHSAT. Let's take a final look at some of the key points for you to keep in mind leading up to the big day, and on test day itself.

- Memorize the math terms, definitions, symbols, and formulas that you will need to use on the test.
- Read a variety of materials in order to expand your vocabulary, and ask yourself questions about the text in order to monitor your own comprehension.
- Taking the practice tests in this book can be helpful for several reasons:
  - You will become familiar with the types of questions that will be on the SHSAT.
  - You will learn which skills you have already mastered and which you would benefit from reviewing.
  - You will find out how to best budget your time on test day.

- Start studying for the test well ahead of time, and then take a break on the day before the test. A quick review on that day should be plenty.
- Getting plenty of sleep, having a good breakfast, and dressing comfortably are important ways to make sure you arrive in tip-top shape for the test!
- Do not start the test if you are at all concerned about whether or not you are feeling well enough to finish. Tell the proctor immediately if you are ill.
- Keep your eye on the time and pace yourself accordingly. It is important to work quickly and carefully, without rushing. Allow yourself more time for the questions or sections that you do not feel are your strength, and move quickly through the areas that are your best skills.
- Try not to spend too much time on any single question. You can always come back later if time allows. Mark your best guess, circle the item number in the test book, and use the time to answer other, possibly easier, questions.
- Read the questions first, then the passages in order to have an idea of what information to look for in the text. Do not, however, actually try to answer the questions before reading the passages. The correct answers are based solely on information in the text, not on what you may already know about the topic.
- Read everything carefully. This includes passages, questions, and answer choices.
- Underline or circle important information in passages, word problems, and questions. This will make it easier to locate the facts needed to select the best answer choice.
- Read every answer choice, then select the one best answer. You may find that two or more of the choices look good, but the correct answer is the one that most completely answers the question. Also, keep in mind that the first answer choice that catches your attention may not be correct. Take the time to carefully consider each and every option.
- Use the scratch paper and your test booklet to complete calculations, draw diagrams, and solve problems. Then, transfer your final answer to the answer sheet.
- Answer every question, even if you have to take your best guess. Any item that is left blank will be marked wrong, so eliminate as many incorrect answer choices as possible, then choose the best option. If you are not sure whether an answer is correct or not, trust your instincts.

A Final Thought

Congratulations! You are taking control of your future and giving yourself the best possible opportunity to do well on the SHSAT by preparing for this test. Doing your best on the SHSAT is an accomplishment you can be proud of. Studying the material, taking the practice tests, and knowing what to expect on the test are beneficial steps in making sure you are well prepared. Now, take a deep breath, smile, and pat yourself on the back for a job well done! Best of luck on the SHSAT!

PART 2

SHSAT Diagnostic Test

CHAPTER 3

Diagnostic Test with Answers

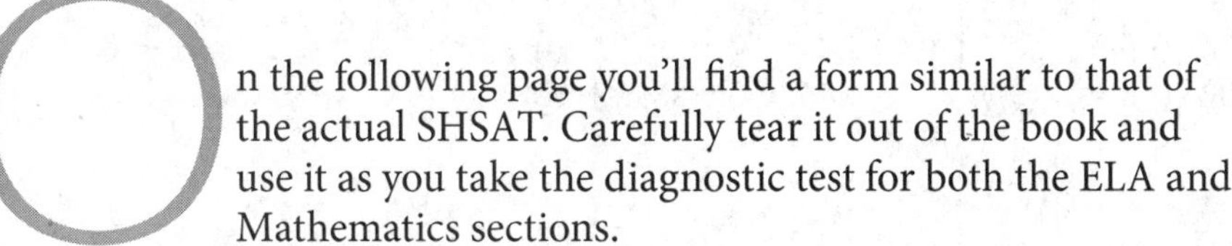

On the following page you'll find a form similar to that of the actual SHSAT. Carefully tear it out of the book and use it as you take the diagnostic test for both the ELA and Mathematics sections.

PART 1 ELA

1 Ⓐ Ⓑ Ⓒ Ⓓ	16 Ⓔ Ⓕ Ⓖ Ⓗ	31 Ⓐ Ⓑ Ⓒ Ⓓ	46 Ⓔ Ⓕ Ⓖ Ⓗ
2 Ⓔ Ⓕ Ⓖ Ⓗ	17 Ⓐ Ⓑ Ⓒ Ⓓ	32 Ⓔ Ⓕ Ⓖ Ⓗ	47 Ⓐ Ⓑ Ⓒ Ⓓ
3 Ⓐ Ⓑ Ⓒ Ⓓ	18 Ⓔ Ⓕ Ⓖ Ⓗ	33 Ⓐ Ⓑ Ⓒ Ⓓ	48 Ⓔ Ⓕ Ⓖ Ⓗ
4 Ⓔ Ⓕ Ⓖ Ⓗ	19 Ⓐ Ⓑ Ⓒ Ⓓ	34 Ⓔ Ⓕ Ⓖ Ⓗ	49 Ⓐ Ⓑ Ⓒ Ⓓ
5 Ⓐ Ⓑ Ⓒ Ⓓ	20 Ⓔ Ⓕ Ⓖ Ⓗ	35 Ⓐ Ⓑ Ⓒ Ⓓ	50 Ⓔ Ⓕ Ⓖ Ⓗ
6 Ⓔ Ⓕ Ⓖ Ⓗ	21 Ⓐ Ⓑ Ⓒ Ⓓ	36 Ⓔ Ⓕ Ⓖ Ⓗ	51 Ⓐ Ⓑ Ⓒ Ⓓ
7 Ⓐ Ⓑ Ⓒ Ⓓ	22 Ⓔ Ⓕ Ⓖ Ⓗ	37 Ⓐ Ⓑ Ⓒ Ⓓ	52 Ⓔ Ⓕ Ⓖ Ⓗ
8 Ⓔ Ⓕ Ⓖ Ⓗ	23 Ⓐ Ⓑ Ⓒ Ⓓ	38 Ⓔ Ⓕ Ⓖ Ⓗ	53 Ⓐ Ⓑ Ⓒ Ⓓ
9 Ⓐ Ⓑ Ⓒ Ⓓ	24 Ⓔ Ⓕ Ⓖ Ⓗ	39 Ⓐ Ⓑ Ⓒ Ⓓ	54 Ⓔ Ⓕ Ⓖ Ⓗ
10 Ⓔ Ⓕ Ⓖ Ⓗ	25 Ⓐ Ⓑ Ⓒ Ⓓ	40 Ⓔ Ⓕ Ⓖ Ⓗ	55 Ⓐ Ⓑ Ⓒ Ⓓ
11 Ⓐ Ⓑ Ⓒ Ⓓ	26 Ⓔ Ⓕ Ⓖ Ⓗ	41 Ⓐ Ⓑ Ⓒ Ⓓ	56 Ⓔ Ⓕ Ⓖ Ⓗ
12 Ⓔ Ⓕ Ⓖ Ⓗ	27 Ⓐ Ⓑ Ⓒ Ⓓ	42 Ⓔ Ⓕ Ⓖ Ⓗ	57 Ⓐ Ⓑ Ⓒ Ⓓ
13 Ⓐ Ⓑ Ⓒ Ⓓ	28 Ⓔ Ⓕ Ⓖ Ⓗ	43 Ⓐ Ⓑ Ⓒ Ⓓ	
14 Ⓔ Ⓕ Ⓖ Ⓗ	29 Ⓐ Ⓑ Ⓒ Ⓓ	44 Ⓔ Ⓕ Ⓖ Ⓗ	
15 Ⓐ Ⓑ Ⓒ Ⓓ	30 Ⓔ Ⓕ Ⓖ Ⓗ	45 Ⓐ Ⓑ Ⓒ Ⓓ	

PART 2 MATHEMATICS

58

59

60

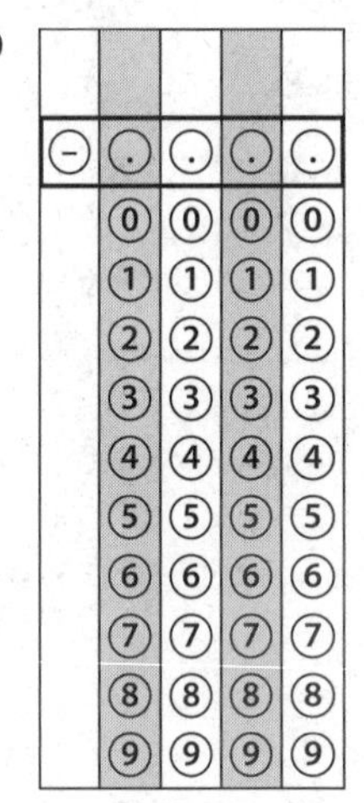

61

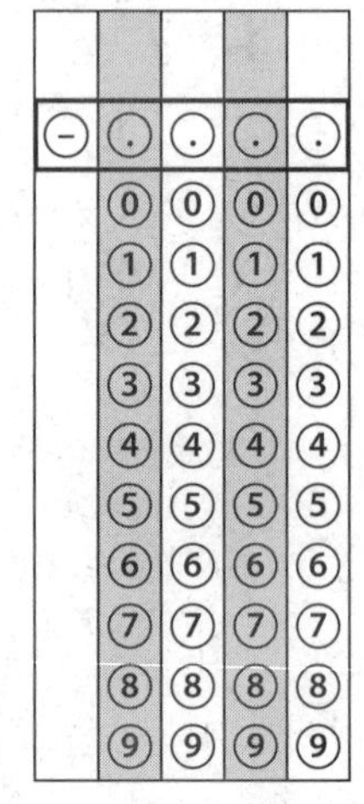

62

63 Ⓐ Ⓑ Ⓒ Ⓓ	76 Ⓔ Ⓕ Ⓖ Ⓗ	89 Ⓐ Ⓑ Ⓒ Ⓓ	102 Ⓔ Ⓕ Ⓖ Ⓗ
64 Ⓔ Ⓕ Ⓖ Ⓗ	77 Ⓐ Ⓑ Ⓒ Ⓓ	90 Ⓔ Ⓕ Ⓖ Ⓗ	103 Ⓐ Ⓑ Ⓒ Ⓓ
65 Ⓐ Ⓑ Ⓒ Ⓓ	78 Ⓔ Ⓕ Ⓖ Ⓗ	91 Ⓐ Ⓑ Ⓒ Ⓓ	104 Ⓔ Ⓕ Ⓖ Ⓗ
66 Ⓔ Ⓕ Ⓖ Ⓗ	79 Ⓐ Ⓑ Ⓒ Ⓓ	92 Ⓔ Ⓕ Ⓖ Ⓗ	105 Ⓐ Ⓑ Ⓒ Ⓓ
67 Ⓐ Ⓑ Ⓒ Ⓓ	80 Ⓔ Ⓕ Ⓖ Ⓗ	93 Ⓐ Ⓑ Ⓒ Ⓓ	106 Ⓔ Ⓕ Ⓖ Ⓗ
68 Ⓔ Ⓕ Ⓖ Ⓗ	81 Ⓐ Ⓑ Ⓒ Ⓓ	94 Ⓔ Ⓕ Ⓖ Ⓗ	107 Ⓐ Ⓑ Ⓒ Ⓓ
69 Ⓐ Ⓑ Ⓒ Ⓓ	82 Ⓔ Ⓕ Ⓖ Ⓗ	95 Ⓐ Ⓑ Ⓒ Ⓓ	108 Ⓔ Ⓕ Ⓖ Ⓗ
70 Ⓔ Ⓕ Ⓖ Ⓗ	83 Ⓐ Ⓑ Ⓒ Ⓓ	96 Ⓔ Ⓕ Ⓖ Ⓗ	109 Ⓐ Ⓑ Ⓒ Ⓓ
71 Ⓐ Ⓑ Ⓒ Ⓓ	84 Ⓔ Ⓕ Ⓖ Ⓗ	97 Ⓐ Ⓑ Ⓒ Ⓓ	110 Ⓔ Ⓕ Ⓖ Ⓗ
72 Ⓔ Ⓕ Ⓖ Ⓗ	85 Ⓐ Ⓑ Ⓒ Ⓓ	98 Ⓔ Ⓕ Ⓖ Ⓗ	111 Ⓐ Ⓑ Ⓒ Ⓓ
73 Ⓐ Ⓑ Ⓒ Ⓓ	86 Ⓔ Ⓕ Ⓖ Ⓗ	99 Ⓐ Ⓑ Ⓒ Ⓓ	112 Ⓔ Ⓕ Ⓖ Ⓗ
74 Ⓔ Ⓕ Ⓖ Ⓗ	87 Ⓐ Ⓑ Ⓒ Ⓓ	100 Ⓔ Ⓕ Ⓖ Ⓗ	113 Ⓐ Ⓑ Ⓒ Ⓓ
75 Ⓐ Ⓑ Ⓒ Ⓓ	88 Ⓔ Ⓕ Ⓖ Ⓗ	101 Ⓐ Ⓑ Ⓒ Ⓓ	114 Ⓔ Ⓕ Ⓖ Ⓗ

PART 1

ENGLISH LANGUAGE ARTS

90 Minutes ■ 57 Questions

Revising/Editing

QUESTIONS 1–20

Revising/Editing Part A

DIRECTIONS: Read and answer each of the following questions. You will be asked to recognize and correct errors in sentences or short paragraphs. Mark the best answer for each question.

(1) The building materials that are native to a region influence the type of homes that are built there. (2) For example, when settling this country, many houses in the East were built of wooden logs because there were plentiful forests. (3) Later, the settlers went west to places that had a plentiful supply of clay. (4) There, they started to build their houses with adobe bricks.

1. Which of these sentences contains a misplaced modifier?

A. Sentence 1
B. Sentence 2
C. Sentence 3
D. Sentence 4

Some settlers in the East lived in areas that had large plentiful stones, so stone houses became the norm especially during the colonial period in those regions.

2. Which edit should be made to correct this sentence?

E. Insert a comma after "East."
F. Insert a comma after "large."
G. Remove the comma after "stones."
H. Insert a comma after "period."

CONTINUE ON TO THE NEXT PAGE ▸

In the early American West, bricks for building houses were made of a mixture of clay and straw that was dried in the sun. Until the bricks were totally hardened and ready for use. Because the climate of these areas was so warm and dry, these simple bricks had a long life.

3. Which is the correct edit for the preceding paragraph?
   - **A.** Remove the comma after "West."
   - **B.** Make two sentences from the first sentence by adding a period after "straw" and capitalizing "That."
   - **C.** Remove the period after "sun" and do not capitalize "until."
   - **D.** Make the last sentence into two sentences by adding a period after "dry" and capitalizing "these."

(1) The science of archaeology grew from one person's fascination with the *Iliad.* (2) You might've heard of it. (3) Its the exciting story of the Trojan War.

4. Which edit needs to be made in the preceding sentences?
   - **E.** Remove the apostrophe from the word "person's."
   - **F.** Move the apostrophe so it comes after the "s" in "person's."
   - **G.** Put the apostrophe in "might've" after the "t."
   - **H.** Put an apostrophe after the "t" in "Its."

A German businessman named Heinrich Schliemann decided to search for the site of ancient Troy in Asia Minor, and actually found the remains of several cities believed to be Troy, one on top of the other.

5. Which edit is needed for the above sentence?
   - **A.** Insert a comma after "Schliemann."
   - **B.** Insert a comma after "site."
   - **C.** Remove the comma after "Minor."
   - **D.** Remove the comma after "Troy."

While Schliemann did much to popularize the science of archaeology, his work was controversial among archaeologists today.

6. Which edit is needed to correct the above sentence?
   - **E.** Change "did" to "had done."
   - **F.** Change "did" to "had been doing."
   - **G.** Change "was" to "is."
   - **H.** Change "was" to "will be."

CONTINUE ON TO THE NEXT PAGE ▶

Revising/Editing Part B

DIRECTIONS: Read the passage below and answer the questions following it. You will be asked to improve the writing quality of the passage and to correct errors so that the passage follows the conventions of standard written English. You may reread the passage if you need to. Mark the best answer for each question.

Passage 1

Dinosaurs in the American West

(1) One hundred and fifty million years ago, dinosaurs roamed the western United States in the area that is now the states of Colorado, Montana, Utah, and Wyoming. (2) At that time, the West was very different than it is today. (3) It was hot and moist and dotted with many lakes and swamps that provided a habitat for the many different types of dinosaurs that existed. (4) The Rocky Mountains did not exist at that time, and much of California was underwater. (5) Covering a good portion of what is considered the American West today, the humid climate was affected by the shallow, warm, inland seas.

(6) One dinosaur species that was prominent in the region during that time was the large Apatosaurus, you might be more familiar with its other name, Brontosaurus. (7) This dinosaur was a plant eater that had a long neck enabling it to reach the top of vegetation. (8) It is believed to have been one of the largest animals to have ever roamed the earth. (9) The average Apatosaurus was 85 feet long and 15 feet tall at the hip. (10) It weighed approximately 18 tons.

(11) A second notable dinosaur was the Allosaurus, a fierce carnivore with sharp teeth and a large head. (12) The Allosaurus was one of the most feared of the dinosaurs in that era. (13) It is thought to have been able to reach speeds of up to 21 miles per hours. (14) Scientists have found fossil evidence pointing to battles between the Allosaurus and the Stegosaurus. (15) In 1991 a team of scientists discovered an Allosaurus fossil that was the most complete to date (about 95 percent intact); they dubbed their finding "Big Al."

(16) In addition to the many dinosaurs who roamed the land, the skies were crowded with flying reptiles who were predators and scavengers. (17) Called pterosaurs, some of these creatures stood as tall as giraffes and had the wingspan of a small plane. (18) In comparison to this era, the American "Wild West" period of 1865 to 1895 seems positively tame.

7. Which sentence is irrelevant to the main idea of the passage?

   A. Sentence 8
   B. Sentence 11
   C. Sentence 15
   D. Sentence 18

CONTINUE ON TO THE NEXT PAGE ▶

8. Which revision of sentence 12 uses the most precise language?

E. The Allosaurus was fairly fast and strong, which enabled it to hunt well.
F. The Allosaurus was a successful predator with short front limbs for grasping prey and strong back legs for speed.
G. The Allosaurus sometimes hunted weaker dinosaurs, using its superior strength to overpower its prey.
H. The Allosaurus was a massive creature, which allowed it to hunt other species successfully.

9. Which sentence would best follow and support sentence 14?

A. One piece of evidence they discovered was a stab wound on an Allosaurus fossil that was the same shape as a Stegosaurus tail spike.
B. They believe that these two species were pretty evenly matched in battle.
C. They consider their evidence irrefutable.
D. In fact, numerous fossilized impressions give the idea that the two species joined in battle frequently.

10. Which transition should be added to the beginning of sentence 4?

E. Nevertheless,
F. Because of this,
G. In contrast,
H. Moreover,

11. What would be the best way to combine sentences 12 and 13 to clarify the relationship between them?

A. Because the Allosaurus was one of the most feared of the dinosaurs in that era, it is thought to have been able to reach speeds of up to 21 miles per hours.
B. The Allosaurus was one of the most feared of the dinosaurs in that era; moreover, it is thought to have been able to reach speeds of up to 21 miles per hours.
C. The Allosaurus was one of the most feared of the dinosaurs in that era although it is thought to have been able to reach speeds of up to 21 miles per hours.
D. The Allosaurus was one of the most feared of the dinosaurs in that era because it is thought to have been able to reach speeds of up to 21 miles per hours.

12. Which edit should be made to sentence 6?

E. Replace the comma after Apatosaurus with a semicolon.
F. Insert a comma after the word "species."
G. Replace the comma after the word "name" with a semicolon.
H. Insert a comma after the word "large."

13. Which of the following sentences contains a dangling modifier?

A. Sentence 1
B. Sentence 3
C. Sentence 5
D. Sentence 7

CONTINUE ON TO THE NEXT PAGE ▶

Passage 2

The Botanist Richard Spruce

(1) Richard Spruce, the son of a poor English schoolmaster, found his life's work and his fame in the jungles of South America. (2) Spruce's mother died when he was young and he was raised by a stepmother who had eight daughters. (3) Plagued with bronchial problems, doctors advised him to spend time out-of-doors. (4) His love of plants developed as he spent time outside in his early years.

(5) When he became an adult, he became a teacher and later a master at a prestigious school. (6) During his time as a teacher, he also worked as a part-time botanical collector. (7) As his interest deepened, he began publishing papers on the subject, and in time his work was brought to the attention of the botanists at Kew Gardens. (8) With their financial backing, he was sent to explore the South American jungles.

(9) While in South America, Spruce explored more of the Amazon jungle than any European before him. (10) Every time Spruce came upon a new plant, he took a specimen of it and labeled it with both the scientific name and the name that the Amazon Indians had given it. (11) He described what the whole plant looked like and what it was used for. (12) After that, he pressed the specimen between pages of blotting paper and sent them back to England to be part of the great plant collection at Kew Gardens in London; in all, Spruce sent 30,000 specimens home.

(13) Spruce had spent 15 years in South America although his poor health made him particularly ill-suited for the job. (14) He suffered with numerous health issues while he was there. (15) Parasitic insects and bouts of malaria plagued him. (16) In addition, he was struck by a mysterious paralysis that left him unable to sit at a desk for the rest of his life. (17) After numerous catastrophes, he returned to England destitute. (18) He returned with volumes of knowledge including the vocabularies of 21 Amazonian languages and maps of three rivers that had never been mapped before. (19) He spent the last 27 years of his life cataloging all the plants he had discovered in his travels.

14. Which edit is needed in sentence 2?

- **A.** Put the apostrophe after the "s" in "Spruce's."
- **B.** Insert a comma after "young."
- **C.** Insert a comma after "stepmother."
- **D.** Replace "daughters" with "daughter's."

15. Which of these sentences contains a misplaced modifier?

- **E.** Sentence 1
- **F.** Sentence 2
- **G.** Sentence 3
- **H.** Sentence 4

16. Which of these choices would best follow and support sentence 9?

- **A.** He mapped the Amazon River and studied its plant life.
- **B.** He was an amazing person.
- **C.** He was meticulous in his dress and in his manners.
- **D.** His personality did not allow him to make mistakes.

CONTINUE ON TO THE NEXT PAGE ▶

17. Which sentence contains an unclear pronoun reference?

E. Sentence 9
F. Sentence 10
G. Sentence 11
H. Sentence 12

18. Which would be the best way to join sentences 14 and 15 to show the relationship of their ideas?

A. Although he suffered with numerous health issues while he was there, parasitic insects and bouts of malaria plagued him.
B. He suffered with numerous health issues while he was there including parasitic insects and bouts of malaria.
C. He suffered with numerous health issues while he was there; in addition, parasitic insects and bouts of malaria plagued him.
D. Because he suffered with numerous health issues while he was there, parasitic insects and bouts of malaria plagued him.

19. Which word or phrase should be added to the beginning of sentence 18 to show the relationship between sentence 17 and sentence 18?

E. Nevertheless,
F. In addition,
G. Furthermore,
H. On the contrary,

20. Which edit is needed in sentence 13?

A. Change “made” to “was making.”
B. Change “made” to “had been making.”
C. Change “had spent” to “was spending.”
D. Change “had spent” to “spent.”

Reading Comprehension

QUESTIONS 21–57

DIRECTIONS: Read the passages below, then answer the questions that appear after each passage. Select the best answer for each question. Reread the passages if necessary. You must base your response **only on information contained in the passage.**

A startling discovery by archaeologists has revolutionized earlier theories about when people first came to the Americas. An excavation at Buttermilk Creek has pushed the date when the first human inhabitants entered the New World back in time some 2,500 years! A huge collection of stone tools such as flint knife blades, chisels, choppers, spears, and other artifacts were found there. The site is a 50 square meter area. It is located 40 miles northwest of Austin, Texas.

These Buttermilk People roamed the plains of North America as early as 15,500 years ago. And they didn't enter the Americas by crossing a land bridge from Siberia, as previously thought. Instead they came by boats crafted from animal skins. Scientists believe this happened at the height of the Ice Age. They think that these people hunted seals along the glaciers and traveled a few miles each day. These early people came with children, babies, and grandparents. They even brought pet dogs. Their first settlements were probably in Washington and Oregon. There is evidence that over centuries they explored all the way to the tip of South America.

For decades scientists had labeled the first inhabitants of the Americas as the Clovis People, also called Paleo-Indians. This was based on the artifacts unearthed near Clovis, New Mexico, in 1936 and 1937. These artifacts dated to 13,000 years ago. At that time these people roamed the Great Plains and the Southwest. Archaeologists must now contend with the new evidence that the Buttermilk People were here much earlier. The evidence of the handcrafted tools and weapons and shreds of flint found alongside the creek is compelling.

The Buttermilk People hunted giant Ice Age mammoths and mastodons, related to present-day elephants, with spears. Spear points were crafted with flint and made with the bones of the mammoths. The hunting of an animal resulted in meat that would last for many weeks. The meat was also dried to provide food through the harsh winter months. Clothing and shelter were made from the hides.

Probably most surprising was the discovery of chunks of hematite (iron oxide). These were worn down along the sides, a sign that they had been rubbed. They were similar to what school chalk looks like after it is used. When mixed with plant oils, hematite produces red ochre. Archaeologists believe the Buttermilk People painted their spears and decorated their clothes and their bodies. This new discovery has given scientists a new way of looking at early people in the Americas.

CONTINUE ON TO THE NEXT PAGE ▶

21. Which of the following best tells what this passage is about?

A. how scientists are able to date human artifacts that are unearthed
B. the relationship between the Buttermilk People and the Clovis People
C. the discovery that people came to the Americas earlier than thought
D. where the artifacts of the earliest settlers to the New World were found

22. The passage suggests that the Buttermilk People

E. had difficulty finding food to eat.
F. were able to record their stories through pictures.
G. were better hunters than the Clovis People.
H. made the most of resources available to them.

23. Which of these statements is true about the Buttermilk People's nature?

A. The Buttermilk People had deep religious beliefs.
B. The Buttermilk People were aggressive against others.
C. The Buttermilk People were curious about their world.
D. The Buttermilk People were serious most of the time.

24. Which of the following best describes what is suggested by the statement that the Buttermilk People "even brought pet dogs" (line 24)?

E. The Buttermilk People were affectionate.
F. The Buttermilk People were well educated.
G. The Buttermilk People feared animals.
H. The Buttermilk People felt animals were spirits.

25. What does the use of hematite suggest about the Buttermilk People?

A. They were fearful of enemies.
B. They were friendly to others.
C. They liked colorful objects.
D. They liked to play games.

26. What was **not** a concern of the Buttermilk People?

E. finding enough food
F. moving from place to place
G. exploring new lands
H. starting a network of trails

CONTINUE ON TO THE NEXT PAGE ▶

Along the floor of the Pacific Ocean, more than a mile beneath the surface of the sea, lives a unique creature. Discovered by scientists in 1977 when they developed a submarine capable of going that deep, this animal lives in an environment that is forever dark; no sunlight penetrates the ocean this deep. And the water always remains just a few degrees above freezing.

But how does this creature survive without the life-giving energy of the sun? The animal, called a giant tube worm, is unlike any other. It is able to thrive in such a hostile environment because of the existence of hydrothermal vents or fissures in the surface of the earth that are powered by volcanic activity. Surprisingly, it does not need the energy of the sun, either to keep it warm or to nourish its food supply. The vents release heated vapors from the earth's core that reach temperatures of over 400 degrees Fahrenheit. The vapors contain hydrogen sulfide. Poisonous to man and other animals, the gas is how the giant tube worm receives its nourishment.

Resembling giant tubes of lipstick, the worms have a soft body surrounded by a hard white shell called chitin (pronounced "kite-in"), the same substance that forms the shells of lobsters and crabs. Tube worms have no mouth or digestive system. They get their food from billions of bacteria that live inside their bodies. The bacteria convert the hydrogen sulfide into food for the worms by oxidizing the gas. The bacteria and worms have a symbiotic relationship, which means that both benefit. The worms get nourishment; the bacteria have a place to live. The giant tube worm anchors itself to the ocean floor. On its uppermost part there is a bright red plume, which is filled with hemoglobin. The plume absorbs the chemicals from the seawater that feed the bacteria. The tube worm has few enemies because not many creatures can survive near the vents, but if it is threatened, it can withdraw the plume inside its shell. Sometimes crabs and crustaceans nibble on the plume for nourishment.

These giant tube worms can reach lengths of eight feet. They grow very slowly. Scientists believe that they are among the longest living animals on earth; some are estimated to be over 250 years old. Scientists think tube worms are born with a mouth, which allows them to absorb bacteria on the ocean floor and in the water. As they grow, the mouth disappears. Giant tube worms have no eyes, but they can sense movement and will pull in their plumes to protect themselves. These giant tube worms are closely related to smaller worms that live in shallow water.

27. Which of the following best tells what this passage is about?

- **A.** why giant tube worms develop
- **B.** how bacteria get their nourishment
- **C.** why giant tube worms have a plume
- **D.** how giant tube worms survive

28. The author implies that most life on earth

- **E.** has a symbiotic relationship with another animal.
- **F.** lives on land rather than in the ocean.
- **G.** can survive vast changes in temperature.
- **H.** needs the energy of the sun to survive.

CONTINUE ON TO THE NEXT PAGE ▶

29. Which of these statements is true about giant tube worms?

A. Giant tube worms are unrelated to any other form of life.
B. Giant tube worms are found in the ocean all over the globe.
C. Giant tube worms are short-lived species that were found by chance.
D. Giant tube worms have taught scientists that organisms can exist without direct or indirect access to light.

30. Which best describes the relationship between giant tube worms and lobsters?

E. They both have hard exteriors.
F. They both live off the hot air vents.
G. They have a protective relationship.
H. They both have bacteria inside them.

31. Which is **not** true of giant tube worms?

A. It is impossible to gain the kind of data needed to fully study them.
B. They are able to live without energy from the sun.
C. They were found when the bottom of the ocean was explored.
D. They do not tolerate extremes in temperature.

32. What might be inferred about why the mature giant tube worm does not have a mouth?

E. The giant tube worm has no need for a mouth after the bacteria are inside.
F. A mouth would not be useful because of the extreme heat.
G. A mouth would get in the way of the plume.
H. The giant tube worm does not require nourishment.

CONTINUE ON TO THE NEXT PAGE ▶

Not all blind people use dogs as guides. A growing number of people who are sightless are turning to miniature horses to ensure their safety and ability to move about. These little animals are equally able to keep a master out of harm's way, and they have certain attributes that may make them more desirable than a Seeing Eye dog.

Miniature horses are no strangers to hard work. Many of their ancestors worked in the coal mines in England and Wales. They have been used for mining in the United States as well. Some of these animals never saw the light of day, living their entire lives underground. The obvious reason for miniature horses working in a mine is their height. They measure 35 inches at their withers. But there were other reasons as well. These little horses are very obedient, easygoing, and able to work long hours. All of these traits make them excellent candidates as guide animals.

And they have other valuable assets. They are hypoallergenic, so people with allergies may prefer them over dogs. They live longer than traditional canine guides, up to 40 years, so people may only have to have one guide animal in their lifetime. They also don't mind spending their downtime out of doors, even though they can be house-trained.

There's another factor to consider as well. Many people are nervous around dogs but feel more comfortable with a small horse. These horses are never aggressive, but they are strong enough to help individuals with physical disabilities, including helping a handler rise from a chair if that is a difficult thing to do. Another good point, say owners, is that dogs are often seen as pets, and it takes some explaining to allow them to act as guides. On the other hand, little horses are recognized quickly as guide animals. And horses are very clean and, unlike dogs, don't get fleas. Plus they are incredibly sweet and willing to take care of their charge.

They are also very adaptable. One sightless person flew with his miniature horse from the farm where she was trained to his home. The horse's name was Cuddles, and she slept beside her master for most of the flight. They also took a trip to New York City, where locals were impressed by this animal and how she was even able to navigate the subway!

Of course dogs and horses are not the only animals that have served as service animals. Pigs are also trained as guide animals from time to time, and monkeys have proved useful to those with serious physical handicaps. So the saying should probably be changed to this: It's not just a dog that is man's best friend.

33. Which of the following best tells what this passage is about?

A. how different animals are used to guide blind people
B. how miniature horses were used in mines
C. why miniature horses are good for those with allergies
D. why miniature horses make good guide animals

34. What trait is **not** mentioned as being an asset for miniature horses serving as guide animals?

E. good stamina
F. good memory
G. calm nature
H. able to live outdoors

CONTINUE ON TO THE NEXT PAGE ▶

35. According to the passage, which of the following statements about miniature horses is accurate?

A. Miniature horses are able to do as much with a handler as dogs are.
B. Miniature horses are easier to train than dogs are.
C. Miniature horses are less likely to injure their handler than dogs are.
D. Miniature horses are less costly to feed than dogs are.

36. The information about miniature horses working in mines was included in order to illustrate

E. how they were misused in the past.
F. why they are obedient.
G. how they behave under stress.
H. what hard workers they are.

37. Which of the following is most likely to choose a miniature horse rather than a dog as a service animal?

A. a person who grew up with cats
B. a person who grew up on a farm
C. a person who likes to live in a city
D. someone who is afraid of dogs

38. Why does the author want to change the saying to "It's not just a dog that is man's best friend"?

E. to make owners of other animals happy
F. to be more politically correct
G. to show that many animals are helpful
H. to make fun of the saying

CONTINUE ON TO THE NEXT PAGE ▶

It was July 20, 1969, and Neil Armstrong took the steps down to the surface of the moon. "That's one small step for man; one giant leap for mankind," he said as people worldwide watched the historic moment on television. It was an event that could not be forgotten. Today some people think that the space exploration program should be cut back or eliminated completely. Still others believe this is a self-defeating attitude.

People who favor future space exploration say that it is vital for many reasons. They say it could be key to the future of the human race. It could open unknown doors in medical treatment. It could provide new kinds of ores and other materials. What exploration of outer space will result in ultimately is not something that can be predicted. But proponents say to let space exploration lapse would be a step backward.

Obviously there is a strong-rooted instinct in people to find out about their universe. Humans have always looked up into the stars and wondered what was out there. Some say that space exploration is an essential extension of this urge. It helps provide some of the answers to the questions about our universe. And those in favor of space exploration say it will continue to do so with technology that allows scientists to reach out further into the universe. For thousands of years, brave people from all cultures have risked voyages into unknown wildernesses and across vast seas to find new lands. Intrepid travelers set out to discover uncharted worlds. Polynesian sailors settled far-flung islands of the Pacific starting more than three thousand years ago. Chinese explorers reached what is now Ethiopia by sea in the second century BCE. And Ferdinand Magellan's expedition, launched in 1519, became the first to sail around the world.

In this spirit, mankind reached out again in 1957 with the launch of *Sputnik* by the Soviet Union. *Sputnik* was the first vessel to travel outside the Earth's atmosphere. It spurred the United States to develop a space program. This program culminated in the *Apollo* missions to the moon. These missions inspired an entire generation of young people.

This exploratory spirit is manifested today by the International Space Station. The ISS conducts intensive environmental research into problems like air quality and climate change. With the population of planet Earth expanding, there is more pressure on the environment and resources. Those who believe in space exploration say the concept of space colonization holds hope for the future of mankind. And they point to what Pulitzer Prize–winning historian William Goetzmann said: "America has indeed been 'exploration's nation,' . . . that . . . continually looks forward in the direction of the new." To many it is imperative to continue space exploration for the good of our world and mankind.

39. Which of the following best tells what this passage is about?

- **A.** the many explorers who wanted to chart unknown lands
- **B.** why people are against space exploration increasing
- **C.** the reasons why people think space exploration is important
- **D.** the history of space travel in this country and the Soviet Union

CONTINUE ON TO THE NEXT PAGE ▶

40. The best reason that the author began the passage by describing the landing on the moon was to

E. remind the reader of what happened.
F. impress the reader with its drama.
G. suggest that space exploration is hard to do.
H. show how difficult it was to reach the moon.

41. Which reason is **not** given for continuing space exploration?

A. improved medical procedures
B. new kinds of materials
C. the possibility of colonization
D. a better food source

42. Why are the explorers in the passage called intrepid?

E. They were driven by hunger.
F. They went by ship.
G. They traveled many miles.
H. They were fearless.

43. The author includes information about explorers to demonstrate

A. the extent of traveling that explorers did.
B. his knowledge of the history of exploration.
C. why space exploration is important.
D. how mankind has always wanted to find new lands.

44. How will ending the space exploration program most negatively affect mankind's future?

E. People will be unaware of the universe around them.
F. No new frontiers will be explored.
G. Mankind will no longer be curious about its origins.
H. Humans may not be able to find other planets to live on.

CONTINUE ON TO THE NEXT PAGE ▶

Mary Cassatt was a famous and critically acclaimed artist, but it was not easy for her to become one. Mary was born in the mid-1800s, a time when young women from well-off families were expected to become educated and then to marry. The education was a polish that would make a woman a charming hostess. But that was not what Mary wanted for herself. At an early age she fell in love with painting. To fulfill her dream, she had to rebel against the wishes of her family, in particular her father.

When Mary was a young girl, her family left the United States to live in Europe. While there, she viewed the work of some of the greatest artists who have ever lived. She even had her first art lesson in Europe. When her family returned home to Pennsylvania, Mary enrolled in the Pennsylvania Academy of Fine Arts in Philadelphia at the age of 17. She was one of a handful of females there. While the other women wanted to learn to paint to round out their education, Mary was a serious student. She soon became frustrated by the slow-paced instruction and vowed to return to Europe once again. Her father did not approve of her pursuing a career as an artist, yet Mary went back to Europe to study painting.

Mary studied painting in Paris. While there she met the famous painter Edgar Degas, and he quickly became her mentor. Soon she joined the Impressionist Movement. This group of artists used bright colors and did not paint in a traditional manner. They painted the "impression" of an object or person. Instead of making something look exactly the way it did, they made it look the way it looked to them.

Mary soon started to become well known. Unlike other artists who painted scenes in nature, Mary chose to paint ordinary people doing ordinary things. She often painted women with children. She returned home to be with her family and to meet with other American artists. She left the Impressionist School and went in her own direction. Her paintings were always distinctive. Sometimes her pictures seem to glow with light. At other times they seem very soft and warm. Mary Cassatt gave the world a new way of looking at people and places. She also showed the world that women could become great artists.

45. Which of the following best tells what this passage is about?

A. the city of Paris in the mid-1800s
B. why Mary Cassatt wanted to be an artist
C. the reasons Mary Cassatt's paintings are popular
D. the life and career of Mary Cassatt

46. How did the experience of living in Europe as a young girl affect Mary Cassatt?

E. She started to show promise as a painter.
F. She became more rebellious.
G. She was exposed to the great masters.
H. She met many artists who helped her develop her art.

47. Which of the following was **not** something that Mary Cassatt wanted?

A. learning more about painting
B. settling down with her family
C. painting the things she loved
D. meeting many artists

CONTINUE ON TO THE NEXT PAGE ▶

48. In what way did the Impressionist Movement change the art of the time?

- **E.** Art became much more expensive than it was before.
- **F.** New standards were set about what could be painted.
- **G.** Fewer members of the public collected paintings.
- **H.** Artists were freer than before in what and how they could paint.

49. Why do you suppose Mary Cassatt left the Impressionist Movement?

- **A.** She did not want to be labeled.
- **B.** She had an argument with Edgar Degas.
- **C.** She wanted to return to America.
- **D.** She was asked to do so by her family.

50. What can be inferred about Mary Cassatt?

- **E.** She worried about her image in society.
- **F.** She did not trust many people.
- **G.** She would do anything necessary to be famous.
- **H.** She was a strong woman who knew what she wanted.

Zoos, as a repository of wild animals, were first established 4,000 years ago by King Shulgi of Mesopotamia. The king wanted to keep lions in his park to amuse himself and his fellow rulers, who would come to visit him often. Shortly thereafter, the Chinese Emperor Wen Wang also amused himself by collecting many strange animals from all parts of his empire. Other notable rulers who continued this tradition of keeping zoos at their courts included Henry the First of England and Montezuma, the last independent Aztec ruler. The oldest zoo still in existence was originally created for the royal family of Vienna in 1752. It was opened to the public in 1779 and has been in operation ever since.

Maintenance, however, of these captive animals has always been a problem. It is hard to determine the right foods for captive animals, even today. Early zoo keepers, who probably had little or no training, were often unsure of even basic facts such as whether the animals they must feed were carnivores or herbivores. Even if the keepers knew their newly captured animals ate special food (such as young bamboo plants), they may have found it impossible to meet such specific dietary needs. In addition, cramped cages and unsanitary conditions were also very common problems. Up through the 1800s, zoos had trouble keeping their animals alive very long because of these issues.

As science advanced, some of the questions about the eating habits and natural behaviors of these animals began to be answered. In the early 1900s, Carl Hagenbeck pioneered the display of zoo animals in cages and pens that more closely resembled their natural habitat. Eventually the focus evolved from simply seeking a better way to showcase the animals to trying to create a habitat that the captive animal was comfortable in. Exhibits became larger and more complex so that the animals could display the natural behaviors that they would in the wild. Foods that the animals would feed on in the wild were obtained. By the end of the twentieth century, animals in zoos were surviving longer than their counterparts in the wilds.

CONTINUE ON TO THE NEXT PAGE ▶

However, by the twenty-first century, zoos had become somewhat controversial. At the heart of the debate was whether or not humans had the right to cage animals for entertainment. Two distinct camps emerged. There were those that called themselves conservationists and championed zoos as a way to rescue animals that might become extinct and to educate new generations on the unique species that make up the world. The other camp consisted of animal activists who protested the captivity of animals for any reason. These activists felt that caging animals that were wild by nature was morally wrong. Despite the ongoing controversy, the zoo industry was alive and well in the twenty-first century. Most major cities had a zoo, and they continued to be a tourist destination, especially for families with children.

51. Which of the following best tells what the passage is about?

A. The reason there are zoos
B. The history of zoos
C. The reason rulers like zoo animals
D. The controversy over caging animals

52. Which is not mentioned as a problem with keeping zoo animals?

E. Knowing what to feed them
F. Keeping animals caged
G. Unsanitary conditions
H. The danger wild animals pose to people

53. According to the passage, which of the following statements about zoos is accurate?

A. Carl Hagenbeck taught people how to properly feed their zoo animals.
B. The first zoos were created by wealthy rulers for their own entertainment.
C. Animal activists are upset by zoos because zoo animals are not well cared for.
D. Zoos are one of the most visited attractions in the United States.

54. The information about early rulers and their zoos was included in order to illustrate

E. that people in power are fascinated by captive animals.
F. that our behavior is learned from our ancestors.
G. that the tradition of displaying wild animals has a long history.
H. that the Mesopotamian civilization was more advanced than most people realize.

55. Based on the information in the passage, which will most likely happen to zoos in the future?

A. They will slowly be phased out as more exciting forms of entertainment take their place.
B. They will continue to be a part of modern society with, perhaps, more freedom for the animals.
C. They will become more interactive and exciting in order to compete with other forms of entertainment.
D. They will be outlawed because of protesting animal rights' activists.

CONTINUE ON TO THE NEXT PAGE ▶

56. Which of these statements can be inferred from the passage?

E. Zoo animals are healthier than animals living in the wild.
F. It makes animals miserable to be caged.
G. Zoo animals can become domesticated after years of living in cages.
H. Early zoo keepers did not care about their animals.

57. Which of the choices best states what is implied by the following sentence from the passage: "Eventually the focus evolved from simply seeking a better way to showcase the animals to trying to create a habitat that the captive animal was comfortable in."

A. The zoo industry continues to evolve and change.
B. It was equally important to display the animals and to treat them well.
C. It was important to show the animals to their best advantage.
D. People began to care more about the comfort of the zoo animals.

CONTINUE ON TO THE NEXT PAGE ▶

PART 2

MATHEMATICS

90 Minutes ■ 57 Questions

Important Notes

(1) No formulas and definitions of mathematical terms and symbols are provided.
(2) Diagrams are not necessarily drawn to scale. Be careful not to make assumptions about relationships in diagrams.
(3) Diagrams can be assumed to be in one plane unless otherwise stated.
(4) Graphs are drawn to scale. Therefore, you may assume relationships according to appearance. This means lines that look parallel can be assumed to be parallel, angles that look like right angles can be assumed to be right angles, and so forth.
(5) All fractions must be reduced to lowest terms.

Grid-In Problems

QUESTIONS 58–62

DIRECTIONS FOR GRID-IN QUESTIONS: In the Mathematics section of the new SHSAT, in addition to the multiple choice questions, there will be five grid-in questions. For these questions, you need to solve a computational question and provide the numerical answer. Once you have found the answer, you must enter it at the top of the grid and then fill in the appropriate circles below to match your answer.

Each grid consists of five columns. Enter your answer beginning at the left. The first column is reserved for the "–" symbol. It only gets used if the answer is a negative number. If your answer is positive, leave that column blank and begin your answer in the second column. For example, if your answer is 28, write 2 in the second column and 8 in the third column. Fill in the circle that contains a 2 below the 2 and the circle that contains an 8 below the 8.

If the answer contains a decimal, enter a "." in the appropriate column. There is a circle that contains a "." that can be filled in. It is important that you do not skip a column in the middle of your answer. For example, if your answer is 203, don't skip the 0 and just leave the column blank! Take time to check your answers carefully. If you forget to write in a digit or fail to fill out the corresponding circle, your answer will be marked wrong even if you calculated the correct answer.

58. What is the value of $5|x| + 3|y|$ if $x = -4$ and $y = -7$?

59. $(\sqrt{36}) \times (\sqrt{(81)}) =$

60. How many integers from 1 to 100 have a factor of 3?

61. Jess wants to build a fence and has 150 feet of wire. Each section of her fence will take $1\frac{1}{4}$ feet of wire. How many complete sections can she build?

62. Assume that m is an even integer and $10 < m < 23$. What is the mean of all possible values of m?

CONTINUE ON TO THE NEXT PAGE ▶

Multiple Choice Problems

QUESTIONS 63–114

DIRECTIONS: Find the solution to each problem; then choose the best answer from the options given. Mark the letter of your answer choice on the answer sheet. You may use your test booklet or paper provided by the proctor as scrap paper for your calculations. However, DO NOT make calculations or put any stray marks on your answer sheet.

63. What is the greatest common factor of 154 and 196?

A. 2
B. 7
C. 11
D. 14

64. Christine, Marylou, and Katy each have a savings account. Marylou has twice as much money in her account as Christine. Katy has three times as much money in her account as Christine. If the total amount in all three accounts is $3,600, how much money does Christine have in her account?

E. $600
F. $720
G. $900
H. $1,200

65. 

In the figure above, points X and Y are on line segment $\overline{WZ}$.

$$XY = 10 \text{ in.}$$
$$XY : XZ = 1:3$$
$$WY : YZ = 5:2$$

What is the length of $\overline{WX}$?

A. 10 in.
B. 20 in.
C. 30 in.
D. 40 in.

66. A truck moves at a rate of 1,100 feet per minute. If the radius of each tire is 2 feet, how much time does it take for a tire to rotate 7,700 times? (Use the fraction 22/7 to approximate pi.)

E. 11 minutes
F. 22 minutes
G. 44 minutes
H. 88 minutes

67. 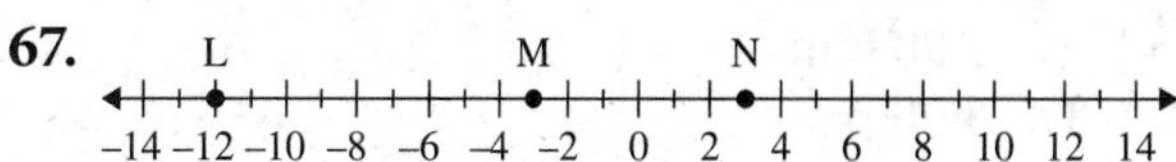

On the number line above, M is the midpoint of $\overline{LO}$. Point O is not shown. What is the length of $\overline{NO}$?

A. 3 units
B. 4.5 units
C. 6 units
D. 9 units

68. A hexagon has two sides each of length $3x$ inches. It has three sides each of length $2x$ inches. The sixth side has a length of 15 inches. If the perimeter of the hexagon is 135 inches, what is the value of x?

E. 4
F. 5
G. 10
H. 15

CONTINUE ON TO THE NEXT PAGE ▶

69. What is the value of $2|x|-9|y|$ if $x=-8$ and $y=-3$?

A. −43
B. −11
C. −9
D. 11

70. $(\sqrt{81})(\sqrt{25})=$

E. 5
F. 9
G. 40
H. 45

71. It will take Fernando 100 hours to completely thaw a frozen turkey in the refrigerator. If he starts thawing the turkey at 9:00 a.m., at what time will the turkey be completely thawed?

A. 6:00 a.m.
B. 8:00 a.m.
C. 1:00 p.m.
D. 3:00 p.m.

72. X is an element of the set {2.8, 3.7, 5.1, 14.0, 20.0} and $\frac{0.3X}{0.25}$ is an integer. What is X?

E. 3.7
F. 5.1
G. 14.0
H. 20.0

73. How many integers from 1 to 135 have 2 as a factor?

A. 67
B. 68
C. 69
D. 70

74. Assume d is an odd integer and $1<d<11$. What is the mean of all possible values of d?

E. 6.0
F. 6.5
G. 12.0
H. 12.5

75.

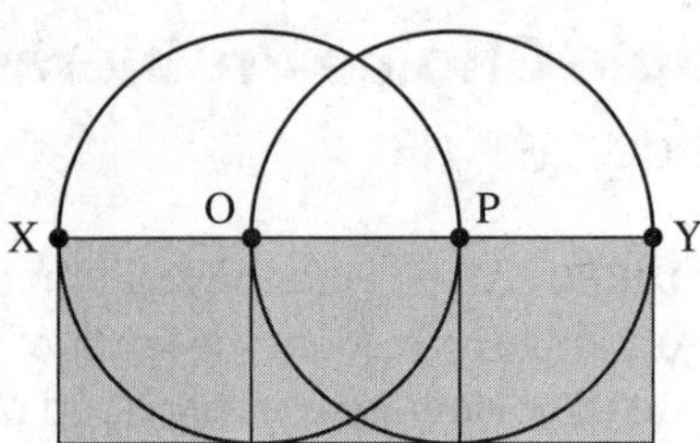

The shaded rectangle in the diagram consists of three squares. The rectangle touches the circles at points X and Y. Points O and P are the centers of the two circles. Both of the circles have a diameter of 18 centimeters. What is the area of the rectangle?

A. 27 sq cm
B. 81 sq cm
C. 243 sq cm
D. 288 sq cm

76. Robyn has 75 feet of copper wire. She needs $\frac{5}{6}$ foot of wire for every electrical circuit she builds. What is the maximum number of electrical circuits Robyn can build?

E. 15
F. 25
G. 90
H. 100

77. Ian earns \$7.36 per hour. If he worked $2\frac{1}{4}$ hours on Saturday and $2\frac{1}{4}$ hours on Sunday, how much did Ian earn in all?

A. \$18.40
B. \$29.44
C. \$31.38
D. \$33.12

CONTINUE ON TO THE NEXT PAGE ▶

78. Assume that the notation $\Psi(o, p, q, r)$ means "Multiply o and p. Subtract q from the product, and then raise to the power of r." What is the value of $\Psi(8,2,16,3) + \Psi(7,7,39,2)$?

E. 18
F. 20
G. 50
H. 100

79. In a marathon, 42 out of 60 runners finished the race. What percentage did **not** finish the marathon?

A. 18%
B. 30%
C. 43%
D. 57%

80. The product of 2 consecutive positive integers is 132. What is their sum?

E. 23
F. 28
G. 37
H. 47

81. A circle has a circumference of s feet and an area of t square feet. If $s = 3t$, what is the radius of the circle?

A. $\frac{1}{6}$ ft

B. $\frac{1}{3}$ ft

C. $\frac{2}{3}$ ft

D. 2 ft

82.

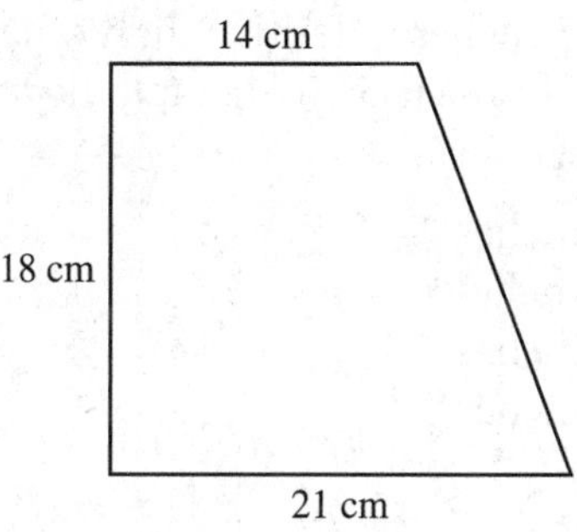

What is the area of the trapezoid above?

E. 21 sq cm
F. 126 sq cm
G. 273 sq cm
H. 315 sq cm

83. For what positive value of x does $\frac{9}{11} = \frac{x^2}{44}$?

A. 3
B. 6
C. 13
D. 36

84. Three consecutive multiples of 3 have a sum of 72. What is the **least** of these numbers?

E. 3
F. 9
G. 21
H. 27

85.

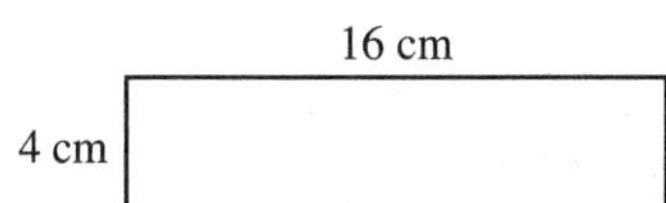

What is the perimeter of a square that has the same area as the rectangle above?

A. 12 cm
B. 20 cm
C. 32 cm
D. 40 cm

CONTINUE ON TO THE NEXT PAGE ▶

86. Lilia is 3 inches taller than half of Jeannie's height. If Lilia is 35 inches tall, how tall is Jeannie?

E. 32 inches
F. 64 inches
G. 70 inches
H. 76 inches

87.

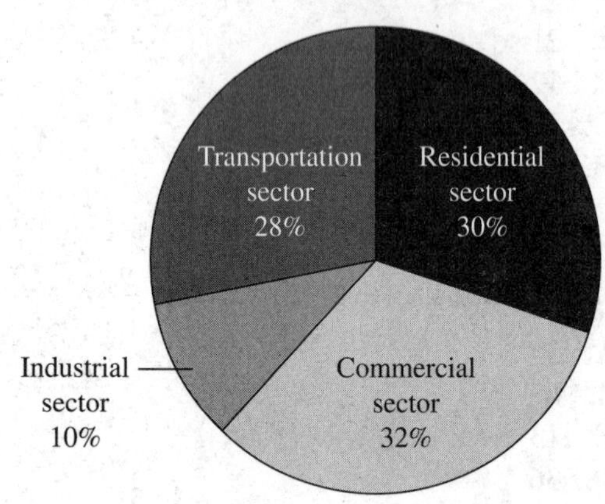

Source: http://www.eia.gov/states/sep_sum/html/pdf/sum_btu_1.pdf

The total energy consumption in New York State in 2008 was about 4,000 trillion btu. About how many trillion btu was consumed by the residential sector?

A. 300
B. 400
C. 1,100
D. 1,200

88. The following table shows the number of calls received by the customer service department.

Day	1	2	3	4	5	6	7
Number of Calls	119	118	122	120	118	118	121

According to the table, what is the median number of calls received by the customer service department in the seven days?

E. 118
F. 119
G. 120
H. 121

89. If $x = 9$ and $y = 3$, what is the value of $\frac{12x}{x-y}$?

A. 6
B. 12
C. 18
D. 36

90. Which of the inequalities are shown on this graph?

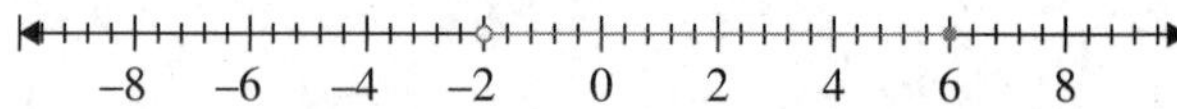

E. $x \leq -2$ and $x > 6$
F. $-2 \leq x < 6$
G. $-2 < x \leq 6$
H. $x < -2$ and $x \geq 6$

91. For what value of q is $5(2+q) = 3(q+4)$?

A. 1
B. 3
C. 4
D. 11

CONTINUE ON TO THE NEXT PAGE ▶

92. Kurt has a jar of marbles. Six of the marbles are blue. The probability of randomly drawing a blue marble is $\frac{1}{5}$. When Kurt adds more blue marbles to the jar, the probability of drawing a blue marble becomes $\frac{1}{4}$. How many blue marbles did Kurt add to the jar?

E. 1
F. 2
G. 3
H. 4

93. Julio is driving from New York to Florida. He drives $\frac{1}{5}$ of the total distance on the first day. He drives $\frac{1}{2}$ of the remaining distance on the second day. What fraction of the total distance does Julio have left to drive?

A. $\frac{2}{5}$

B. $\frac{3}{5}$

C. $\frac{1}{10}$

D. $\frac{3}{10}$

94.

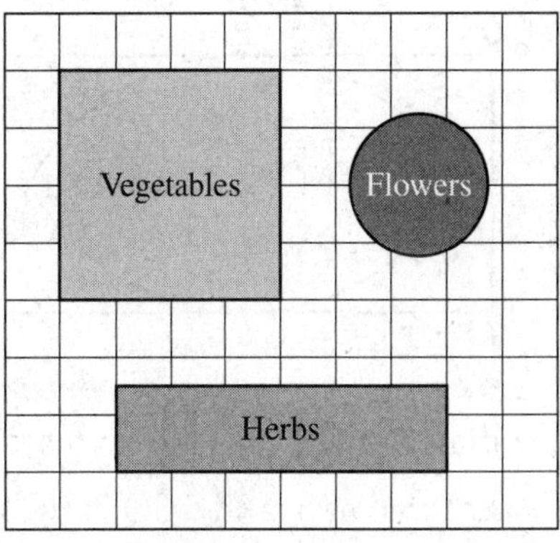

Scale: 1 in. = 3 ft

The diagram above shows a plan for a community garden. The plan is drawn on a grid made up of 1-inch squares. About how many square yards will be used to grow herbs?

E. 4.5 sq yd
F. 9.0 sq yd
G. 13.5 sq yd
H. 18.0 sq yd

95. Tanisha's website had x visitors on Friday. On Saturday, it had 500 more visitors than it did on Friday. The total number of visitors on Friday and Saturday was twice the number on Sunday. In terms of x, how many visitors did Tanisha's website have on Sunday?

A. $x + 250$

B. $2x + 250$

C. $2x + 1,000$

D. $\frac{x + 250}{2}$

CONTINUE ON TO THE NEXT PAGE ▶

96.

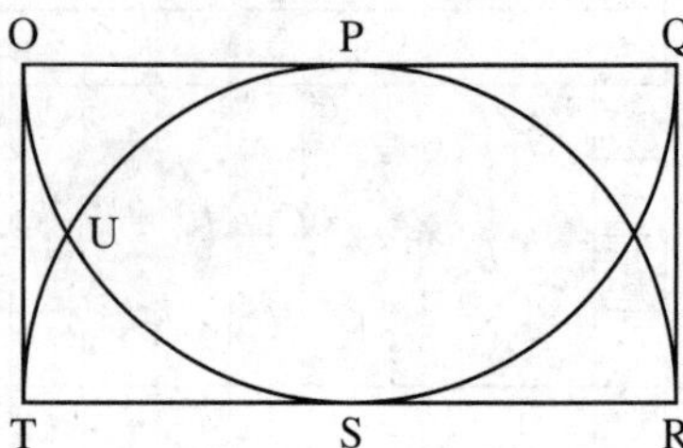

In the diagram above, TPR is an arc of a circle centered at S, and OSQ is the arc of a circle centered at P. $\overline{OQ}$ passes through point P, and $\overline{RT}$ passes through point S. The perimeter of triangle PSU (not shown) is 15 centimeters. OQRT is a rectangle, and the length of $\overline{OQ}$ is twice the length of $\overline{OT}$. What is the area of the rectangle?

E. 20 sq cm
F. 30 sq cm
G. 40 sq cm
H. 50 sq cm

97. Kelly is 3 times the age that Allie was seven years ago. Allie is now 18. How old is Kelly?

A. 14
B. 21
C. 25
D. 33

98. In 2000, the population of Utica, NY, was about 60,000. The number of females was 53% of the population. About how many more females than males lived in Utica in 2000?

E. 3,600
F. 4,000
G. 17,000
H. 28,200

99. Javier poured a total of 128 fluid ounces of lemonade into cups. He poured 11 fluid ounces into all but the last cup. How many fluid ounces did he pour into the last cup?

A. 5
B. 6
C. 7
D. 8

100.

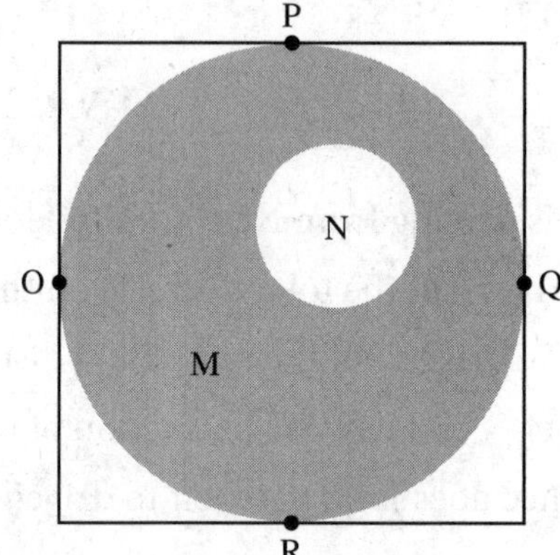

Circle M touches the square at points O, P, Q, and R. Circle N lies inside circle M. The area of circle N is 3π sq cm. The area of the shaded portion is 22π sq cm. What is the area of the square?

E. 25 sq cm
F. 66 sq cm
G. 100 sq cm
H. 121 sq cm

101. There are 25 links in 1 rod and 0.22 yards in 1 link. How many feet are there in 1 rod?

A. 5.5 ft
B. 7.5 ft
C. 16.5 ft
D. 66 ft

102. If $x = 5$ and $\frac{4x+6y}{2y} = 8$, what is the value of y?

E. 2
F. 4
G. 6
H. 8

CONTINUE ON TO THE NEXT PAGE ▶

103. Substance A has a mass of 60 grams. The ratio of the masses of substance A to substance B is 3:5. The ratio of the masses of substance B to substance C is 4:7. What is the sum of the mass of substance B and the mass of substance C?

A. 75 grams
B. 100 grams
C. 175 grams
D. 275 grams

104.

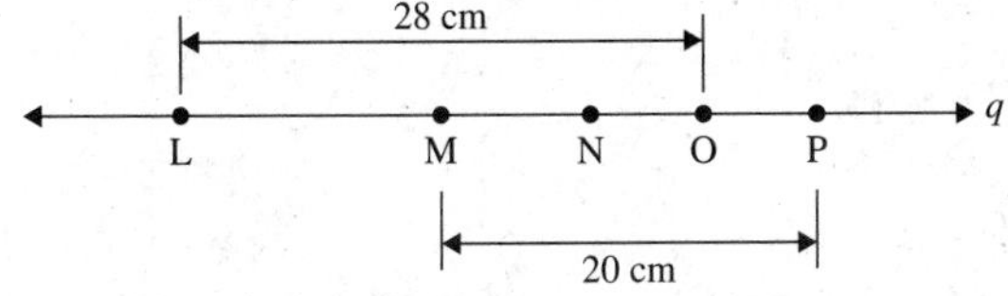

On line q, LP = 37 centimeters. If MN = 3 cm, what is the length of $\overline{NO}$?

E. 8 cm
F. 9 cm
G. 10 cm
H. 11 cm

105. A camera costs x dollars at Store X and y dollars at Store Y. The camera at Store Y costs $9 less than $\frac{2}{3}$ the cost at Store X. What is the value of y in terms of x?

A. $\frac{2}{3}x + 9$

B. $\frac{2}{3}x - 9$

C. $9 - \frac{2}{3}x$

D. $9x + \frac{2}{3}$

106.

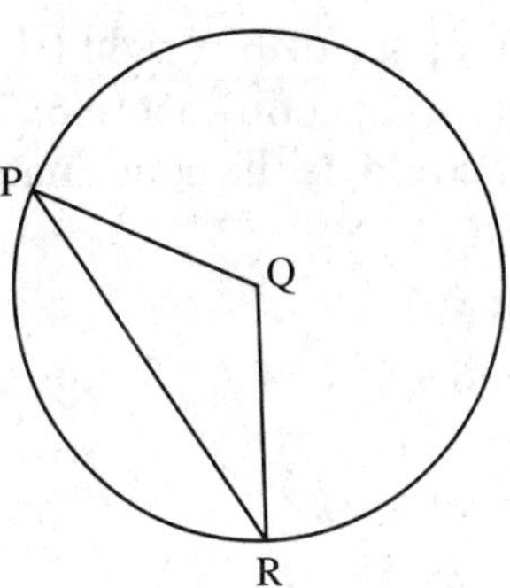

Q is the center of the circle. P and R are points on the circle. The perimeter of triangle PQR is 39 centimeters, and PR is 21 centimeters. What is the area of the circle?

E. 18π sq cm
F. 24π sq cm
G. 81π sq cm
H. 90π sq cm

107. $\left(\frac{3}{4} - \frac{1}{3}\right) \div \frac{5}{8} =$

A. $\frac{2}{3}$

B. $\frac{1}{4}$

C. $\frac{4}{3}$

D. $\frac{4}{15}$

108. Each member of the Cobb family packed a suitcase for a trip. Mark's suitcase weighed 51 pounds. Brenda's suitcase weighed 45 pounds. Jonathan's suitcase weighed 31 pounds. How much did Leah's suitcase weigh if the mean weight for the 4 suitcases was 40 pounds?

E. 25 pounds
F. 31 pounds
G. 33 pounds
H. 42 pounds

CONTINUE ON TO THE NEXT PAGE ▶

109. The longest side of a right triangle has endpoints at coordinates (6, 0) and (0,−6). What **could** be the coordinates of the third vertex?

A. (6,6)
B. (−6,−6)
C. (6,−6)
D. (−6,0)

110. Nicholas had a jar containing 12 quarters, 3 dimes, 7 nickels, and 14 pennies. He removed 6 quarters, and then randomly drew another coin. What is the probability that the coin was a dime?

E. $\frac{1}{2}$
F. $\frac{1}{4}$
G. $\frac{1}{10}$
H. $\frac{1}{12}$

111. Brandy painted $\frac{1}{2}$ of a wall on the first day. On the second day, she painted $\frac{1}{3}$ as much as she did on the first day. What is the ratio of the painted portion of the wall to the unpainted portion?

A. 1:2
B. 1:3
C. 2:1
D. 2:3

112. If $3x + 1$ is an odd integer, which of the following is also an odd integer?

E. $2x$
F. $5x$
G. $x + 4$
H. $2x + 7$

113. What is the greatest common factor of 204 and 135?

A. 3
B. 9
C. 12
D. 14

114. Adam, Chris, and Jerry went in together to buy a car. However, Adam paid twice as much as Chris did, and Jerry paid three times as much Chris. If altogether they paid $4,800, how much did Adam pay?

E. $600
F. $800
G. $1,600
H. $2,000

THIS IS THE END OF THE TEST. IF TIME REMAINS, YOU MAY CHECK YOUR ANSWERS. BE SURE THAT THERE ARE NO STRAY MARKS, PARTIALLY FILLED ANSWER CIRCLES, OR INCOMPLETE ERASURES ON YOUR ANSWER SHEET.

Diagnostic Test Answer Key

1. B
2. F
3. C
4. H
5. C
6. G
7. C
8. F
9. A
10. H
11. B
12. E
13. C
14. B
15. G
16. A
17. H
18. B
19. E
20. D
21. C
22. H
23. C
24. E
25. C
26. H
27. D
28. H
29. D
30. E
31. D
32. E
33. D
34. F
35. A
36. H
37. D
38. G
39. C
40. F
41. D
42. H
43. D
44. H
45. D
46. G
47. B
48. H
49. A
50. H
51. B
52. H
53. B
54. G
55. B
56. E
57. D

58. 41

59. 54

60. 33

61. 120

62. 17

63. D
64. E
65. D
66. H
67. A
68. G
69. B
70. H
71. C
72. H
73. A
74. E
75. C
76. G
77. D
78. H
79. B
80. E
81. C
82. H
83. B
84. G
85. C
86. F
87. D
88. F
89. C
90. G
91. A
92. F
93. A
94. F
95. A
96. H
97. D
98. E
99. C
100. G
101. C
102. E
103. D
104. E
105. B
106. G
107. A
108. G
109. C
110. G
111. C
112. H
113. A
114. G

Explanation of Answers—ELA Section

Revising/Editing

1. **(B)** The question asks you to identify the sentence with a misplaced modifier. In sentence 2 the phrase "when settling this country" precedes "many houses." Of course, "many houses" can't settle a country. The sentence needs to be revised so that the phrase can modify "people." In all the other sentences, the modifiers correctly modify the words that they should, so the answer is Option B.

2. **(F)** No comma should be added after "East" (Option E) because that would separate a subject from its verb. Options G and H are incorrect because the comma after "stones" is needed to separate two independent clauses and there does not need to be a comma after the word "period." Option F, however, is needed. When two or more adjectives are describing something, they should be separated by a comma.

3. **(C)** Option A is incorrect. That comma is needed because it comes after an introductory prepositional phrase of four or more words. Options B and D create sentence fragments. Option C is correct because "Until the bricks were totally hardened and ready for use" is a sentence fragment. It doesn't contain a complete thought and needs to be connected to the preceding sentence.

4. **(H)** The word "person's" is already punctuated correctly. It is a single noun showing possession, so Options E and F are not correct. Also, there is no problem with "might've," so Option G is incorrect. The mistake is in "Its." This should be a contraction, so it needs an apostrophe. Therefore, Option H is the answer.

5. **(C)** Inserting a comma after "Schliemann" would separate the subject from the verb, so Option A is incorrect. There is no reason to insert a comma after "site," so Option B is incorrect. The comma after the word "Troy" is needed. It separates a nonessential phrase from the rest of the sentence, so Option D is incorrect. The answer is Option C. That comma indicates that two independent clauses are being joined, but they are not. The second part of the sentence can't stand on its own. That comma needs to be removed.

6. **(G)** All the options are dealing with changes of verb tense. Option E puts "did" into the past perfect tense, which makes it seems as if it is no longer true. That edit is not needed. Option F makes "did" past progressive, which is also wrong. Option H changes "was" to the future tense. That can't be right because the sentence says "today." Option G is the answer because the sentence is indicating that the work is controversial right now.

7. **(C)** The question asks which sentence is irrelevant to the main idea of the passage. The passage is describing what the American West was like during the time of dinosaurs. Option A is relevant because it supports a description of the Apatosaurus. Option B is relevant because it introduces another type of dinosaur that was found there. Option D is relevant because it sums up the passage. Option C, however, simply states a fact about a current discovery. It relates to the main topic, dinosaurs, but does not add significantly to the information about what dinosaurs in the American West were like.

8. **(F)** Sentence 12 needs to be revised because it uses very generalized information. Although all the options are better choices than the sentence in the passage, Options E, G, and H still use vague descriptions such as "fairly fast and strong," "superior strength," and "massive creature." Option F uses specific images such as "short front limbs" and "strong back legs" that give the reader a picture of the creature being described.

9. **(A)** The question asks for a sentence to support sentence 14, which states that scientists have discovered fossilized evidence of battles between the two species. Option B simply offers a new, although related, idea. Option C tells us what the scientists think, and Option D continues with the idea of sentence 14 but does not support it with fact. Option A gives the reader a fact to support the detail given in sentence 14 so it is the best choice.

10. **(H)** Sentence 4 is adding support to the idea that the West was very different. Options E and G make it appear to contradict the earlier statements, and Option F indicates that the sentence is a result of the earlier statements. Option H is the only option that reinforces the idea that another fact is being given.

11. **(B)** Sentences 12 and 13 both give facts about the Allosaurus. Option A suggests that sentence 13 happens because of sentence 12. Option C suggests that sentence 12 happens in spite of sentence 13, and Option D suggests that sentence 12 happens because of sentence 13. None of these is correct; the sentences do not have a causal relationship with each other. They are equal ideas and therefore are joined by a semicolon and a conjunctive adverb. The conjunctive adverb "moreover" suggests that another reason or fact will follow. Therefore, Option B is the correct choice.

12. **(E)** Sentence 6 has a comma splice in it and needs to be punctuated in a way that shows the joining of two independent clauses. Options F and H insert unnecessary commas in ways that break up the flow of ideas. Option G replaces a necessary comma with a semicolon, which would be incorrect, also. Option E combines two independent clauses using a semicolon, which is the proper way for them to be joined.

13. **(C)** The question asks that you locate a dangling modifier. Options A, B, and D all offer sentences with modifying phrases or clauses that are placed next to the words that they modify. In sentence 5, however, the phrase "covering a good portion of what is considered the American West today" comes right before "humid climate," which causes confusion. That phrase is really modifying "inland seas." The sentence needs to be revised so that that relationship is clear.

14. **(B)** In this sentence, the apostrophes are used correctly, so neither Option A nor Option D is correct. Also, there is no need for a comma after "stepmother," so Option C is incorrect. A comma after the word "young" is necessary, however. The conjunction "and" joins two independent clauses and needs a comma to help it.

15. **(G)** This question asks you to look for a misplaced modifier. Sentences 1, 2, and 4 are correct, but there is a misplaced modifier in sentence 3. "Plagued with bronchial problems" is placed so that it seems to be describing doctors, but the doctors were not the ones with bronchial problems. This sentence needs to be revised so that it is clear that "Plagued with bronchial problems" refers to Spruce. Therefore, Option G is correct.

16. **(A)** This sentence asks you to find the sentence that best supports sentence 9. Sentence 9 tells about Spruce exploring South America. Although Options B, C, and D all might be true, they don't support what is said in sentence 9. Option A, however, does support sentence 9. It gives more detail about Spruce's explorations.

17. **(H)** The question asks you to look for a sentence that has an unclear pronoun reference. The unclear reference is in sentence 12, where it states Spruce "sent them back to England," referring to the specimen. "Specimen" is singular, and so the pronoun should be "it." All the other pronouns in the sentences mentioned are used correctly, so the answer is Option H.

18. **(B)** The question asks you to pick the choice that will show the relationship between sentences 14 and 15. Options A and D make sentence 14 a dependent clause, but they both distort the meaning. Parasitic insects and bouts of malaria didn't plague him "although" or "because" he had health issues. They were a part of his health issues. This is also why Option C is wrong. Parasitic insects and bouts of malaria weren't in addition to his health problems; they were a part of them. The best answer is Option B, which clearly shows that the health issues included parasitic insects and bouts of malaria.

19. **(E)** The sentence asks for a transitional word that will show the relationship between sentence 17 and sentence 18. Sentence 17 says he returned destitute, and sentence 18 says he returned with knowledge. Although Options F and G would be true, they make it seem like he returned with two similar things. Option H is also incorrect because sentence 18 doesn't refute sentence 17. Option E is the correct answer. It means that although one thing happened, another did also.

20. **(D)** The question asks you to look at the verb usage in sentence 13. Sentence 13, as well as the rest of the passage, is written in the past tense, and there is no reason to change that. Options A, B, and C all change the verb into a progressive form, which is incorrect. There is not an ongoing action in the sentence. Option D is correct. The verb doesn't need to be in the past perfect. It should just be in the past for this sentence.

Reading Comprehension

21. **(C)** This question asks you to determine the general theme of the passage. Option A is not discussed in the passage. Option B, though both people are mentioned, is not the theme of the passage. Option D is a detail that is mentioned, but not the focus of the entire passage. The passage describes the discovery that humans came to the Americas earlier than previously thought. Thus, the best answer is Option C.

22. **(H)** This question asks you to make an inference based on the information in the passage. Option E does not agree with the information in the passage that says the Buttermilk People hunted mastodons and seals. Option F might appeal, but the passage only says that the Buttermilk People used hematite to decorate their clothes, spears, and bodies. It does not mention them using it to tell a story through pictures. Option G could also appeal, since it seems as though the Buttermilk People were good hunters. But this does not mean they were better hunters than the Clovis People. The Buttermilk People seemed to make broad use of the mastodon, using it for food as well as clothing and shelter. Option H is the best answer.

23. (C) The question asks specifically about the Buttermilk People's nature, which is not directly discussed in the passage. In order to answer the question, you must look at the information in the passage and use it to infer the answer. Option A may be true, but there is nothing to support this idea in the passage. Option B could be true or false, but the passage does not discuss this possibility. Option C is supported by the passage, which states, "There is evidence that over centuries they explored all the way to the tip of South America" (lines 26–28). There is no evidence that Option D is true.

24. (E) The phrase "even brought pet dogs" implies a people who cared about animals and, in particular, their own animals. The fact that these early people would even have pets suggests that they were affectionate (Option E). There is no evidence for Option F. The concept of being well educated probably did not exist at that time. There is no support for either Option G or H.

25. (C) This is an inference question. It is necessary to look for information that supports one of the options. Neither Option A nor B is supported by the passage. There is no evidence of the Buttermilk People being fearful of enemies or being friendly to others. Option C is supported by the passage. The fact that the Buttermilk People liked to decorate their spears and themselves does suggest that they liked colorful objects. Option D is not supported. There is nothing in the passage about these people playing games.

26. (H) To answer this question you have to go through the passage and try to find the one topic that is not discussed. Option E and F are discussed in the paragraph. So is Option G. The topic of where the Buttermilk people settled would suggest that they were concerned with creating places to live. That leaves Option H. There is no mention of them creating a network of trails.

27. (D) This question asks you to determine the general theme of the passage. Option A is not discussed in the passage. Options B and C are mentioned, but they are details, not the theme of the passage. The passage describes how giant tube worms survive. Thus, the correct answer is Option D.

28. (H) This is an inference question. You need to make an inference based on the information in the passage. Option E is not supported by the passage. While the giant tube worm has a symbiotic relationship with the bacteria inside it, this is not necessarily true of "most life." Option F is not suggested by the passage. This is not a topic of discussion. Option G seems to be refuted by the passage since it seems that giant tube worms are unusual because they can stand vast changes in temperature. Option H is supported by the passage, which states, "Surprisingly, it does not need the energy of the sun," suggesting that most life does.

29. (D) To answer this question, you need to read the passage carefully to see which option is correct. Option A is a misstatement, since the passage tells the reader that giant tube worms "are directly related" to another form of worm. Option B is not directly refuted in the passage, but the passage suggests that giant tube worms are possibly only found in the Pacific Ocean. Since giant tube worms live until they are 250 years old, they are hardly "short-lived." Option D is the correct answer. This can be inferred from the passage because giant tube worms do exist without access to light.

30. **(E)** To answer this question, you need to reread the section of the passage that talks about lobsters. If you do this, you will find that only Option E is an accurate description of the relationship between giant tube worms and lobsters. Their exteriors are made of the same hard material. Option F might appeal, but there is nothing in the passage to suggest that lobsters live off the hot air vents. There is no mention either of Options G or H. The giant tube worms have a relationship with bacteria that benefits them both, not with lobsters.

31. **(D)** To answer this question you need to review the passage and find what is true of the giant tube worms. You will also need to use the information to infer the correct answer. Option A does not seem likely because there seems to be a great deal of data on giant tube worms in the passage. Option B is something that is directly stated in the passage, so it can be eliminated. Option C is also correct according to the passage. However, Option D does not seem to be correct. There are both very hot and very cold temperatures in the giant tube worms' environment. So Option D is the correct answer.

32. **(E)** To make an inference, you need to weigh all the information in a passage and come to the most logical conclusion. Options F and G don't seem to be likely. While Option H may appeal, the passage does say the giant tube worm gets nourishment from the bacteria inside it. Option E seems to be the only logical reason. Therefore, it is the correct answer.

33. **(D)** This question asks you to determine what the main idea or general theme of the passage is. Option A is mentioned in the passage, but it is only a detail, not a general theme. Options B and C are also details in the passage, not the main focus of it. The passage describes why miniature horses make good guide animals. Therefore, the correct answer is Option E.

34. **(F)** Check back through the passage to answer this question. Review the traits that are mentioned. Although the word *stamina* is not used, the passage says that these horses can work long hours, so Option E can be eliminated. Options G and H can also be eliminated because they are mentioned in the passage. So that leaves Option F. There is no mention of the horses' memories.

35. **(A)** Option A seems to be a logical conclusion from the information in the passage. There is no suggestion that Option B or C is correct. The subject of how much it costs to feed a miniature horse is not discussed. Thus Option A is the correct answer.

36. **(H)** You have to figure out why the author used this information in the passage. Option E might be a possibility, although that particular theme is not addressed in the passage. Option F is off the mark. The horses were obedient, and that is one reason they were used. There is no suggestion that Option G is correct. Option H is the best answer.

37. **(D)** You need to use your best judgment to answer this question. Option A does not seem to be a candidate for either a dog or a horse guide. Option B may or may not be a factor in choosing a horse guide, but it is difficult to judge. The same is true of Option C. Option D is the most likely answer.

38. **(G)** To answer this question you have to examine each option carefully. Option E is appealing, but is that really the reason that the author changed the saying? Option F might be possible, but the passage does not seem to be about political correctness. Option G seems to be correct. This seems to be a good reason. Option H does not seem likely. Option G is the best answer.

39. (C) This question asks you to determine what the main idea or general theme of the passage is. Option A is mentioned in the passage, but it is only a detail, not a general theme. Option B is not really discussed in the passage. Option D is only discussed in passing. The passage gives the reasons why people think that space exploration is important. Therefore, the correct answer is Option C.

40. (F) After describing the landing, the passage continues, "It was an event that could not be forgotten" (lines 6–7). Option F best explains what the author means: the event was dramatic. None of the other options explain why the author used this description.

41. (D) You will need to review the passage to answer this question. Scan through the passage to find what reasons are mentioned for continuing space exploration. Options A, B, and C are definitely mentioned. There is no mention of finding a better food source; hence Option D is the correct answer.

42. (H) A clue to the answer is stated in line 34: "*brave* people" have searched to find new lands. Option H restates this definition. The others do not mean what intrepid means.

43. (D) You will need to analyze the author's intent from what the passage says. It talks about how mankind has always wanted to know about the world. This is the reason for including information about explorers. Option A is not the reason, nor is Option B. This information has no bearing on the importance of space exploration, so Option C is not correct. Option D is the answer.

44. (H) While some of the options may occur should space exploration cease, such as Option G, the most important impact must be Option H. Neither Option E nor Option G would probably be an impact of the loss of the program.

45. (D) This question asks you to determine what the main idea or general theme of the passage is. Option A is mentioned in the passage, but it is only a detail, not a general theme. Options B and C are details in the passage, not the main focus of it. The passage describes how Mary Cassatt happened to become a unique artist. Thus, the correct answer is Option D.

46. (G) Use the information in the passage to find the answer to this question. While the passage says that Mary took her first art class in Europe, it does not say she showed promise, so Option E can be eliminated. There is no reason to believe she became more rebellious, although it appears she always had a mind of her own, so Option F is not correct. Option G is something that the passage supports. Therefore it is the correct answer. Option H may or may not be true, but not according to the passage.

47. (B) A careful review of the passage will help answer this question. Option A is something that Mary wanted to do, as is Option C. Option D probably happened because she was in Paris. That leaves Option B. Mary did not seem to want to settle down. She wanted to become an artist.

48. (H) The passage talks about how the Impressionists used bright colors and did not paint things exactly the way they looked. The option that fits best with this information is Option H. Artists were freer to do what they wanted. There is no evidence for Option E or G. Again, the Impressionists were more about breaking rules than setting standards, so Option F can be eliminated.

49. (A) You have to use the information and your own prior knowledge to answer this question. Option A is appealing. Mary did not seem to want to be part of any organization. There is no evidence that Option B is correct. While she did return to America, she did not necessarily have to leave the Impressionist Movement to do so. There is no suggestion that Mary was asked by her family to leave the movement, so Option D can be eliminated. The best answer is Option A.

50. (H) You need to use the information in the passage to make an inference about Mary Cassatt. Options E and F do not seem to fit with her personality. Mary did not seem to be worried about her image, nor did she seem not to trust people. While Mary wanted to be a famous artist, it doesn't seem as though she would do anything to achieve this goal. Option H seems to fit her personality best. She was a strong woman who knew what she wanted.

51. (B) This question asks you to determine what the main idea or general theme is of the passage. Option A is not really discussed in the passage; it is definitely not the general theme. Options C and D are details of the passage, not the main focus. The passage details the first known zoos and explains how they evolved from then until present day. Therefore, the correct answer is Option B.

52. (H) Check back through the passage to answer this question. Review what is mentioned about the problems people had keeping zoo animals. These included Options E, F, and G, so these can be eliminated. There is no mention, however, of the danger wild animals pose to people, so Option H is the correct answer.

53. (B) Option A is not true. Hagenbeck introduced the idea of natural habitats, not proper food. Option C is also not substantiated by the passage. The passage just says that animal activists are upset because the animals are caged. The passage says that zoos are a tourist attraction, but it doesn't rank them as an attraction, so Option D is also false. That leaves Option B. The passage tells us this is in the first paragraph by mentioning the first zoos, telling about who created them, and saying what their purpose was.

54. (G) For this question, you have to decide why the author used this information in the passage. Option E doesn't seem to be the reason that early rulers and their zoos were included because that idea was not developed in the passage. Although we may learn our behavior from our ancestors, that point is never made in the passage either, so Option F is not correct. Option H is also probably true, but not elaborated on in the passage. The most reasonable choice is Option G, as the passage covers the history of zoos.

55. **(B)** You have to use your best judgment to answer this question, but your answer has to be based on the passage. Options A and C both seem very plausible, but they have little to do with the information in the passage. Other types of entertainment were never mentioned. Option D is a possibility, but it doesn't seem likely from the passage. The passage states that the zoo industry was alive and well despite protests, and it never indicates that the protests had a negative impact on zoos. The answer is Option B, because, from the passage, you know that the tradition of zoos has gone on for the last 6,000 years. From that fact, and without any opposing facts, you can assume that the tradition will continue.

56. **(E)** To answer this question, you have to examine each option carefully. Many of the options are appealing, but it is important to pick the one option that seems most likely based on the information at hand. Option F is probably true, but the way animals feel is not discussed in the passage. The same is true of Option G; it is not discussed in the passage. Early zoo keepers are discussed. They did not know much about their animals. However, their *feelings* about the animals are never discussed, so Option H can't be the correct choice. However, you can infer from the passage that zoo animals are healthier than animals in the wild. Although this is not explicitly stated in the passage, the inference is supported by this sentence: "By the end of the twentieth century, animals in zoos were surviving longer than their counterparts in the wilds." Therefore, Option E is the answer.

57. **(D)** To answer this question, you simply have to look closely at the sentence in question and make sure you understand its meaning. To begin with, you can eliminate Options B and C, as both of them are blatantly false when considering the meaning of the sentence. Both Options A and D are true interpretations of the sentence, but Option D is the more specific one. It doesn't just tell us a change was made in the zoo industry; it tells us what that change was: a more caring attitude toward the animals. Therefore, Option D is the correct answer.

Explanation of Answers—Mathematics Section

58. Substitute the values of x and y into the expression (remember that $||$ means that you take the absolute value of that number):

$$5|x|+3|y|=5|-4|+3|-7|$$
$$=5(4)+3(7)$$
$$=20+21$$
$$=41$$

59. Solve by finding the square roots:

$(\sqrt{36})=6$; $(\sqrt{(81)}=9$; $(6)\times(9)=54$

60. The easiest way to figure this out is to simply divide 100 by 3. This will give us the number of times that 3 goes into 100 evenly, and it will also tell us how many numbers there are that 3 lands on as it climbs to 100.

$$\frac{100}{3}=33$$

61. First, turn the mixed number into an improper fraction: $1\frac{1}{4}=\frac{5}{4}$.
Then divide to find the number of $\frac{5}{4}$ sections Jess can build from 150 feet.

$$150\div\frac{5}{4}$$

To divide with a fraction, multiply using the reciprocal: $\frac{150}{1}\times\frac{4}{5}$.
Multiply:

$$\frac{150}{1}\times\frac{4}{5}=\frac{600}{5}$$

Divide:

$600 \div 5 = 120$

So, Jess could build 120 complete sections.

62. The even integers between 10 and 23 are 12, 14, 16, 18, 20, and 22. To determine the mean, add the 6 integers and divide by 6:

$$\frac{12+14+16+18+20+22}{6}=17$$

63. (D) Factor each number into its prime factors:

$154=2\bullet7\bullet11$

$196=2\bullet2\bullet7\bullet7$

The common prime factors are 2 and 7:

$154=\boxed{2}\bullet\boxed{7}\bullet11$

$196=\boxed{2}\bullet2\bullet\boxed{7}\bullet7$

The greatest common factor (GCF) is the product of the common prime factors:

$GCF=2\bullet7=14$

64. (E) Let x represent the amount of money that Christine has in her account. Marylou has twice as much as Christine, so Marylou has $2x$ in her account. Katy has three times as much as Christine, so Katy has $3x$ in her account. Together, they have \$3,600, so $x+2x+3x=\$3{,}600$. Solve for x:

$$x+2x+3x=\$3{,}600$$
$$6x=\$3{,}600$$
$$x=\$600$$

65. (D) The ratio of XY: XZ is 1:3 and XY = 10 in. Set up a proportion to find XZ:

$$\frac{XY}{XZ}=\frac{1}{3}$$
$$\frac{10}{XZ}=\frac{1}{3}$$
$$10\bullet3=XZ$$
$$30=XZ$$

Solve for YZ:

$$\begin{aligned} YZ &= XZ - XY \\ &= 30 - 10 \\ &= 20 \end{aligned}$$

Set up another proportion to find WY:

$$\frac{WY}{YZ} = \frac{5}{2}$$

$$\frac{WY}{20} = \frac{5}{2}$$

$$WY \bullet 2 = 5 \bullet 20$$

$$WY = 50$$

Solve for WX:

$$\begin{aligned} WX &= WY - XY \\ &= 50 - 10 \\ &= 40 \end{aligned}$$

66. (H) In one rotation of the tire, the truck moves through one circumference of the circle:

One rotation: $C = 2\pi r = 2\pi(2\text{ ft}) = 4\pi$ feet

In 7,700 rotations, the truck moves a distance of 7,700 circumferences:

Distance = (7,700)4π feet

At a rate of 1,100 ft/min, one sets up the following proportion:

$$\frac{1{,}100\text{ feet}}{1\text{ minute}} = \frac{(7{,}700)4\pi\text{ feet}}{\text{time}}$$

Cross multiplying and solving for time:

$$\text{time} = \frac{(7{,}700)4\pi}{1{,}100}\text{ minutes}$$

time = 28π minutes

Substituting the fraction $\frac{22}{7}$ for π:

$$\text{time} = 28\left(\frac{22}{7}\right)\text{ minutes}$$

time = 88 minutes

67. (A) The formula for the midpoint between two numbers a and b on a number line is $\frac{a+b}{2}$. Use the formula to find the location of point O:

$$\text{midpoint} = \frac{a+b}{2}$$

$$M = \frac{L+O}{2}$$

$$-3 = \frac{-12+O}{2}$$

$$-6 = -12 + O$$

$$6 = O$$

The formula for the distance between two points is $b - a$. Use the formula to find the length of $\overline{NO}$:

$$\begin{aligned} \text{distance} &= b - a \\ &= O - N \\ &= 6 - 3 \\ &= 3 \end{aligned}$$

68. (G) The sum of all six sides of the hexagon is 135, so $2(3x) + 3(2x) + 15 = 135$. Solve for x:

$$2(3x) + 3(2x) + 15 = 135$$

$$6x + 6x + 15 = 135$$

$$12x = 120$$

$$x = 10$$

69. (B) Substitute the values of x and y into the expression:

$$\begin{aligned} 2|x| - 9|y| &= 2|-8| - 9|-3| \\ &= 2(8) - 9(3) \\ &= 16 - 27 \\ &= -11 \end{aligned}$$

70. (H) $(\sqrt{81})(\sqrt{25}) = (9)(5) = 45$

71. **(C)** Since there are 24 hours in a day, it will be 9:00 a.m. after 24 hours, 48 hours, and 96 hours. Therefore, 100 hours after Fernando starts thawing the turkey will be 9:00 a.m. plus 4 more hours, or 1:00 p.m.

72. **(H)** First, simplify the fraction:

$$\frac{0.3X}{0.25}=\frac{30X}{25}=\frac{6X}{5}$$

For $\frac{6X}{5}$ to be an integer, the product of 6 and X must end in a 0 or 5. For example:

if $6X=30$, then $\frac{6X}{5}=6$

if $6X=32$, then $\frac{6X}{5}=6.4$

if $6X=35$, then $\frac{6X}{5}=7$

The only number in the set for which $6X$ will end in a 0 or 5 is 20.0. Therefore $X=20.0$.

73. **(A)** All even integers have 2 as a factor. There are five even integers from 1 to 10, five even integers from 11 to 20, and so on:

1–10	2, 4, 6, 8, 10
11–20	12, 14, 16, 18, 20
. . .	. . .
121–130	122, 124, 126, 128, 130
131–135	132, 134

There are 13 consecutive groups of 10 integers. Each of these groups has five even integers, so the number of even integers from 1 to 130 is $13\times5=65$. There are two more even integers from 131 to 135. Therefore, the total number of even integers is $65+2=67$.

74. **(E)** The odd integers between 1 and 11 are 3, 5, 7, and 9. The mean of these integers is

$$\frac{3+5+7+9}{4}=6.$$

75. **(C)** Each circle touches the center of the other circle, so the length of the rectangle is equal to the length of the diameter of one circle plus the length of the radius of the other circle: $18+9=27$ cm.

The rectangle is made up of three squares, so the side length of each square is $27\div3=9$ cm.

The width of the rectangle is equal to the side length of a square, so the area of the rectangle is $27\times9=243$ sq cm.

76. **(G)** Divide to find the number of $\frac{5}{6}$ foot pieces of wire Robyn can cut from 75 feet:

$$75\div\frac{5}{6}=75\times\frac{6}{5}=90.$$

77. **(D)** The total number of hours Ian worked is $2\frac{1}{4}\times2=4.5$. Therefore, the total amount that he earned is $\$7.36\times4.5=\$33.12$.

78. **(H)** Translate $\Psi(o,p,q,r)$ into an algebraic expression:

$$\Psi(o,p,q,r)=[(o\times p)-q]^r$$

Substitute the values of o, p, q, and r into the expression and solve:

$$\Psi(8,2,16,3)=[(8\times2)-16]^3=(16-16)^3=0^3=0$$

$$\Psi(7,7,39,2)=[(7\times7)-39]^2=(49-39)^2=10^2=100$$

$$\Psi(8,2,16,3)+\Psi(7,7,39,2)=0+100=100$$

79. (B) The number of runners who did not finish the marathon is $60-42=18$.

The fraction of runners who did not finish the marathon is $\frac{18}{60}$.

Reduce the fraction to lowest terms and then multiply by 100 to find the percentage who did not finish the marathon:

$$\frac{18}{60}=\frac{3}{10}\times 100=30\%$$

80. (E) Through quick estimation, we can conclude that the two consecutive positive integers are 11 and 12: $11\times 12=132$. The sum of 11 and 12 is $11+12=23$.

81. (C) The formula for the circumference of a circle is $C=2\pi r$. The formula for the area of a circle is $A=2\pi r$. Substitute the formulas into the equation $s=3t$ to solve for the radius of the circle:

$$s=3t$$
$$2\pi r=3(\pi r^2)$$
$$\frac{2}{3}\pi r=\pi r^2$$
$$\frac{2}{3}r=r^2$$
$$\frac{2}{3}=r$$

82. (H) The formula for the area of a trapezoid is $A=\frac{1}{2}\times$ height (base_1 + base_2), where base_1 and base_2 are the lengths of the parallel sides of the trapezoid. Substitute the given values into the equation and solve:

$$A=\frac{1}{2}\times \text{height }(\text{base}_1+\text{base}_2)$$
$$=\frac{1}{2}\times 18(14+21)$$
$$=9(35)$$
$$=315$$

83. (B) Cross multiply and then solve for x:

$$\frac{9}{11}=\frac{x^2}{44}$$
$$11x^2=9(44)$$
$$x^2=\frac{9(44)}{11}$$
$$x^2=9(4)$$
$$x^2=36$$
$$x=6 \text{ or } -6$$

84. (G) Let x represent the smallest of the three numbers. In terms of x, the next two consecutive multiples of 3 are $x+3$ and $x+6$. The sum of the three numbers is 72, so $x+(x+3)+(x+6)=72$. Solve for x:

$$x+(x+3)+(x+6)=72$$
$$3x+9=72$$
$$3x=63$$
$$x=21$$

85. (C) The area of the rectangle is $16\times 4=64$ sq cm. Therefore, the area of the square is 64 sq cm, and the side length of the square is $\sqrt{64}=8$ cm. The perimeter of the square is $8\times 4=32$ cm.

86. (F) Let j represent Jeannie's height in inches:

$$\frac{1}{2}j+3=35$$
$$\frac{1}{2}j=32$$
$$j=64$$

87. (D) The residential sector consumed 30% of the total energy:

$$4{,}000\times 30\%=4{,}000\times 0.30=1{,}200$$

88. (F) The median is the middle value in a list of numbers. To find the median, list all the numbers in order from least to greatest. The number in the middle is 119.

118, 118, 118, $\boxed{119}$, 120, 121, 122

89. (C) Substitute the values of x and y into the expression:

$$\frac{12x}{x-y}=\frac{12(9)}{9-3}=\frac{108}{6}=18$$

90. (G) The number line is shaded between -2 and 6. That means x includes all values between -2 and 6. The open circle at -2 indicates that -2 is not included in the range for x. The closed circle at 6 indicates that 6 *is* included in the range for x, thus the use of the "$\leq$" symbol.

91. (A)

$$5(2+q)=3(q+4)$$
$$10+5q=3q+12$$
$$2q=2$$
$$q=1$$

92. (F) Let x represent the original number of marbles in the jar. There are 6 blue marbles, and the probability of randomly drawing one of them is $\frac{1}{5}$. Set up a proportion to solve for x:

$$\frac{6}{x}=\frac{1}{5}$$
$$x=30$$

Let y represent the number of blue marbles Kurt added to the jar. When Kurt adds the blue marbles, the probability becomes $\frac{1}{4}$. Set up another proportion to solve for y:

$$\frac{6+y}{30+y}=\frac{1}{4}$$
$$4(6+y)=30+y$$
$$24+4y=30+y$$
$$3y=6$$
$$y=2$$

93. (A) Julio drives $\frac{1}{5}$ of the distance on the first day, so the fraction of the total distance that remains after the first day is $1-\frac{1}{5}=\frac{4}{5}$.

The fraction of the total distance that Julio drives on the second day is $\frac{1}{2}\times\frac{4}{5}=\frac{2}{5}$.

After two days, the fraction of the total distance that Julio has driven is $\frac{1}{5}+\frac{2}{5}=\frac{3}{5}$.

Therefore, the fraction of the total distance that Julio has left to drive is $1-\frac{3}{5}=\frac{2}{5}$.

94. (F) The drawing of the herb garden has a width of about 1.5 inches and a length of about 6 inches. The scale is 1 in. = 3 feet, so the width of the actual herb garden is $1.5 \times 3 = 4.5$ feet and the length is $6 \times 3 = 18$ feet.

One yard is equal to 3 feet, so the width is $4.5 \div 3 = 1.5$ yd and the length is $18 \div 3 = 6$ yd. Therefore, the area of the herb garden is $1.5 \times 6 = 9$ sq yd.

95. (A) If x represents the number of visitors on Friday, then the number of visitors on Saturday is expressed as $x+500$. The total number of visitors on Friday and Saturday is $x+x+500=2x+500$.

The total number of visitors on Friday and Saturday is twice the number on Sunday, so the number of visitors on Sunday is expressed as $\frac{2x+500}{2}=x+250$.

96. **(H)** The sides of triangle PSU are the radii of circle P and circle S: $\overline{SU}$ is a radius of circle S, $\overline{PU}$ is a radius of circle P, and $\overline{PS}$ is a radius of both circles. Since both circles share $\overline{PS}$, their radii are all the same length. This means that triangle PSU is an equilateral triangle, and the length of the radii of both circles is $15 \div 3 = 5$ cm.

$\overline{OQ}$ is the diameter of the circle P and a side of rectangle OQRT. Since the radius is 5 cm, OQ is $5 \times 2 = 10$ cm. The length of $\overline{OQ}$ is twice the length of $\overline{OT}$, so OT is $10 \div 2 = 5$ cm. Therefore, the area of the rectangle is $10 \times 5 = 50$ sq cm.

97. **(D)** Allie is now 18 years old. Her age seven years ago was $18 - 7 = 11$. Therefore, Kelly's age is $3 \times 11 = 33$.

98. **(E)** The number of females was $60{,}000 \times 0.53 = 31{,}800$. The percentage of males in the population was $100\% - 53\% = 47\%$, so the number of males was $60{,}000 \times 0.47 = 28{,}200$.

Subtract to find how many more females than males lived in Utica in 2000:

$31{,}800 - 28{,}200 = 3{,}600$

99. **(C)** Divide 128 by 11 to find the number of cups Javier filled with 11 fluid ounces of lemonade. The remainder represents the amount he poured into the last cup:

$128 \div 11 = 11R7$

100. **(G)** The area of circle M is the area of the shaded portion plus the area of circle N: $22\pi + 3\pi = 25\pi$. The formula for the area of a circle is $A = \pi r^2$. Solve for the radius:

$$\pi r^2 = 25\pi$$
$$r^2 = 25$$
$$r = 5$$

The radius of circle M is 5 cm, so its diameter is 10 cm. The diameter of circle M is equal to the side length of the square, so the area of the square is $10 \times 10 = 100$ sq cm.

101. **(C)** There are 3 feet in one yard and 0.22 yard in 1 link, so the number of feet in one link is $0.22 \text{ yd} \times 3 = 0.66$.

Since 1 rod = 25 links and 1 link = 0.66 ft, the number of feet in 1 rod is $25 \times 0.66 = 16.5$.

102. **(E)** Substitute the value of x into the expression and solve for y:

$$\frac{4(5) + 6y}{2y} = 8$$
$$\frac{20 + 6y}{2y} = 8$$
$$20 + 6y = 16y$$
$$20 = 10y$$
$$2 = y$$

103. **(D)** Substitute the mass of substance A into this ratio and solve for the mass of substance B:

$$\frac{A}{B}=\frac{3}{5}$$
$$\frac{60}{B}=\frac{3}{5}$$
$$3(B)=5(60)$$
$$B=100 \text{ grams}$$

Substitute the mass of substance B into this ratio and solve for the mass of substance C:

$$\frac{B}{C}=\frac{4}{7}$$
$$\frac{100}{C}=\frac{4}{7}$$
$$4(C)=100(7)$$
$$B=175 \text{ grams}$$

Add the mass of B and C to get the sum: 100 grams + 175 grams = 275 grams.

104. **(E)** Subtract to find the missing lengths:

$$\begin{aligned}\text{OP}&=\text{LP}-\text{LO}\\&=37-28\\&=9\text{ cm}\\\text{MO}&=\text{MP}-\text{OP}\\&=20-9\\&=11\text{ cm}\\\text{NO}&=\text{MO}-\text{MN}\\&=11-3\\&=8\text{ cm}\end{aligned}$$

105. **(B)** Translate the verbal description into an algebraic equation:

If the cost of the camera at Store Y is \$9 less than $\frac{2}{3}$ the cost at Store X, then $y=\frac{2}{3}x-9$.

106. **(G)** $\overline{PQ}$ and $\overline{QR}$ are two sides of triangle PQR. They are also the radii of the circle, so they have the same length. The perimeter of the triangle is 39 cm and PR is 21 cm, so because the sum of the three sides of the triangle equals its perimeter, you can solve for the radius, which is equal to PQ and QR:

$$\begin{aligned}21+r+r&=39\\2r&=39-21\\2r&=18\\r&=9\end{aligned}$$

The radii PQ and QR are each 9 cm. Therefore, the circumference of the circle is $C=9^2\pi=8\,1\pi$ sq cm.

107. **(A)**

$$\begin{aligned}\left(\frac{3}{4}-\frac{1}{3}\right)\div\frac{5}{8}&=\left(\frac{9}{12}-\frac{4}{12}\right)\div\frac{5}{8}\\&=\frac{5}{12}\div\frac{5}{8}\\&=\frac{5}{12}\times\frac{8}{5}\\&=\frac{40}{60}\\&=\frac{2}{3}\end{aligned}$$

108. **(G)** Let x represent the weight of Leah's suitcase, and solve for x using the formula for the mean.

$$\begin{aligned}\frac{51+45+31+x}{4}&=40\\\frac{127+x}{4}&=40\\127+x&=160\\x&=33\end{aligned}$$

109. **(C)** Look at the coordinate plane below. There are two possible coordinates for the third vertex, (0, 0) and (6, −6). Of the two, only (6, −6) is offered as an answer choice.

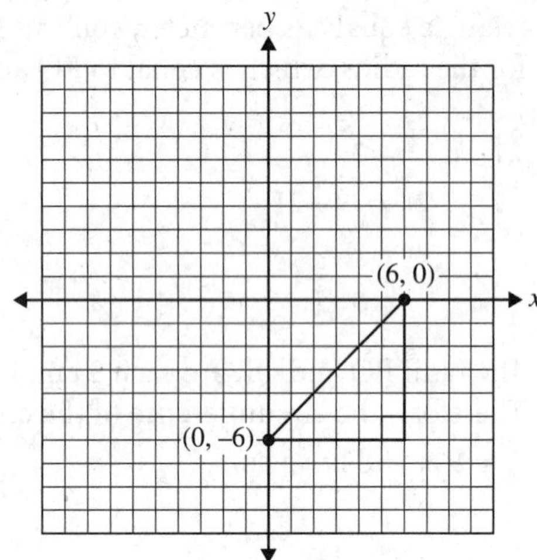

110. **(G)** There were 36 coins in the jar, and then Nicholas removed 6 quarters. This leaves 30 coins in the jar. Three of those coins are dimes, so the probability of randomly drawing a dime is $\frac{3}{30}=\frac{1}{10}$.

111. **(C)** Brandy painted $\frac{1}{2}$ of the wall on the first day. On the second day, she painted $\frac{1}{3}\times\frac{1}{2}=\frac{1}{6}$ of the wall. The fraction of the wall that is painted is $\frac{1}{2}+\frac{1}{6}=\frac{2}{3}$. The fraction of the wall that is unpainted is $1-\frac{2}{3}=\frac{1}{3}$. The ratio of painted to unpainted is $\frac{\frac{2}{3}}{\frac{1}{3}}$ or 2:1.

112. **(H)** If $3x+1$ is an odd integer, then $3x$ must be an even integer (because one less than an odd integer must be even), and x must also be an even integer (or $3x$ could not be even). For example:

$3(2)+1=7$

$3(3)+1=10$

$3(4)+1=13$

$3(5)+1=16$

You can see that $3x+1$ is only odd when an even integer is substituted for x. Substitute an even integer into each of the answer options. Only $2x+7$ produces an odd integer.

113. **(A)** Factor each number into its prime factors:

$204 = 2 \times 2 \times 3 \times 17$

$135 = 3 \times 3 \times 3 \times 5$

The common prime factor is 3.

The greatest common factor (GCF) is the product of the common prime factors. In this case, there is just 3, so that is the answer.

114. **(G)** Let x represent the amount of money that Chris paid. Adam paid twice as much as Chris, so Adam paid $2x$. Jerry paid three times as much as Chris did, so Jerry paid $3x$. All together, they paid $4,800, so $x + 2x + 3x =$ $4,800. Solve for x:

$x + 2x + 3x = \$4,800$

$6x = \$4,800$

$x = \$800$

If Adam paid $2x$, then he paid $1,600.

PART 3

SHSAT Topic Reviews

CHAPTER 4

Revising/Editing Questions

As you know, the ELA section of the SHSAT test includes revising/editing questions. The purpose of these questions is to determine the level of your writing skills. In addition, this section tests your analytical thinking as you choose the correct answers for some of these questions. Some people think that this section is the most difficult part of this test, but don't let that make you nervous. Once you understand exactly what the questions require and learn a few key strategies for approaching this section, you will be well prepared and able to tackle these items.

There will be two nonfiction passages in this section. Following each passage will be 6–8 questions that relate to the content. The questions will be multiple choice, and you will be asked to pick the best response. Some of the questions will refer to the passage as a whole, and some will refer to a specific sentence in the passage. There will also be 5–8 stand-alone questions in this section. The scope of the questions will range from correct verb usage to comma placement to paragraph organization. In this chapter, we will review a few of the rules that standard written English follows and provide you with some tips for spotting errors.

Organization

One of the most important tools in writing is organization. The SHSAT tests you on this in a few ways. You might be asked to choose which sentence best follows and supports a paragraph, which sentence is irrelevant to the argument presented in a paragraph, which would be the best transition from one sentence to the next, or other similar tasks. In other words, you are going to be asked to improve a writing passage.

When you get to the revising/editing section of the test, the best thing to do is to have a strategy in place. This will help you face the questions with confidence, and sometimes that is the best tool of all!

First, read over the passage. You will probably notice that it seems like a hastily written first draft. You don't have to read it slowly and carefully at this point; instead, just see if you can skim it to get the main idea. Unlike the reading comprehension passages, in this section you are not going to be asked about the purpose or deeper meaning of the selection. Instead, you will be focusing on correcting grammar and logic, supporting the argument, and eliminating irrelevant details. As you read, some errors in grammar or logic may jump out at you. If they do, take a minute and underline them. That way, you can find them again easily if you are asked to later.

After you have skimmed the passage, ask yourself a few questions: What was the author's point, or purpose, of writing the passage? How do the paragraphs relate to one another? Do you recognize an organizational style? Again, do not spend a lot of time on this step, but if you can, underline the main point and mark any sentence that obviously does not fit with the argument presented. If anything was confusing or glaringly out of place, mark it.

These things might seem obvious, but most of the questions will relate to the passage's mistakes. If you can easily mark them as you read through, it will save you time when you are answering the questions. However, do not spend time looking for mistakes before you read the questions. That will just slow you down, as you don't know what the questions are yet.

After you have read the passage, look at the first question. Many of the questions might ask about a specific sentence in the passage. If they do, you need to go back and read that sentence slowly and carefully as well as the sentences before and after it. This method helps make sure you understand the sentence's context. Context is often what the question is testing you on. As you look through the possible answers, you need to remember to make sure the answer you choose is a complete sentence, is grammatically correct, and is the most concise.

The strategies so far have applied to all the questions you might encounter in this section. Let's go into a little more detail about the particular types of questions you might be asked.

Question Types

Questions that ask you to support another sentence or the passage as a whole, delete an irrelevant sentence, or add a concluding sentence are all testing you on your organizational writing skills. These are probably the most common types of questions in the revising/editing section of the SHSAT. Before you answer any of these types of questions, you should understand what the main point of the passage is. If you don't already know it, go back and read the passage carefully. Then look at your choices.

If you are picking a sentence to support another sentence in the passage, study your options. Often you will be able to quickly eliminate any choices that contradict the main idea or mention the topic but don't align with the argument. Remember, if you are asked to insert a sentence to support another sentence, the answer must contain information that strengthens the sentence already there. It can't contradict or just introduce irrelevant, although topic-centric, information.

If you are asked to pick a sentence that offers a concluding idea, look carefully at the choices given. You don't want to pick a sentence that just addresses a part of the passage if it should conclude the whole passage. You also don't want a concluding sentence that addresses the topic, but doesn't directly focus on the main argument of the passage. The concluding sentence should clearly sum up the author's argument.

You can apply the same strategy when you are removing an irrelevant sentence. You may be given four sentences and have to eliminate one of them as irrelevant. The irrelevant sentence often strays from the topic or just adds useless information. However, be sure to read each sentence. You might think you know the answer before you read them all, and it is tempting to just mark it down and move on, but you should take the time to read each sentence choice. This way, you will be sure not to make a mistake because you were in a hurry and didn't notice the all-important negative or other word that gave the sentence a meaning you didn't expect at first glance.

Some of these questions will probably ask you what the best transition would be from one sentence to the next. These transitions might be a single word, or they might be a short phrase. For example, the question might be "Which transition should be added to the beginning of sentence 5?" You will be able to choose from four different transitional words or phrases. In order to answer this question correctly, you need to look back at the sentence in question and at sentence 4 also. What kind of relationship do they have to one another? Does the second sentence contradict the first? Does it support it? Does it reach a conclusion? Transitional words and phrases help to clarify that relationship.

If the second sentence supports the first by adding another fact or example, you might use a transition such as:

In addition
Furthermore,
Moreover,
Also,

or another similar phrase or word.

If the second sentence contradicts the first, you should use a transition such as:

On the other hand
Although
Nevertheless

or some other phrase or word that shows opposition.

If the second sentence is summarizing or making a conclusion from the first, use a transition such as:

Therefore
In fact
Ultimately
After all

or similar concluding word or phrase.

Similarly, the SHSAT might ask you which would be the best way to combine two sentences in order to clarify the relationship between their ideas. This also deals with transitional words or phrases. Again, you need to carefully read the two sentences in question and identify what type of relationship those ideas have. Once you understand what the author is trying to say, pick a transitional word that supports that relationship. Did the first idea happen *because* of the second idea? Or did it happen *in spite of* the second idea? After you have determined the relationship between the two ideas, look at the multiple choice options given to you and pay special attention to the transitional words or phrases that were added to the sentences. Choose the sentence with the transitions that best align with what you think the author was trying to say.

Shifting Sentences Around

Another way the SHSAT might test your writing skills is to ask you where best a sentence would fit in the passage. This has to do with your logic skills. If a sentence gives information about a topic that hasn't been introduced yet in the paragraph, it should be moved. If it is between two sentences that are the same topic and it is a different topic, it should be moved. If it sums up a paragraph, it should go at the end of that paragraph; but if it is a supporting detail, it needs to come before the concluding sentence. This seems like a complicated thing to decide, but it really is not. You just have to ask yourself what makes the most sense. Writing is really all about making sense, and that starts with good organization.

Finally, the SHSAT might test your writing skills by asking you to pick the most precisely worded sentence. If that is that case, examine the sentence choices that are given. Which one uses exact verbs and specific nouns? Don't be misled into choosing the option that you think would best fit in the passage. That is not what the question asked. If the question asks which sentence is most **precise**, then that is what you are looking for. Choose the sentence that uses exact and specific words.

All of this sounds like a lot of information to process, but as you try to do some practice tests, you might be surprised by how much of this comes naturally to you. Let's try a practice passage right now. Remember to use the strategies given to help you answer the questions.

Read the following passage:

Arteriosclerosis and Its Treatment

(1) In developed countries, a large proportion of all deaths are due to a disease that is called arteriosclerosis. (2) Arteriosclerosis is a condition in which fatty material (plaque) collects on the walls of the arteries, causing hardening of the arteries and possible blockage. (3) This narrowing of the artery walls can cause vital organs to not receive enough blood flow. (4) It can lead to pieces of plaque breaking off and causing damage. (5) Depending on which arteries are affected, this disease can cause angina (heart pain), a heart attack, or a stroke.

(6) Many different things are believed to contribute to arteriosclerosis. (7) It has been linked to having a sedentary lifestyle as well as to smoking and to diets high in cholesterol. (8) High amounts of sugar in the blood, whether from insulin resistance or diabetes, are believed to contribute to the disease. (9) Having a family history of arteriosclerosis can be a factor as well.

(10) Medical researchers believe that every man or woman, if he or she lives long enough, will inevitably suffer from arteriosclerosis. (11) This is because arteriosclerosis is caused by the wear and tear resulting from the constant flow of blood through the arteries over the course of a lifetime.

(12) There are many procedures and medicines to help keep this disease under control should it develop. (13) Doctors may use certain drugs to reduce your risk. (14) They may perform surgery to clean out the affected arteries. (15) Any medical procedure that uses anesthesia is considered risky.

(16) Many people can avoid these drastic measures by taking matters into their own hands in a timely manner. (17) Before the disease has progressed too far, a change in diet can make a dramatic difference. (18) Including fresh vegetables and fruits in your diet and removing processed foods will go a long way toward reducing your risks. (19) Perhaps most importantly, exercising regularly can lower blood pressure and bad cholesterol as well as strengthen your arteries.

Now, let's see if you can answer some questions about the best way to organize and revise that passage. Look at question 1:

1. Which revision of sentence 13 uses the most precise language?
   - **A.** Prescriptions are available that can help to keep you healthy.
   - **B.** Your general physician may prescribe blood pressure medicine or cholesterol-lowering statins in hopes of reducing damage to your arteries.
   - **C.** Your general physician has many prescription options available that can keep your blood flowing smoothly.
   - **D.** A medical professional may suggest you use prescription drugs to prevent blockages.

Do you think you know? The trick is to find the most **precise** language used. Some of the other sentences might be okay, but it is important to pay attention to what the question is asking you to choose. Options A, C, and D all use vague language like "medical professional" or "prescriptions." In contrast, Option B uses the precise language of "general physician," "blood pressure medicine," and "cholesterol-lowering statins." That is the sentence with the most precise language, so that is the correct answer.

Let's try another one. See if you can answer the following question:

2. Which transition best shows the relationship between sentence 3 and sentence 4?
   - **A.** Notwithstanding,
   - **B.** Therefore,
   - **C.** Similarly,
   - **D.** Furthermore,

As with all questions, it is important to read it carefully to make sure you know what it is asking for. This question asks you to choose a transition that shows the relationship between sentence 3 and sentence 4. The first thing you should do is look back and read the two sentences carefully. You will see that each sentence lists a possible effect of arteriosclerosis. Because sentence 4 is adding another fact to the one already given in sentence 3, you should look for an "addition" transitional word.

Option A is a contrast transition. That would be great if sentence 4 contradicted sentence 3, but it doesn't. Option B is a summarizing transition, but sentence 4 doesn't summarize sentence 3. Option C is a comparison transition, and that doesn't work either. The two sentences are not showing a comparison. Option D is the only addition transition available, and it clearly indicates that another fact will follow. Option D is the right choice.

Let's keep going. Try question 3:

3. Which sentence would best follow sentence 18 to support the argument presented in the passage?
   - **A.** In fact, studies have shown that a change in diet can actually reverse damage caused by arteriosclerosis.
   - **B.** There are many additional benefits to maintaining a healthy diet.
   - **C.** It is hard to make a dietary change, but the hard work is worth it.
   - **D.** The risk of arteriosclerosis is not something to be taken lightly.

As always, the first step is to make sure you understand what the question is asking. This question asks you to pick the sentence that will follow sentence 18 and best support the argument in the passage. Those are two different requirements. It doesn't just have to fit in after sentence 18; it has to support the overall argument of the passage. To find the answer, you first need to have a general idea of what the argument of the passage is. This passage is arguing that although arteriosclerosis is a deadly disease, changes in lifestyle can reduce the risks associated with it. Options B and C both make general statements about the benefits of a healthy diet, but they don't address its effect on arteriosclerosis. Option D identifies the seriousness of the disease but does not mention lifestyle changes. Option A, however, supports the argument. It gives a fact about how a change in lifestyle can reduce your risk. Option A, therefore, is the answer.

4. Which sentence would best follow and support sentence 11?

A. Over time, cholesterol builds up in the arteries of your heart or head like rust and debris build up in the pipes under your sink.
B. Arteriosclerosis is one of the most serious diseases in the Western world.
C. Because it is a silent disease, many people do not take the risks of arteriosclerosis seriously enough.
D. More studies need to be conducted on this disease so that treatments become more effective.

The question asks you to pick the option that supports sentence 11. Unlike with the previous question, with this one you don't have to worry about supporting the whole passage. That was not included in the sentence. So, what is sentence 11 doing? It is describing arteriosclerosis. Options B, C, and D all refer to the disease in general, but they do not necessarily support sentence 11. Option A, however, gives us an analogy of arteriosclerosis that helps to describe the disease. Therefore, Option A is the correct answer.

Let's keep going and review a few more scenarios that you might come across in the SHSAT:

5. Which sentence strays from the main idea of the passage and should be removed?

A. Sentence 6
B. Sentence 9
C. Sentence 11
D. Sentence 15

This question is a little different. However, like some of the other ones you have done, it is easy to figure out if you understand the main point of the passage. The question asks you to look for the sentence that strays from the main idea of the passage. The passage tells what arteriosclerosis is, what it does, and how to treat it. Options A, B, and C all relate to those ideas. Option D, however, which states that surgery is dangerous, is not relevant in this passage. It can be removed, so Option D is the answer.

Here is another type of question you might encounter on the SHSAT. See if you can work it out:

6. Which of the following would be the best concluding sentence for the above passage?

A. Arteriosclerosis is a deadly disease that you cannot escape.
B. Although you can't eliminate your risk of arteriosclerosis, with a combination of self-discipline and medical treatment you can certainly reduce your chances of experiencing its deadly consequences.
C. So many things contribute to arteriosclerosis that it is impossible to avoid them all.
D. The majority of heart attacks that happen in the United States are caused by unchecked arteriosclerosis.

Again, first look at what the question is asking you. You need to choose the sentence that will sum up the whole passage. Now look at the choices. Option A is true, but it really just addresses a part of what the passage is about. Options C and D may also be true, and they refer to the topic "arteriosclerosis," but they don't address the main argument of the passage. Option B does sum up the ideas in the passage. It mentions that arteriosclerosis is a constant risk, but also that it can be treated. Therefore, Option B is the answer.

The hope is that you are beginning to get the hang of this. If not, just go back and read over the explanations a few more times. Practice makes perfect! There are just a couple more types of questions you need to review in this chapter.

Try this one:

7. Consider this sentence: "In addition, being overweight and having high blood pressure can also contribute to the disease." Where would it best fit into the passage?

   A. After sentence 4
   B. After sentence 8
   C. After sentence 16
   D. After sentence 19

To answer this question, first read the sentence given. Then, look at each of the sentence options. Should it be placed after sentence 4, which talks about the dangerous effects of arteriosclerosis? Should it go after sentence 8, which gives causes of arteriosclerosis? Should it go after sentence 16, which talks about doing things to prevent arteriosclerosis, or should it go after sentence 19 and act as a concluding sentence to the whole passage? The answer is that it should go after sentence 8, because it also lists things that can contribute to the disease. (A hint is the transitional phrase "in addition" at the beginning of the sentence.) The answer, therefore, is Option B.

There's just one last question, so give it one more try:

8. Which is the best way to combine these two sentences to show the correct relationship between them?

   A. Doctors may use certain drugs to reduce your risk; on the contrary, they may perform surgery to clean out the affected arteries.
   B. Because doctors may use certain drugs to reduce your risk, they may perform surgery to clean out the affected arteries.
   C. Doctors may use certain drugs to reduce your risk; nevertheless, they may perform surgery to clean out the affected arteries.
   D. Doctors may use certain drugs to reduce your risk; in addition, they may perform surgery to clean out the affected arteries.

Which would the best choice be? To decide, you must understand what the two sentences are saying. In Option A, "on the contrary" is used. That shows ideas that conflict, but these ideas don't conflict, so Option A isn't right. Option B tells us that the doctors perform surgery because of the drugs! That can't be correct. Option C uses "nevertheless" to combine the sentences; that is also false—one is not in spite of the other. Option D is the correct answer because it uses the transition "in addition." These are two things that doctors do, so the second is in addition to the first.

The next chapter reviews some grammatical and mechanical rules that you might be tested on in the SHSAT.

CHAPTER 5

Grammar and Mechanics

In this chapter, we will review some common grammar and mechanics (punctuation) rules that you might be tested on in the SHSAT. As you know if you have studied English, the rules can sometimes seem endless. Don't despair! You probably have more of an understanding of these rules than you give yourself credit for, and for those rules you don't understand, this guide can help. Take a little time to study this chapter. Brushing up on these simple concepts will make you much more confident when you go to take the test.

Modifiers

One thing you might be tested on is your ability to locate a misplaced modifier. Modifiers are words that are used to describe, or modify, something else in the sentence. One type of error that people make with modifiers is placing them incorrectly.

For example, look at this sentence:

> The store gave coupons to its customers that would expire at the end of the month.

The coupons are what will expire, but the way the sentence is worded, it seems as though it is the customers that are going to expire. The modifying phrase "that would expire at the end of the month" needs to be placed as closely as possible to the word it describes, which is "coupons." The correct way to phrase this sentence would be:

> The store gave coupons that would expire at the end of the month to its customers.

Look at this sentence:

> A scientist named Alfred Wegener noticed that a map of the world about 80 years ago resembled a giant jigsaw puzzle.

Which is the misplaced modifier?

A. named Alfred Wegener
B. that a map of the world
C. about 80 years ago
D. resembled a giant jigsaw puzzle

Do you see the mistake? Can you locate the misplaced modifier? If you picked Option C, you are correct. Because the phrase "about 80 years ago" comes right after "map of the world," readers could be confused and think the map had to be about 80 years old. "About 80 years ago" should be at the beginning of the sentence. Then it would be clear that "80 years ago Wegener noticed."

Good job. Now let's move on to another type of modifier mistake that you might be asked to identify: the dangling modifier. A dangling modifier occurs when there is no specific word for the modifier to describe. When you are trying to locate dangling modifiers, pay special attention to the beginning and ending of the sentence because that is often where they are found.

Look at this sentence:

> Realizing it was going to rain, the picnic was canceled.

The picnic did not realize that it was going to rain. That sentence does not tell us who realized it was going to rain. In order to fix this type of modifier problem, the whole sentence has to be revised. You could add a noun for the phrase to modify:

Realizing it was going to rain, the organizers canceled the picnic.

Or you could change the modifying phrase to an adverb clause:

Because the organizers realized it was going to rain, the picnic was canceled.

Either change works. Just make sure the modifier has something to describe.

Let's try a few practice questions to make sure you can locate these misplaced modifiers on your own. Look at the following paragraph:

(1) My sister is the genealogist of the family. (2) She notifies everyone in the family whenever she finds a piece of information she thinks we will enjoy. (3) One interesting story was about an ancestor who had bequeathed some beautiful, antique furniture to his descendants. (4) This furniture is apparently still owned by some distant family relatives. (5) They agreed to bring some pieces, reluctantly, to the next family reunion.

Which sentence has a misplaced modifier in it?

A. Sentence 2
B. Sentence 3
C. Sentence 4
D. Sentence 5

Did you catch it? The answer is Option D, sentence 5. The word "reluctantly" describes the verb "agreed." "Reluctantly" needs to be placed either at the beginning of the sentence, right before the word "agreed," or right after. Any of those places would make the meaning of the sentence clearer.

Let's try another one. Look at this paragraph:

(1) The Arctic fox is comparable in size to the domestic cat. (2) Living in the region midway between Norway and the North Pole, scientists are fascinated by this mammal. (3) This canine predator can adapt to its environment. (4) In the summer, its fur is a brown color, but during the winter months, its coat turns white. (5) Its fur is the thickest of all Arctic mammals. (6) The Arctic fox can roam all winter without hibernating.

Which sentence has a dangling modifier?

A. Sentence 1
B. Sentence 2
C. Sentence 3
D. Sentence 5

If you chose sentence 2, you are correct. Although it is possible that the scientists live in the region between Norway and the North Pole, it is far more likely that the author meant the Arctic fox lived in that region. The sentence could be corrected with a little rearranging. The modifying phrase needs to be beside the word it modifies. Either of these solutions would work:

This mammal, living in the region midway between Norway and the North Pole, fascinates many scientists.

Or:

Scientists are fascinated by this mammal, which lives in the region midway between Norway and the North Pole.

Verbs

Now that you have modifiers under your belt, let's move on to another common trouble area: correct verb usage. This is something that might also be tested on the SHSAT.

It is important to use the correct verb tense when you are writing. Misusing verbs can cause a lot of confusion for readers. In addition, you need to make sure that the subject and verb always agree. If the subject is plural, the verb must be plural; if the subject is singular, the verb must be singular.

In addition to the regular verb tenses (past, present, and future), there are progressive tenses, which indicate continuing movement and end in "ing." Then there are perfect tenses. These tenses give depth to verbs by placing them further into the past. For example, "had" is often part of a perfect tense. It is used to place a verb further into the past. This sentence, "I ate, so I was not hungry," has two past tense verbs. From that sentence, all we know is that both things happened sometime in the past. If we say instead that "I had eaten, so I was not hungry," we know that "had eaten" took place sometime before "was not hungry." Using a perfect tense can be useful sometimes, but it can also just distort a sentence when the tense is not necessary.

One easy way to spot a mistake is to look for a verb that is not the same tense as the verbs in the rest of the paragraph. Usually, the verb tenses in a paragraph should match. If most of the verbs in the paragraph are in the past tense, but one is in the present tense, you should take a second look to make sure that is not an error. Perfect and progressive tenses added to a paragraph are common because they give a sentence depth, but it is not common for a writer to switch between past and present tenses. That should be a red flag, so watch out for it!

This seems simple, but it can be tricky, so let's do a few practice questions.

Look at the following paragraph:

(1) I've had a terrible cold for several days. (2) Besides feeling bad, I've been bored. (3) I've watched every terrible movie that came on the TV and talked on the phone to my mom every day. (4) I wonder when I was well and can go back to work. (5) I'm tired of the coughing, sneezing, and complaining.

Which of these changes should be made to sentence 4?

A. Change "wonder to "have wondered."
B. Change "was" to "will be."
C. Change "can go" to "may go."
D. Change "wonder" to "am wondering."

Both Option A and Option D offer changes that would be incorrect; there is nothing wrong with the original subject/verb "I wonder." There is no reason to either put it in the past tense like Option A does, or put it in the progressive tense like Option D does, so these changes are unnecessary. Option C would not be correct. "May" indicates permission; "can" indicates ability. This person doesn't need permission to go back to work. He or she needs to feel well enough to go back. Option B is the answer you are looking for. "Was" is past tense, but this person is wondering about the future. The future tense of "was" is "will be." "Will be" makes more sense than "was" in this sentence.

Let's practice correct verb usage one more time. Consider the following paragraph:

(1) My seventh grade teacher defined the word eccentric. (2) Every day, she wandered into our classroom and had caused us to giggle. (3) She always sported the strangest combination of clothing, and her breath reeked of garlic and cigarettes. (4) Little strands of red hair frizzed out from beneath the kerchief that always covered her head. (5) She was absolutely unbelievable.

Which change should be made to sentence (2)?

A. Change "wandered" to "had wandered."
B. Change "had caused" to "was caused."
C. Change "had caused" to "caused."
D. Change "wandered" to "was wandering."

In this example paragraph, there is no need for the perfect tense. All the other verbs are in the past tense, and putting "had caused" in the sentence instead of just "caused" does not add anything. "Caused" did not happen at an earlier time than the rest of the paragraph. Similarly, there is no need to put "wandered" into the past perfect tense [Option A] or the past progressive [Option D]. It is fine as it is. Therefore, Option C is correct.

Pronoun Error

Another thing that can get confusing in writing is pronoun reference. A pronoun must agree with its *antecedent* (the word it is taking the place of) in number and gender. That might sound complicated, but it is not. Think of it this way: if you are talking about a man, say "he," not "she." If you are talking about more than one person, say "they" or "them" not "he" or "she." You already knew that, didn't you? Although it is simple, it is also simple to make a mistake if you aren't careful because many times multiple phrases and clauses are separating the two.

Consider the following paragraph:

(1) The human eye is a very sensitive organ since so much of it is exposed to the environment. (2) Luckily, the facial structure around the eye is designed to protect the exposed parts of the eye from harm or at least keep it to a minimum. (3) The eyelid is essential, since they shut over the eye and this protects it from dust or other airborne materials that could irritate. (4) Tear ducts perform an important role because they provide the fluids that keep the eye moist, which is necessary to the well-being of the organ.

Which sentence contains a pronoun that does not agree with its antecedent?

A. Sentence 1
B. Sentence 2
C. Sentence 3
D. Sentence 4

If you picked Option C, you are correct. In sentence 3, the pronoun "they" takes the place of the word "eyelid." However, "eyelid" is singular, so "they" should be "it." All the other pronouns in the paragraph are correct.

Another way to misuse a pronoun is with an unclear pronoun reference. Take a look at the following example:

Sam told William that he was an excellent student.

It is probably easy to spot the pronoun "he," but who is the word "he" taking the place of? Was Sam telling William that Sam was an excellent student, or that William was? In situations like this, even though it seems redundant, it is always best to make it very clear:

Sam told William that William was an excellent student.

Remembering these few rules of grammar will go a long way toward helping you through your SHSAT exam!

Dealing with Mechanics

Students often get confused by the many punctuation rules in standard written English. Those rules can feel overwhelming sometimes. You don't have to panic, though. Punctuation follows specific rules, and brushing up on a few of the most important rules can help you to breeze right through this test.

Commas

Probably the biggest mechanics problem students face is understanding commas. The rules for comma usage can seem endless, and some students resort to just inserting commas randomly in the hope that they have chanced upon the right spot. You don't have to rely on luck. There really are rules for proper comma usage, and they aren't too hard to remember. The most important rules, and the ones you might be tested on, can be summed up in six guidelines:

1. Use commas when you have a list of three or more things. For example: "Hats, coats, and scarves are winter accessories."
2. Use a comma with a conjunction to join two complete sentences. For example: "I went to town, and you stayed home."
3. Use a comma to set off a phrase that is not essential to the sentence. For example: "Krista, my friend, has a great job."
4. Use a comma to separate adjectives before the noun they modify. For example: "I saw a tiny, white pony."
5. Use a comma to separate a city and its state or country. For example: "I live in Atlanta, Georgia, but I have been to Paris, France."
6. Use a comma to set off an introductory word, long phrase, or clause. For example:
   A. "Today, we are happy."
   B. "Among the many choices, this was the best."
   C. "If you are unhappy, please let me know."

Most comma usage falls into one of these six categories. Once you understand these six uses, you should be able to look carefully at a sentence and know positively where the commas go. Let's go a little deeper into some of these rules and practice identifying common comma errors.

The most common comma error might be the "comma splice." The comma splice occurs when two independent sentences are joined by a comma. These are actually very easy to spot after just a little practice.

Here is an example of this kind of mistake:

> Rachel is very smart, she began reading when she was three years old.

"Rachel is very smart" and "she began reading when she was three years old" are each a complete thought that could stand alone as a sentence. Sometimes the easiest fix for this is just to replace the comma with a period and capitalize the first word of the next sentence like this:

> Rachel is very smart. She began reading when she was three years old.

Alternatively, you could replace the comma with a semicolon. That would also make the sentence correct:

> Rachel is very smart; she began reading when she was three years old.

Another solution would be to add a conjunction after the comma. A comma and a conjunction can work together to join two complete sentences:

> Rachel is very smart, and she began reading when she was three years old.

Additionally, you could fix this sentence by removing the comma and adding whichever subordinating conjunction makes sense. For example:

> Rachel is very smart because she began reading when she was three years old.

Or:

> Since Rachel is very smart, she began reading when she was three years old.

Notice that when the subordinating conjunction is put at the beginning of the sentence, we still need the comma after "smart." That is because an **introductory** subordinating clause is always followed by a comma. In the first example, no comma is needed because the subordinating clause does not begin the sentence.

There is one more solution to the comma splice. The comma can be replaced by a semicolon followed by a conjunctive adverb and a comma. Conjunctive adverbs include words or phrases such as "however," "moreover," "on the other hand," "nevertheless," "instead," "also," "therefore," "consequently," "otherwise," and "as a result." Just make sure to pick the conjunctive adverb that shows the correct relationship!

For example:

> Rachel is very smart; therefore, she began reading when she was three years old.

To review: Two independent sentences cannot be joined by a comma alone. You can make two separate sentences with them by separating them with a period and a capital letter, or you can join them by using one of the following strategies:

A semicolon
A comma and a conjunction
A subordinating conjunction
A semicolon followed by a conjunctive adverb and a comma

Why don't you try to identify the comma splice? Look at the following paragraph:

> (1) My name is Marie, and I am from France. (2) Now, I live in Chicago. (3) I have one child, a son named Pierre. (4) He is a doctor at a large hospital in Chicago, he is planning to get married.

Which sentence contains a comma splice?

A. Sentence 1
B. Sentence 2
C. Sentence 3
D. Sentence 4

Read each sentence carefully and pay attention to the punctuation. Let's check each comma to see if it has been used correctly. In the first sentence, a comma is used with the conjunction "and" to join "My name is Marie" and "I am from France." These are both complete thoughts and could stand alone, so that comma is correct. Two independent sentences need a comma with a conjunction to join them.

The next comma comes in the second sentence after the word "Now." That comma is correct because introductory words, phrases, and clauses should be followed by a comma.

The third sentence has a comma after the word "child." That is correct also. It is separating a nonessential phrase from the rest of the sentence.

Look at the comma in sentence 4: "He is a doctor at a large hospital in Chicago, he is planning to get married." Is that a comma splice? Again, separate the two parts of the sentence: "He is a doctor at a large hospital in Chicago" and "he is planning to get married." Are these both complete sentences that could stand by themselves? The answer is yes.

Joining two complete sentences with just a comma breaks the rules. Commas do not have the authority to join sentences on their own; they need a conjunction to help them. The sentence could be fixed by making it two sentences or using one of the four strategies we discussed earlier:

> *A semicolon:* He is a doctor at a large hospital in Chicago; he is planning to get married.
>
> *A comma and a conjunction:* He is a doctor at a large hospital in Chicago, and he is planning to get married.
>
> *A subordinating conjunction:* Since he is a doctor at a large hospital in Chicago, he is planning to get married.
>
> *A semicolon followed by a conjunctive adverb and a comma:* He is doctor at a large hospital in Chicago; moreover, he is planning to get married.

(All these solutions correct the punctuation problems, although the subordinating conjunction changes the meaning of the sentence in this case and so that correction should be avoided.)

Let's try one more. Look at this paragraph:

> (1) Rochelle has been applying for full-time jobs for several months. (2) Last week she received a response from a company she is very interested in. (3) The company's human resources director asked her to come in for an interview. (4) She is very excited, but also nervous. (5) She is worried that she will be too nervous to make a good impression, and she is concerned that she does not have enough experience to get hired.

Do you see the comma splice?

There are only two commas in this paragraph. Look at the first one. Should it be there? Which rule does it follow? At first glance, it seems to be working with the conjunction "but" to join two sentences. Look again. On one side of the comma-conjunction is "She is very excited"; that is a complete thought. On the other side is "also nervous"; that is not a complete thought. If both sides aren't complete thoughts, then it does not need a comma to join it. That comma needs to be removed.

Look at the second comma. Is that joining two complete thoughts? Separate the sentence parts: "She is worried that she will be too nervous to make a good impression," and "she is concerned that she does not have enough experience to get hired." Yes, the sentence part on each side of the comma-conjunction could stand by itself. That comma is correct.

One trick to determining if a conjunction is joining two complete sentences or not is to place your finger on the conjunction. Could the part of the sentence on each side of your finger stand alone as its own sentence? If so, put a comma before that conjunction! If one side or the other is not a complete thought, then that conjunction does not need a comma.

More Commas

Most of what we have focused on so far is the comma splice, but let's not forget the other uses for commas. Look at this sentence:

> If a plate moves the land above it can shift which explains how one original landmass became multiple continents over time.

Where should a comma be inserted? Remember the six rules of commas? One of those rules says that a comma needs to follow an introductory word, phrase, or clause. Do you see that clause?

It is "If a plate moves," so a comma is needed after "moves."

There is another comma needed though. Did you pick it instead? Another rule of comma usage says that commas are used to separate nonessential clauses from the rest of the sentence. "Which explains how one original landmass became multiple continents over time" is a nonessential clause. It should be separated from the rest of the sentence by a comma.

Let's look at another example:

> The brow nose and cheekbones give the eye protection from the top at the sides and below.

Do you know where the commas go in this sentence? Don't just guess; remember the rules. One of the six rules listed earlier states that commas are used to separate items in a series. Commas are needed to separate "brow nose and cheekbones," changing it to "brow, nose, and cheekbones." Using the same rule, you should also insert commas in "from the top at the sides and below," making it much more readable as "from the top, at the sides, and below."

Let's do one more to make sure we have all the common comma uses covered:

> The handsome hopeful man stood waiting patiently for the girl.

Do you know where the comma should go in the above sentence? It follows another of the six rules: commas separating coordinating adjectives. There are two adjectives describing the man in the sentence. They should be separated by a comma: "handsome, hopeful man."

Okay! If you have worked through commas and understand their uses, you are in good shape. The rest of mechanics is a breeze! Let's review just a few more mechanics rules that you might be tested on.

Apostrophes

Apostrophes are used to show possession. For singular words, simply add an apostrophe and an "s." For example:

> The dog's bone was lost.

This rule is still true if the singular word ends in "s," like "bus."

> This bus's schedule is erratic.

If you want to show possession on a plural word ending in "s," the apostrophe comes after the "s." For example:

> The dogs' bone was lost.

If the word is already plural and does not end in "s," treat it as if it were a singular word. For example:

> The child's food was gone.
> The children's food was gone.

All these rules apply to nouns; however, they don't apply to possessive pronouns. Possessive pronouns are already possessive! "My," "mine," "our," "ours," "his," "hers," "its," "your," "yours," "their," and "theirs" are all possessive pronouns and never need an apostrophe to show ownership.

Look at this sentence and see if you can find the correct answer:

My grandmothers cabin is next to his' cabin.

A. My grandmothers cabin is next to his cabin.
B. My grandmother's cabin is next to his cabin.
C. My grandmothers' cabin is next to his cabin.
D. My grandmother's cabin is next to his' cabin.

First, look at the apostrophe in the sentence. Is that right? Does a possessive pronoun ever need an apostrophe to show possession? The answer is no, and so Option D cannot be correct. Next, decide if there is any other ownership in the sentence. Do you see it? Grandmother owns the cabin. Option A can't be correct because "grandmothers" does not show ownership. So, is it Option B or Option C? Most likely, only one grandmother owns that cabin, so we don't want to pick the plural possessive in Option C. The answer must be Option B, where the apostrophe comes after the singular noun "grandmother."

There are two main uses for apostrophes: to show possession and to create a contraction. We have already covered showing possession, but let's delve into creating contractions for just a moment. A simple trick to finding misused apostrophes is to realize that if they are not showing possession, they must be creating a contraction.

Here is a list of pronouns that are commonly mixed up:

Their, they're
Your, you're
Its, it's

Once you know that possessive pronouns do not use apostrophes, it is easy to know what the right word to use is. Look at the following example:

Its raining outside, so the dog stayed in its house.

A. It's raining outside, so the dog stayed in its house.
B. Its raining outside so the dog stayed in its house.
C. It's raining outside so the dog stayed in it's house.
D. Its raining outside so the dog stayed in it's house.

Which is the correct answer? Possessive pronouns don't take apostrophes, so simply decide which "its" could mean "it is"; that one will need the apostrophe.

Think of it this way:

It is raining outside, so the dog stayed in it is house.

Does that make sense? The first "it is" makes sense in the sentence, but the second "it is" doesn't. Options C and D must be incorrect, then, because "it is house" doesn't make sense. Option B also has to be incorrect because "Its raining" doesn't have an apostrophe, so it is not a contraction of "it is raining." Option A is the correct answer.

Let's do one more:

(*Their/They're*) house is always well-kept because (*their/they're*) very particular about details.

A. Their house is always well-kept because their very particular about details.
B. They're house is always well-kept because they're very particular about details.
C. They're house is always well-kept because their very particular about details.
D. Their house is always well-kept because they're very particular about details.

Which is the right answer? Again, simply ask yourself, where does it mean "they are"? Say it this way:

They are house is always well-kept because they are very particular about details.

The first "they are" does not make sense. That one cannot be a contraction, so it shouldn't have an apostrophe. The second "they are" does make sense. That is the one that is a contraction and should have an apostrophe. Therefore, the answer has to be Option D.

One final note on apostrophes: Apostrophes are used to show ownership or to create a contraction (it is = it's). They are never used to make something plural.

CHAPTER 6

Reading Comprehension

There will be six passages with five to seven comprehension questions after each. These 30–40 items measure how well you are able to understand and interpret information you have read. All of the passages you read in this section will be nonfiction. The topics of the passages may include:

- Biographies
- Historical events
- Science
- Art
- Human interest stories
- Discussions sharing a point of view

As with any reading test, the key is to read the information carefully. After reading each passage, you will be given six multiple choice questions. The first question will always ask you to identify the main idea of the passage. The other questions can be answered based on the facts, details, and information given in the passage, or on inferences that can be drawn based on this information.

You may find that more than one of the answer choices looks correct. Your task is to choose the one best answer, based solely on the information you have read. You may need to combine ideas found in different parts of the text to come up with the best answer to a question.

You also must be careful not to base your answer choice on information you previously knew about the topic. For example, you might be given a passage to read about the Statue of Liberty. Perhaps you have written research papers on this remarkable monument and have even visited on several occasions. You might even consider yourself an expert on the topic. However, none of the information you have learned elsewhere is to be used to answer the questions on the SHSAT. The one best answer is based only on the facts and details that are included in the passage.

> Make sure you separate information you already know about a topic from the ideas you read in a passage. Questions on the SHSAT must be answered based only on the information you are given in the passage.

Most likely, you have already learned a number of reading comprehension skills in the past, so much of what you read in this chapter may be review. This section of the test could be a great place for you to earn points that will increase your overall score on the test. Just make sure you read each word carefully, know exactly what each question is asking, and select the best answer for the questions.

With that in mind, let's go over some of the skills you will need to correctly answer the reading comprehension questions on the SHSAT.

Main Idea and Supporting Details

Every passage you read, whether fiction or nonfiction, has a **main idea**. The main idea, sometimes referred to as the *big idea*, tells what the passage is mostly about. It is the most important information, key concept, or main message that the author wants you to gain by reading the text.

For example, if you were to read a passage about Mount Rushmore, the main idea might be:

> Mount Rushmore is a national memorial that features the faces of several presidents carved into the side of a mountain.

This would be the key piece of information that the author wants you to learn by reading the text. His or her main reason for writing the passage is to tell readers that Mount Rushmore is a national memorial that shows the faces of some of our leaders carved into the side of a mountain.

The main idea may be the author's opinion about the subject matter or a general idea. Be careful not to confuse the main idea of a passage with the **topic**. The topic, or subject, is a single word or short phrase that tells what the passage is about. In the example above, the topic is *Mount Rushmore*. The main idea, on the other hand, is a complete sentence that tells the most important information about the topic. Often, the main idea is introduced in the **topic sentence**. This sentence is usually near the beginning of the text and tells what the passage will be about.

> Identifying the topic first can be a helpful way to determine the main idea of a passage. To find the topic, ask yourself, *What or who is the subject of the passage?* Then, to find the main idea, ask, *What is the most important thing the author wants me to know about this topic?*

In a passage that includes several paragraphs, each paragraph will have its own main idea. Often, the main idea of a paragraph is found in the first sentence; however, it can be anywhere in the paragraph. These paragraphs work together to explain and support the main idea of the entire passage as a whole. The main idea of the entire passage will tell the central message that is being explained by all of the paragraphs together. In this case, you will have to read the full passage, then determine the most important idea that the author wanted to relay.

As you read, you will find **supporting details** that explain, prove, or give more information about the main idea. They help to make the main idea stronger and clearer so that the reader is better able to fully understand its importance. Types of details often used to support the main idea are:

- Examples
- Reasons
- Definitions
- Facts
- Descriptions

In the passage discussed earlier about Mount Rushmore, supporting details could include statements such as those shown below.

> This monument is located in the Black Hills of South Dakota.
>
> The cost of creating the memorial was nearly $1 million, the majority of which was provided by the U.S. government.
>
> The rock carving features 60-foot-high likenesses of Presidents Washington, Jefferson, Roosevelt, and Lincoln.

Each of these details helps readers more fully understand the main idea that *Mount Rushmore is a national memorial that features the faces of several presidents carved into the side of a mountain.* Notice that the supporting details tell more about the main idea, such as *where* the monument is located, *how* much it cost to build, *who* was responsible for funding the project, and *which* presidents are represented. This information helps to explain Mount Rushmore.

Supporting details often answer the questions:

- Who?
- What?
- Where?
- How?

- When?
- Why?

Being able to recognize the main idea and identify supporting details will help you better understand what you read. You will know what message the author is trying to share and be able to organize the information in the passage in a way that helps you understand the topic.

Read the following paragraph. As you read, look for the main idea and supporting details.

> While his name may be unfamiliar to many, Gutzon Borglum was an artist who was responsible for a number of works that have become parts of American history. Born around 1867, Borglum spent his teens and twenties studying art. After painting a portrait of a wealthy general, he was introduced to Theodore Roosevelt. Several years later, the artist created a bust of Abraham Lincoln, which Roosevelt displayed in the White House, giving Borglum a reputation around the country. As a result, he was commissioned to carve his first mountain sculpture, a bust of Robert E. Lee on Georgia's Stone Mountain. Although he was not the artist to complete this project, he did develop techniques that would be useful in his following, and most famous, carving. After leaving what he felt was a project that would only be supported by people in a limited area of the country, Borglum went on to create a masterpiece that he felt would gain national support: carving the faces of four United States presidents into Mount Rushmore.

First, let's find the topic. Ask:

> What or who was the subject of the paragraph?

Since all of the information is about the life and work of artist Gutzon Borglum, he is the topic of the paragraph.

Now that we know the topic, let's identify the main idea. Ask, *What was the passage about?* Remember, the main idea is a complete sentence. The key concept that the author wanted us to know is that *Gutzon Borglum was an artist whose works are an important part of American history.* This sentence tells the big idea of the whole paragraph. All of the other information you read gives information, facts, details, and examples that explain the main idea.

Finally, let's find the supporting details in the paragraph that help to build a complete understanding of the main idea. Ask, *What information did the author include that helped to explain the main idea?*

The main idea is that Borglum's work is an important part of American history. Details that explain this include:

- He created a bust of Abraham Lincoln, which Roosevelt displayed in the White House.
- He worked on a carving of Robert E. Lee in the side of Georgia's Stone Mountain.
- He carved the faces of four United States presidents into Mount Rushmore.

As you probably noticed, the main idea is a small part of the passage. The majority of the passage is made up of supporting details. As you read, think about how each supporting detail tells more about the main idea. You will probably find that some supporting details are more informative and helpful than others.

> Some questions on the SHSAT may ask you to determine which statement best tells what the passage is about, but will not actually include the words *main idea*. In this case, you are still looking for the answer choice that tells the general point the author was trying to make throughout the passage. Select the answer choice that most closely states the main idea, since the main idea tells what the passage is about.

Fact and Opinion

As you already know, **facts** are true statements that can be proven. **Opinions** are someone's personal views or thoughts, which may or may not be able to be verified.

The average rainfall in June is 6.8 inches.
There was too much rain in July.
This was the wettest summer on record.

All of these statements tell about summertime rain; however, only two of the statements can be verified. The first and third statements could be proven using rainfall data from weather reports. Therefore, these statements are facts. The second statement is an opinion, because we cannot prove that there was too much rain. A statement that says that there was too much, too little, or just the right amount of rain expresses a personal viewpoint. Not everyone would agree that there was too much rain. Some people might have enjoyed the wet weather and believe that July had the perfect amount of rain.

As you read, it is important to be able to distinguish between facts and opinions. Since all of the passages on the SHSAT are nonfiction, the majority of the information included will be facts. But it is still possible that an opinion will occasionally appear in the text, especially when the purpose of the passage is to share a point of view.

As you know, facts can be used as supporting details. While an opinion may agree with the main idea of a passage, it will not be the strongest statement supporting the main idea.

As you read the following paragraph, look for facts and opinions. Notice which statements best support the main idea of the text.

Not only was Wolfgang Amadeus Mozart a renowned composer, he was also an accomplished musician who mastered a number of instruments. Mozart's father, Leopold, was a composer and violinist. By the time he was three, the younger Mozart had learned to play the piano. Within a short time, he had also mastered the harpsichord, organ, and violin. By the time he was six years old, he performed concerts for European royalty on these instruments, which his father had taught him to play. Later in life, he wrote a number of piano concertos, which allowed him to be recognized as both the composer and soloist when performing. Many of these concertos featured the piano and wind instruments of the orchestra working together to create some of his most beautiful compositions.

Which fact from the passage best supports the main idea?

A. Wolfgang Amadeus Mozart, composer and musician
B. Mozart's father, Leopold, was a composer and violinist.
C. Within a short time, he had also mastered the harpsichord, organ, and violin.
D. Not only was Wolfgang Amadeus Mozart a renowned composer, he was also an accomplished musician who mastered a number of instruments.

Let's look at each of the answer choices and see how well you did identifying the fact that best supports the main idea. You probably recognized that answer choice A is the topic rather than a supporting fact.

Now, take a look at answer choice B. This is a fact. It can be verified by checking the information in a biography or a book about musical history. However, even though this fact is in the passage, it does not support the main idea. It is definitely interesting, and it offers insight into Mozart's family, but it does not help to explain the main idea of the passage.

Answer choice D is the main idea. This piece of information is the key concept that the author wanted to share when he or she wrote the paragraph. In this question, we are looking for the fact that best supports this statement.

Let's go back to answer choice C. This statement is a fact that could also be verified through a quick look at a biography or musical history book. This statement also supports the main idea. So, as you probably recognized, this is the correct answer to the question.

Certain words may offer clues that a statement contains an opinion. Look for words such as *better, best, worst, beautiful, awful, easiest, too difficult, too much, terrific,* and *should*. Often, these indicate a personal viewpoint, rather than a verifiable fact.

Inferences

Suppose you come home an hour past your curfew. Mom is standing in the doorway with her eyebrows furrowed, arms folded across her chest, foot quickly tapping on the ground. Without her ever saying a word, you can read between the lines to figure out that she's angry. You have just made an **inference**.

There are times when an author expects you to read between the lines as well. He or she will make suggestions, give information, or offer clues about something but never directly state what it is that he or she wants you to know. Readers have to make an inference, or read between the lines to discover information that is implied or suggested in the passage.

When making an inference, be sure to reflect on:

- Clues and hints in the text
- Details and information given
- What the author does and does not say
- The word choice of the author
- Your own prior knowledge and observations

An inference is not a random, wild guess that is made out of the blue. It is a logical conclusion based on information that is suggested or implied. Take a look at the following example.

> Rebecca put down her pompons and nervously climbed to the top of the human pyramid, trying to put aside her fear of performing in front of a stadium full of football fans.

You've probably figured out that Rebecca is a cheerleader. The following facts are all clues that would lead you to this inference:

- She has pompons.
- Rebecca is climbing to the top of a human pyramid.
- She is performing in a stadium full of football fans.

Let's look at another example:

> Every Friday night, the football stadium is packed with high school students anxiously watching their aggressive peers toss the ridiculously shaped ball to each other while running from a herd of oversized, helmet-wearing thugs who want nothing more than to pummel them into the ground.

What does the author's word choice in this sentence suggest? Words and phrases such as *aggressive peers, ridiculously shaped ball, helmet-wearing thugs*, and *pummel them into the ground* suggest that the author is not exactly a football fan. Often, an author's word choice can be used to make inferences about his or her feelings on the topic. Based on this sentence, it would be logical to infer that the author does not like football and probably does not attend these games.

Sometimes, what an author does *not* say can offer information as well. Read the paragraph below, then choose the best inference.

> Four exciting touchdowns clinched the win for the Northside Mustangs last night! Number 24, freshman Christopher Young, intercepted a pass by the Tigers, and the crowd was on their feet! Young barreled more than 40 yards down the field, dodging and outmaneuvering his opponents, to score the team's first points of the night. Undoubtedly, cheers could be heard for miles! In the second half of the game, Darnell Thompson carried the ball into the end zone, adding another touchdown to the Mustangs' score. Jonathan Atkins also scored two touchdowns in the final quarter.

Which inference could be made, based on the passage?

A. The author is a fan of Christopher Young.
B. Most of the players on the team are freshmen.
C. The passage was written by the coach of the Mustangs.
D. Darnell Thompson is the most valuable player on the team.

You were probably able to infer that the author is a fan of Christopher Young. The author included information such as Young's jersey number and class, as well as details about the touchdown he made, but did not mention this information about any of the other players. By reading between the lines, you could logically conclude that the author thinks highly of Young.

Let's consider each of the other answer choices and determine why these would not be the best inference. Although Young is a freshman, there is no evidence to indicate that any of the other players are in the same class, so answer choice B is not correct. And while the paragraph may have been written by the coach, this is not a logical inference, since there is no evidence to imply who wrote the passage. Therefore, answer choice C is not correct. Darnell Thompson did make a touchdown; however, nothing suggests that he is more valuable than any of the other players, so answer choice D is not the best inference.

For whatever reason, the author appears to believe that Christopher Young and the touchdown he made were more important than the other players and the points they scored for the team.

Drawing Conclusions

In many ways, **drawing conclusions** is similar to making inferences. To draw a conclusion, you must look at the information given and make a reasonable guess about what is happening.

Suppose you walk past a hospital. A happy young man is carrying a fistful of pink balloons that read "Congratulations." In his other hand, he has a gift bag with a pink teddy bear sticking out of it and a bouquet of flowers. Beside him, a nurse is pushing a smiling young woman in a wheelchair. The woman has a hospital band on her arm and is gently cradling a tiny bundle wrapped in a pink blanket. Using the information you have gained through observation, as well as what you already know, you can logically conclude that this couple has just welcomed a baby girl into their lives.

> His use of light and shadow causes the images to come to life on the canvas. The uniqueness of the brushstrokes gives each piece a distinctive quality that is only found in his artistic style.

Let's look at the facts and details mentioned in the paragraph:

- Use of light and shadow
- Images come to life on the canvas
- Brushstrokes
- His artistic style

By looking at the information given, and using what you already know, you were probably able to conclude that the author is referring to an artist. And since the artist uses a canvas and brushstrokes, it would be logical to in turn conclude that the artist being discussed in this instance is a painter.

Now it's your turn. As you read the following sentences, look for information that offers clues about the passage. Combine these clues with your own prior knowledge and draw a logical conclusion about the text.

> The structure of Russia's Kizimen has been compared to Mt. St. Helens in the United States. It is approximately 12,000 years old and nearly 8,000 feet high, and it is made of layers of ash, lava, and rocks from earlier eruptions. Although ash emissions have been recently recorded, the only explosive eruption in recorded historical time occurred in 1928.

Which statement best describes Kizimen?

A. It is a volcano.
B. It is a mountain.
C. It is nearly 100 years old.
D. It erupts on a regular basis.

Let's take a look at the clues in the paragraph that offer information about Kizimen.

- It has been compared to Mt. St. Helens.
- It is made of ash, lava, and rocks from earlier eruptions.
- There have been recent ash emissions.
- There was an explosive eruption in 1928.

Now, let's think about the prior knowledge you probably already have related to this topic.

- Mt. St. Helens is a volcano.
- Ash, lava, and rocks come from volcanoes.
- Volcanoes erupt.

Based on the information given as well as your own prior knowledge, it is likely that you were able to conclude that Kizimen is a volcano. You may have figured that out without too much thought. In fact, when you read the question and answer choices, you might have even thought that answer choice A was actually stated in the paragraph. Notice that the word *volcano* is not used in the passage at all. If you knew that Kizimen is a volcano, it is because you drew that conclusion. Good for you!

Context Clues

The purpose of reading is to gain understanding of the passage. In order to understand the passage, you have to understand the meanings of the words. Occasionally, when you are reading, you will come across a word that is unfamiliar. Sometimes you can grab a dictionary to find the definition. But this is not always convenient, or even possible. For example, if you find a word you do not know on the SHSAT, you will not have access to a dictionary, so you'll have to find another way to determine the word's meaning.

Often authors will include **context clues**, which are hints that can help you determine the meanings of words. Types of clues that can be helpful in figuring out meaning include

- Synonyms
- Antonyms
- Definitions
- Explanations
- Examples

As you know, **synonyms** are words that have the same or similar meanings, such as *small* and *tiny*.

> Following the merger of the companies, Miss Winchester is hoping to retain, or keep, her current position.

In this sentence, the synonym *keep* is included to explain the meaning of the less familiar word, *retain*. By including this context clue, the author is helping readers to understand the text.

Antonyms, or opposites, are another type of context clue that can help readers determine meaning. Consider this example:

> All of the community members' concerns, whether petty or important, were addressed during the city council meeting.

In this case, the words *petty* and *important* are stated as being words with different meanings. The sentence tells that the concerns were either *petty* or *important*, so these words must mean different things. We can determine that *petty* must be the opposite of *important*. So *petty* means "something that is unimportant, insignificant, or trivial."

An author may include a **definition** that states the meaning of a word that he or she feels could be unfamiliar to readers:

> Lola's exuberant reaction to the election results proved that she was full of enthusiasm about being the new class president.

In this example, the definition of *exuberant* is found later in the same sentence when the author explains that Lola was full of enthusiasm. A reader who was unfamiliar with the word would be able to tell what type of reaction Lola had to the news. Similarly, an **explanation** may also be included to clarify a word's meaning:

> When he attends college, Samuel plans to take classes in horticulture to learn about the science of growing plants.

Reading the beginning of this sentence, you might wonder what Samuel will study in horticulture classes. Then the second half of the sentence explains that he will learn about the science of growing plants in these classes. This explanation tells readers the meaning of *horticulture*.

Examples are also used to clarify the meaning of words that readers might find unfamiliar:

> The types of organisms, such as plants and animals, that are found in a habitat vary depending on the environment.

In this sentence, plants and animals are given as examples of types of organisms. From this, readers can figure out that organisms are living things.

Often, context clues are found within the same sentence as the word they are helping to explain. Other times, they may be found in the surrounding sentences. As you read, be sure to look at information in sentences before and after the unfamiliar word in order to determine what the word means. Take a look at the following sentence.

> It generally takes three business days for a requisition to be processed. Department managers must approve all official written requests for needed materials prior to the supplies being ordered.

What is the meaning of the word *requisition*? By reading the first sentence, we can tell that it is something that must be processed. Context clues in the second sentence explain that this is an official written request for needed materials.

Now you try it. Read the following sentences, then use context clues to help you answer the question.

> Some may find the work of the researcher to be provincial. However, experts in the field disagree with this claim and state that his latest journal is not at all unsophisticated and simple. He uses scientific facts as well as his own investigations and experiments to explain which outcomes are plausible and which are unachievable.

Which is the meaning of *provincial*?

A. expert
B. investigations
C. researcher
D. simple

Did you choose answer choice D? Great! The second sentence uses the definition "unsophisticated and simple" to explain the meaning of *provincial.* Pay close attention when you read! The paragraph says that some find the researcher to be *provincial.* Then, it states that experts disagree; his work is *not* unsophisticated and simple, as others claim. In other words, some think it is unsophisticated and simple. These are the people who said it is provincial. Be careful not to overlook words such as *however* and *disagree* that point out an alternate point of view.

Let's try another one. Answer the following question, based on the same paragraph.

Which has the same or nearly the same meaning as *plausible*?

A. impossible
B. reasonable
C. result
D. unachievable

This question takes a little more thinking. You have to use context clues to determine the meaning of *plausible*, then figure out which of the answer choices has a similar meaning. First, let's find the meaning of *plausible.* The paragraph states that the researcher explains "which outcomes are plausible and which are unachievable." This sentence includes antonyms to explain the two types of outcomes: plausible and unachievable. So, *plausible* is the opposite of *unachievable. Plausible* means achievable, or possible.

Which of the answer choices could explain an outcome that is achievable or possible? *Impossible* and *unachievable* are opposites of *plausible. Plausible* is an adjective, so its synonym will also be an adjective. *Result* is a noun that means the same as *outcome.* An outcome that is plausible would be reasonable. *Reasonable* is also an adjective, and it has a meaning that is similar to that of *plausible.* So the correct answer is B.

Multiple-Meaning Words

As mentioned earlier, in order to be able to understand what you read, you must know the meaning of the words. As you are aware, some words have more than one meaning. For example, think about the meaning of the word *breach.* You might have thought that *breach* means "failure to obey or preserve something." Or you may have thought that a *breach* is "a gap or hole."

Maybe you thought that the meaning of *breach* is "the leap a whale makes out of the water." Actually, all of these are correct definitions. But in order to comprehend text that includes multiple-meaning words, you must know which definition the author has in mind. Think about how the word *breach* is used in the following sentence:

> Dr. Thompson's discussion of Kylie's condition was a *breach* of confidentiality.

The only way to know which meaning is correct is to consider how the word is used. In this example, the doctor's discussion did not create a hole, nor did any large mammals leap out of the water, so these are not the correct definitions. The discussion did, however, fail to preserve the confidentiality between a doctor and his patient.

Read the following sentence. Look at how *faculty* is used in the sentence to determine which of the word's meanings is correct.

> The principal expected Mrs. Ramirez, the Spanish teacher, to attend a meeting after school with all of the other members of the school's *faculty.*

In this sentence, the principal expects a teacher to attend a meeting. The school's *faculty* will be at this meeting. Using clues in the sentence, we can determine that in this case, the correct meaning of *faculty* is "the teaching staff at a school."

Now, consider the following sentence containing the word *faculty.*

> One reason Ling does so well on tests is that she has a great faculty for memorizing facts quickly.

In this sentence, *faculty* does not refer to a teaching staff. The meaning of the word in this case is "a capacity or ability."

As you read, make sure to look at how the words are used, and pay attention to context clues in order to determine which definition of a multiple-meaning word is being used. Assuming the incorrect definition of a word can hinder you from fully comprehending the passage.

Read the sentence below. Look at how the italicized word is used to help you determine which meaning is correct.

> Following the storm, a contractor was asked to give a *quote* for repairing the damage to Mr. Patel's roof.
>
> Which is the correct meaning of *quote* in this sentence?
>
> **A.** to copy someone's exact words
> **B.** reuse of art or written material
> **C.** to refer to something as support or proof
> **D.** an estimate of the cost for providing a service

The sentence tells that the contractor gave a quote for repairing the roof. Although all of the answer choices give definitions for *quote,* only answer choice D makes sense in the context of the sentence. He would have given an estimate of the cost for making the repairs.

> Remember, the part of speech can be helpful in determining which of a word's meanings is being used. In the sample question, *quote* is a noun, so the correct meaning must also be a noun. Since answer choices A and C give definitions of verbs, these are not correct.

Summarizing

Think about the last research paper or book report you wrote. In order to complete the project, you probably read information in books or online, then restated the most important points using your own words. What you did was **summarize.**

Being able to summarize what you have read is one way to demonstrate how well you understood the text. To summarize, you have to focus on the main idea and most important supporting details, then state or explain them in your own words. On the SHSAT, you may be asked to choose a statement that best summarizes the passage you have read. The answer choices will probably all include facts from the passage. Some of the choices might even summarize a particular paragraph. However, the best summary will focus on the most important information from the entire passage.

Read the following paragraph. As you read, look for the main idea and most important details. Then, select the statement that best summarizes the passage.

> Hurricanes are large storms that swirl around a center, or eye. These storms have maximum sustained winds of at least 74 miles per hour. At this speed, a hurricane is classified as a Category 1, the slowest, weakest type of hurricane. The strongest of the storms are classified at Category 5 and have winds exceeding 155 miles per hour.
>
> These powerful weather systems form over the warm waters of the ocean, which provide the energy needed for the storms to strengthen. Typically, the surface temperature of the ocean water must be at least 79 degrees Fahrenheit to be favorable for the growth of a hurricane. Hurricanes rapidly weaken once they have moved onto land. The rain bands, which are the outermost part of the storm, may reach for hundreds of miles and contain thunderstorms and the possibility of tornadoes.

Which statement best summarizes the passage?

A. Ocean waters must generally be at least 79 degrees Fahrenheit in order for a hurricane to form.
B. Hurricanes form and strengthen over warm ocean waters, but quickly weaken once they are over land.
C. Rain bands are the outermost part of a hurricane, and the thunderstorms can reach hundreds of miles.
D. Hurricanes are strong, swirling storms that form over warm ocean waters and have winds of at least 74 miles per hour.

To select the best summary, first identify the main idea:

> Hurricanes are large storms that swirl around a center, or eye.

Then, identify the most important supporting details:

- Hurricanes have winds of at least 74 miles per hour.
- Hurricanes form over the warm waters of the ocean.

Now, determine which of the answer choices includes this information. Answer choices A and C are supporting details from the passage. Answer choice B summarizes the second paragraph; however, the correct answer for this question must summarize the entire passage. If you selected answer choice D, you found the best summary of the passage!

> Be sure you read each question carefully. You may be asked to choose a statement that summarizes the entire passage, or you may be asked to choose a statement that summarizes a specific paragraph. Make sure you know exactly what you are being asked to find.

Synthesis

Sometimes, in order to fully comprehend a passage, you will need to consider information given in different parts of the text. **Synthesis** means combining information from various parts of a passage, or from different passages. Let's consider the passage about hurricanes. Suppose you wanted to find the answer to the following question:

> What wind speeds would you expect to find in a Category 1 hurricane that has already reached land?
>
> **A.** 73 mph
> **B.** 95 mph
> **C.** 101 mph
> **D.** 150 mph

Take a look at information found in different parts of the passage. The following sentences are from the first paragraph:

> These storms have maximum sustained winds of at least 74 miles per hour. At this speed, a hurricane is classified as a Category 1, the slowest, weakest type of hurricane.

This statement is from the second paragraph:

> Hurricanes rapidly weaken once they have moved onto land.

By synthesizing this information, we know that a Category 1 hurricane has winds of at least 74 mph, but that the storm would weaken quickly once it moves onto land. That tells us that the winds would be slower after the storm has reached land, and that answer choice A would be the most likely wind speed.

As you read, be sure to consider each piece of information as it relates to the rest of the passage. Often, the facts and bits of information will work together to help create a full, complete understanding of the text.

Organizational Structure

When an author writes a passage, he or she arranges the ideas in a particular order, depending on the type of information being included. Not only does this help the information to make sense, but it also helps readers to follow the thoughts and best understand the text.

Organizational structure refers to the way ideas are arranged in a passage. Types of organizational structures that authors often use are listed below.

- Sequence
- Order of importance
- Cause and effect
- Compare and contrast
- Problem and solution
- Description

Being able to recognize organizational structure can help you to make better sense of the material you read. You will be able to mentally organize information as you read it, and anticipate what type of information might be presented in the text. For example, if you are reading a cause and effect passage, you can expect to find events that happen as a result of other occurrences. If you are reading a passage that uses a problem and solution structure, you will know to look for possible ways to solve a given problem.

Recognizing the organizational structure can also help you to determine the types of questions you might be asked about the passage. If you read a passage that compares and contrasts two countries, for example, you can assume that you will be asked to identify similarities and differences between the places you read about. Knowing this, you can look for the answers to the anticipated questions as you are reading.

Let's review the types of organizational structures you might find on the SHSAT.

Sequence

Authors may choose to use sequence to organize the information in a passage. In this case, ideas and events are arranged in numerical or chronological order. Sequence may also be used to indicate a particular order of steps in completing a process, such as when giving directions or explaining how to do something. Some signal words that indicate a sequential structure are listed below.

after	meanwhile
before	next
during	preceding
finally	second
first	soon
following	then
immediately	today
initially	until
later	when

Dates may also be used to indicate a sequential text structure. Take a look at the sequential paragraph below. Notice the signal words that help readers to recognize the chronological order of the events.

Initially, the United States began with 13 colonies. *During* the early years of our country, the number of states grew quickly. *By 1900,* a total of 45 states were a part of the U.S. *Within the first few years of the twentieth century,* three more states were added: Oklahoma *in 1907* and New Mexico and Arizona *in 1912.* Approximately 47 years *later,* Alaska became the forty-ninth state in *1959,* with Hawaii *following* only a few months *later* to bring the total to the 50 states that are part of our country today.

Order of Importance

Authors may also present ideas in the order of importance. The author may explain the most important idea first, followed by the second most important, and so on, ending with the least significant of the set.

> Veterans Day is a day on which we remember all of those who have served our country and honor them for their patriotism and sacrifice. This holiday is celebrated in the United States each year on November 11, the anniversary of the day that World War I fighting ceased. For several years, observation of the holiday was moved to a Monday, like Memorial Day and Presidents' Day; however, the November 11 date was reestablished as Veterans Day in 1978.

In this paragraph, the explanation of Veterans Day contains the most important facts, and it is stated at the beginning. This strategy introduces the strongest facts first and captures the attention of the readers. The ideas that follow are of lesser importance.

On the other hand, the author may begin by explaining the least important idea and build to the idea that he or she feels is most important. This strategy leaves readers with the strongest idea in their minds when they finish reading.

> For several years, Veterans Day was observed on a Monday, like Memorial Day and Presidents' Day; however, November 11 was reestablished as Veterans Day in 1978. The holiday is celebrated in the United States on this day each year because it is the anniversary of the day that World War I fighting ceased. Veterans Day is a day on which we remember all of those who have served our country and honor them for their patriotism and sacrifice.

Notice that this paragraph is arranged with the least important fact first, and the most important fact making a final impact on readers.

Cause and Effect

As you know, a *cause* is what makes something happen, or the reason another event takes place. This resulting event is an *effect.*

> If you study and answer the practice questions for the SHSAT, you'll be better prepared for the test.

In this example, studying and answering the practice questions are the causes; being prepared for the test is the effect.

When an author uses a cause and effect organizational structure, the causes of an event and the resulting effects are presented in the passage. The text explains how facts, ideas, or events happen or exist because of something else. Words that often signal cause and effect relationships include those in the following list.

accordingly	if . . . then
as a result	in order to
because	leads to
consequently	so that
due to	therefore
for this reason	thus
hence	

> A single cause may have more than one effect. Likewise, a single effect may have more than one cause.

Keep in mind that these signal words may not be included to alert you to every cause and effect relationship in a passage. You may have to determine how events are connected based on the facts and the context of the reading.

When you recognize a cause and effect structure in a passage, be on the lookout for ways that one event impacts others, as well as for reasons that events take place. Being able to recognize how events are related will help you anticipate what information will be important, and help you to fully understand the reading. Look at the example below, and determine the cause and effect.

> Abby's current school only includes grades six through eight, so she will be attending a new school next year for ninth grade.

In this example, the word *so* signals a cause and effect relationship. The fact that her current school only goes through eighth grade is the cause, or the reason, she will attend a new school for ninth grade. Attending the new school is the effect. Now, read the following example.

> Abby will be attending a new school next year for ninth grade because her current school only includes grades six through eight.

This sentence explains the same cause and effect relationship; however, the effect is stated first, and the cause is stated afterward. As you can see, either the cause or the effect can come first. Look for signal words and clues about how events are related in order to determine which is the cause and which is the effect.

Compare and Contrast

When an author compares and contrasts, he or she explains similarities and differences between events, concepts, objects, places, or people.

> John F. Kennedy, like Ronald Reagan, was a twentieth-century U.S. president. Unlike Reagan, however, Kennedy was a member of the Democratic Party, whereas Reagan was a Republican.

This example compares ways in which the two men were alike: both were presidents. It also contrasts differences between them: Kennedy was a Democrat, and Reagan was a Republican. When you recognize a compare and contrast organizational structure, look for similarities and differences that can help you fully understand the topic. Some signal words that may be used to indicate this structure are shown below.

although	in contrast
as opposed to	instead of
as well as	nevertheless
both	on the other hand
but	similar to
different from	similarly
however	unlike
in common	yet

There are different ways that authors may arrange texts using a compare and contrast format. Authors may completely discuss one of the subjects, then completely discuss the other. For example, an author might present all of the information about John F. Kennedy, then present all of the information about Ronald Reagan.

On the other hand, the author may compare and contrast the two subjects one characteristic at a time. He or she might tell which state Kennedy was from, then tell which state Reagan was from. The author might then discuss the political affiliation of each of these presidents. Then, he or she might present the most significant achievements of each man.

Now, read the paragraph below. Look for similarities and differences between the topics, and find any signal words that indicate ways in which the two are alike or different.

> Pointillism is an artistic style in which artists, such as Seurat, create paintings using only dots. When seen from a distance, the dots blend together to form the intended colors and images. Surrealism is also an artistic style used by painters, including Dali. However, this style was not intended to provide viewers with a realistic image, but rather a dreamlike creation that does not make logical sense.

You probably recognized that pointillism and surrealism are both artistic styles. The word *also* is used to indicate the similarity between the subjects. You probably also recognized a few differences, such as the fact that Seurat used pointillism, and that the works are created using dots that form the realistic images. Surrealism was used by Dali, and the images are dreamlike and do not make logical sense. Signal words such as *however* and *but* indicate that differences between the styles are being presented.

Problem and Solution

When a problem and solution organizational structure is used, a problem is stated, then one or more solutions to problem are presented. As you read passages with this structure, you can anticipate that possible solutions will be included and can be on the lookout for them.

Each year, approximately 1,500 people are stung by stingrays in the United States. While most of these cases are not serious, it is possible for the sting to be fatal, and even minor stings can be extremely painful, nonetheless. Since stingrays are often found buried in the sand, beachgoers should shuffle their feet as they enter the water in order to scare the animals away and avoid stepping on them. Divers should avoid hovering above stingrays, which not only can cause the marine creatures to feel trapped, but also places the diver in the ray's strike zone. Also, anyone spending time in the water should be aware of the location of stingray habitats and exercise caution in these areas.

What problem and solution(s) did you notice in this paragraph? You probably recognized that the problem is people being stung by stingrays. After this issue was introduced, several possible solutions were presented: beachgoers should shuffle their feet, divers should not hover above the animals, and anyone near the water should be careful near stingray habitats.

Description

As you might expect, a description describes a topic. The author introduces the topic, then describes it by listing characteristics, attributes, features, or examples. Readers who recognize this organizational structure know to look for details that will help to explain or describe the topic. Signal words to look for in this type of structure are listed below.

above	between	near
along	for example	onto
appears to be	for instance	over
as in	including	such as
beside	looks like	under

Built in 1672, the Castillo de San Marcos is the oldest masonry fort in the United States. Located in St. Augustine, Florida, near the Atlantic Ocean, this fort was built using coquina, a type of stone that was formed from tiny coquina clam shells, and a mortar made from oyster shells, sand, and water. The walls of the fort are 12 feet thick in most places, and 19 feet thick on the sides facing the harbor. The fort, once surrounded by a moat, has two drawbridges, rooms with vaulted ceilings, and three fireplaces, originally used for heat, light, and cooking. On each corner of the fort is a four-sided structure in a shape that looks like a diamond. These allowed soldiers to fire in any direction, if needed. A courtyard in the middle of the fort was once used to protect the townspeople during attacks.

Notice that the first sentence in this paragraph introduces the topic, the Castillo de San Marcos. This is then followed by several features and attributes that explain the fort to readers.

You Try It!

In this chapter you've reviewed a number of reading comprehension skills. Now it's time to put these skills into practice. Use the skills you have learned to select the correct answers to the questions that follow the passage below.

Arizona's well-known Grand Canyon was created by the flow of the Colorado River; however, another significant U.S. chasm was also the result of many years of extensive erosion. Waimea Canyon, located on the west side of the Hawaiian island of Kauai, is known as "The Grand Canyon of the Pacific." Although it is smaller than the better-known gorge in Arizona, this geological wonder is 14 miles long, one mile wide, and in excess of 3,600 feet deep, making it the largest canyon in the Pacific Ocean.

The island of Kauai is nearly 6 million years old and was originally a volcano. Thousands of years ago, the flood waters and rivers flowing from Mount Wai'ale'ale carved Waimea Canyon, which today is the home of the Waimea River. Weathering and erosion continue to break down the ancient rocks within the canyon, revealing layers of red lava from early volcanic eruptions, and carry these bits of rock into the nearby ocean. This process causes the river water to appear red, giving the name *Waimea* to the river and the canyon: *Wai* means "fresh water," and *mea* means "red."

In 1792, an English sea captain, George Vancouver, introduced goats to Kauai. Since that time, the animals have helped to accelerate the erosion of the walls of Waimea Canyon. Today, goats are wild in the canyon. Between wind, water, and these four-legged creatures, layers upon layers of ancient rock have been revealed along the sides of the canyon. The multicolored cliffs not only include red hues from the lava, but also green and gold from the plant life growing along the sides of the canyon. Visitors to Waimea Canyon can observe this magnificent gorge from three scenic lookout areas. The most striking views occur during the early sunrise hours.

Access to Waimea Canyon allows visitors to get an up-close view of the natural result of erosion, from top to bottom. The road that leads into the canyon reaches nearly 4,000 feet above sea level. Waimea Canyon sits inside of Koke'e State Park, which includes 45 miles of hiking and horse trails, some of which lead to the floor of the valley. One trail in particular, Kukui Trail, offers hikers and horseback riders a two-mile, steep path from an elevation of 2,700 feet down to the bottom of the canyon. From the valley, these visitors can follow the Waimea River out to the Pacific Ocean to see firsthand the path taken by the red waters that carry rock away from the lava-layered walls of the canyon.

1. Which of the following best tells what this passage is about?
   A. the history of the Waimea River
   B. how erosion created Waimea Canyon
   C. hiking and horseback riding in Waimea Canyon
   D. the introduction of goats to the Hawaiian Islands

Remember, the main idea tells what a passage is mostly about. In order to answer question 1, we need to first identify the main idea. In this case, the main idea of the passage is that *Waimea Canyon is a large canyon on Kauai that was created by weathering and erosion of the layers of an ancient volcano.* So the answer choice that best tells what the passage is about will reflect the information in the main idea. You probably recognized that answer choice B best accomplishes this.

So, what makes the other answer choices incorrect? Let's find out. While the Grand Canyon was mentioned in the passage, it is not what the passage is mostly about, so answer choice A is incorrect. Answer choice C does tell what the final paragraph is mostly about; however, it does not reflect the main idea of the entire passage. This is a detail that supports the main idea but is not the main idea itself. Similarly, answer choice D is discussed in the third paragraph but is not the topic of the passage as a whole.

Generally, there is not a single correct way to state the main idea. In this case you might have said that the main idea was *Waimea Canyon is a large canyon on Kauai that was created by weathering and erosion of the layers of an ancient volcano.* On the other hand, you might have said the main idea was *Waimea Canyon is the "Grand Canyon of the Pacific" and is the result of many years of wind and water washing away the layers of lava and rock.* Either one of these is correct. Both explain the same basic idea, just in different words.

2. Which of the following best summarizes the second paragraph?

E. Waimea Canyon contains many layers of lava rock because the island on which it is found was once a volcano.
F. Waimea Canyon is 14 miles long, one mile wide, and in excess of 3,600 feet deep, making it the largest canyon in the Pacific Ocean.
G. Kauai was once a volcano, so water flowing through and eroding the canyon is red, giving Waimea Canyon a name meaning "red waters."
H. Goats, wind, and water work together to erode the walls of Waimea Canyon, revealing layers of red, which are covered by green and gold plants.

As you know, a summary restates the main idea and most important details from a passage. Answer choice E is the main idea of the paragraph and is not a summary of the text. The correct answer will include information from this answer choice, though. Answer choice F contains information found in the first rather than the second paragraph. Also, the majority of this sentence was copied directly from the passage. A summary should restate, or use different words, to give the information. Answer choice G contains the main idea and important details from the third paragraph, and it summarizes that section of the passage rather than the second paragraph. Answer choice H includes the main idea and most important details from the second paragraph. This information is restated, rather than copied, making this the correct answer choice.

3. In what ways are the Grand Canyon and Waimea Canyon similar?

A. Both are the same size.
B. Both are the result of water flow.
C. Both contain plant and animal life.
D. Both offer hiking and horseback trails.

In order to answer this question, you had to synthesize facts stated in the first and second paragraphs. By combining information from different locations, you were probably able to determine that both canyons were created by rivers, making answer choice B the correct answer.

The first paragraph explains that Waimea Canyon is much smaller than the Grand Canyon, making answer choice A incorrect. And while plants, animals, and trails may be found in the Grand Canyon, these facts are not mentioned in this particular passage, so answer choices C and D cannot be the correct choices. Remember, you must base your SHSAT answer choices solely on information given in the passage.

4. Which inference can be made based on the passage?

E. Erosion is often accelerated by animal life.
F. Kauai is the oldest of the Hawaiian Islands.
G. Waimea Canyon is the only canyon in the Pacific.
H. The Grand Canyon is more than 3,600 feet deep.

Keep in mind that an inference must be based on information that is stated. Since there is no mention of how often animals affect erosion, answer choice E cannot be correct. The ages of the other islands of Hawaii are not mentioned, making answer choice F incorrect as well. We do know that Waimea is the largest canyon in the Pacific, but we do not know if it is the only canyon in the Pacific, so answer choice G must be incorrect. What we do know is that Waimea Canyon is 3,600 feet deep, and that it is smaller than the Grand Canyon. Based on this information, we can infer that the Grand Canyon must be more than 3,600 feet deep, making answer choice H the correct option.

5. Which fact best supports the main idea of the passage?

A. The most striking views occur during the early sunrise hours.
B. The Grand Canyon was created by the flow of the Colorado River.
C. From the valley, visitors can follow the Waimea River out to the Pacific Ocean.
D. Flood waters and rivers flowing from Mount Wai'ale'ale carved Waimea Canyon.

The question asks you to identify a fact that supports the main idea. Remember, a fact can be verified, or proven. The idea in answer choice A is an opinion rather than a fact. Not everyone would agree with this statement, and it cannot be verified, so this is not the correct answer. Answer choice B is a fact; however, it does not support the main idea since it is gives information about the Grand Canyon rather than Waimea Canyon. Answer choice C does contain a fact about the topic, Waimea Canyon, but it does not strongly support the main idea, which relates to how the canyon was formed. Answer choice D, on the other hand, is a fact that helps to explain how Waimea Canyon was formed, which strongly supports the main idea. So this is the correct choice.

6. Which of the following conveys the same or nearly the same meaning as the word *gorge* in the first paragraph?
   - **E.** The stray puppy appeared to gorge himself after not eating in so long.
   - **F.** The hawk hunted for its meal, then stored the food in the gorge in its throat.
   - **G.** Soldiers were able to enter the fort through the narrow gorge at the rear of the structure.
   - **H.** From the bridge spanning the gorge, we could clearly see the base of the valley far below.

In the first paragraph, *gorge* is a noun meaning "a deep, narrow valley with steep rocky sides." Only answer choice H uses the same meaning. The meaning of *gorge* in answer choice E is "to greedily overeat." In this sentence, *gorge* is a verb. As you reviewed earlier in the chapter, the correct answer would need to be the same part of speech as the meaning of the word as it was used in the passage. In answer choice F, a gorge is a pouch in the neck of a hawk where it stores food. As it is used in answer choice G, a gorge is a military entrance found in the rear of a fortification.

Let's Review!

In this chapter, you've reviewed a number of strategies that can help you to improve your understanding of text and to answer the reading comprehension questions on the SHSAT. Let's take a final look at what you have learned:

- Every passage has a **main idea**, which is the most important information, main message, or key concept that the author wants to share. The main idea can generally be stated in a complete sentence. If a passage has more than one paragraph, each paragraph will have a main idea.
- The main idea is often introduced in the **topic sentence**, located near the beginning of the passage. This sentence tells what the passage will be about.
- The **topic** of a passage is the subject of the material. It may be a single word or a short phrase that tells what the material is about, such as *killer whales*, *dentistry*, or *the Revolutionary War.*
- **Supporting details** are facts, examples, reasons, definitions, or descriptions that help to explain and give more information about the main idea. These supporting details help the reader to gain a more complete understanding of the main idea.
- **Facts** are statements that are true and can be proven or verified. **Opinions**, on the other hand, are someone's personal views or thoughts and can be disputed.
- Authors often expect readers to make **inferences**, or read between the lines to discover information that is implied or suggested in the writing.
- Readers often have to draw **conclusions** about a passage. A conclusion is a reasonable, educated guess based on given information.
- **Context clues** are hints that help readers determine the meanings of unfamiliar words. Types of context clues include:
  - Synonyms
  - Antonyms
  - Definitions
  - Explanations
  - Examples
- Many words have more than one meaning. Context clues can be helpful in determining which definition of a multiple-meaning word is being used.
- A **summary** is a restatement of the main idea and most important details in a text. To

summarize, readers must relay the information using their own words rather than using the words and phrases given by the author.

- In order to gain a full understanding of the text, readers may have to **synthesize**, or combine information from various parts of a passage.
- The **organizational structure**, or the ways ideas are arranged in a passage, can help readers recognize what information will be important and help them to know what types of information to anticipate in the text. Common organizational structures used by authors include
  - Sequence
  - Order of importance
  - Cause and effect
  - Compare and contrast
  - Problem and solution
  - Description

CHAPTER 7

Arithmetic

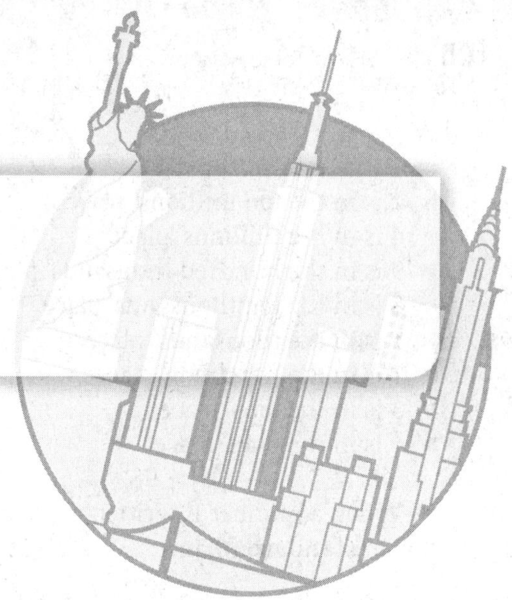

Some of the questions on the mathematics section of the SHSAT will assess your knowledge of arithmetic. These questions will be mixed in with the other types of mathematics questions: algebra, probability, statistics, and geometry.

As you read this chapter, pay close attention to not only the strategies we review, but also the vocabulary and formulas. You will need to be familiar with these to do well on the test; however, they will not be provided for you on test day.

Number Sense

Let's start by reviewing the types of numbers. Knowing the correct terms for these will be important when answering arithmetic questions.

- **Natural numbers.** These are the counting numbers you first learned when you were much younger. Notice that these start with the number 1: 1, 2, 3, 4, 5, 6, 7 . . .
- **Whole numbers.** Whole numbers are the natural numbers, along with zero: 0, 1, 2, 3, 4, 5, 6, 7 . . .
- **Integers.** This group of numbers includes the whole numbers as well as the negatives of the natural numbers: . . . −7, −6, −5, −4, −3, −2, −1, 0, 1, 2, 3, 4, 5, 6, 7 . . .
- **Rational numbers.** Rational numbers include integers as well as fractions that are formed when one integer is divided by another integer. These numbers can be written as a fraction or a ratio. This group includes not only fractions, but also decimals, repeating decimals, and terminating decimals. A few examples of rational numbers are $\frac{1}{4}$, 0.67, 0.343434, 4.2, $12\frac{15}{16}$, 178.03.
- **Irrational numbers.** Irrational numbers cannot be written as a fraction. Nonterminating decimals and nonrepeating decimals are a part of this group. Any square root that is not a perfect square root is also irrational. Examples of irrational numbers are shown below: pi, 0.745092335071224 . . . , $\sqrt{3}$.
- **Real numbers.** These are any numbers that can name a position on a number line. This includes all rational and irrational numbers.

> Not all numbers with a radical sign are irrational. For example, $\sqrt{16}$ and $\sqrt{25}$ are rational since $\sqrt{16} = 4$ and $\sqrt{25} = 5$.

Now that you have reviewed the types of numbers within our number system, let's look at different ways numbers may be written.

Expanded Form

Each digit of a number has a different place value name.

24,987,136

As you know, this number is twenty-four million, nine hundred eighty-seven thousand, one hundred thirty-six. In this example, the:

- 2 is in the ten millions' place
- 4 is in the millions' place
- 9 is in the hundred thousands' place
- 8 is in the ten thousands' place
- 7 is in the thousands' place
- 1 is in the hundreds' place
- 3 is in the tens' place
- 6 is in the ones' place

When a number is written as we usually see it, it is in **standard form**:

24,987,136

Expanded form is seen when a number is written as an addition sentence, with each digit showing its place value:

Standard form: 365
Expanded form: $300 + 60 + 5$

Since place value tells us that 365 has 3 hundreds, 6 tens, and 5 ones, we use expanded form to show each of these values.

3 hundreds = 300
6 tens = 60
5 ones = 5

Now you try it. What is the following number, written in expanded form?

73,902

You probably knew that 73,902 has 7 ten thousands, 3 thousands, 9 hundreds, and 2 ones. Notice that there is a zero in the tens' place. That means the number has zero tens. So, in expanded form, the number is

$70{,}000 + 3{,}000 + 900 + 2$

Notice that we simply omitted the number of tens, since there was a 0 in the tens place.

Scientific Notation

Scientific notation is a way to express large numbers as a multiplication sentence including a small number and a power of 10. Each number in scientific notation will have a **coefficient** that is a number greater than or equal to 1 and less than 10. Each number will also have a **base**, which is the number 10. Following the number 10, there will be an **exponent**, or the power of ten.

Let's take a look at an example. The number below is extremely large: 327 billion, to be exact. It is shown in standard form and in scientific notation.

$327{,}000{,}000{,}000 = 3.27 \times 10^{11}$

To write 327 billion in scientific notation, we need to place a decimal after the first digit, then drop the zeros.

3.27~~000000000~~

Now, count the number of places from the decimal to the end of the row of zeros. Since there are two digits after the decimal (the 2 and 7) and nine zeros, there are a total of 11 places between the decimal and the end of the number. That means our exponent will be 11.

So, in this example, our coefficient is 3.27, our base is 10, and our exponent is 11.

Now it's your turn. What is the number below, written in scientific notation?

94,500,000

The first step is to place the decimal and determine the coefficient. In this case, the coefficient will be 9.45. Next, count the places between the decimal and the end of the row of zeros. Since there are seven digits, the exponent will be 7. As always, the base is 10. So, in scientific notation, the number is:

$94{,}500{,}000 = 9.45 \times 10^{7}$

We know that scientific notation can be used to write large numbers; however, did you know that it can be used to write extremely small numbers as well? The steps in writing a small number are very similar to those used to write large numbers. The only differences are that we will count the numbers to the *left* of the decimal, rather than those to the right, and the exponent will be negative.

$0.000\,000\,000\,072\,5 = 7.25 \times 10^{-11}$

First, move the decimal to the right to create a number between 1 and 10. Then, drop the zeros between the original placement of the decimal and the new placement of the decimal.

0.~~000 000 000 0~~7.2 5

Count the zeros that were crossed off, as well as the number to the left of the decimal. Ten zeros plus the number 7 is a total of 11, so the exponent will be 11. We moved the decimal to the right rather than the left because this is a very small number, so the exponent will be negative.

Let's try one more. Write the following in scientific notation.

0.000 005 46

In this example, the coefficient will be 5.46. There are a total of six digits between the original placement of the decimal point and the placement of the decimal point to the right in the coefficient, so our exponent will be −6. As always, the base will be 10.

5.46×10^{-6}

What if you need to convert a number from scientific notation to standard notation? Simple! Move the decimal point in the coefficient. The exponent tells how many places to move it. If the exponent is positive, move the decimal to the right to make the number larger. If the exponent is negative, move the decimal to the left to make the number smaller.

What is the following number in standard notation?

2.9×10^{8}

Write the coefficient, then move the decimal eight places to the right.

2.9 _ _ _ _ _ _ _

290,000,000.

Operations

In arithmetic, you can expect to perform four basic types of operations on numbers:

- Addition
- Subtraction
- Multiplication
- Division

These are things that you began learning at an early age, and they are the foundation of most of your math skills. These operations are used in nearly every area of math, in one way or another. On the SHSAT, you will be using these skills to answer computation and word problems, not only in the area of arithmetic, but also in algebra, geometry, probability, and statistics.

Choosing an Operation

When you see a computation problem, it is pretty simple to determine which operation, or operations, you will need to use. For example, the addition sign here indicates that you need to add.

$734 + 609 =$

Word problems, on the other hand, can require a little more thought. Often you will have to read a problem and figure out if you need to add, subtract, multiply, divide, or use a combination of these skills to correctly solve the problem. The good news is there are often hints within the question that can help you select the correct operation to use.

Some key words that may indicate **addition** include:

add	combined	in all	raise
additional	extra	increase	sum
altogether	gain	plus	total
both			

Signal words that often indicate **subtraction** include:

change	fewer	more than
decrease	have left / were left	nearer
difference	less / less than	reduce
drop	loss	remain
fall	lost	take away
farther	minus	

Key words that often indicate the need for **multiplication** include:

a factor of	increased by	times
as much	of	total
by	product	triple
double	multiplied by	twice

> Notice that some of the words may also be used to indicate addition. That is because multiplication is the same as repeated addition. Multiplication may be used as a shortcut to find the total of many. Be sure to consider the situation before selecting an operation, rather than relying completely on the signal words.

Some words that may let you know that **division** is required include:

average	equal parts	per
break up	every	quotient of
cut into	into	ratio of
divide evenly	out of	split into
each		

When choosing an operation, pay attention to the context, and determine what type of answer would make sense. If a larger number is needed, use addition or multiplication. If a smaller number is needed, use subtraction or division. After you have found the answer, check to make sure that the amount is reasonable for the situation. For example, if a pair of shoes costs $35, and you need to find the cost of 7 pairs, $5 would not be a reasonable answer. The correct answer would need to be greater than, not less than, the cost of a single pair of shoes.

Order of Operations

Some arithmetic questions may require a combination of addition, subtraction, multiplication, and division.

$10 + 5 \times 3 =$

If we were to complete these steps in order from left to right, the answer would be 45.

$10 + 5 \times 3 = 15 \times 3 = 45$

The only problem is, this is not the correct answer! There is a set of rules, known as the **order of operations**, that states the order in which the operations in math problems must be solved. According to these rules, math problems must be solved according to the following sequence:

1. Parentheses
2. Exponents
3. Multiplication and division (from left to right)
4. Addition and subtraction (from left to right)

So, according to this set of rules, how would we correctly solve the example?

$10 + 5 \times 3 =$

Since there are no parentheses or exponents, we'll start with the multiplication, then complete the addition.

$10 + \underline{5 \times 3} = 10 + 15 = 25$

> To help you remember the order of operations, take a look at the first letter in each of the steps: P, E, M, D, A, S. These are also the first letters of the words in the phrase *Please excuse my dear Aunt Sally.* Keep this phrase in mind, and you'll be sure to solve the operations in the correct order!

Let's try another one. Remember to use the order of operations to solve the steps in the proper sequence.

$39 \div (15 - 2) + 4^2 =$

First, solve anything in parentheses.

$39 \div \underline{(15 - 2)} + 4^2 = 39 \div \underline{13} + 4^2$

Next, solve the exponent.

$39 \div 13 + \underline{4^2} = 39 \div 13 + \underline{16}$

Now, complete any multiplication or division. In this example, there is only one division step. If there were more than one multiplication or division step, we would solve them from left to right.

$\underline{39 \div 13} + 16 = \underline{3} + 16$

Finally, complete any addition or subtraction. Again, if there were more than one addition or subtraction problem to solve, we would begin at the left of the equation and work toward the right.

$3 + 16 = 19$

It's your turn. Use the order of operations to solve the problem below.

$8 \times 7 - (2 + 4)^2 \div 9 =$

A. 2.2
B. 7.7
C. 24
D. 52

Although there are many ways to solve this problem, only one way is correct. First, solve what is in the parentheses.

$8 \times 7 - \underline{(2 + 4)}^2 \div 9 = 8 \times 7 - \underline{6}^2 \div 9$

Next, solve the exponent.

$8 \times 7 - \underline{6^2} \div 9 = 8 \times 7 - \underline{36} \div 9$

This leaves multiplication, subtraction, and division. According to the order of operations, we must solve the multiplication and division next, working from left to right.

$\underline{8 \times 7} - 36 \div 9 = \underline{56} - 36 \div 9$

$56 - \underline{36 \div 9} = 56 - \underline{4}$

Finally, we can solve the subtraction.

$\underline{56} - \underline{4} = \underline{52}$

Did you select answer choice D? Awesome!

Estimation

At times, it is not necessary to find an exact answer to a math problem. In these circumstances, we can use **estimation**, which is an educated guess of about what the actual answer is.

A computer costs \$1,470. A business owner wants to purchase 105 of the computers for his employees. About how much will the computers cost?

The words *about how much* tell you that you can estimate the amount rather than try to find the exact cost. Rounding is one strategy you can use to estimate. The price of each computer is about \$1,500, and the business owner needs about 100 computers.

$\$1,500 \times 100 = \$150,000$

So the total cost of the computers will be about \$150,000.

> Estimation is a great way to quickly determine whether your answer to a math problem is reasonable or not. If estimation shows that your answer is not reasonable, you know to go back and look for mistakes.

Multiplication

You probably learned how to multiply when you were in the second or third grade, so by now you're a pro! But it's a good idea to refresh your memory on a few things related to multiplication that you will need to know before taking the SHSAT.

Prime Numbers

As you learned when you were much younger, *factors* are the numbers being multiplied, and the *product* is the answer.

$5 \times 7 = 35$

In this example, 5 and 7 are the factors, and 35 is the product.

Prime numbers are those numbers greater than 1 whose only factors are 1 and the number itself. These numbers cannot be evenly divided by any other numbers. For example, what numbers could be multiplied in order to have a product of 3? Only 1 and 3. That means 3 is a prime number since the only factors are 1 and the number itself, 3. That is, 3 is only evenly divisible by 1 and 3.

The prime numbers between 0 and 100 are 2, 3, 5, 7, 11, 13, 17, 19, 23, 29, 31, 37, 41, 43, 47, 53, 59, 61, 67, 71, 73, 79, 83, 89, 97.

Notice that 2 is the first number in the list. Since 1 is not greater than 1, it is not considered prime. The only factors of 2 are 1 and 2, so 2 is a prime number. Obviously, since 2 is a factor of any even number, all other prime numbers are odd.

Is 133 a prime number? No, because $7 \times 19 = 133$. And $133 \div 19 = 7$.

Is 157 a prime number? Yes, because it can only be evenly divided by 1 and 157.

Composite Numbers

Composite numbers, unlike prime numbers, have more than two factors. For example, 12 is a composite number. Factors of 12 include 1, 2, 3, 4, 6, and 12.

You just learned that 1 is not a prime number. So does that make it a composite number? Well, let's take another look at the definition: *composite numbers have more than two factors.* How many factors does 1 have? One. So 1 is not a composite number or a prime number.

To determine whether a number is prime or composite, you may have to see whether or not it is divisible by another number. But here are a few ways to quickly identify composite numbers.

- All even numbers, with the exception of 2, are composite. Even numbers are all divisible by at least 1, 2, and the number itself.
- All numbers with a 5 in the ones place are composite. Any number that ends with a 5 is a multiple of 5 and is divisible by at least 1, 5, and the number itself. Think about the factors of 25, 175, and 495 as examples.
- All numbers whose digits have a sum that is divisible by 9 are composite. If the sum of the digits is divisible by 9, the number itself is divisible by 9. For example, 243 is divisible by 9 because $2 + 4 + 3 = 9$. And $243 \div 9 = 27$. Also, 685 is divisible by 9 because $5 + 6 + 7 = 18$, which is divisible by 9: $567 \div 9 = 63$. So any of these numbers are at least divisible by 1, 3, 9, and the number itself.
- Likewise, all numbers whose digits have a sum that is divisible by 3 are composite. If the sum of the digits is divisible by 3, the number itself is divisible by 3. For example, 102 is divisible by 3 because $1 + 0 + 2 = 3$. So $102 \div 3 = 34$. Also, 411 is divisible by 3 because $4 + 1 + 1 = 6$, and 6 is divisible by 3. So $411 \div 3 = 137$.

> It is true that if the sum of the digits of a number is divisible by 9, the number itself is divisible by 9, and if the sum of the digits of a number is divisible by 3, the number itself is divisible by 3. However, this trick does not work with other numbers. Just because the sum of the digits of a number is divisible by 7, that does not mean that the number is divisible by 7. This only works with multiples of 9 and multiples of 3, but it can come in very handy when determining composite numbers.

You know that even numbers are composite. So, to find out if an odd number is prime or composite:

1. See if it is divisible by 3 by finding the sum of the digits.
2. See if it is divisible by 5 by looking at the number in the ones' place.
3. See if it is divisible by 9 by finding the sum of the digits.
4. If the number is not divisible by 3, 5, or 9, try dividing it by the only remaining odd factor: 7.

If the number is evenly divisible by 7, it is composite. If not, it is a prime number.

Use what you've learned so far to answer the following question.

Which is the greatest odd composite integer between 485 and 499?

A. 498
B. 497
C. 495
D. 493

To answer this, we have to check each of the answer choices to determine if it meets the requirements of the question. Answer choice A, 498, is a composite number; however, it is even. Since the question asks for an odd integer, this is incorrect.

Take a look at answer choice B, 497. This number does not have a 5 or 0 in the ones' place, so it is not divisible by 5. The sum of the digits is not divisible by 3 or 9, so the number itself is not divisible by 3 or 9. To determine if it is composite, divide 497 by 7. Since $497 \div 7 = 71$, this is the greatest odd composite integer between 450 and 499.

Let's check the other answer choices as well. Since answer C, 495, has a 5 in the ones' place, this number is divisible by 5 and is a composite number. However, since 495 is not greater than 497, which is also composite, this is not the correct answer choice.

Answer choice D, 493, is the greatest prime number in the list, but since we are looking for the greatest composite number, this is not the correct option.

Greatest Common Factor

The **greatest common factor**, also known as the GCF, is the largest number that is a factor of two or more numbers. To find the GCF of a pair of numbers, list all of the prime factors of each number. Then, multiply the factors that both numbers have in common.

Let's find the GCF of 12 and 18. First, list all of the prime factors of both numbers.

Prime factors of 12: $2 \times 2 \times 3$

Prime factors of 18: $2 \times 3 \times 3$

Next, identify which factors are shared by both numbers.

Prime factors of 12: $\underline{2} \times 2 \times \underline{3}$

Prime factors of 18: $\underline{2} \times \underline{3} \times 3$

These numbers share two factors: 2 and 3. So, we'll multiply 2 and 3 to find the greatest common factor.

$2 \times 3 = 6$

So, 6 is the greatest common factor of 12 and 18.

Now you try it. Find the GCF and select the correct answer.

What is the greatest common factor of 72 and 90?

A. 2
B. 3
C. 6
D. 18

First, list the prime factors of 72 and 90. Then identify which factors the numbers have in common.

Prime factors of 72: $\underline{2} \times 2 \times 2 \times \underline{3} \times \underline{3}$

Prime factors of 90: $\underline{2} \times \underline{3} \times \underline{3} \times 5$

Both numbers have at least one 2, and two 3s. Notice that the prime factorization of 72 has two 2s, and the prime factorization of 90 only has one 2. We have to find how many factors 72 and 90 have in common, so we only underlined one 2 in each list of factors. However, since both 72 and 90 have two 3s, we were able to underline both 3s in each list.

Now, we can multiply the factors that are shared by both numbers.

$2 \times 3 \times 3 = 18$

So, the GCF of 72 and 90 is 18. Did you select answer choice D? Great job!

> If two numbers do not share any common factors, the GCF is 1, because 1 is a factor of all numbers.

Least Common Multiple

A **multiple** is a number that can be divided evenly by another number. For example, multiples of 4 include 4, 8, 12, 16, 20, 24, 28, 32 . . . because each of these numbers can be evenly divided by 4.

A **common multiple** is a number that is evenly divisible by two or more given numbers. For example, 24 is a common multiple of both 3 and 4 since it can be evenly divided by both of these numbers.

The **least common multiple,** or LCM, is the lowest common multiple shared by two or more numbers. We already know that 24 is a common multiple of 3 and 4; however, it is not the least common multiple because there is a smaller number that is a multiple of both.

To find the least common multiple, list the multiples of both numbers. Look for numbers that appear on both lists.

Multiples of 3: 3, 6, 9, 12, 15, 18, 21, 24, 27...

Multiples of 4: 4, 8, 12, 16, 20, 24, 28...

Since 12 is the lowest number that is included on both lists, it is the least common multiple of 3 and 4.

> Notice that when you list multiples of the two numbers, you only have to write numbers until you find one that is on both lists. There really is no reason to continue listing extra numbers once you find a match.

What if you need to find the LCM of more than two numbers? Follow the same steps, just be sure to include lists of multiples of all of the numbers in question. See how well you can do answering the following question.

What is the lowest common multiple of 8, 12, and 15?

A. 4
B. 24
C. 60
D. 120

The first step in solving this is to list the multiples of each number.

Multiples of 8: 8, 16, 24, 32, 40, 48, 56, 64, 72, 80, 88, 96, 104, 112, 120

Multiples of 12: 12, 24, 36, 48, 60, 72, 84, 96, 108, 120

Multiples of 15: 15, 30, 45, 60, 75, 90, 105, 120

Notice that the smallest number to appear in each of the lists is 120, so D is the correct answer. Answer choice A is the greatest common factor of 8 and 12. Answer choice B is the lowest common multiple of 8 and 12, but it is not a multiple of 15, so this choice is incorrect. Answer choice C is the lowest common multiple of 12 and 15, but it is not a multiple of 8, so it is also incorrect.

Let's check out another way to find the least common multiple of 8, 12, and 15. First, list the prime factors of each of the numbers.

Prime factorization of 8: $2 \times 2 \times 2$

Prime factorization of 12: $2 \times 2 \times 3$

Prime factorization of 15: 3×5

Take a look at the prime factors. The least common multiple of 8, 12, and 15 will be the product of these factors, multiplied by the greatest number of times it appears on any list. For example, 2 is a factor of both 8 and 12. It appears three times in the prime factorization of 8 and twice in the prime factorization of 12. Since the most times it appears in a list is three, we will include it three times. Since the most times 3 appears on any list is once, we will include one 3. And, since the most times 5 appears on any list is once, we will include one 5.

Prime factorization of 8: $\underline{2} \times \underline{2} \times \underline{2}$

Prime factorization of 12: $2 \times 2 \times \underline{3}$

Prime factorization of 15: $3 \times \underline{5}$

Now, let's multiply these factors.

$\underline{2} \times \underline{2} \times \underline{2} \times \underline{3} \times \underline{5} = 120$

This shows us that the least common multiple of 8, 12, and 15 is 120.

Exponents (Grade 9 Test Only)

An **exponent** indicates repeated multiplication.

$4^2 = 4 \times 4$

$5^3 = 5 \times 5 \times 5$

As you can see in these examples, when the exponent is 2, we multiply the number by itself 2 times. When the exponent is 3, we multiply the number by itself 3 times.

When the exponent in an expression is 2, we say the number is *raised to the second power.* Another way to say this is to say that the number is *squared.* For example, 4^2 is *four to the second power,* or *four squared.*

When the exponent is 3, we say that the number is *raised to the third power,* or we can say that the number is *cubed.* So, 5^3 is *five to the third power,* or *five cubed.*

So, what is the correct answer to the following example?

$15^2 = ?$

To find this answer, multiply 15×15. So, $15^2 = 15 \times 15 = 225$.

What if a term has a zero exponent? Anything to the power of zero equals 1.

$23^0 = 1$

Sometimes in math, we need to multiply terms that have exponents.

$y^4 \times y^6 =$

In this example, both terms have the same base, *y*. So these can be multiplied. To multiply terms that have the same base, we simply add the exponents.

$y^4 \times y^6 = y^{4+6}$

$y^{4+6} = y^{10}$

Let's take a closer look at how that works. Remember, exponents stand for repeated multiplication.

$y^4 = y \times y \times y \times y$

$y^6 = y \times y \times y \times y \times y \times y$

So, when we multiply $y^4 \times y^6$, we are really multiplying 4 *y*'s and 6 *y*'s.

$y^4 \times y^6 = y \times y \times y \times y \times y \times y \times y \times y \times y \times y$

That shows *y* multiplied by itself 10 times. This is equal to y^{10}, which is the same result we found by adding the exponents.

So, how do we divide terms with exponents? Well, we already know that division is the opposite of multiplication. Since we multiply terms with exponents by adding, we divide terms with exponents by subtracting.

$m^9 \div m^2 = m^{9-2}$

$m^9 \div m^2 = m^7$

Remember, to multiply or divide terms with exponents, the terms must have the same base.

$a^3 \times b^5 = a^3 \times b^5$

Since a and b are not the same base, we cannot add these exponents to multiply.

Roots (Grade 9 Test Only)

Roots, also known as **radicals**, are the opposite of exponents. For example, $5^2 = 25$, or *five squared equals 25.* Since 5 times itself equals 25, 5 is the **square root** of 25.

$\sqrt{25} = 5$

The symbol used to indicate square root is known as a *radical symbol.* The term $\sqrt{25}$ is read *the square root of 25.*

What is $\sqrt{81}$?

We know that $9 \times 9 = 81$. That means that 9 is the square root of 81.

$9^2 = 81$

$\sqrt{81} = 9$

Simplifying Radicals

To simplify a radical, or find the square root, we take any perfect squares out from under the radical sign.

$\sqrt{144} = \sqrt{12^2} = 12$

Not all numbers under a radical sign will be perfect squares. That means, they are not the result of multiplying a whole number by itself. For example, $\sqrt{48}$ is not a whole number. We know that $6 \times 6 = 36$ and $7 \times 7 = 49$, but no number times itself equals 48. So how do we solve $\sqrt{48}$? We need to find a factor of 48 that is a perfect square. Since 16 is a perfect square ($4^2 = 16$) and is a factor of 48, we can use it to help us find the square root of 48.

$\sqrt{48} = \sqrt{16 \times 3}$

Next, we find the square root of the factor that is a perfect square, 16. We will move the square root of 16 out from under the radical sign.

$\sqrt{48} = \sqrt{16 \times 3} = 4\sqrt{3}$

Since 3 is not a perfect square, and no factor of 3 is a perfect square, 3 will stay under the radical sign. The answer, $4\sqrt{3}$, is read *four times the square root of three.*

> If you haven't already done so, it would be a great idea to memorize all of the perfect squares from $2^2 = 4$ through $15^2 = 225$. Knowing these will help you find square roots in the same way that memorizing multiplication facts helps you solve division problems.

Now you try it!

Simplify the expression $\sqrt{150}$.

First, determine whether the number under the radical sign is a perfect square. Since no number times itself equals 150, determine whether any factor of 150 is a perfect square. Think of the perfect square numbers, and figure out if they are factors of 150: 4, 9, and 16 are not; however, 25 is a factor of 150, so we can use that.

$\sqrt{150} = \sqrt{25 \times 6}$

Now move the root of the perfect square out from under the radical sign.

$\sqrt{150} = \sqrt{25 \times 6} = 5\sqrt{6}$

Since 6 does not have a factor that is a perfect square, we have simplified the expression.

Multiplying Square Roots

Sometimes, to simplify an expression, we will need to multiply radicals.

$(\sqrt{20})(\sqrt{5})$

Neither of these factors is a perfect square, so let's multiply them together first, then find the square root of the product.

$(\sqrt{20})(\sqrt{5}) = \sqrt{100}$

$\sqrt{100} = \sqrt{10^2} = 10$

Let's try another one. Use multiplication to simplify the following expression.

$(\sqrt{24})(\sqrt{10})(\sqrt{3})$

Start by multiplying the numbers and writing the expression using a single radical symbol.

$(\sqrt{24})(\sqrt{10})(\sqrt{3}) = \sqrt{720}$

Next, find factors that are perfect squares. You probably recognized that since 72 is divisible by 9, then 720 is as well. And since 9 is a perfect square, we can start simplifying by using that number.

$$\sqrt{720} = \sqrt{9 \times 80}$$

Now, we can move the square root of 9 out from under the radical symbol.

$$\sqrt{9 \times 80} = 3\sqrt{80}$$

Next, determine whether any factors of 80 are a perfect square. Since 16 is both a factor and a perfect square, we can use that to further simplify the expression.

$$3\sqrt{80} = 3\sqrt{16 \times 5}$$

When we move the square root of 16 out from under the radical sign, we will multiply it by the number that is already outside of the radical, 3.

$$3\sqrt{16 \times 5} = 4 \times 3\sqrt{5} = 12\sqrt{5}$$

Since 5 does not have any perfect square factors, the expression has been completely simplified.

Adding and Subtracting Radicals

As we just reviewed, square roots can be multiplied. Now let's review how to add and subtract these numbers. In order to add and subtract square roots, the radicals must be the same.

$$3\sqrt{7} + 5\sqrt{7}$$

Since both terms include the same number under the radical sign, we can simply add the numbers by which square roots are being multiplied.

$$\underline{3}\sqrt{7} + \underline{5}\sqrt{7} = \underline{8}\sqrt{7}$$

Square roots can be subtracted in the same way.

$$12\sqrt{15} - 2\sqrt{15} = 10\sqrt{15}$$

Take a look at the equation below. Notice that the middle term does not have a number outside of the radical sign. That means that there is *one* of that radical. In other words, the term is being multiplied by 1. When this happens, we will add or subtract 1 as needed.

$$20\sqrt{2} + \sqrt{2} - 14\sqrt{2} = 21\sqrt{2} - 14\sqrt{2} = 7\sqrt{2}$$

Often before being able to add or subtract square roots, the expressions must first be simplified. After that, if the radicals are the same, the terms can be added or subtracted.

$$\sqrt{27} + \sqrt{75} =$$

First simplify the radicals.

$$\sqrt{27} + \sqrt{75} = \sqrt{9 \times 3} + \sqrt{25 \times 3} = 3\sqrt{3} + 5\sqrt{3}$$

The terms have the same square root, so now we can add.

$$3\sqrt{3} + 5\sqrt{3} = 8\sqrt{3}$$

Now it's your turn. Simplify the expression.

$$4\sqrt{54} + \sqrt{24} + \sqrt{98}$$

Remember, the first step is to simplify each of the terms. If there is already a term outside of the radical sign, as seen in the first term in this example, be sure to multiply this number by the square root that you take out from under the radical sign.

$$4\sqrt{54} + \sqrt{24} + \sqrt{98} =$$
$$4\sqrt{9 \times 6} + \sqrt{4 \times 6} + \sqrt{49 \times 2}$$

$$(3 \times 4)\sqrt{6} + 2\sqrt{6} + 7\sqrt{2} =$$
$$12\sqrt{6} + 2\sqrt{6} + 7\sqrt{2}$$

Now, add to combine like radicals. Notice that two of the terms have the same number under the radical sign. These can be combined. However, the unlike term cannot be combined with the others.

$$\underline{12\sqrt{6}} + \underline{2\sqrt{6}} + 7\sqrt{2} = 14\sqrt{6} + 7\sqrt{2}$$

Fractions, Mixed Numbers, and Decimals

Let's review a few things you probably learned about fractions during elementary school. As you know, a **fraction** names parts of a whole. The number on the top of the fraction is the **numerator**, and the number on the bottom is the **denominator**. For example, if you ate $\frac{3}{8}$ of a pizza, the denominator tells that the pizza was divided into 8 equal parts, and the numerator tells that you ate 3 of those equal parts.

Equivalent fractions are fractions that name equal amounts, such as $\frac{1}{2}$, $\frac{2}{4}$, and $\frac{8}{16}$.

A **mixed number** is a whole number and a fraction combined. For example, if you studied at the library for $2\frac{1}{3}$ hours, you were there for 2 whole hours plus $\frac{1}{3}$ of another hour.

On the SHSAT, you may need to add, subtract, multiply, or divide fractions. We'll review how to perform each of these operations.

Adding and Subtracting Fractions

To add or subtract fractions with like denominators, we simply add or subtract the numerators. The denominator stays the same.

$$\frac{5}{12}+\frac{6}{12}=\frac{11}{12}$$

If the fractions have unlike denominators, we must first find a common denominator.

$$\frac{1}{3}+\frac{5}{12}=$$

In this case, we can multiply the first fraction by $\frac{4}{4}$ to make the denominator the same as the second fraction. Since $\frac{4}{4}$ is equal to 1, the value of the fraction does not change; the new fraction will be equivalent to the original.

$$\frac{1}{3}\left(\frac{4}{4}\right)=\frac{4}{12}$$

Now we can add.

$$\frac{4}{12}+\frac{5}{12}=\frac{9}{12}$$

The numerator and denominator are both multiples of 3, so we can simplify the fraction by dividing the numerator and denominator both by 3.

$$\frac{9}{12}=\frac{3}{4}$$

Let's subtract fractions.

$$\frac{5}{7}-\frac{1}{6}=$$

Before we can subtract, we must first find a common denominator. Here is where finding the lowest common multiple comes in handy. Both denominators can evenly divide 42, so we will multiply the first fraction by $\frac{6}{6}$ and the second by $\frac{7}{7}$ to give them the same denominator. Then we can subtract.

$$\frac{5}{7}\left(\frac{6}{6}\right)-\frac{1}{6}\left(\frac{7}{7}\right)=$$

$$\frac{30}{42}-\frac{7}{42}=\frac{23}{42}$$

When performing operations involving a fraction and a whole number, be sure to write the whole number as a fraction with a denominator of 1. For example, 12 is the same as $\frac{12}{1}$.

Multiplying and Dividing Fractions

To multiply fractions, the denominators do not have to be the same. Simply multiply the numerators, multiply the denominators, and simplify the product.

$$\frac{3}{16}\times\frac{2}{3}=\frac{6}{48}$$
$$\frac{6}{48}=\frac{1}{8}$$

To divide fractions, invert the second fraction and multiply.

$$\frac{5}{8}\div\frac{15}{16}=\frac{5}{8}\times\frac{16}{15}=\frac{80}{120}=\frac{2}{3}$$

Let's try multiplying a fraction and a mixed number.

$$\frac{7}{9}\times3\frac{1}{12}=$$

First, convert the mixed number into an **improper fraction**. An improper fraction is simply a fraction that has a numerator that is greater than the denominator. To change a mixed number to an improper fraction, multiply the denominator by the whole number, then add the numerator. The result is the new numerator. The denominator stays the same. So, to change $3\frac{1}{12}$ to an improper fraction, multiply 12×3, then add the numerator, 1. The result is 37, which is the numerator of the improper fraction. The denominator is still 12.

Now multiply.

$$\frac{7}{9}\times\frac{37}{12}=\frac{259}{108}$$

The result is an improper fraction. To simplify this, convert it back to a mixed number. First, divide the numerator by the denominator to find the whole number. Then, write the remainder as the numerator of the fraction.

$$\frac{259}{108}=2\frac{43}{108}$$

> Remember to do all of your calculations on scrap paper or in your SHSAT test book. Do not work any of the problems on the answer sheet. This sheet should only be used to mark your final answer.

Now you try it. Use what you know about fractions to answer the question below.

For her science fair project, Nicolette is testing the effect of adding plant food to potted vegetables. She has $3\frac{7}{8}$ pounds of plant food and will dissolve $\frac{1}{2}$ ounce of the food in one cup of water daily for each plant. How many servings of plant food will she be able to make?

A. $1\frac{15}{16}$

B. $7\frac{3}{4}$

C. 31

D. 124

Let's see how well you did! First, we have to find how many ounces of plant food she has. Notice that the item states that she has $3\frac{7}{8}$ *pounds* of the food. We need to find how many *ounces*. To do this, we need to multiply $3\frac{7}{8}$ by 16 since there are 16 ounces in a pound. So, convert $3\frac{7}{8}$ to an improper fraction, then multiply it by 16.

$$3\frac{7}{8}\times16=\frac{31}{8}\times\frac{16}{1}=\frac{496}{8}=62$$

So, Nicolette has 62 ounces of plant food. Next, divide this amount into $\frac{1}{2}$ ounce servings.

$$\frac{62}{1} \div \frac{1}{2} = \frac{62}{1} \times \frac{2}{1} = 124$$

She can make 124 servings of plant food for her project.

Converting Fractions and Decimals

Decimals are another way to write amounts that are part of a whole.

$$\frac{1}{4} = 0.25$$

$$\frac{1}{2} = 0.5$$

$$\frac{60}{10} = 0.6$$

$$\frac{3}{4} = 0.75$$

$$\frac{95}{100} = 0.95$$

$$1\frac{1}{2} = 1.5$$

To convert a fraction to a decimal, divide the numerator by the denominator.

Convert $\frac{3}{4}$ to a decimal.

$3 \div 4 = 0.75$

$$\frac{3}{4} = 0.75$$

To convert a decimal to a fraction, place the decimal as the numerator over a denominator of 100. Then, simplify the fraction.

Convert 0.35 to a fraction.

$$0.35 = \frac{35}{100} = \frac{7}{20}$$

Percentages

Like fractions and decimals, percentages also refer to part of a whole. However, **percent** means "out of 100" or "per 100." For example, 85 percent, or 85%, means 85 out of 100.

$$85\% = \frac{85}{100} = 0.85$$

Changing a fraction to a percent is the same as changing a fraction to a decimal, only you will use a percent symbol (%) rather than a decimal point.

Mei Ling scored $\frac{32}{40}$ on her math quiz. What percent of the questions did she answer correctly?

To solve this, divide the numerator by the denominator.

$$\frac{32}{40} = 32 \div 40 = 0.8 = 80\%$$

> Be careful not to confuse decimals that only have one digit to the right of the decimal point. Remember that the first place value is tenths, then hundredths. That means 0.8 = 80% and 0.08 = 8%.

To convert a percent to a decimal, move the decimal two places to the left.

43% = 0.43

7% = 0.07

135% = 1.35

Notice that percents can be greater than 100%. Take a look at the following example.

The number of students attending Lincoln Junior High School has increased by 178% over the past 10 years. If there were 650 students originally, how many students currently attend the school?

To solve this, we need to first change the percent to a decimal.

178% = 1.78

Next, we can multiply the original number by the decimal number.

$650 \times 1.78 = 1{,}157$

Over the past 10 years, the number of students has increased from 650 to 1,157.

Very small amounts may be described as percents that are less than 1%.

A survey of 800 students showed that only 0.5% of students would like to have more homework. How many students surveyed responded that they would like more homework?

To solve this, first change the percent to a decimal by moving the decimal point two places to the left.

$0.5\% = 0.005$

Now, multiply the number of students surveyed by the decimal number.

$800 \times 0.005 = 4$

So only 4 students out of 800 surveyed would like more homework.

Let's use what we've reviewed about percents to solve the following example.

A pair of jeans is priced $85. They are on sale for 30% off. What is the final price of the jeans, including 6% sales tax?

First, we need to find the discounted price. To do this, we need to find 30% of $85. Convert 30% to a decimal and multiply by the price of the jeans.

$30\% = 0.30$

$0.30 \times 85 = 25.5$

So, the discount is $25.50. Next, we need to subtract the discount from the original price in order to find the sale price.

$85 - 25.5 = 59.50$

Next, to find the sales tax, we need to determine 6% of 59.50. Again, convert the percent to a decimal, then multiply.

$6\% = 0.06$

$59.50 \times 0.06 = 3.57$

Finally, add the sales tax to the discounted price to find the total cost.

$59.50 + 3.57 = 63.07$

So the final price, including the discount and sales tax, is $63.07.

Ratios and Proportions

A **ratio** is a way to compare two different numbers. For example, suppose there are 25 students in your math class. Of those, 15 are boys and 10 are girls. The ratio of boys to girls is 15:10. In the statement *ratio of boys to girls*, the word *boys* was listed first, therefore, the number of boys must be listed first in the ratio. Ratios can be stated in words, numbers, or as a fraction.

There were 15 boys and 10 girls.

The ratio of boys to girls is 15 to 10.

15:10

$\frac{15}{10}$

Notice that the numbers included in the ratio are the number of boys and the number of girls. The total number of students is not included.

Just like fractions, ratios can also be reduced, or simplified.

The ratio of boys to girls is $\frac{15}{10}$, or 15:10

The ratio of boys to girls is $\frac{3}{2}$, or 3:2.

This shows that for every three boys there are two girls.

Let's use what we've discussed about ratios to solve a problem.

In Mr. O'Rourke's third period class, the ratio of freshmen to sophomores is 7:5. How many of the 24 students are freshmen?

The ratio 7:5 indicates that for every 7 freshmen, there are 5 sophomores. That means that in every 12 students, 7 are freshmen and 5 are sophomores. So, the fraction $\frac{7}{12}$ shows that 7 out of 12 students are freshmen. We can multiply this fraction by the total number of students to find how many freshmen are in the class.

$$\frac{7}{12} \times 24 = 14$$

So, there are 14 freshmen. That also means that since there are a total of 24 students, the remaining 10 are sophomores.

Ratios are important to properly setting up and solving proportions. A **proportion** is an equation that has equivalent ratios on each side.

$$\frac{2}{3} = \frac{4}{6}$$

Since the two ratios are equal, this is a proportion. When one value in a ratio is missing, solving a proportion is a way to determine the unknown number.

$$\frac{x}{12} = \frac{1}{2}$$

Since you know that $\frac{6}{12}$ is equivalent to $\frac{1}{2}$, you probably already figured out that the missing number in this proportion is 6. One way to solve a proportion is to cross multiply. This means, multiply the denominator on the left by the numerator on the right. Then, multiply the numerator on the left by the denominator on the right. Basically, you multiply across the equals sign.

$$\frac{x}{12} = \frac{1}{2}$$
$$x(2) = 12(1)$$
$$2x = 12$$
$$x = 6$$

Let's try another example.

The ratio of teachers to students at West Lake Junior High School is 1:14. How many teachers are there if the school has a total of 882 students?

First, write the ratio of teachers to students as a fraction. Remember, since teachers are listed first, the number of teachers comes first.

$$1:14 = \frac{1}{14}$$

Now write the ratio of the total number of teachers to the total number of students. Since the actual number of teachers is unknown, use a variable in the ratio.

$$\frac{t}{882}$$

Next, set up the ratios as a proportion. Remember, the ratios are equivalent.

$$\frac{t}{882} = \frac{1}{14}$$

Cross multiply to solve for t and find the total number of teachers.

$$\frac{t}{882} = \frac{1}{14}$$
$$14(t) = (1)882$$
$$14t = 882$$
$$14t \div 14 = 882 \div 14$$
$$t = 63$$

So, the total number of teachers at the school is 63.

You Try It!

In this chapter, you've reviewed a number of skills that will help you answer the arithmetic questions on the SHSAT. Use what you have learned to answer the questions below.

1. What is the greatest composite odd integer less than 50 that is not a perfect square?

A. 49
B. 47
C. 45
D. 39

To find the correct answer, let's start with the greatest odd integer less than 50, which is 49. Since 49 is a perfect square ($7^2 = 49$), this is not the correct answer. Since 47 is a prime number, it is not correct either. Answer choice C, 45, is correct because it is composite (factors of 45 include 1, 3, 5, 9, 15, and 45), odd, and not a perfect square. Answer choice D, 39, is also composite; however, it is not the greatest composite odd integer.

2. Elliot began a new job working in his aunt's day care center. He will work $12\frac{1}{2}$ hours each week and will earn $8.60 per hour for the first three weeks. He will earn a 20% raise after that. How much will Elliot's paycheck be for his work the fourth week?
   A. $21.50
   B. $86.00
   C. $107.50
   D. $129.00

First, convert $12\frac{1}{2}$ to a decimal, 12.5. Next, multiply the hours Elliot will work by his rate per hour, $8.60.

$$12.5 \times 8.6 = 107.5$$

So, we know he will make $107.50 per week for the first three weeks. Next, find 20% of this amount to determine the amount of his raise. Convert 20% to a decimal, 0.2, then multiply by the amount he earned prior to the raise.

$$107.5 \times 0.2 = 21.5$$

He will earn an additional $21.50 per week. Add this to his previous wages to find the amount of his paycheck for the fourth week.

$$\$107.50 + \$21.50 = \$129.00$$

3. $(\sqrt{45})(\sqrt{5})(\sqrt{32}) =$
   A. $12\sqrt{10}$
   B. $60\sqrt{2}$
   C. $72\sqrt{10}$
   D. $100\sqrt{72}$

To simplify square roots, multiply the numbers underneath the radical sign, then look for factors that are perfect squares.

$$(\sqrt{45})(\sqrt{5})(\sqrt{32}) = \sqrt{7{,}200} = \sqrt{72 \times 100}$$

Pull the square root of the perfect square to the outside of the radical sign, and look for perfect square factors of the number remaining under the radical sign.

$$10\sqrt{72} = 10\sqrt{36 \times 2}$$

Move the square root of the perfect square to the outside of the radical sign, and multiply it by the factor that is already there.

$$10\sqrt{36 \times 2} = 6 \times 10\sqrt{2} = 60\sqrt{2}$$

4. Marquez is making a scale model of his school for a project. According to his scale, 2 cm is equal to 3 meters. If the length of the building is 120 meters, what will be the length of the model, in cm?
   A. 40
   B. 60
   C. 80
   D. 120

To find the length of the model, we will need to set up a proportion. First, find the ratio of cm to meters Marquez is using for his scale. According to the scale, the ratio of cm to meters is 2:3.

$$\frac{2}{3}$$

We do not know how many cm the model will be in length, so let's use the variable *s* to represent the unknown value. We do know that the building is 120 meters long, so this will be the bottom number of the ratio.

$$\frac{s}{120} = \frac{2}{3}$$

Cross multiply to find the value of the variable.

$$3(s) = 2\,(120)$$
$$3s = 240$$
$$3s \div 3 = 240 \div 3$$
$$s = 80$$

So Marquez's model will have a length of 80 cm.

Let's Review!

In this chapter, you've reviewed arithmetic vocabulary and skills that will be helpful for correctly answering questions on the SHSAT Math test. Let's take another quick look at some of the information that will help you do your best on this section of the test.

- **Expanded form** uses the place values of the digits to write a number as an addition sentence: 4,376 = 4,000 + 300 + 70 + 6.
- **Scientific notation** is a way to write very large or very small numbers as a multiplication sentence including a number between 1 and 10 and a power of 10: $920{,}000{,}000{,}000 = 9.2 \times 10^{11}$. In this example, 9.2 is the **coefficient**, 10 is the **base**, and 11 is the **exponent**. Remember to move the decimal point to the left when converting large numbers to scientific notation, and to the right when converting small numbers.
- Look for key words when selecting which operation is required to solve word problems. Clues such as *both*, *combined*, and *total* often indicate that you need to add. *Decrease*, *difference*, and *fewer* often suggest subtraction. *Times*, *product*, and *triple* may tell you to multiply. *Average*, *quotient of*, and *per* sometimes indicate division.
- The **order of operations** is a set of rules that tell you the sequence in which operations must be completed. Always solve math problems according to the following order: parentheses, exponents, multiplication and division, addition and subtraction.
- **Prime numbers** are those that have exactly two factors: 1 and the number itself. Examples of prime numbers include 2, 3, 5, and 7. On the other hand, composite numbers have three or more factors. Examples of **composite numbers** include 6, 10, and 15. All even numbers, with the exception of 2, are composite.
- The **greatest common factor** (GCF) is the largest number that is a factor of two or more numbers. The **least common multiple** (LCM) is the lowest multiple shared by two or more numbers.
- An **exponent** indicates repeated multiplication: $7^4 = 7 \times 7 \times 7 \times 7$. In this example, the exponent, 4, tells that 7 is multiplied by itself 4 times. This is read *seven to the fourth power.* When a number has an exponent of 2, we say the number is *squared.* When the exponent is 3, we say the number is *cubed.*
- To multiply terms containing exponents, first make sure they have the same base, then add the exponents. To divide terms with the same base, subtract the exponents.

  $$q^4 \times q^8 = q^{12}$$
  $$w^9 \div w^7 = w^2$$

- **Roots**, or **radicals**, are the opposite of exponents. To find the square root of a number, determine what number when multiplied by itself equals the number under the radical sign.

  $\sqrt{144} = 12$

- To simplify radicals, find any factors of the number that are perfect squares, and move the square root of the factor to the outside of the radical sign.

  $\sqrt{300} = \sqrt{100 \times 3} = 10\sqrt{3}$

  To multiply radicals, multiply the numbers under the radical signs first, then find the square root of the product.
- Terms that have the same number under the radical sign can be added or subtracted. We cannot add or subtract terms with different numbers under the radical sign.

- **Fractions** name parts of a whole. To add or subtract fractions, first find a common denominator. To multiply fractions, multiply the numerators, then multiply the denominators. To divide fractions, invert one of the fractions, then multiply.
- **Decimals** also name part of a whole. To convert fractions to decimals, divide the numerator by the denominator.
- Percents refer to part of 100. For example, 76% means 76 out of 100, or 76 per 100. Percents can be written as a decimal: $\frac{76}{100} = 76\% = 0.76$.
- **Ratios** compare two different numbers. A **proportion** is an equation that sets two ratios equal to one another. Cross multiplication is one way to solve a proportion containing a ratio with an unknown value.

CHAPTER 8

Algebra

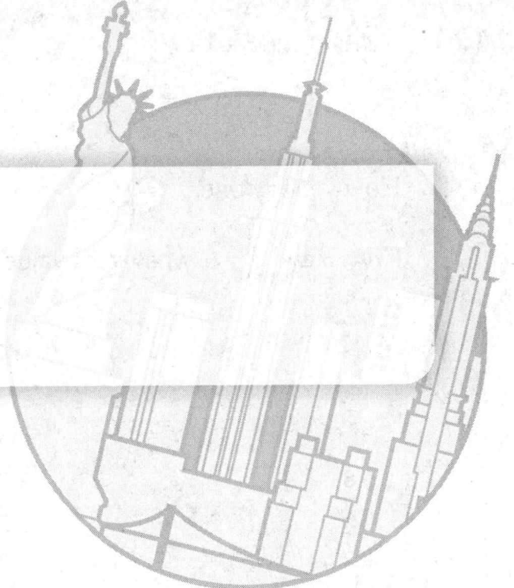

The Math section of the SHSAT will include questions to assess your knowledge of arithmetic, geometry, probability and statistics, and algebra. In this chapter, we will review some of the skills that will help you answer the algebra questions. Keep in mind that as you work through algebra questions, you may need to use skills reviewed in other chapters. For example, we will be using exponents to solve some of the algebra questions. Exponents are reviewed in the arithmetic chapter. Be sure to refer to other sections of the book as needed.

As you work through the chapter, also remember that any vocabulary or formulas you need to solve the problems must be memorized. You will be expected to use these to answer the questions; however, they will not be provided for you on the test.

Variables

When you think of algebra, the first thing that probably comes to mind is letters. **Variables** are letters or symbols that take the place of an unknown value in math.

$7x + 3y = 15$

In this equation, the variables x and y represent unknown values. In this chapter, we will review strategies for solving equations, expressions, and inequalities that include variables. In other words, we'll review ways to figure out what values are represented by these letters or determine the values of the expressions in which the variables are included.

Sometimes the values of the variables are given, and we can use substitution to answer the question.

What is the value of $4x - 2y$ if $x = 7$ and $y = 3$?

In this question, the values of the variables are given. All we have to do is substitute these values into the expression.

$x = 7$ and $y = 3$

$4x - 2y = 4(7) - 2(3) = 28 - 6 = 22$

Let's try another one.

What is the value of $5\,|w| \div 10\,|q|$ if $w = 8$ and $q = -1$?

First, take a look at the terms $|w|$ and $|q|$. The vertical lines on either side of the variables indicate absolute value. The **absolute value** of a number is its distance from zero on a number line. For example, -3 is three units from zero, so the absolute value of -3 is 3. Absolute value is always positive.

So, to solve the example, the absolute value of the variables will be positive numbers. Let's start by substituting the values into the expression, then solve the expression.

$w = 8$ and $q = -1$

$5\,|w| \div 10\,|q| = 5\,|8| \div 10\,|-1| = 5(8) \div 10(1) =$
$40 \div 10 = 4$

Now you try one.

If $a = 3$ and $b = 6$, what is the value of $\frac{a^b}{b^a}$?

A. $\frac{1}{12}$

B. $\frac{4}{7}$

C. $\frac{8}{27}$

D. $3\frac{3}{8}$

First, substitute the given values for each variable.

$$\frac{a^b}{b^a} = \frac{3^6}{6^3}$$

Then solve the expression.

$$\frac{3^6}{6^3} = \frac{729}{216}$$

Both the numerator and the denominator are divisible by 9, so simplify the fraction.

$$\frac{729}{216} = \frac{81}{24}$$

Since both 81 and 24 are divisible by 3, reduce the fraction further. Then, convert the improper fraction to a mixed number.

$$\frac{81}{24} = \frac{27}{8} = 3\frac{3}{8}$$

Solving Algebraic Equations

When we use substitution, the values of the variables are given. Many times, though, this is not the case. Take a look at the equation below.

$$7 + x = 15$$

Here, rather than being told the value of the variable, we have to figure that out. At a quick glance, you can probably tell that $x = 8$ because you already know that $7 + 8 = 15$. But many equations are not solved that easily.

In order to solve equations, we must isolate the variable. That means we have to get the variable alone on one side of the equation.

As you know, the values on either side of the equals sign are the same.

$$7 + x = 15$$

$$7 + 8 = 15$$

As we work to isolate the variable, the values on both sides of the equation must remain equal. That means the same operations must be performed to both sides. So how do we know what operations to perform? In order to solve equations, we will use the operations that are opposite of those that are included in the equation. For example, addition and subtraction are opposite operations because we can use addition to undo subtraction.

$$7 + 8 = 15$$

$$15 - 8 = 7$$

Multiplication and division are also opposite operations.

$$3 \times 4 = 12$$

$$12 \div 4 = 3$$

Let's go back to our original example.

$$7 + x = 15$$

This equation uses addition. In order to isolate the variable, we will use the opposite operation, subtraction. And we will perform the same subtraction to both sides of the equation so the two sides remain equal. In order to get the *x* by itself on one side of the equation, we need to subtract 7. So we will subtract 7 from both sides in order to maintain equality.

$$7 + x - 7 = 15 - 7$$

$$x = 8$$

By subtracting 7 from both sides, not only do we isolate the variable, we also discover the value of *x*.

Let's try another one.

$$9y = 108$$

This equation involves multiplication because $9y$ means $9 \times y$. Since division is the opposite of multiplication, we will divide both sides of the equation by 9 to isolate the variable.

$$\frac{9y}{9} = \frac{108}{9}$$
$$y = 12$$

To check your work, substitute the value of the variable back into the original equation.

$$9y = 108$$
$$9(12) = 108$$
$$108 = 108$$

Since the two sides of the equation are equal, we know we solved the equation correctly and found the value of the variable.

Let's try an equation that is a little more complex.

What is the positive value of the variable in the equation $\frac{k^2}{40} = \frac{9}{10}$?

Since the variable is part of a division expression, we must use multiplication to isolate it. If we multiply both sides of the equation by 40, we can eliminate the division on the right side of the equals sign.

$$\frac{k^2}{40} = \frac{9}{10}$$
$$40 \times \frac{k^2}{40} = 40 \times \frac{9}{10}$$
$$k^2 = \frac{360}{10}$$
$$k^2 = 36$$

Since the variable is squared, the next step is to eliminate the exponent. Finding the square root will isolate the variable. Be sure to find the square root of the values on both sides of the equation in order to maintain equality.

$$\sqrt{k} = \sqrt{36}$$
$$k = 6$$

In order to make sure we solved the equation correctly, let's plug the value of the variable back into the original equation.

$$\frac{k^2}{40} = \frac{9}{10}$$

Substituting 6 for k:

$$\frac{6^2}{40} = \frac{9}{10}$$
$$\frac{36}{40} = \frac{9}{10}$$
$$\frac{9}{10} = \frac{9}{10}$$

Perfect! The value of k is 6!

Let's use what you've reviewed about algebraic expressions to solve an equation that involves substitution as well as finding the unknown value of a variable.

If $s = 5$ and $2s(8t - 4s) = 40$, what is the value of t?

In this case, the value of s is given, so begin by substituting this value into the equation.

$$2s(8t - 4s) = 40$$
$$2 \times 5(8t - 4 \times 5) = 40$$
$$10(8t - 20) = 40$$

Now, we can work on solving for t. Since the variable is part of a multiplication expression, use division as the first step in getting the variable alone on the left side of the equation. Be sure to divide both sides by 10 to keep them equal.

$$10(8t - 20) = 40$$
$$\frac{10(8t - 20)}{10} = \frac{40}{10}$$
$$8t - 20 = 4$$

Look at the left side of the equation. It involves subtracting 20. We can add 20 to both sides to isolate the term $8t$.

$$8t - 20 = 4$$

$$8t - 20 + 20 = 4 + 20$$
$$8t = 24$$

We know that $8t$ means *8 multiplied by t*, so we will use division to undo the multiplication. So the next step is to divide both sides of the equation by 8.

$$\frac{8t}{8} = \frac{24}{8}$$
$$t = 3$$

Let's check our work. Substitute the value of t back into the original equation. We know that $s = 5$ and $t = 3$.

$$2s(8t - 4s) = 40$$
$$2 \times 5(8 \times 3 - 4 \times 5) = 40$$
$$10(24 - 20) = 40$$
$$10(4) = 40$$
$$40 = 40$$

Since $40 = 40$ is true, we know that the equation was solved correctly!

Now you try it! Use what you have learned about solving equations to answer the question below.

For what value of m is $4(m + 6) = 9(m - 4)$?

A. 2
B. 5
C. 10
D. 12

Let's solve the equation to check your work. The 4 outside of the parentheses on the left side of the equation means we have to multiply 4 by each of the terms inside those parentheses. So, we will multiply $4 \times m$, then multiply 4×6. The same is true of the 9 on the right side of the equation. The 9 must be multiplied by m, then by 4.

$$4(m + 6) = 9(m - 4)$$
$$4m + 24 = 9m - 36$$

Next, we need to isolate the terms with variables on the same side of the equation. Let's subtract $4m$ from both sides of the equation. That will eliminate the variable from the left side, and place the only terms with a variable on the right.

$$4m + 24 \underline{- 4m} = 9m - 36 \underline{- 4m}$$
$$24 = 5m - 36$$

When isolating a variable, it does not matter which side of the equation contains the variable. However, it is usually easier to work with positive variables than negative. When deciding where to isolate the variable, take a look at which side of the equation contains the greatest coefficient. By subtracting the lesser coefficient from both sides, the variable ends up on the side with the greatest coefficient, and the term is positive.

Now, the only term with a variable is on the right side of the equation. To isolate the variable, we need to move the constant, 36, to the left side of the equation. Since 36 is negative, we need to add 36 to both sides of the equation, since $-36 + 36 = 0$. That way, the only constants are on the left of the equation.

$$24 \underline{+ 36} = 5m - 36 \underline{+ 36}$$
$$60 = 5m$$

We're almost there! The term $5m$ is the same as *5 multiplied by m*. That means, we need to use division to eliminate the coefficient and get the variable alone. So, we will divide both sides of the equation by 5.

$$\frac{60}{5} = \frac{5m}{5}$$
$$12 = m$$

So the value of m is 12. Did you select answer choice D? Great job! Remember to substitute the value of the variable into the original equation to check your work.

$$4(m+6)=9(m-4)$$
$$4(12+6)=9(12-4)$$
$$4(18)=9(8)$$
$$72=72$$

The equation is true, so we know the answer is correct!

> If you are completely stuck on an SHSAT question asking you to find the value of a variable, try substituting each of the answer choices into the equation to see which makes the equation true. This will probably take more time than solving the equation as you've learned here; however, the strategy can be useful in finding the correct answer if you are confused and worried about getting the question wrong.

Monomials and Polynomials (Grade 9 Test Only)

In the previous section, we worked with variables and exponents. Now let's review some definitions that will come in handy on the SHSAT. In algebra, you will work with monomials and polynomials. A **monomial** is one term and may contain a constant, a variable, an exponent, or the product of a constant and one or more variables:

$$3x^2$$

A **constant** is a single number. In this example, the constant is 3. As you know, the variable is a letter or symbol, which in this example is x. A monomial can contain more than one variable as long as they are being multiplied. Here are some examples of monomials:

$$4mn$$
$$xy^3z$$

Notice that monomials do not contain addition or subtraction signs. A **polynomial**, on the other hand, is the sum or difference of more than one term.

$$6y^2+3$$
$$7qrs^3-2s+8$$
$$9a^2+4b+e$$

Notice that each of these polynomials contains plus and/or minus signs. Polynomials can also contain positive exponents, but they do not contain negative exponents or square roots. The typical format of a polynomial lists terms with the greatest exponents first, followed by other exponents in decreasing order.

$$12x^3+2x^2-4x+5$$

Each part of the polynomial is called a **term**. The example above has four terms, each separated by a plus or minus sign.

Monomials

A monomial can contain multiplication. For example, $10b^2$ means $10 \times b^2$. Also, $6st$ means $6 \times s \times t$. Suppose we need to multiply two monomials.

$$4c^3 \times 5d^2$$

What this really means is $4 \times c^3 \times 5 \times d^2$. To solve this, multiply the coefficients. Since we can't combine unlike terms, we will list the variables beside each other, which indicates multiplication.

$$4c^3 \times 5d^2 = 20c^3d^2$$

Let's try another example. Simplify:

$$3(a^4)(-6a^2)$$

As you know, terms beside each other in parentheses indicate multiplication. First, multiply the coefficients, keeping in mind that multiplying a positive by a negative results in a negative product. Also, remember that to multiply like terms containing exponents, add the exponents.

$$3(a^4)(-6a^2)=-18a^{4+2}=-18a^6$$

Polynomials

In order to evaluate polynomials, we will combine like terms. For terms to be alike, the variable part must be exactly the same.

$5\underline{x^2} + 7\underline{x^2} =$

Since the variable part of the first two terms is the same, x^2, these terms can be combined by adding the coefficients.

$5\underline{x^2} + 7\underline{x^2} = 12\underline{x^2}$

At times, some terms in a polynomial will be alike and can be combined, while others can't.

$8\underline{y^3} + 2\underline{y^3} + 4xy =$

In this example, the first two terms can be combined because the variable part is exactly the same, y^3. However, the third term has a different variable part, so it cannot be combined.

$8y^3 + 2y^3 + 4xy = 11y^3 + 4xy$

Let's simplify the following by combining like terms.

$10a^2 + 3a^2 - a^2$

Since all of the variable parts of these terms are the same, a^2, we can add and subtract the coefficients to combine the like terms. The third term does not include a coefficient. In this case, it is understood that the coefficient is 1 because $1 \times a^2 = a^2$.

$10a^2 + 3a^2 - a^2 = 12a^2$

Let's try another one. Remember, we can only combine terms that are exactly alike to simplify the polynomial.

$5k^2 + 7k - 3 - 2k + 4k^2 + 6$

First, group the like terms together. Keep the plus and minus signs with the term that follows them. For example, since the polynomial above indicates that we should subtract $2k$, we will move the minus sign with the $2k$ when we group the like terms.

$(5k^2 + 4k^2) + (7k - 2k) + (-3 + 6)$

$9k^2 + 5k + 3$

Remember to arrange the terms in order of descending exponents.

It's your turn. Combine like terms in the equation below.

$(15 + 5z) - (7 - 2z) =$

A. $8 + 7z$
B. $8 + 3z$
C. $8 - 3z$
D. $22 - 7z$

Did you select answer choice A? Great job! Let's review why this is the correct answer choice. To combine the like terms, first remove the parentheses. Keep in mind that the negative sign between the sets of parentheses must be applied to both terms within the second set. So $7 - 2z$ becomes $-7 + 2z$.

$(15 + 5z) - (7 - 2z) = 15 + 5z - 7 + 2z$

Next, combine the like terms.

$15 + 5z - 7 + 2z = 5z + 2z + 15 - 7 = 7z + 8$

Now that we've reviewed adding and subtracting polynomials, let's try multiplying a monomial and a polynomial. In this case, there are two factors: one outside the parentheses and one inside.

$4w(5w^2 + 2w - 3)$

This multiplication sentence has two factors. The first factor is $4w$. The second factor is $(5w^2 + 2w - 3)$. Notice that the term $4w$ is outside of the parentheses, and the other terms are inside. This means that $4w$ must be multiplied by each of the terms within the parentheses. Start by multiplying $4w$ by the first term, $5w^2$. Then multiply $4w$ by each of the other terms.

$4w(5w^2 + 2w - 3) = (4w \times 5w^2) + (4w \times 2w) + (4w \times -3)$

$20w^3 + 8w^2 - 12w$

Now you try it. Remember to multiply the monomial by each of the terms of the polynomial.

Simplify $-7q^2(4q^3 - 9q^2 + q - 3)$.

A. $-28q^6 + 63q^4 - 7q^2 + 21q^2$
B. $-28q^5 + 63q^4 - 7q^3 + 21q^2$
C. $-28q^5 - 63q^4 + 7q^3 - 21q^2$
D. $-28q^4 + 63q^3 - 7q^2 + 21q$

Did you choose answer choice B? Awesome! Let's check to see why this was the correct answer. Start by multiplying $-7q^2$ by each of the terms of the other factor.

$-7q^2(4q^3 - 9q^2 + q - 3) = (-7q^2 \times 4q^3) + (-7q^2 \times -9q^2) + (-7q^2 \times q) + (-7q^2 \times -3)$

Remember that to multiply terms with exponents, the exponents are added.

$(-7q^2 \times 4q^3) + (-7q^2 \times -9q^2) + (-7q^2 \times q) + (-7q^2 \times -3) = -28q^5 + 63q^4 - 7q^3 + 21q^2$

Solving Inequalities

The symbols $>$, $<$, $\geq$, and $\leq$ are often used to compare values:

MEANING
$>$ is greater than
$<$ is less than
$\geq$ is greater than or equal to
$\leq$ is less than or equal to

Inequalities use greater than and less than symbols to compare values that are not equal.

$6 > 3$

$-4 < 2 < 7$

$x > 9$

$y \leq 14$

Each of these inequalities compares values that are not the same. For example, the first inequality tells that *6 is greater than 3.* The next tells that *−4 is less than 2, and 2 is less than 7.* The third tells that *the value of* x *is greater than 9.* The last example tells that *the value of* y *is less than or equal to 14.*

Inequalities are solved in much the same way as equations. We are trying to find the value of the variable. The only difference is that the result will not tell the exact value of the variable, rather it will tell that the value is greater than or less than the solution. Take a look at the following inequality.

$n + 7 > 10$

To solve the inequality, isolate the variable. Since 7 is added to *n*, we will subtract 7 from both sides of the inequality.

$n + 7 > 10$

$n + 7 \underline{- 7} > 10 \underline{- 7}$

$n > 3$

While the solution to this inequality does not give us an exact value for *n*, we do know that the value of *n* is greater than 3.

Let's try another example.

Which is equivalent to the following inequality?

$15 \leq d - 9$

A. $6 \leq d$
B. $6 \geq d$
C. $24 \geq d$
D. $d \geq 24$

Since 9 is subtracted from the value on the right side of the inequality, we will add 9 to both sides to isolate the variable.

$15 \leq d - 9$

$15 + 9 \leq d - 9 + 9$

$24 \leq d$

Notice that *24* $\leq$ d is not one of the answer choices; however, d $\geq$ *24* is. Answer choice D means d *is greater than or equal to 24*. The solution we found when solving the inequality was *24 is less than or equal to* d. Both of these have the same meaning, since the terms are reversed as well as the inequality symbol. Watch carefully! Make sure your answer has the same meaning as the answer choice you select.

As you can see, solving inequalities is very much like solving equations. The only difference occurs when the inequality involves multiplying or dividing negative numbers. Any time we have to multiply or divide the inequality by a negative number, the inequality sign reverses. Check out the example below.

$$6x > 18$$

To solve this inequality, we will divide both sides by 6.

$$6x > 18$$

$$\frac{6x}{6} > \frac{18}{6}$$

$$x > 3$$

Now let's solve a similar inequality that includes *negative* 6*x* rather than positive 6*x*.

$$-6x > 18$$

In order isolate the variable and solve this inequality, we need to divide both sides by −6. When dividing or multiplying an inequality by a negative number, the inequality symbol reverses. Take a look.

$$-6x > 18$$

$$\frac{-6x}{-6} < \frac{18}{-6}$$

$$x < -3$$

We solved the inequality in the same way, with the exception of reversing the symbol. Let's try another example.

$$\frac{5y}{-3} + 4 < 19$$

First, subtract 4 from both sides so the term with the variable is alone on the left side of the inequality.

$$\frac{5y}{-3} + 4 < 19$$

$$\frac{5y}{-3} + 4 - 4 < 19 - 4$$

$$\frac{5y}{-3} < 15$$

The term $\frac{5y}{-3}$ involves division. This term means 5y ÷ −3. In order to undo the division, we need to multiply both sides of the inequality by −3, which reverses the inequality sign.

$$\frac{5y}{-3} < 15$$

$$\frac{(-3)5y}{-3} > (-3)15$$

$$5y > -45$$

Notice that the inequality symbol reversed when we multiplied by a negative number. Now we can finish solving the inequality by dividing both sides by 5. Since we are now dividing by a positive number, the inequality symbol does not change again.

$$\frac{5y}{5} > \frac{-45}{5}$$

$$y > 9$$

In order to isolate the variable in $\frac{5y}{-3} < 15$, we could multiply both sides by the fraction $\frac{-3}{5}$, since this is the inverse of the fraction in the inequality. Multiplying by the inverse results in a product of 1. Since we would have been multiplying by a negative number, the inequality sign would still have been reversed following this step.

Writing Algebraic Equations

At times, in order to solve word problems, the problems need to be written as algebraic expressions. The key words that suggest which operation to use in solving the problem can be helpful in correctly writing the expression. Several examples of how to translate words into expressions are shown below.

Addition	the sum of 9 and x 10 more than s	$9+x$ $s+10$
Subtraction	7 less than q the difference of 8 and d	$q-7$ $8-d$
Multiplication	y multiplied by 12 the product of 6 and h	$12y$ $6h$
Division	the quotient of t and 5 k divided by 3	$\frac{t}{5}$ $\frac{k}{3}$

In a word problem, the word *is* often means *equals*. The word *of* often indicates multiplication. For example, *half of twelve is six* translates to $\frac{1}{2} \times 12 = 6$.

In algebra, it is common for word problems to require that they be written as algebraic expressions in order to be solved. Don't let this make you nervous. Just think about what the question is asking, and pay close attention to clues given in the words.

Write an expression to show that q is equal to three times the value of r.

The phrase *three times the value of* r tells that we need to multiply by 3 and *r*. So we know that *q* equals 3 multiplied by *r*.

$q = 3r$

Let's try another example.

The quotient of a and 9 is less than the sum of 8 and b.

The word *quotient* indicates division, and the word *sum* indicates addition. Notice that we are told that one of the values *is less than* the other, rather than the values being equal. That means we will be using an inequality symbol, not an equals sign.

Let's look at each part of the statement separately.

The quotient of a *and* 9 translates to $\frac{a}{9}$.

. . . *is less than* translates to the symbol <.

. . . *the sum of 8 and* b translates to 8 + *b*.

So *the quotient of* a *and 9 is less than the sum of 8 and* b translates to the inequality below.

$\frac{a}{9} < 8 + b$

Now you try it. Look for key words that indicate which operations and symbols to include.

Which shows that one-third the value of h is less than the value of j, and j is less than or equal to 7?

A. $\frac{h}{3} < j \leq 7$

B. $\frac{h}{3} > j \geq 7$

C. $\frac{h}{3} \leq j < 7$

D. $3h < j \leq 7$

This problem involves two inequalities, so let's take a look at them one at a time. The first part of the problem states that *one-third the value of* h *is less than the value of* j. One-third the value of *h* is $\frac{1}{3}$ of *h*. This can be expressed as $\left(\frac{1}{3}\right)h$ or $\frac{h}{3}$. So *one-third the value of* h *is less than the value of* j is expressed as $\frac{h}{3} < j$. The first half of the correct inequality is shown below.

$$\frac{h}{3} < j$$

The second part of the problem includes other inequality. It tells that j *is less than or equal to 7.* This is expressed as $j \leq 7$. The second half of the inequality is shown below.

$$j \leq 7$$

So *one-third the value of* h *is less than the value of* j, *and* j *is less than or equal to 7* is expressed as the inequality below, which is answer choice A.

$$\frac{h}{3} < j \leq 7$$

In the examples we just reviewed, you had to translate a word problem into an algebraic expression. Sometimes, you will need to not only write the expression, but also find the value of the variable in order to answer a question. Take a look at the following example.

Mackenzie is twice as old as Luke. Luke is 8 years old. How old is Mackenzie?

To solve this problem, you will write an algebraic expression to represent the situation, then solve the expression to answer the question:

- First, think about what we know: Luke is 8 years old. Mackenzie is twice as old as Luke.
- Next, think about what we need to find out: How old is Mackenzie?
- Now let's use the information to write an expression. We'll use the variable *M* to represent Mackenzie's age. The words *twice as old* tell us that we will need to multiply Luke's age by 2 to find Mackenzie's age. Let's use the variable *L* to stand for Luke's age.

$$M = 2L$$

This equation tells us that Mackenzie's age is twice Luke's age. Since we know his age already, we can substitute this value for *L*.

$$M = 2L$$

$$M = 2(8)$$

Now, we can solve to find the value of *M*.

$$M = 2(8)$$

$$M = 16$$

So Mackenzie is 16 years old.

Let's try another one.

Reggie spent $\frac{5}{6}$ of an hour working on his math homework. Suri spent $2\frac{1}{2}$ times as many hours completing her homework. How many hours did Suri spend doing homework?

What we know is that:

- Reggie spent $\frac{5}{6}$ of an hour doing homework.
- Suri spent $2\frac{1}{2}$ times as long doing her homework.

What you need to find is how many hours Suri spent on homework. The key words *$2\frac{1}{2}$ times* indicate that you will need to multiply. Let *R* stand for the time Reggie spent, and *S* represent the time Suri spent. Suri's time is equal to $2\frac{1}{2}$ times as long as Reggie spent.

$$S = \left(2\frac{1}{2}\right)R$$

Since we know how long Reggie spent, let's substitute his time for the variable *R*.

$$S = \left(2\frac{1}{2}\right)R$$

$$S = \left(2\frac{1}{2}\right)\left(\frac{5}{6}\right)$$

Now we can multiply the fractions to solve for *S*.

$$S = \left(2\frac{1}{2}\right)\left(\frac{5}{6}\right)$$

$$S = \left(\frac{5}{2}\right)\left(\frac{5}{6}\right)$$

$$S = \frac{25}{12}$$

$$S = 2\frac{1}{12}$$

So Suri spent $2\frac{1}{12}$ hours doing her homework.

> Remember that when multiplying mixed numbers, such as $2\frac{1}{2}$, the mixed number needs to first be converted to an improper fraction.

Each of the previous two examples involved only multiplication. Some word problems will require algebraic expressions involving more than one step. Read the problem below, and determine how to write the information as an algebraic expression in order to answer the question.

> Marco and Adam play on the same basketball team. The number of points Marco scored in the district tournament was 6 less than 4 times the number of points Adam scored. If Adam scored 9 points, how many points did Marco score?

We know that:

- Marco scored 6 less than 4 times the number of points Adam scored.
- Adam scored 9 points.

We need to find how many points Marco scored.

> It can be helpful to underline key information in a math problem. On the SHSAT, feel free to underline, circle, or put stars by important facts and numbers in the test booklet. Just be careful not to make any extra marks on your answer sheet.

Let's use the information to write an algebraic expression. We can use the variable M for Marco's points and A for Adam's points. The phrase *6 less than* tells that we will need to subtract 6. The phrase *4 times* indicates multiplying by 4. Take another look at this sentence from the problem:

> The number of points Marco scored in the district tournament was 6 less than 4 times the number of points Adam scored.

So Marco's points are equal to 6 less than 4 times Adam's points.

$$M = 4A - 6$$

Since we know that Adam scored 9 points, we can substitute this value for A.

$$M = 4(9) - 6$$

Now we can solve the equation to find the value of M.

$$M = 4(9) - 6$$

$$M = 36 - 6$$

$$M = 30$$

Marco scored 30 points in the tournament. Substitute this value back into the equation to make sure the answer is correct.

$$M = 4A - 6$$

$$30 = 4(9) - 6$$

$$30 = 36 - 6$$

$$30 = 30$$

The equation is true, so we solved it correctly!

Not all word problems that require writing an algebraic expression will involve a real-life scenario. Sometimes the problems will simply be mathematical situations. Take a look at the following example.

> Three consecutive multiples of 5 have a sum of 240. What is the greatest of these numbers?

To write an expression that will help us solve the problem, let's start by figuring out what we know. *Three consecutive multiples of* 5 tells us that each of the numbers is divisible by five and is five more than the previous number. For example, the numbers could be 5, 10, and 15 or possibly 25, 30, and 35. Let's call the first of the consecutive numbers x. The second of the consecutive numbers is five more than the first, so its value is $x + 5$. The third of the consecutive numbers is five more than that, or $x + 5 + 5$, which is the same as $x + 10$. So our three numbers are x, $x + 5$, and $x + 10$.

The problem states that these three consecutive multiples of five, which we are calling x, $x + 5$, and $x + 10$, have a sum of 240. The word *sum* indicates that the numbers are added together. So we can write the equation shown here.

$$x + (x + 5) + (x + 10) = 240$$

The question asks what the greatest of the numbers is. We have named the greatest number $x + 10$. To find its value, we need to first solve for x, then add 10.

To solve for x, start by combining like terms.

$$x + (x + 5) + (x + 10) = 240$$

$$x + x + x + 5 + 10 = 240$$

$$3x + 15 = 240$$

Next, subtract 15 from both sides to leave the term containing the variable alone on the left side of the equation.

$$3x + 15 - 15 = 240 - 15$$

$$3x = 225$$

Now we can divide both sides by 3 to isolate the variable.

$$\frac{3x}{3} = \frac{225}{3}$$

$$x = 75$$

Now we know that the value of x is 75. So the least of the consecutive multiples of 5 is 75. The question asked for the greatest of these numbers, which is $x + 10$.

$$x + 10 = 75 + 10 = 85$$

So the correct answer is 85.

You Try It!

In this chapter, you've reviewed a number of skills that will be helpful in answering the algebra questions on the SHSAT. Now, use what you have learned to select the best answer choice to each of the questions below.

1. What is the value of $f + g(g + 2f)$ when $f = 3$ and $g = 5$?
   A. 34
   B. 44
   C. 53
   D. 58

Did you choose D? Excellent! To find the value of the expression, substitute the given values of the variables.

$$f + g(g + 2f) = 3 + 5(5 + 2 \times 3)$$

Remember that the order of operations states that operations within parentheses must be completed first, and that multiplication and division are applied before addition and subtraction. That means the first step is to multiply 2×3 in the parentheses, then add the 5.

$$3 + 5(5 + 2 \times 3) = 3 + 5(5 + 6) = 3 + 5(11)$$

Now multiply 5×11, then add 3 to the product.

$$3 + 5(11) = 3 + 55 = 58$$

2. What is the value of q in $15(q - 7) = 4(q + 4)$?
   A. 0
   B. 1
   C. 8
   D. 11

Let's solve the equation to find the value of the variable. First, multiply the constant outside of each set of parentheses by each term inside the parentheses.

$$15(q-7)=4(q+4)=15q-105=4q+16$$

Since the largest term containing the variable is on the left of the equals sign, let's move all of the variable terms to that side. To do so, subtract $4q$ from both sides of the equation. Then combine like terms.

$$15q-105=4q+16$$
$$15q-105-4q=4q+16-4q$$
$$11q-105=16$$

Next, add 105 to both sides of the equation to isolate $11q$ on the left.

$$11q-105=16$$
$$11q-105+105=16+105$$
$$11q=121$$

Now divide both sides of the equation by 11 to find the value of q.

$$11q=121$$
$$\frac{11q}{11}=\frac{121}{11}$$
$$q=11$$

So the value of q is 11. Substitute this back into the original equation to verify the answer.

$$15(q-7)=4(q+4)$$
$$15(11-7)=4(11+4)$$
$$15(4)=4\,(15)$$
$$60=60$$

The equation is true, so the answer was correct! The value of the variable is 11.

3. Simplify $(24c^2+9)-(-6+3c^2)+2c$.

A. $24c^2+2c+17$

B. $21c^2+2c+15$

C. $21c^2+2c+3$

D. $29c^2+3$

Start by removing the parentheses. Be sure to apply the negative sign to all terms in the second set of parentheses.

$$(24c^2+9)-(-6+3c^2)+2c=$$
$$24c^2+9+6-3c^2+2c$$

To simplify the expression, combine like terms. Remember, for terms to be alike, they must have the exact same variable and exponent. Remember to arrange the terms in order of descending exponents.

$$24c^2+9+6-3c^2+2c$$
$$24c^2-3c^2+2c+9+6$$
$$21c^2+2c+15$$

So answer choice B is correct.

4. Simplify $-12x+4<-9x+25$.

A. $x>-7$

B. $x<-7$

C. $x<7$

D. $x>7$

The symbol for *is less than* (<) tells that this is an inequality. As you know, inequalities are solved in much the same way as equations. First, use opposite operations to collect like terms on either side of the inequality. Let's move the terms with variables to the left, and the terms without variables to the right.

$$-12x + 4 < -9x + 25$$

$$-12x + 4 + 9x < -9x + 25 + 9x$$

$$-3x + 4 < 25$$

$$-3x + 4 - 4 < 25 - 4$$

$$-3x < 21$$

Next, we have to divide both sides of the inequality by −3 in order to isolate the variable. This is the step where things are slightly different from solving an equation. Since we will be dividing by a negative number, the inequality sign will reverse. So, instead of being the symbol for *is less than*, it will become the symbol for *is greater than* (>).

$$-3x < 21$$

$$\frac{-3x}{-3} > \frac{21}{-3}$$

$$x > -7$$

5. Three friends each earned babysitting money over the weekend. Keisha earned \$2.50 more than Chloe. Chloe earned three times as much as Sydney. If the total the friends earned was \$46.25, how much did Keisha earn?

A. \$6.25
B. \$8.75
C. \$18.75
D. \$21.25

In order to solve this word problem, we need to write it as an algebraic expression. First, think about what we know:

- Keisha earned \$2.50 more than Chloe.
- Chloe earned 3 times more than Sydney.
- The total earned was \$46.25.

We don't know how much Sydney earned, so we'll use the variable s to represent the amount of money she made. We do know that Chloe earned 3 times as much as Sydney. The words *3 times as much* indicate that we will multiply Sydney's earnings by 3 to find Chloe's earnings. So, Chloe's money is represented by $3 \times s$, or $3s$. Keisha earned \$2.50 more than Chloe. The phrase *\$2.50 more than* tells that we will add this amount to Chloe's total. So, Keisha made $3s + 2.50$.

The total the friends earned was \$46.25. That means Sydney's money + Chloe's money + Keisha's money = \$46.25.

$$s + 3s + (3s + 2.50) = 46.25$$

Now we can combine like terms and solve for the variable. First, combine all terms containing the variable.

$$s + 3s + (3s + 2.50) = 46.25$$

$$s + 3s + 3s + 2.50 = 46.25$$

$$7s + 2.50 = 46.25$$

Next, subtract 2.50 from both sides to get the variable term alone on the left side of the equation.

$$7s + 2.50 = 46.25$$

$$7s + 2.50 - 2.50 = 46.25 - 2.50$$

$$7s = 43.75$$

Finally, divide both sides of the equation by 7.

$$7s = 43.75$$

$$\frac{7s}{7} = \frac{43.75}{7}$$

$$s = 6.25$$

We have found the value of the variable!

However, we're not quite finished. The question asked how much Keisha earned. The variable represents the amount Sydney earned. Take another look at the information given in the problem.

Keisha earned \$2.50 more than Chloe. Chloe earned three times as much as Sydney.

Solving for the variable, s, showed us that Sydney earned \$6.25. Chloe earned three times this amount. So, she earned $3 \times \$6.25$.

$$3 \times \$6.25 = \$18.75$$

Chloe earned \$18.75. Keisha earned \$2.50 more than Chloe. So Keisha earned \$18.75 + \$2.50.

\$18.75 + \$2.50 = \$21.25

So Keisha earned \$21.25, which means answer choice D is correct.

Let's Review!

In this chapter, you've reviewed vocabulary and skills that will be helpful in answering the algebra questions on the SHSAT Math test. Let's go over some of the key points that you will need to remember in order to do your best on this section of the test.

- **Variables** are letters or symbols that take the place of unknown values in math. In the equation $9x = 27$, x is the variable.
- **Absolute value** is the distance of a number from zero on the number line. The absolute value of a number is always positive. The absolute value of 17 is shown as $|17|$.

  $|-45| = 45$

- When the value of a variable is given, the value can be substituted into an equation or expression. Substitution can also be used to check your answer when solving for the value of a variable.
- To find the value of a variable, the variable must be isolated on either side of the equation. Use opposite operations of those included in the equation, being sure to perform the same operation on both sides of the equals sign.
  - Addition and subtraction are opposite operations.
  - Multiplication and division are opposite operations.
  - Squared numbers and square roots are opposites.
- Inequalities are solved in the same way as equations. The only difference is that the inequality symbol is reversed when multiplying or dividing by a negative number. These symbols may be included in inequalities: $<, >, \leq, \geq$.
- A **monomial** is a single term that may contain a constant, a variable, an exponent, or the product of a constant and one or more variables. $15x^2y^3$ is an example of a monomial.
- A **polynomial** is the sum or difference of more than one term. In other words, it is a group of two or more monomials being added or subtracted. $15x^2y^3 + 32x - 14$ is an example of a polynomial. It contains three terms.
- In order to solve some word problems, they must be written as algebraic expressions. Key words in the problem indicate which operation, or operations, must be used to solve the problem.

CHAPTER 9

Geometry

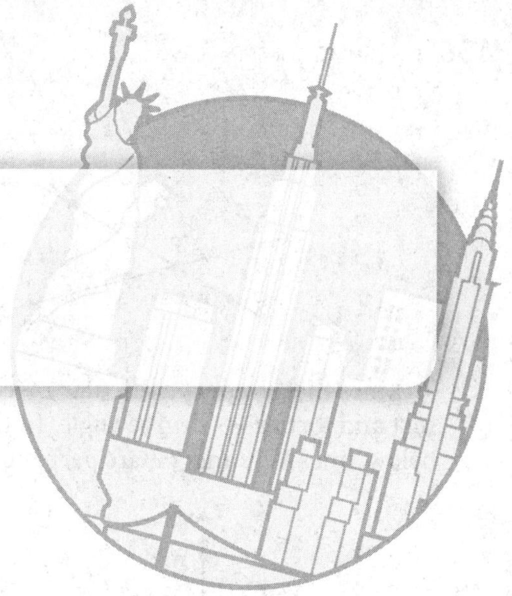

Some of the questions on the Math section of the SHSAT will assess how well you understand geometry. As you know, geometry questions deal with lines, angles, and shapes. There are a number of important vocabulary words and formulas you will need to know in order to answer these questions. Pay close attention to each of these. It is important that you not only memorize the formulas, but also be comfortable applying them to solve problems.

Lines and Angles

There are quite a few important terms to understand in geometry. While you will not have to define these words on the SHSAT, it will be important to recognize and understand each of them. Let's start by reviewing the types of lines and angles that are the building blocks of many geometric figures.

Lines, Segments, and Rays

Lines are one of the basic geometrical terms. By definition, a line continues forever in both directions. For this reason, the ends of lines have arrows on them.

A line that passes through two points is often named for those points. In the following example, the line passes through points C and D, so it can be named *line CD*. The symbol $\overleftrightarrow{CD}$ represents this line.

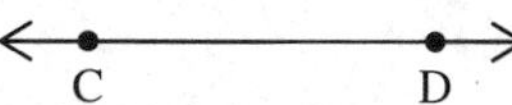

A **point** identifies an exact location on a line. The point has no length or width. It is simply a specific location. The line above contains points C and D.

As we just discussed, lines continue indefinitely in a specific location. **Line segments**, on the other hand, have two definite end points. The end of a line segment is identified by a point. Line segment FG, also known as $\overline{FG}$, is shown below. Notice that it begins at exactly point F and ends at exactly point G.

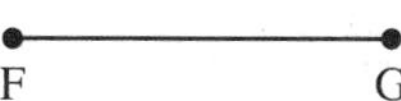

Like line segments, **rays** also have a specific beginning point; however, they continue forever in one direction. So one end of a ray is indicated by an endpoint, and the other is indicated by an arrow, pointing in the direction in which the ray continues. The ray below would be known as *ray HJ*, or $\overline{HJ}$.

Intersecting lines, segments, and rays share a common point. In other words, the lines cross one another. For example, in the following diagram, lines MN and PQ intersect, or cross, at point R.

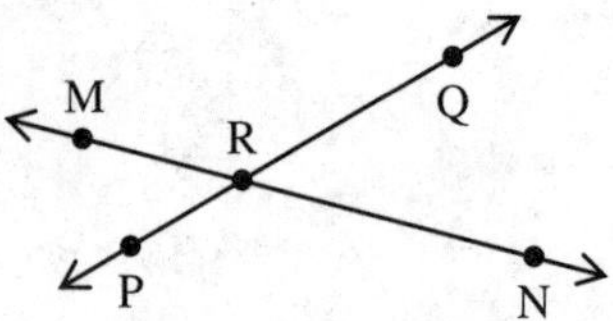

Lines that are **perpendicular** meet or intersect and form a 90-degree angle. In the diagram below, lines WX and YZ are perpendicular.

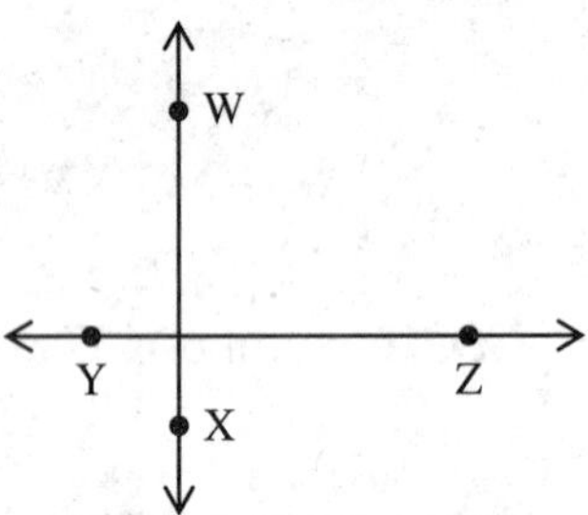

Lines, segments, or rays that are **parallel** never intersect, or cross each other. The lines can go on forever, and they will never touch. They remain the same distance apart at all points. Line segments ST and UV below are parallel. This is written as segment ST || segment UV, or ST || UV, and is read *segment ST is parallel to segment UV.*

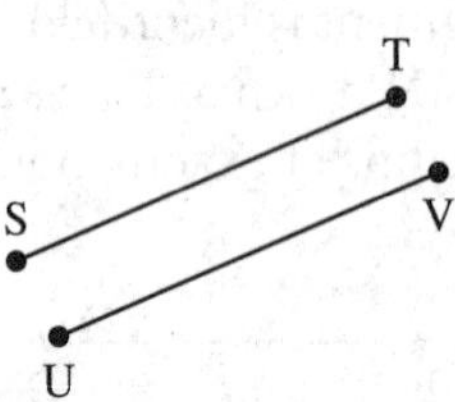

Having trouble remembering the difference between perpendicular and parallel lines? Take a look at the two l's in parallel. They look like parallel lines. Notice that they never cross each other, and they remain the same distance apart.

Types of Angles

Two rays that share an endpoint are called an **angle**. The rays are the sides of the angle. The endpoint where the rays meet is called the **vertex**. An angle can be named by a point on each of the rays and the vertex. In the example below, points E and G are located on the rays, and point F is the vertex. This angle would be called *angle EFG* or *angle GFE*. The name of the vertex is always in the middle. Angle EFG can be named by the symbol ∠EFG.

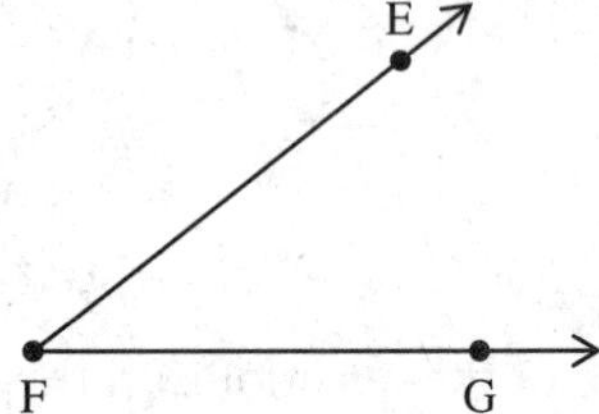

There are several types of angles, each named for the size of the space between the rays. If the rays are closer together, with a narrow space between them, the angle has a smaller measure. If the rays have a wide space between them, the angle has a larger measure. Two rays that are perpendicular to each other form a 90-degree angle, which looks like the letter L. A 90-degree angle is known as a **right angle**.

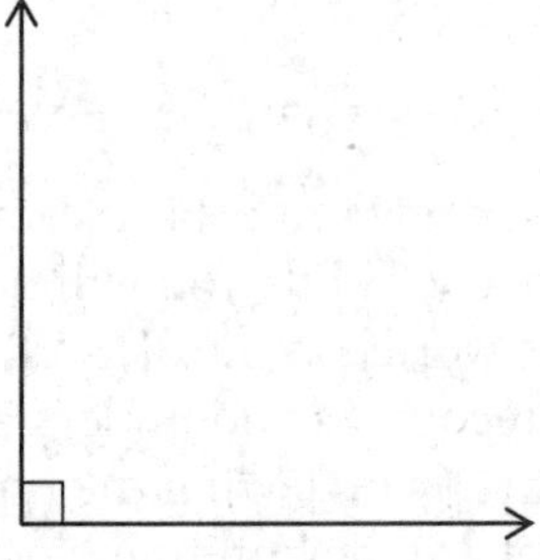

The small square symbol (□) in the corner of an angle indicates a right angle. Take a look at the symbol in the example of the right angle. When you see the little square, you know that the angle measures 90 degrees.

An angle that measures less than 90 degrees is known as an **acute** angle. Each of the following angles is an acute angle.

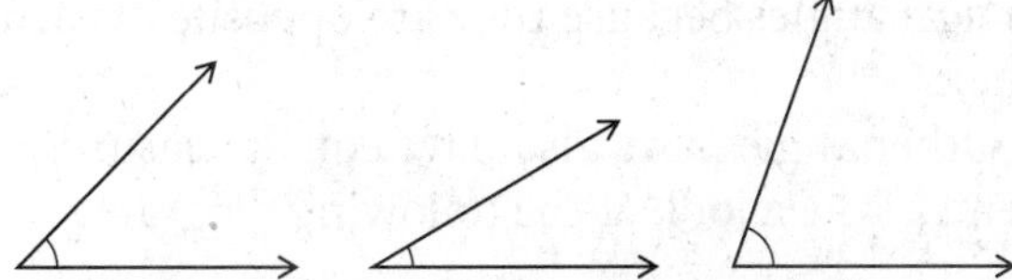

An angle that that measures greater than 90 degrees is known as an **obtuse** angle. Each of the following angles is an obtuse angle.

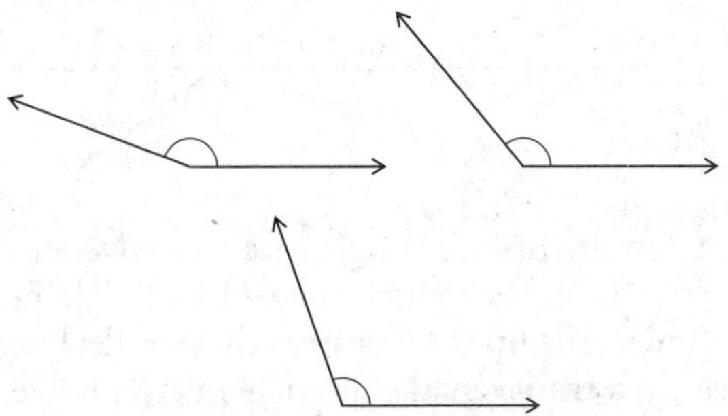

An angle that is completely **straight** measures 180 degrees.

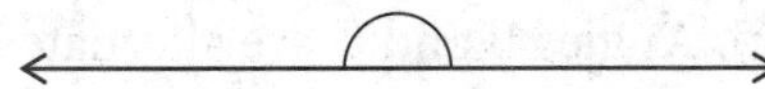

Sometimes, a ray divides an angle into two equal parts. A ray that does this is called an **angle bisector**. The angle on the left below measures 50 degrees. On the right, an angle bisector divides it into two 25-degree angles.

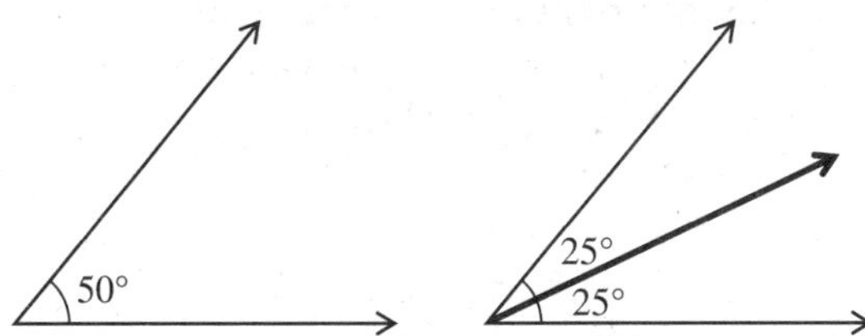

Relationships Between Angles

Understanding the relationship between types of angles can help in solving problems and determining the unknown measurement of an angle.

Two angles are said to be **complementary** if the sum of the angles equals 90 degrees. For example, an angle measuring 30 degrees and an angle measuring 60 degrees are complementary because their sum is 90 degrees: $30 + 60 = 90$.

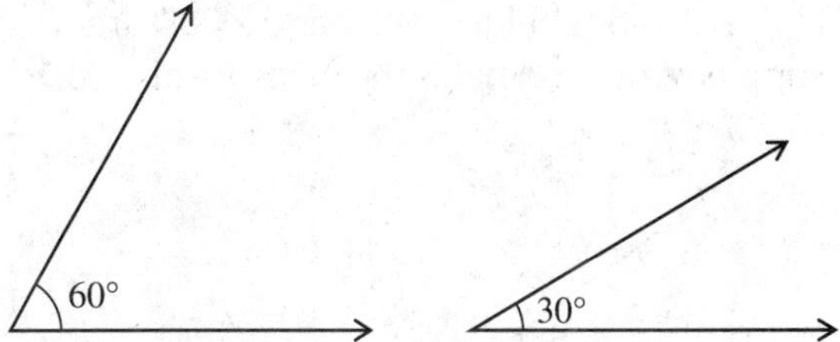

When put together, the complementary angles equal a right angle.

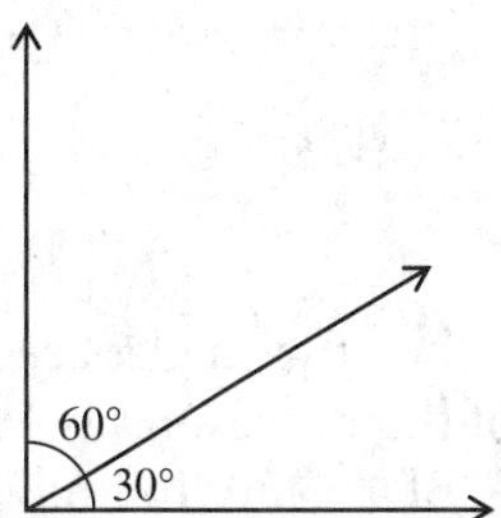

Two angles are said to be **supplementary** if the sum of the angles equals 180 degrees. For example, an angle measuring 70 degrees and an angle measuring 110 degrees are supplementary because their sum is 180 degrees: $70 + 110 = 180$.

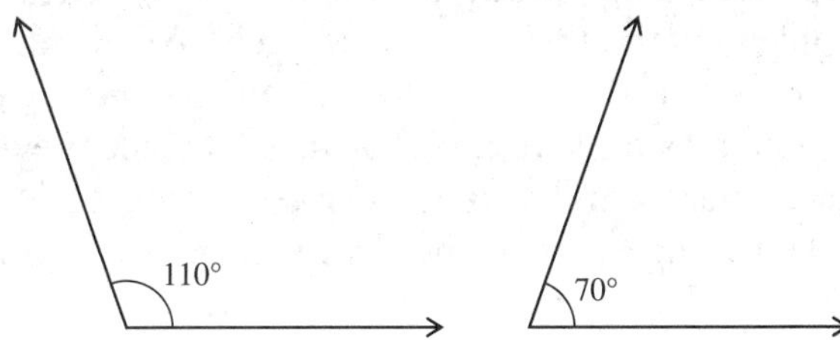

When put together, the supplementary angles form a 180-degree angle, or a straight line.

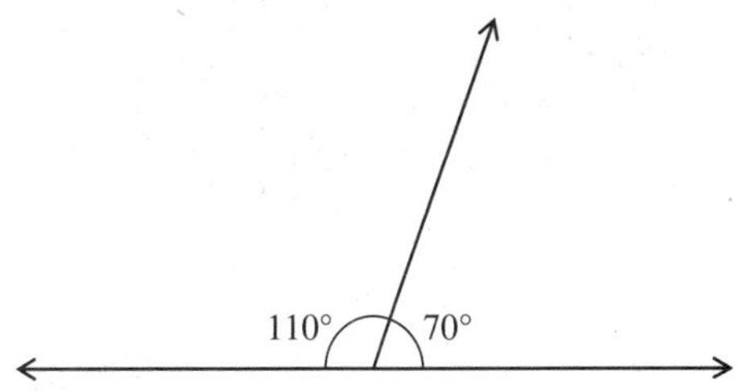

Let's use some of this information to answer a question.

In the diagram below, ∠ABC and ∠CBD are supplementary. What is the measure of ∠CBD?

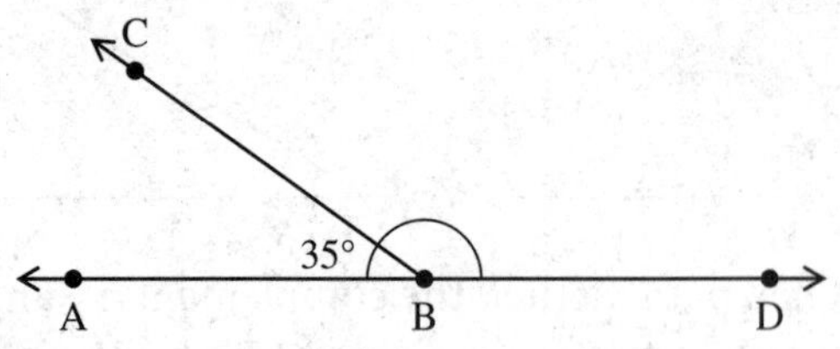

A. 55°
B. 90°
C. 145°
D. 155°

We know that when two angles are supplementary, the sum of their measures is 180 degrees. So $\angle ABC + \angle CBD = 180$. To find the missing measurement, we can subtract the measure of ∠ABC from 180.

$180 - 35 = 145$

The measure of ∠CBD is 145 degrees.

In the example above, not only are the angles supplementary, they are also adjacent. **Adjacent angles** share a vertex and a common side. Angles divided by a bisector are also adjacent since they share a vertex and a common side.

Many angles are formed by lines that meet or intersect. **Vertical angles** are opposite of each other when two lines intersect. The important thing to remember about vertical angles is that their measurements are equal. In the diagram below, ∠QRS and ∠TRV are vertical angles. So, $\angle QRS = \angle TRV$.

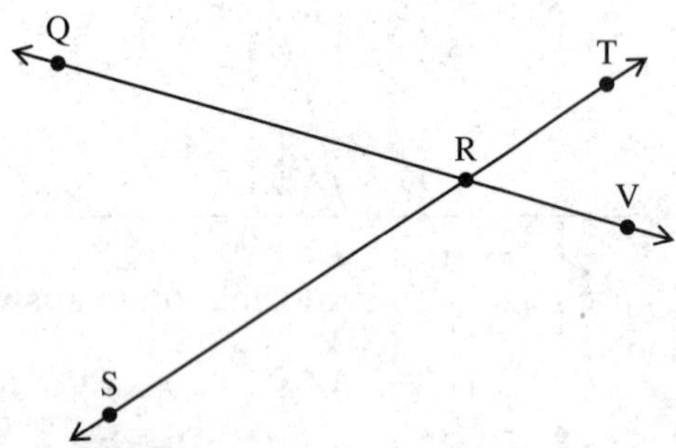

Suppose ∠QRS measures 48 degrees. That means ∠TRV also measures 48 degrees. Notice that in this example, ∠QRT and ∠SRV are also vertical angles because they are opposite of each other.

Other angle pairs also have equal measurements. Take a look at the following diagram.

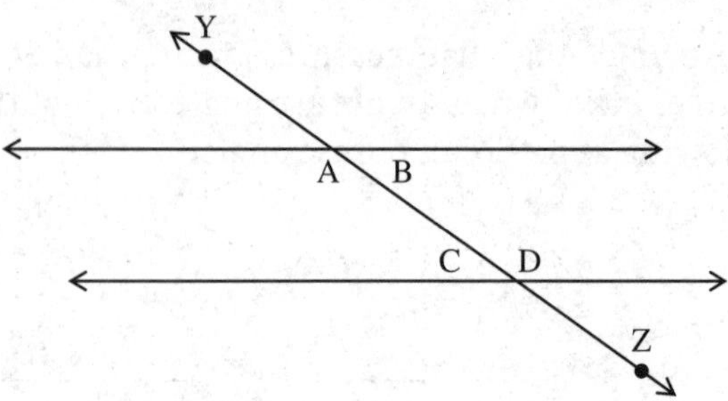

Alternate interior angles are created when two parallel lines are intersected by a third line, as shown. The line that crosses the parallel lines is called a **transversal**. Alternate interior angles are a pair of angles on opposite sides of the transversal, and they have the same measurement. They are located inside, or between, the set of parallel lines. In the diagram, line YZ is the transversal. Angles B and C are alternate interior angles. Since angle B has a measure of 35 degrees, angle C also has a measure of 35 degrees. (Angles A and D are also alternate interior angles.)

> Alternate interior angles are on alternate, or opposite, sides of the transversal. They are on the interior, or inside, of the parallel lines.

Like alternate interior angles, alternate exterior angles also have the same measurement. **Alternate exterior angles** are on opposite sides of the transversal, but they are on the outside of the parallel lines.

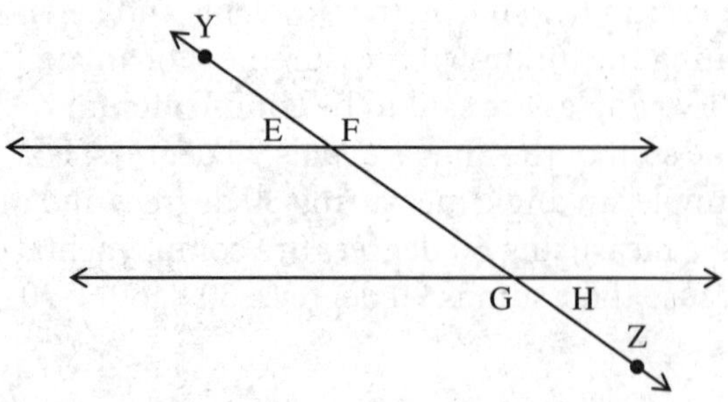

In the previous diagram, line YZ is the transversal. Angles E and H are on opposite sides of the transversal and are outside the set of parallel lines. So angles E and H are alternate exterior angles, and they have equal measurements. Likewise, angles F and G are alternate exterior angles.

Let's use what we've reviewed about angles to answer the following question.

> Line segment AB is a transversal intersecting a pair of parallel lines. Angle M has a measurement of 118 degrees.
>
> 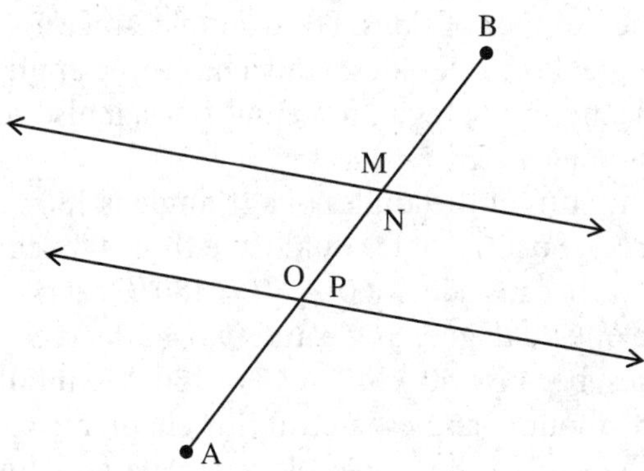
>
>
> What is the measure of angle P?
>
> **A.** 28°
> **B.** 62°
> **C.** 72°
> **D.** 118°

We know that angle M has a measurement of 118. Since angles M and N are vertical angles, they have the same measurement. So, ∠M and ∠N are both 118 degrees. Angle N and angle O are alternate interior angles, which means they also have the same measurement. Since we know that ∠N measures 118 degrees, ∠O also measures 118 degrees. Angle O and angle P are supplementary angles, so the sum of ∠O and ∠P equals 180 degrees. To find the measurement of ∠P, subtract 118 from 180.

$180 - 118 = 62$

So the measure of angle P is 62°.

As you know, variables represent unknown values. We worked with variables in the chapter of this book that reviews algebra skills. There will be questions on the SHSAT that require you to use skills from several areas of mathematics. For example, you will need to rely on your knowledge of both algebra and geometry to answer the following question.

> The four lines in the diagram intersect at a single point.
>
> 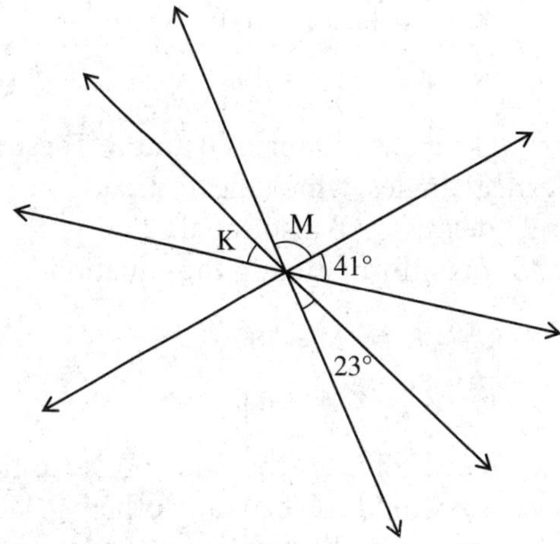
>
>
> What is the measure of ∠K in terms of M?
>
> **A.** 180 − M
> **B.** 157 − M
> **C.** 139 − M
> **D.** 116 − M

In order to discuss each of the angles in the diagram, let's label them. We'll label them A through F, although you could use any letters or numbers you choose. The purpose of labeling them is simply for our discussion of how to solve the problem.

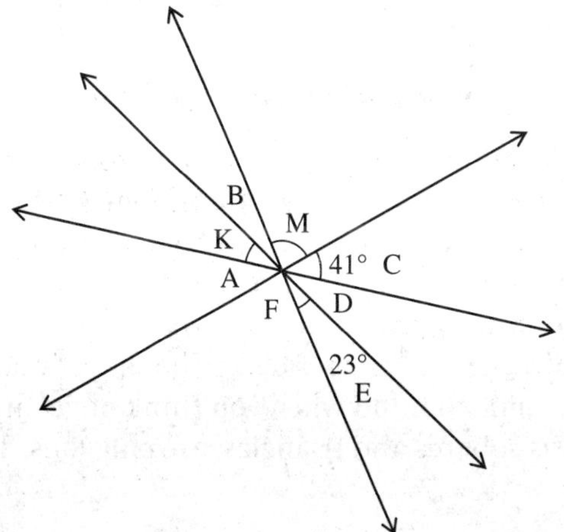

Angles A, K, B, and M are on the same straight line. That means, the sum of these angles is 180 degrees. In other words, $\angle A + \angle K + \angle B + \angle M = 180$.

Angle A and angle C are vertical angles, which means they have the same measurements. Since we know from the diagram that $\angle C$ equals 41 degrees, we know that $\angle A$ also equals 41 degrees. Let's substitute this value into the equation.

$$\angle A + \angle K + \angle B + \angle M = 180$$

$$41 + \angle K + \angle B + \angle M = 180$$

Next, take a look at angles B and E. These are also vertical angles, which means that since $\angle E$ equals 23 degress, $\angle B$ also equals 23 degrees. Let's add this information to the equation as well.

$$41 + \angle K + \angle B + \angle M = 180$$

$$41 + \angle K + 23 + \angle M = 180$$

Now we can solve for the value of $\angle K$ in the same way we would solve for any other variable. Begin by combining like terms and isolating $\angle K$ on one side of the equation.

$$41 + \angle K + 23 + \angle M = 180$$

$$41 + 23 + \angle K + \angle M = 180$$

$$64 + \angle K + \angle M = 180$$

$$64 - 64 + \angle K + \angle M = 180 - 64$$

$$\angle K + \angle M = 116$$

$$\angle K + \angle M - \angle M = 116 - \angle M$$

$$\angle K = 116 - \angle M$$

So in terms of M, $\angle K = 116 - M$.

Two-Dimensional Figures

When you think of geometry, you probably think of shapes, such as squares and triangles. Much of geometry does deal with polygons. A **polygon** is a two-dimensional figure made from three or more straight sides. In fact, the word *polygon* actually means "many sided." The shapes that often come to mind when you think of geometry, such as squares and triangles, are polygons. The list of polygons below tells how many sides each of the figures contains.

NUMBER OF SIDES	
Triangle	3
Quadrilateral	4
Pentagon	5
Hexagon	6
Heptagon	7
Octagon	8
Nonagon	9
Decagon	10

The number of angles in any polygon is equal to the number of sides. For example, since a triangle has three sides, it also has three angles. And since an octagon has eight sides, it also has eight angles.

The sum of the angles of a triangle is 180 degrees. So a triangle could have three 60 degree angles, because $60 + 60 + 60 = 180$. Or it could have one 90 degree angle and two 45 degree angles, because $90 + 45 + 45 = 180$. We'll talk more about triangles later in this chapter.

The sum of the angles of a quadrilateral, however, is 360 degrees. As you know, a square has four sides, so it is a quadrilateral. A square has four 90 degree angles, and $90 + 90 + 90 + 90 = 360$. The sum of the interior angles of any quadrilateral equals 360 degrees.

The sum of the interior angles of a pentagon is 540 degrees, and the sum of the interior angles of a hexagon is 720 degrees. But rather than trying to remember a list of polygons and the sums of their interior angles, all you have to memorize is the formula below.

$$(n - 2) \times 180°$$

In the formula, the variable n represents the number of sides of the polygon. So what the formula tell us is that the number of sides of a polygon, minus 2, multiplied by 180 equals the sum of the interior angle of the figure. Let's prove this using a triangle. Since we know a triangle has 3 sides, we'll substitute 3 for n.

$(n - 2) \times 180°$

$(3 - 2) \times 180°$

$(1) \times 180°$

$180°$

As we already reviewed, the sum of the interior angles of a triangle is 180 degrees. Let's try this formula again to find the sum of the angles of an octagon.

$(n - 2) \times 180°$

$(8 - 2) \times 180°$

$(6) \times 180°$

$1{,}080°$

The sum of the interior angles of an octagon is 1,080 degrees.

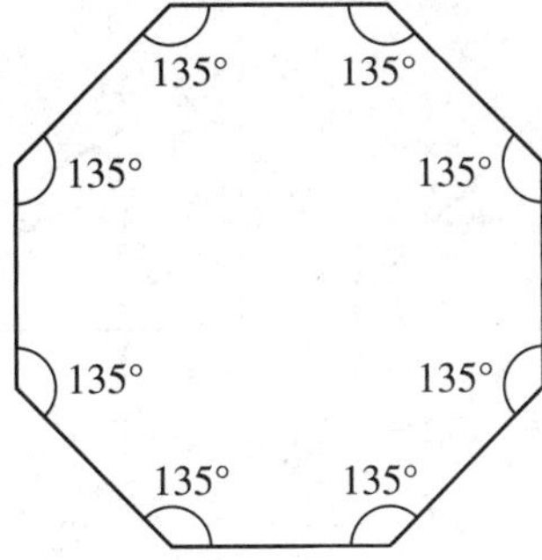

Now that we've reviewed the number of sides and the sum of the angles of polygons, let's go over the types of triangles and quadrilaterals.

Triangles

All triangles have three sides and three angles, but the lengths of the sides and the measures of the angles can vary. The sum of all of the angles is always 180 degrees, but the individual angles can be quite different. Triangles can be classified by the length of their sides or by their angle measurements.

A triangle that has three equal sides and three equal angles is called an **equilateral triangle**. Each of the angles of an equilateral triangle measures 60 degrees.

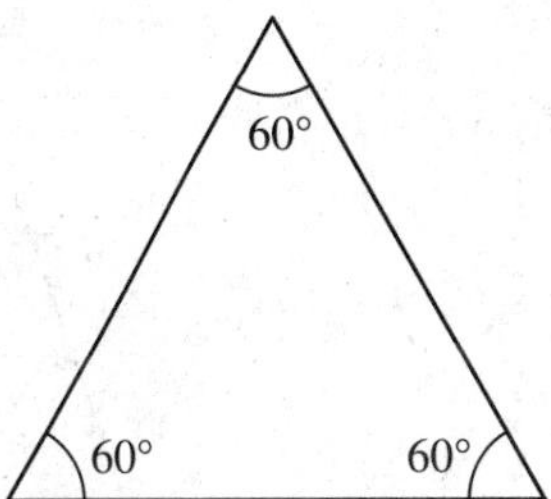

An **isosceles triangle** has two sides that are equal and two angles that are equal. Notice that in each of the isosceles triangles below, two angles have the exact same measure and two of the sides have the exact same length.

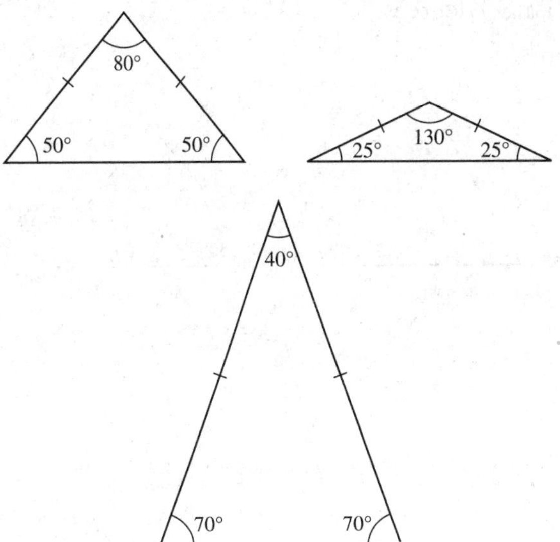

Notice the little lines marking two of the sides on each of the isosceles triangles. In geometry, these marks indicate that the lines are the same length. So, in an equilateral triangle, all three sides would be marked since all three sides are equal in length.

A triangle with no equal sides is called a **scalene triangle**. Since each of the sides of a scalene triangle has a different length, each of the three angles in a scalene triangle also has a different measure.

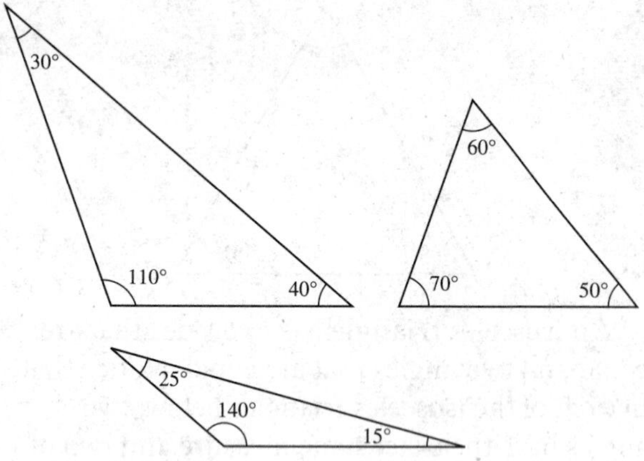

The angles of an **acute triangle** are all less than 90 degrees.

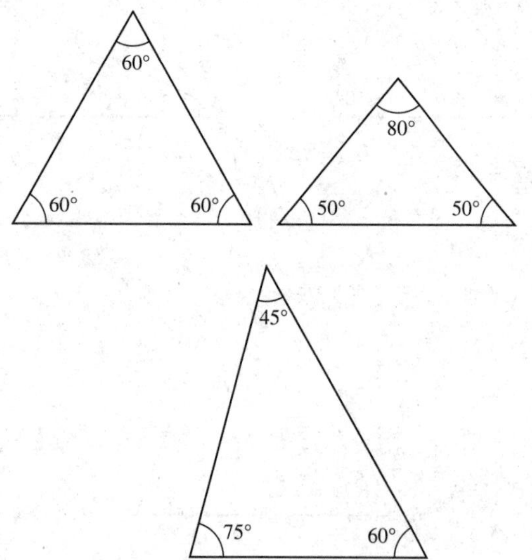

An **obtuse triangle** has one angle that measures greater than 90 degrees.

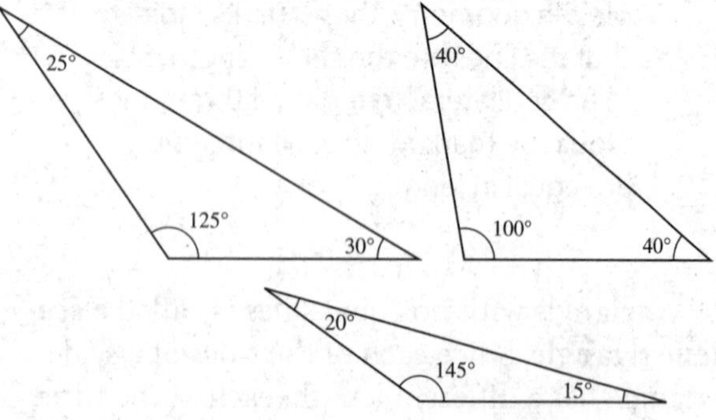

> Triangles can be classified in more than one way. For example, an equilateral triangle is also an acute triangle, since all of the angles are less than 90 degrees. A triangle that is classified as a scalene obtuse triangle has one angle that is greater than 90 degrees, and each of the sides is a different length.

A **right triangle** has one right angle, which measures 90 degrees. The other angles may or may not be equal to each other, and the other sides, or legs, of the triangle may or may not be equal to each other. Notice that each of the right triangles below is different from the others.

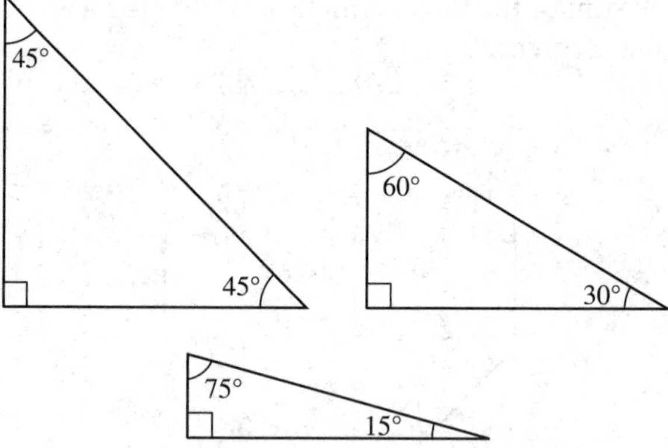

The side of the triangle that is across from the right angle has the greatest length and is called the **hypotenuse**. The other two sides of the triangle are called **legs**.

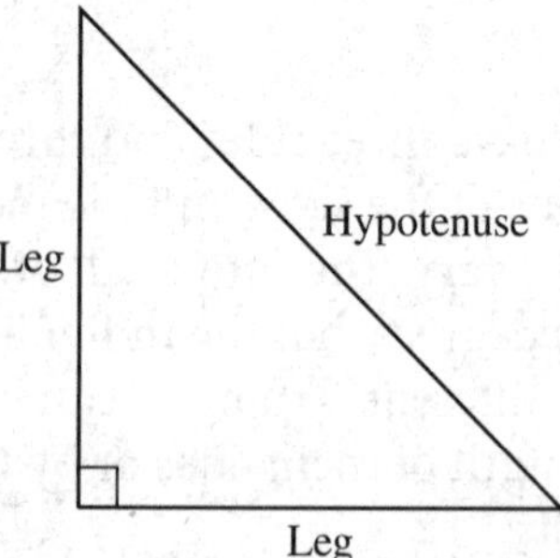

Let's use what you've learned about triangles to answer the following question.

In the diagram, line segment EF is perpendicular to line segment CD. The measure of ∠FED is 48 degrees.

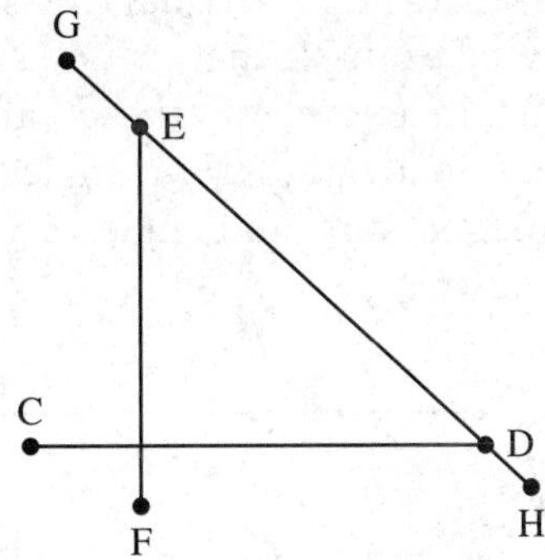

What is the measure of ∠CDE?

A. 32
B. 42
C. 90
D. 138

Perpendicular lines form a right angle, so the triangle formed by the three line segments is a right triangle. We know that the angle formed by lines EF and CD is a right angle, which measures 90 degrees, and that the measure of angle FED is 48 degrees. The sum of the interior angles must equal 180 degrees.

$$90 + 48 + \angle CDE = 180$$

$$138 + \angle CDE = 180$$

$$138 - 138 + \angle CDE = 180 - 138$$

$$\angle CDE = 42$$

Therefore angle CDE has a measurement of 42 degrees.

Pythagorean Theorem (Grade 9 Test Only)

If the lengths of two sides of a right triangle are known, the length of the third side may be found using the Pythagorean Theorem:

$$a^2 + b^2 = c^2$$

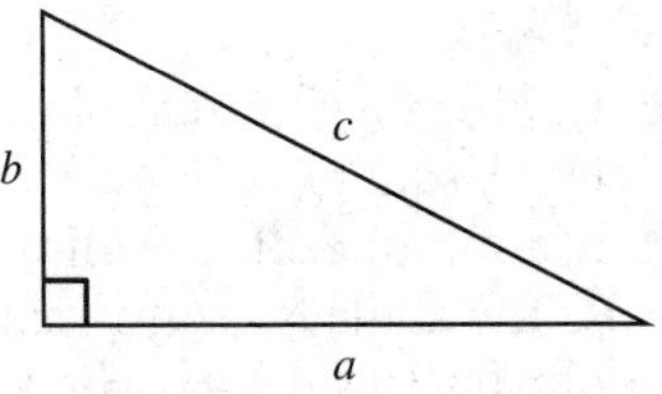

In this expression, "a" and "b" must be the legs of the right triangle and "c" must be the hypotenuse.

For example, if a = 4 cm and b = 3 cm, the hypotenuse (c) may be found as follows:

$$4^2 + 3^2 = c^2$$
$$16 + 9 = c^2$$
$$25 = c^2$$
$$5 = c$$

This type of triangle is called a "3-4-5" triangle and is very common. Triangles with similar ratios between their sides are also called "3-4-5" triangles. For example, 6-8-10 and 30-40-50 triangles have the same ratios.

Try this question: Find the length of the unknown side (b) in this triangle:

A. 8 cm
B. 9 cm
C. 10 cm
D. 12 cm

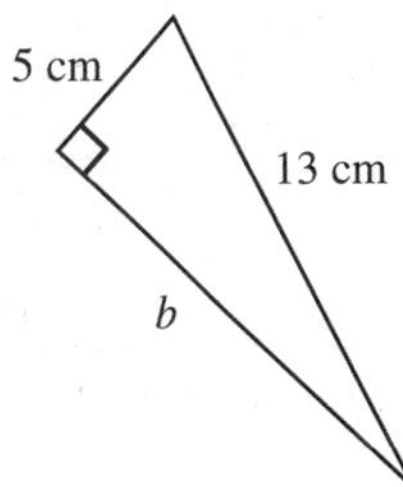

The correct answer is D.

$$5^2 + b^2 = 13^2$$
$$25 + b^2 = 169$$
$$b^2 = 169 - 25$$
$$b^2 = 144$$
$$b = 12 \text{ cm}$$

Quadrilaterals

Quadrilaterals are polygons that have four sides and four angles. A square, rectangle, rhombus, parallelogram, and trapezoid are all types of quadrilaterals. The angle measures, side length, and number of parallel sides vary between each of these figures; however, the sum of the interior angles of all quadrilaterals equals 360 degrees.

A **rectangle** is probably one of the first figures you ever learned about. As you know, rectangles have four right angles and two pairs of equal, parallel sides.

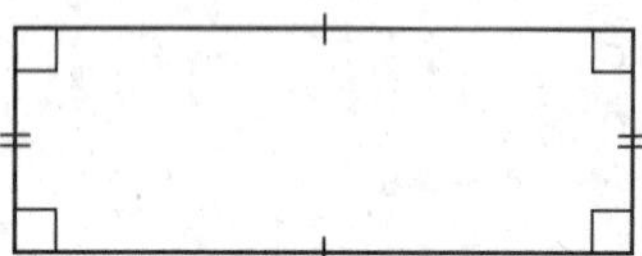

A **square** also has four right angles and is actually a type of rectangle. But the sides of a square are all the same length.

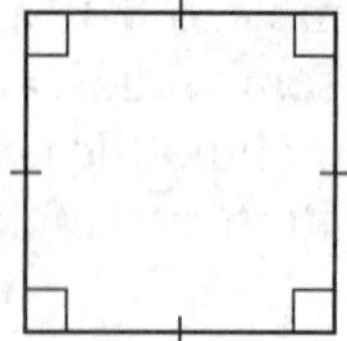

Like a square, a **rhombus** also has four sides of equal length, and the opposite sides are parallel. The corners of a rhombus can be angles of any size; however, opposite angles are equal. In the following example, corners A and C have equal measures, and corners B and D have equal measures.

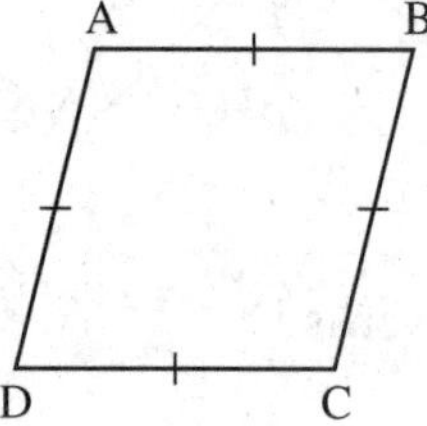

Not only does a square match the definition of a rectangle, it also matches the definition of a rhombus: it has four sides of equal length, opposite sides are parallel, and opposite angles are equal.

Squares, rectangles, and rhombuses are all examples of another type of quadrilateral, the **parallelogram**. The opposite sides of a parallelogram are parallel and have equal lengths. Notice in the following example that the top and bottom sides are equal in length, and the left and right sides are equal in length. Again, angles A and C have the same measure, and angles B and D have the same measure.

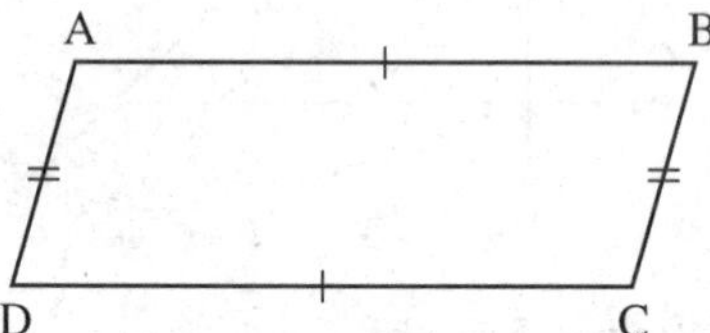

A **trapezoid** is a quadrilateral that has one pair of parallel sides. Notice that the sides do not have to be equal in length.

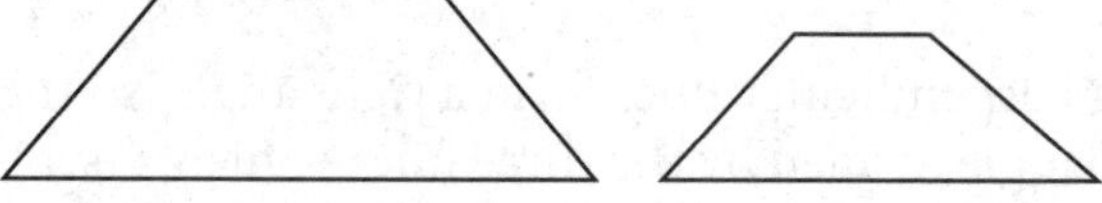

Congruence and Similarity (Grade 9 Test Only)

Figures that have exactly the same shape and size are **congruent**. The lengths of the sides of congruent figures are equal, and the angle measures of congruent figures are equal.

The figures can be positioned differently and still be congruent, as long as the lengths and angle measures are the same.

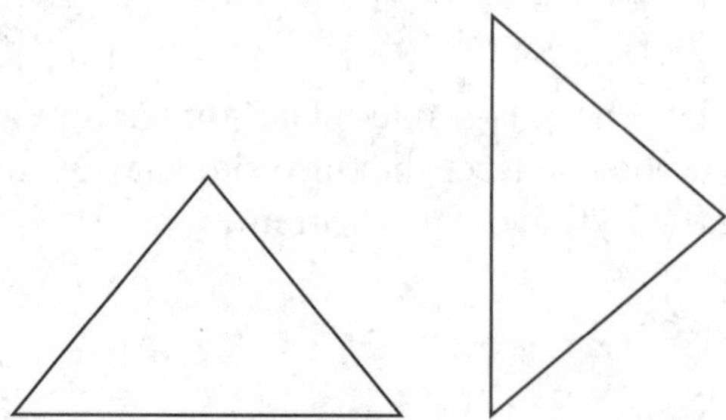

Sometimes a pair of figures will have exactly the same shape, but be different sizes. These figures are said to be **similar**. Take a look at the similar triangles. Both are right isosceles triangles. Both have the exact same angle measures. However, one is larger than the other. They are not congruent since the lengths of the sides are not equal; however, they are similar to one another.

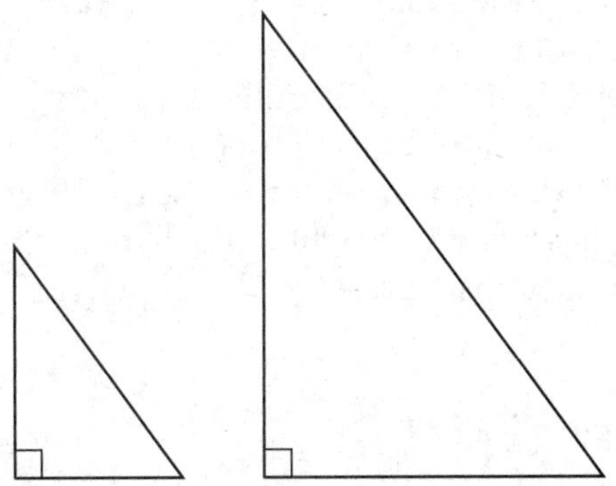

Understanding similarity and congruence can help you solve problems regarding the measurements of geometric figures. Let's take another look at the similar right triangles above. Suppose we know the measurements of the larger triangle, but do not know the length of the hypotenuse of the smaller triangle.

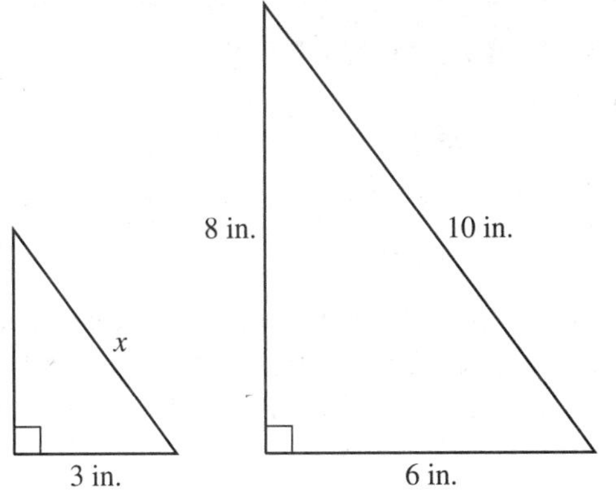

Because the triangles are similar, we can use a ratio of the corresponding sides to find the length of the hypotenuse of the smaller triangle. We know that the ratio of the shorter leg to the hypotenuse of the large triangle is 6:10, or $\frac{6}{10}$. We know that the ratio of the shorter leg to the hypotenuse of the smaller triangle is 3:x, or $\frac{3}{x}$. We can use the ratios to set up a proportion and solve for x to find the length of the hypotenuse.

$$\frac{6}{10}=\frac{3}{x}$$

Now cross multiply and solve for the variable.

$$\frac{6}{10}=\frac{3}{x}$$

$$6(x)=10(3)$$

$$6x=30$$

$$\frac{6x}{6}=\frac{30}{6}$$

$$x=5$$

So, the hypotenuse of the smaller triangle is 5 inches.

Perimeter and Area

Measurement of figures is an important part of geometry. We've already discussed angle measurements. Now let's review what you need to know about perimeter and area of two-dimensional figures.

Perimeter is the distance around a figure. To find the perimeter, simply add the lengths of each of the sides. Take a look at the square below.

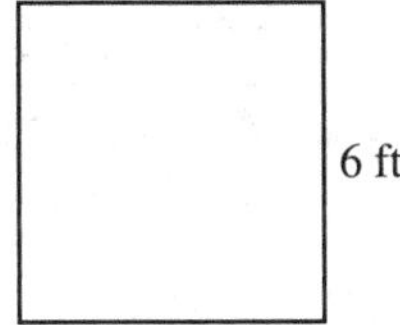

The length of each of the sides of the square shown is 6 feet. So the distance around the entire figure would be 24 feet, because $6+6+6+6=24$.

Since a square and a rhombus have four equal sides, we can simply multiply the length of one of the sides by 4 to find the perimeter. For other polygons, add to find the sum of the side lengths to determine the perimeter of the figure.

What is the perimeter of the hexagon?

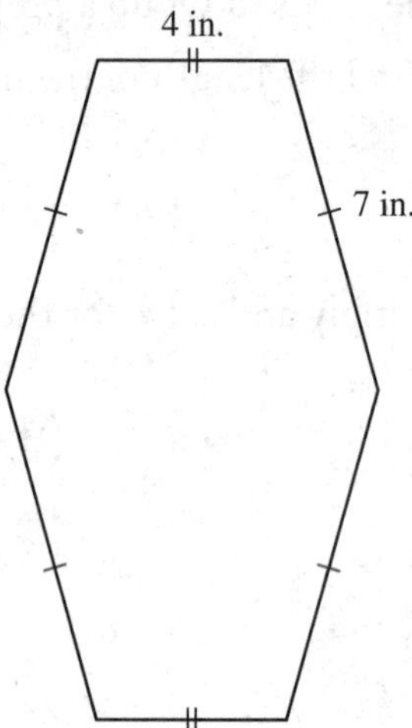

To find the perimeter of the figure, find the sum of the lengths of the sides. The symbols for equal side lengths indicate that four of the sides have a length of 7 inches each, and two of the sides have a length of four inches each. Add the side lengths to find the perimeter.

$$7 + 7 + 7 + 7 + 4 + 4 = 36$$

So the perimeter of the figure is 36 inches.

While perimeter measures the distance around shapes, **area** measures the space within two-dimensional figures. For example, the rectangle below contains 12 square units. So we would say that the area of the rectangle is 12 square units.

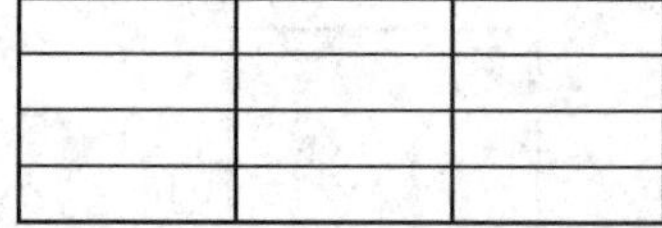

Examples of common square units often used to measure area include square inches, square feet, square yards, or square miles. If you were measuring the area of your bedroom, you would likely measure in square feet. If you were telling someone about the size of New York City, you would report the area in square miles.

To find the area of a rectangle or a square, we can simply multiply the length times the width of the figure.

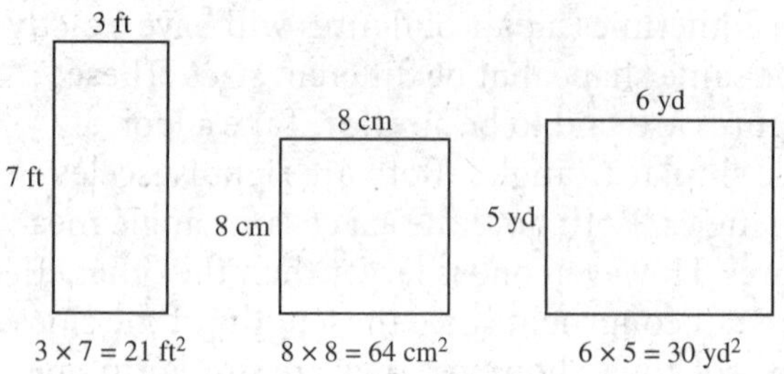

The area of the first rectangle is 21 square feet. The area of the square is 64 square centimeters. The area of the final rectangle is 30 square yards.

There are different formulas for finding the areas of each type of two-dimensional figure. In the formulas for area, you will use the length, width, base, and/or height of the figures. Each measurement is represented by the letter shown.

Area	A
Length	l
Width	w
Base	b
Height	h

The formulas for area are listed below. On the SHSAT, you will need to know the formulas and be able to apply them to solve problems. Make sure you memorize the following list and are comfortable using each formula.

FORMULAS FOR AREA

Rectangle and square	$A = l \times w$
Parallelogram	$A = b \times h$
Trapezoid	$A = \frac{1}{2} h(b_1 + b_2)$
Triangle	$A = \frac{1}{2} b \times h$

Now let's practice applying these formulas to find the areas of various figures. To find the area of a parallelogram, we must multiply the base by the height. The **base** is the line on the bottom of the figure. The **height** measures how tall the figure is.

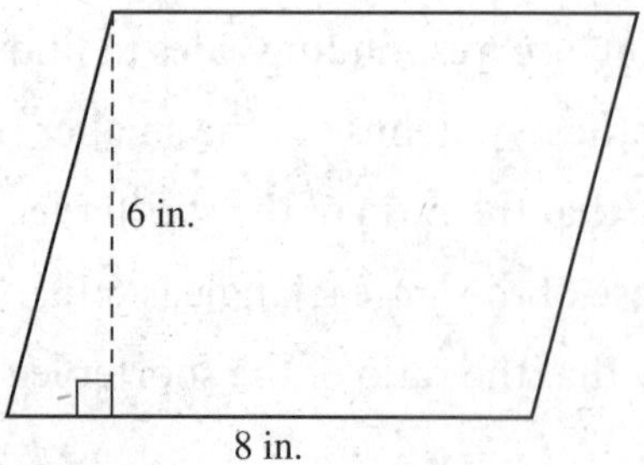

Notice that the height is different from the length of the sides. The dotted line indicating the height is called an **altitude** and is perpendicular to the base. According to the diagram, the base of the parallelogram is 8 inches, and the height is 6 inches. Multiply these lengths to find the area: $8 \times 6 = 48$. So the area of the parallelogram is 48 square inches.

> The area of a figure is always stated in square units. The words *square feet* or *square meters* may be used, for example, or the abbreviation for the unit of measure may be included, with an exponent of 2, such as ft² or m².

The formula for the area of a trapezoid included the measures of two bases.

$$A = \frac{1}{2}h(b_1 + b_2)$$

As you know, a trapezoid has two parallel lines. These are both considered to be bases, and the symbols b_1 and b_2 refer to base 1 and base 2. It does not matter which measurement you use for base 1 and which you use for base 2. The important thing is that we will be using the sum of the lengths of the two bases to find the area. So let's try it. Use the formula for the area of a trapezoid to determine the area of the figure shown.

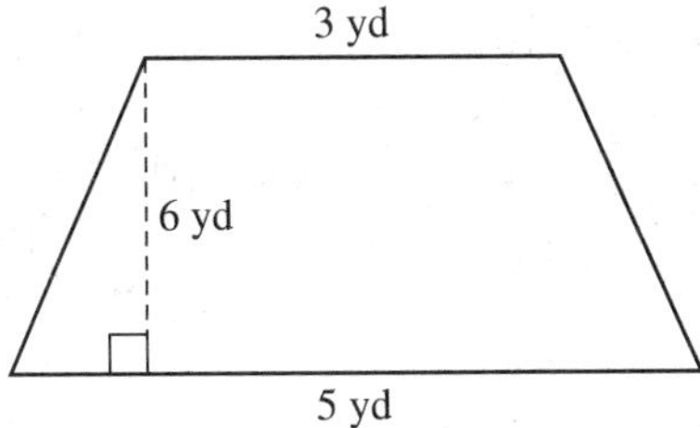

The altitude line is labeled 6 yards, so we know this is the height of the trapezoid. One base is labeled 3 yards, and the other is labeled 5 yards, so we will put these measurements into the formula.

$$A = \frac{1}{2}h(b_1 + b_2)$$

$$A = \frac{1}{2}6(3 + 5)$$

$$A = \frac{1}{2}6(8)$$

$$A = \frac{1}{2}(48)$$

$$A = 24$$

So the area of the trapezoid is 24 square yards.

In the examples of parallelograms and trapezoids we have worked with so far, the height has been indicated by a line that is not one of the sides of the figure. Sometimes, when finding the area of a triangle, the height is the same as one of the legs. Take a look at the following right triangle.

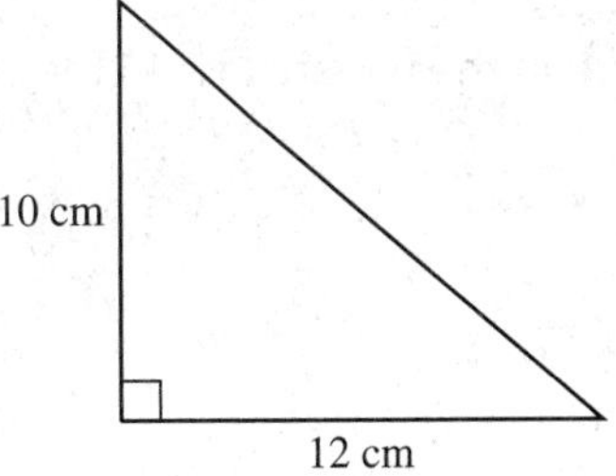

Notice that one leg of the triangle indicates the height. An altitude line is not needed. We can use the given measurements to find that the area of the right triangle is 60 cm^2.

$$A = \frac{1}{2}b \times h$$

$$A = \frac{1}{2}(12 \times 10)$$

$$A = \frac{1}{2}(120)$$

$$A = 60$$

There will be times when the altitude of a triangle is drawn within the figure, as shown in the following example on the left. There will be other times when the altitude is beside the triangle, as shown in the example on the right. Regardless of where the altitude is drawn, it still represents the height of the figure and is used in the formula to find the area.

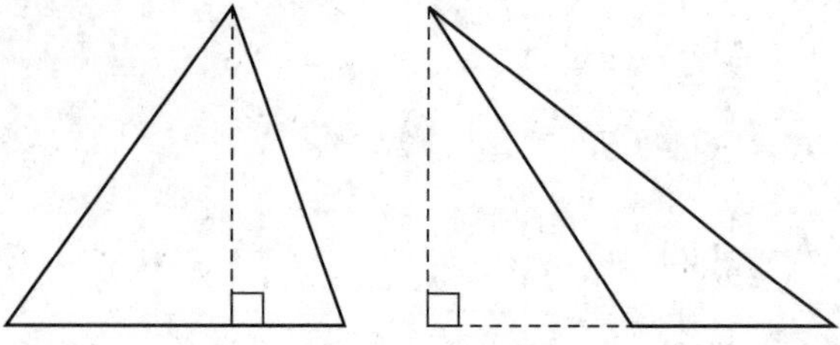

Let's practice using what you have learned.

A rectangle has the same area as the triangle below.

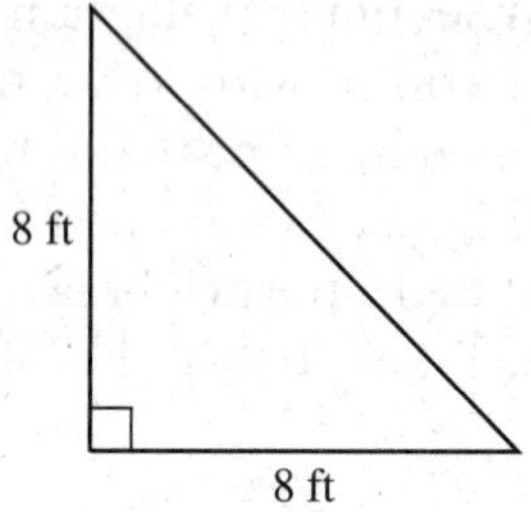

The length of the rectangle is 16 feet. What is the width?

A. 2 feet
B. 4 feet
C. 18 feet
D. 32 feet

We know that the area of the rectangle is the same as that of the triangle. Let's start by finding the area of the triangle.

$A = \frac{1}{2}b \times h$

$A = \frac{1}{2}(8 \times 8)$

$A = \frac{1}{2}(64)$

$A = 32$

The area of both figures is 32 square feet. We also know that the length of the rectangle is 16 feet. Since the area of a rectangle is equal to the product of the length times the width, we can use this formula to help us find the width.

$A = lw$

$32 = 16w$

$\frac{32}{16} = \frac{16w}{16}$

$2 = w$

So the width of the rectangle is 2 feet.

Circles

So far, the two-dimensional figures we have discussed in this chapter have all been polygons. Circles are also two-dimensional figures, but since they do not have any straight sides, they are not polygons. As you know, a **circle** is a geometric figure that is a curve on which every point is an equal distance from the center. A **radius** is the distance from the center of a circle to any point on its edge. The **diameter** of a circle is the distance across the center of a circle, from one edge to the other. The length of the diameter is twice that of the radius.

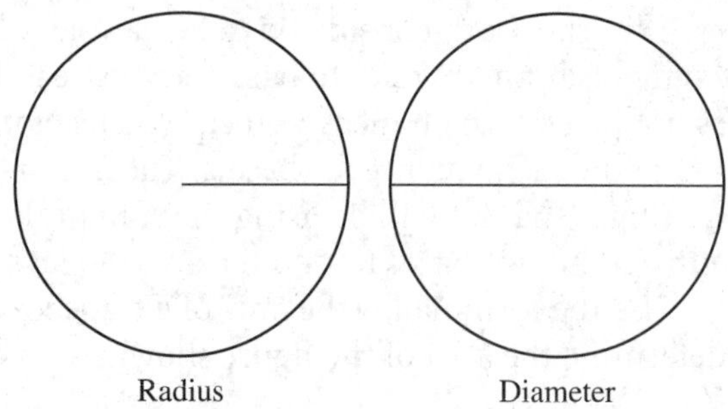

The formulas to find the measurements of circles include **pi**, which is represented by the symbol π. Pi is actually an example of an irrational number, as discussed earlier in this book, because it is a nonterminating decimal. Since the decimal never ends and never repeats, we use the approximation 3.14 for pi. We use the approximation 3.14 for pi, but the actually number goes on forever, something like 3.141592653589793238 462643383279502884197169399375105820974944 592307816406286208998628034825342117067982 148086 . . . you get the idea.

$\pi = 3.14$

As you know, perimeter is the distance around a polygon. **Circumference** is the distance around a circle. The following formula is used to find circumference, where *C* represents circumference and *r* represents radius.

$C = 2\pi r$

Since the diameter is equal to twice the radius, you can also use the formula $C = \pi d$, where *d* represents diameter, to find the circumference of a circle.

The circle below has a radius of 7 inches. Let's find the circumference.

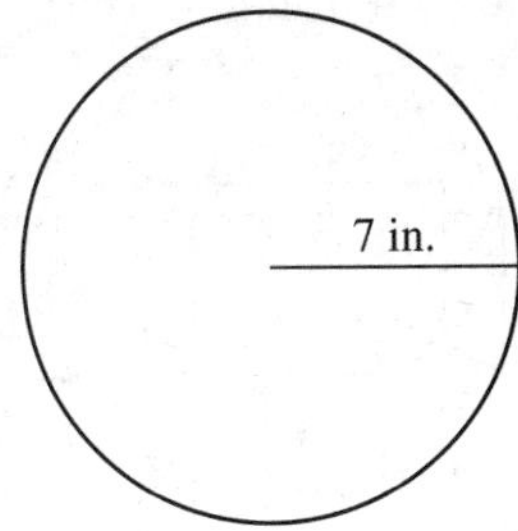

Substitute the measurement of the radius into the formula. Remember to use the decimal 3.14 for pi, then find the distance around the figure.

$C = 2\pi r$

$C = 2\pi(7)$

$C = 2(3.14)(7)$

$C = 43.96$

So the circumference of the circle is 43.96 inches.

To find the area of a circle, we will also use pi and the measurement of the radius. The formula is shown below.

$A = \pi r^2$

Let's find the area of the same circle. Remember, the radius is 7 inches.

$A = \pi r^2$

$A = \pi(7)^2$

$A = (3.14)(7)^2$

$A = (3.14)(49)$

$A = 153.86$

So the area of the circle is 153.86 in^2.

Some of the math questions on the SHSAT may ask you to simply find the perimeter, area, or circumference of a figure. Others will require you to apply several geometric skills in order to solve a problem. For example, in order to answer the following question, you will need to use what you know about circles and the area of right triangles in order to determine the area of the circle. Use what you have reviewed in this chapter to answer the question.

In the diagram shown, the area of triangle PQR is 48 cm^2, and line segment QR is a diameter of the circle.

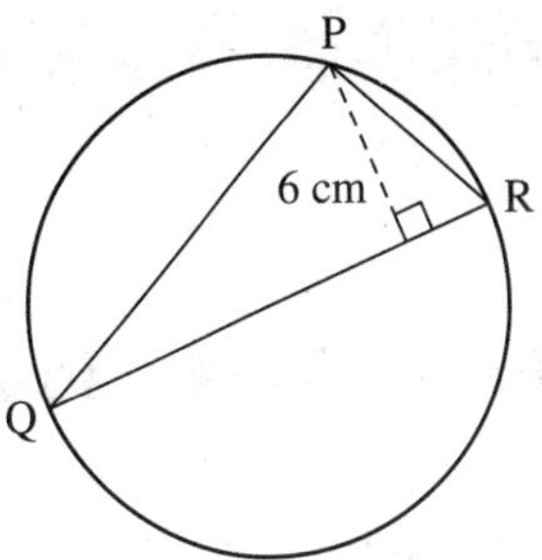

What is the area of the circle?

A. 50.24 cm^2
B. 100.48 cm^2
C. 200.96 cm^2
D. 256.0 cm^2

To find the area of the circle, we need to know the length of the radius. Since line segment QR is a diameter, we can use this measurement to find the radius. But first we must determine the length of the diameter. We know that the area of the triangle is 48 square centimeters, and that the height is 6 centimeters. We can use this to determine the length of line segment QR, the base of the triangle.

$$A = \frac{1}{2}bh$$

$$48 = \frac{1}{2}b(6)$$

$$48 = \frac{1}{2}(6)(b)$$

$$48 = 3b$$

$$\frac{48}{3} = \frac{3b}{3}$$

$$16 = b$$

So the length of line segment QR, the diameter of the circle, is 16 centimeters. Since the radius is half the length of the diameter, the radius of the circle is 8 centimeters. Now we have the information needed to find the area of the circle.

$$A = \pi r^2$$
$$A = (3.14)(8)^2$$
$$A = (3.14)(64)$$
$$A = 200.96$$

So the area of the circle is 200.96 square centimeters.

Three-Dimensional Figures

So far in this chapter, all of the geometric figures we have discussed have been two-dimensional, or flat. Now let's talk about **three-dimensional figures**, which are known as such because they have three dimensions: length, width, and height. When discussing these figures, it is important to understand a few vocabulary words.

- **Face.** The flat side of a three-dimensional figure.
- **Vertex.** The corner points of a three-dimensional figure.
- **Edge.** Where two faces meet.
- **Volume.** The capacity of a three-dimensional figure; how much the shape can hold.
- **Surface area.** The total area of the surface of a three-dimensional figure.

Now let's review a few common geometric solids. A **cube** is a three-dimensional figure that has six faces. Each side is an identical square. The length, width, and height of a cube are all equal.

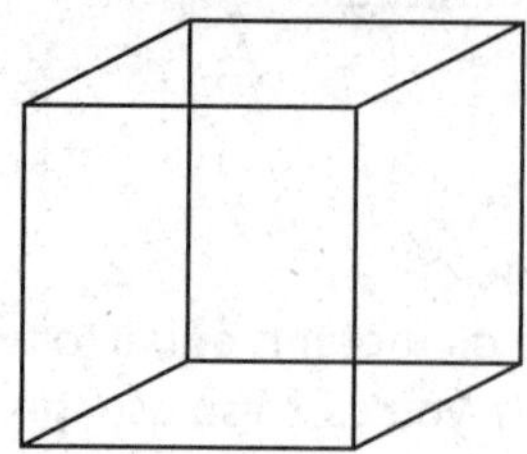

A **rectangular prism**, often called a **rectangular solid**, also has six faces, each of which is a rectangle. The length, width, and height of a cube are all equal, however, the length, width, and height of a rectangular solid may be different. Also, notice in the examples below that the opposite faces are identical.

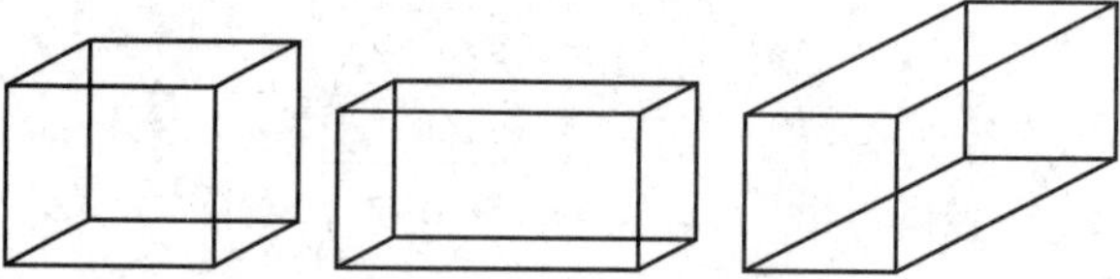

Prisms, such as the rectangular prisms above, have two congruent parallel bases that are polygons. The number of faces of a prism depends on the shape of the bases. Each will have two bases, then a number of faces equal to the number of sides of the base. For example, since a rectangle has four sides, a rectangular prism has 4 side faces, plus the two bases, for a total of 6 faces. A triangular prism has 3 side faces, plus the two bases, for a total of 5 faces. A pyramid with hexagons as bases would have 6 side faces, plus two bases, for a total of 8 faces. Take a look at the following examples.

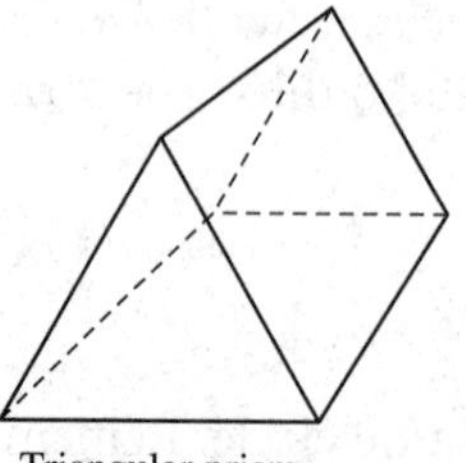

Triangular prism

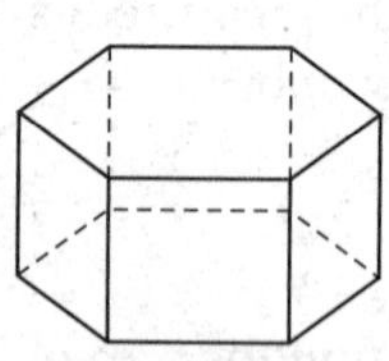

Hexagonal prism

A **cylinder** has two parallel bases that are congruent circles. The bases are joined by a curved surface.

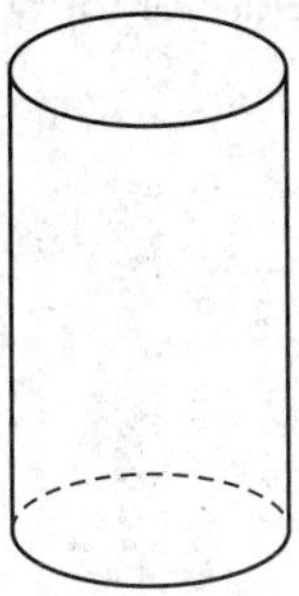

A **cone** has one circular base and a curved surface that connects the base to the vertex.

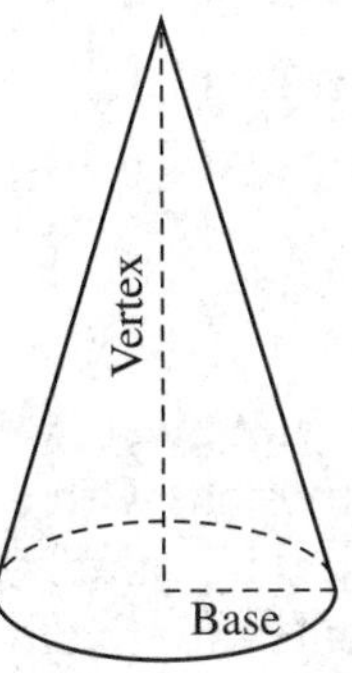

Pyramids have triangle shaped faces that connect the base and the vertex. The base of a pyramid may be any kind of polygon. The number of sides of a pyramid depends on the shape of the base. For example, a **square pyramid** has a square base. Since a square has 4 sides, a square pyramid has four triangular faces plus the square base, for a total of 5 faces. **A triangular pyramid** has a triangle shaped base. Since a triangle has 3 sides, a triangular pyramid has 3 triangle shaped faces plus the triangular base, for a total of 4 faces.

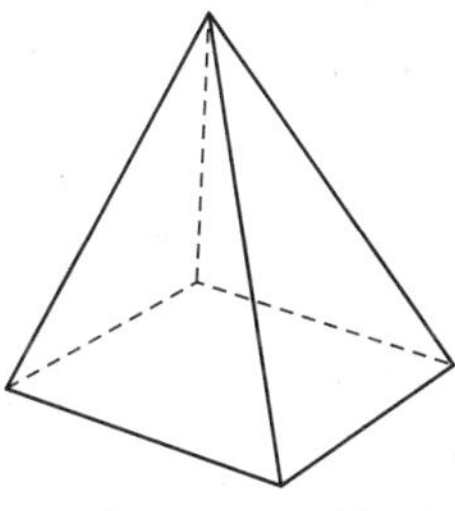

Square pyramid

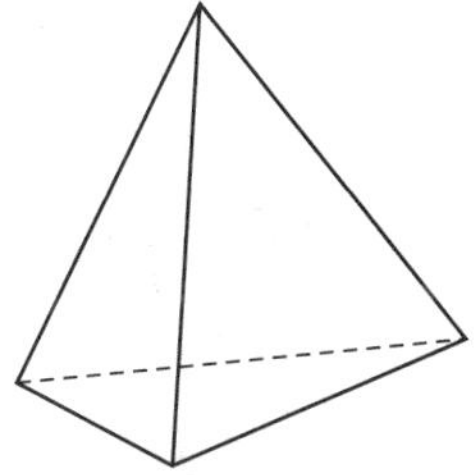

Triangular pyramid

> Many polygons could serve as the base of a pyramid. Just remember that the number of sides the pyramid has depends on how many sides the polygon base has.

Each three-dimensional shape has a different formula for determining its surface area and volume. Make sure you know each of these formulas before taking the SHSAT, and be comfortable using each. Let's take a look at the formulas for determining these measurements. In these, *s* represents the length of one side of a cube, *V* represents volume, and *l*, *w*, and *h* represent length, width, and height. *SA* represents surface area.

FORMULAS FOR VOLUME

Cube	$V = s^3$
Rectangular solid	$V = lwh$
Prism	$V = \text{area of base} \times \text{height}$

FORMULAS FOR VOLUME (GRADE 9 TEST ONLY)

Cylinder	$V = \pi r^2 h$*
Cone	$V = \frac{1}{3}\pi r^2 h$**
Pyramid	$V = \frac{1}{3} \times \text{area of base} \times \text{height}$

*Notice that this is the same as area of the base × height.

**This is the same as $\frac{1}{3}$ × area of the base × height.

FORMULAS FOR SURFACE AREA

Cube	$SA = 6s^2$
Rectangular solid	$SA = 2(lw + wh + lh)$
Cylinder	$SA = 2\pi r^2 + 2\pi rh$

> Surface area is the sum of the areas of each of the faces. Remember, s^2 tells the area of a square. Since a cube is made up of six identical squares, $6s^2$ tells the area of all six of the squares, which is the surface area.

Let's try applying some of these formulas.

The height of the cone is four times the measure of the radius of the base. The diameter of the base is 6 inches. What is the volume of the cone?

To find the volume of the cone, we need to know the radius and the height. Neither of these is given in the problem; however, we have the information we need to determine both measurements. The height is four times the measure of the radius. We don't know the radius, but we do know that it equals half the diameter. So, if the diameter is 6 inches, the radius is 3 inches. And if the height is four times the radius, the height is equal to 4×3.

Diameter = 6 in.
Radius = 3 in.
Height = 4 × radius = 4 × 3 = 12

Now we can insert the length of the radius and the height into the formula for determining the volume of a cone.

$$V = \frac{1}{3}\pi r^2 h$$

$$V = \frac{1}{3}\pi(3)^2\,(12)$$

$$V = \frac{1}{3}\pi(9)\,(12)$$

$$V = \frac{1}{3}(3.14)\,(9)\,(12)$$

$$V = \frac{1}{3}(339.12)$$

$$V = 113.04$$

Now you try it! Use the formulas reviewed in this section to answer the following question.

A rectangular solid with a surface area of 712 cubic centimeters has a length of 8 centimeters and a width of 12 cm. What is the sum of the width and the height of the solid?

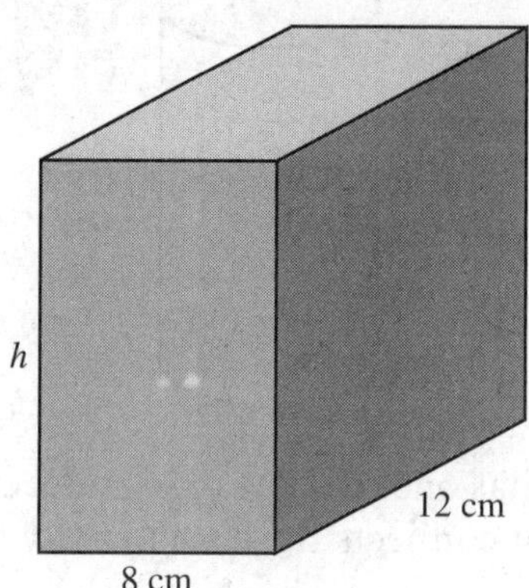

A. 12 cm
B. 13 cm
C. 20 cm
D. 25 cm

Since the height is not given, we will need to represent this measurement with a variable and use algebra skills to find its value. Let's substitute the given measurements into the formula for surface area of a rectangular solid and substitute the variable *h* for the unknown height.

$$SA = 2(lw + wh + lh)$$

$$712 = 2[(8 \times 12) + 12h + 8h]$$

$$712 = 2(96 + 12h + 8h)$$

Next, combine like terms.

$$712 = 2(96 + 12h + 8h)$$

$$712 = 2(96 + 20h)$$

Now multiply the terms inside parentheses by 2, and solve for the variable.

$$712 = 2(96 + 20h)$$

$$712 = 192 + 40h$$

$$712 - 192 = 192 - 192 + 40h$$

$$520 = 40h$$

$$\frac{520}{40} = \frac{40h}{40}$$

$$13 = h$$

So, the height of the figure is 13 cm. But the question did not ask for the height; it asked for the sum of the width and the height. Since the width is 12 cm and the height is 13 cm, the sum of these measurements is 25 cm, making answer choice D correct.

Coordinate Planes

A coordinate plane is created by a horizontal number line and a vertical number line. The point on the plane where the two lines intersect is called the **origin** and is point 0 on both number lines. The horizontal number line is called the ***x*-axis**; the vertical number line is the ***y*-axis**.

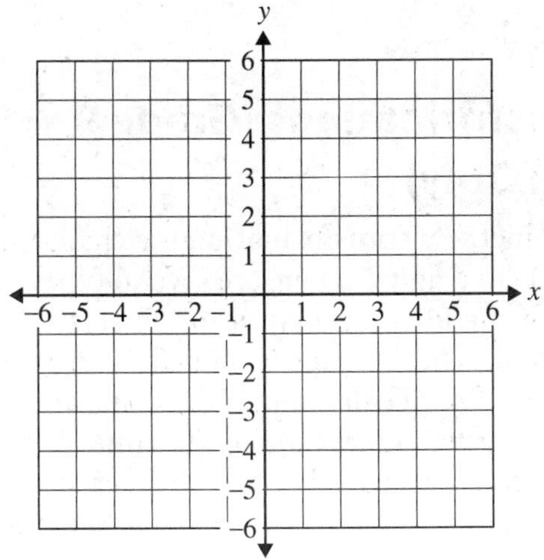

Notice that values to the right of the origin and those above the origin are positive numbers; values to the left of the origin and values below the origin are negative numbers.

Each point on the coordinate plane can be named by its location. Take a look at the point on the plane below.

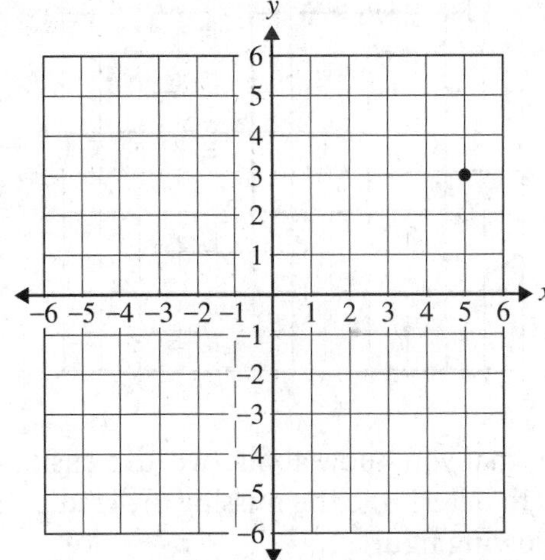

To locate this point, begin at the origin. Move to the right along the *x*-axis to the number 5, then move up to the number 3 on the *y*-axis. Since we moved over 5 spaces and up 3 spaces to reach this point, we say that it is located at (5, 3). This **ordered pair** of numbers tells the location of the point on the plane. Since the origin is located at 0 on both axes, the ordered pair that names this point is always (0, 0).

The numbers in the ordered pair are called the **coordinates**. The first coordinate in an ordered pair always names the location along the horizontal axis, or the *x*-axis. For this reason, the first number is the ***x*-coordinate**. Likewise, the second number in an ordered pair always names the location along the vertical axis, or the *y*-axis, and is known as the ***y*-coordinate**.

Two-dimensional figures may be shown on a coordinate plane. The four vertices of the following rectangle are located at (–4, –2), (–4, 3), (1, 3), and (1, –2). Notice that point Q is located to the left of and below the origin, so both coordinates are negative. Point S is to the right of and above the origin, so both coordinates are positive.

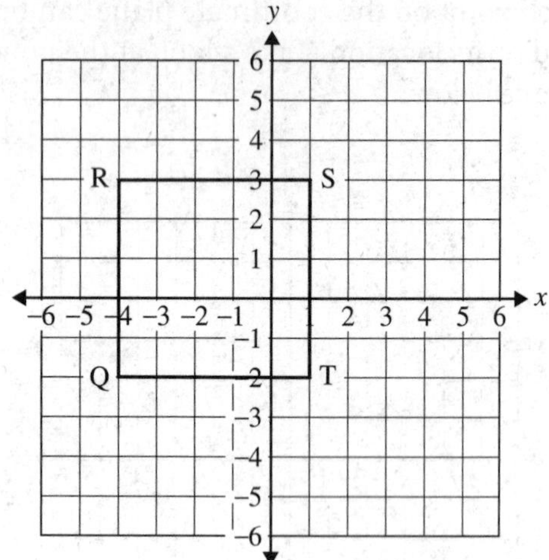

Use what you know about two-dimensional figures to determine the missing ordered pair for the following figure.

Points J, K, and L form a right triangle. Points J and K are shown.

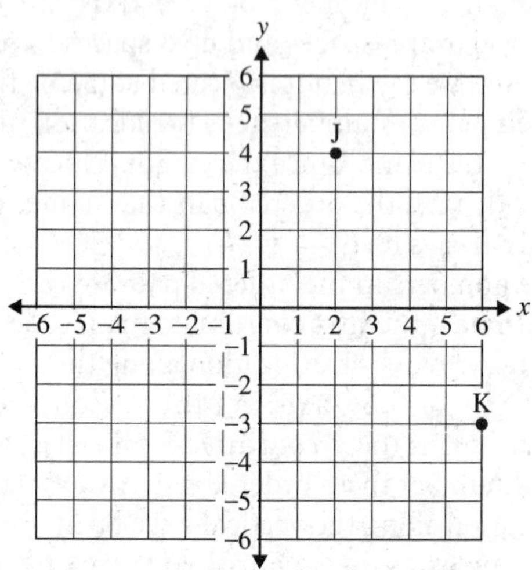

Which could be the coordinates of point L?

A. (−6, 4)
B. (−4, 6)
C. (−2, 3)
D. (2, −3)

To find the location of point L, we must determine which of the given ordered pairs will form a right angle with points J and K. Any of the points will form a triangle, but we specifically need to find the coordinates that will form a right triangle. Each of the answer choices is shown on the coordinate plane. Notice that only answer choice D (2, −3) forms a right triangle with points J and K.

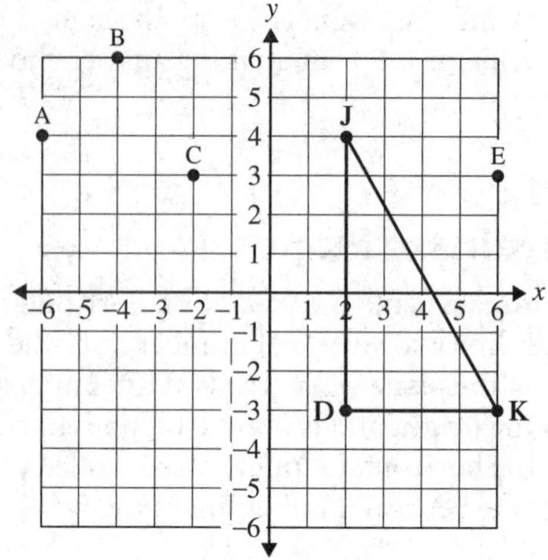

Transformations (Grade 9 Test Only)

In geometry, a **transformation** is a change that is made to a figure. There are several types of transformations that may occur. First is a **rotation**. When a shape is rotated, it turns around a fixed center point. The shape and size of the original figure remain the same. A figure can be rotated as much as 360 degrees around the center of rotation, or the fixed point around which the figure rotates.

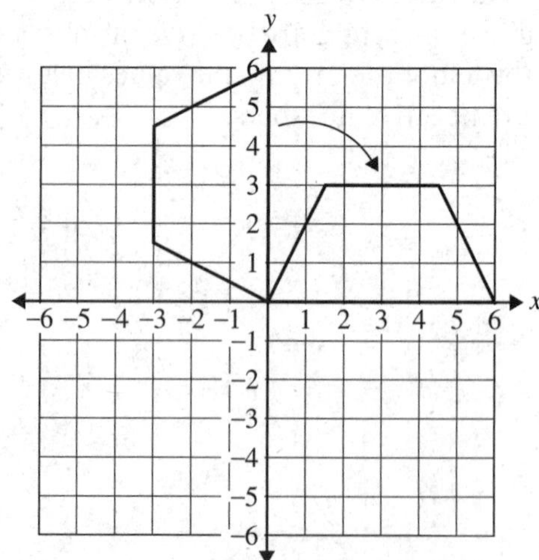

Look at the example above. Imagine there is a pin in the corner of the first figure, holding the figure in place at that point. Then imagine turning the figure clockwise, without moving the pin. The figure has rotated around the pin, and the new position is shown on the right. The trapezoid on the right has been rotated 90 degrees from its original position.

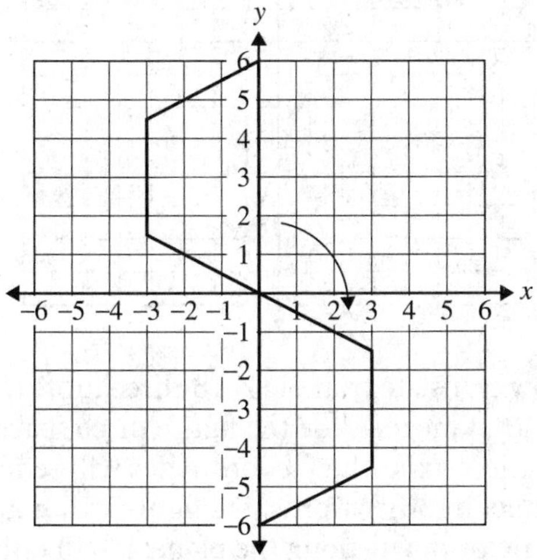

Think of a rotation as being hands on a clock. A figure that has been rotated 90 degrees has moved one-quarter of an hour; a figure that has been rotated 180 degrees has moved one-half of an hour.

A **reflection** results when a figure is flipped over a central line. In its new position, the figure is the same distance from the central line as it was prior to being reflected. Figures may be reflected in any direction and create symmetry within the plane. The size and shape of the figures do not change.

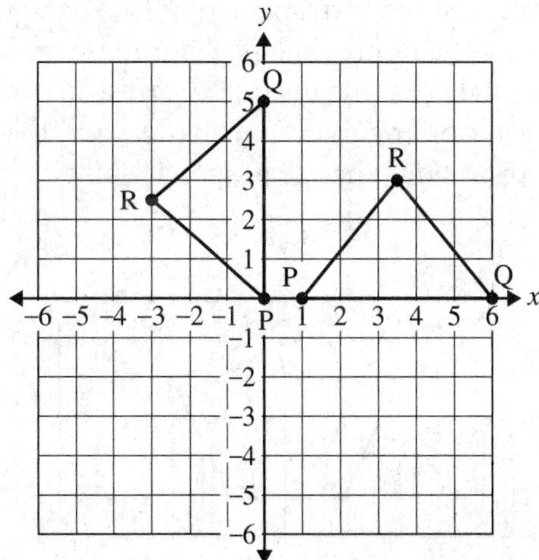

In this example, the triangle on the left was reflected across the *y*-axis. Notice that point P in both triangles is an equal distance from the *y*-axis. The same is true for points Q and R. The new triangle is a mirror image of the original. If we were to stand the edge of a mirror along the central line, this is the image we would see.

A **translation** happens when a shape is moved to another position without being turned. In elementary school, you may have called a translation a *slide*, since it shows the new position of the figure if we were to slide it across the plane. When a shape is translated, every point of the figure moves the same distance in the same direction. The new image is congruent to the original.

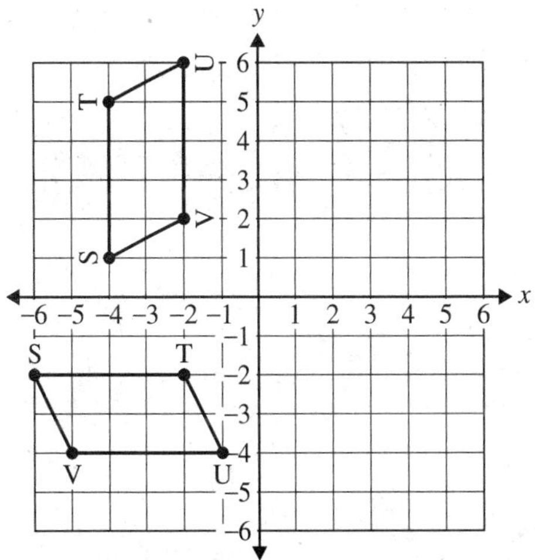

A **dilation** is a transformation that changes the size of the figure. The new figure is similar to the original. That means that the measurements of the interior angles do not change, and the corresponding sides change proportionally.

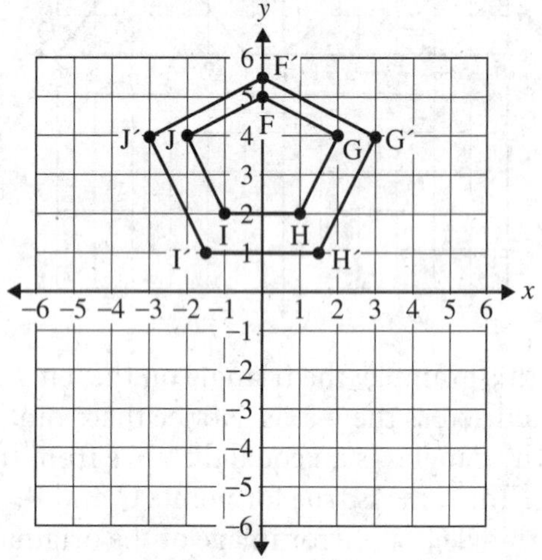

Point X in right triangle XYZ is located at (−5, 8). Rotate the figure 180 degrees. Point X becomes point A on the new triangle, and Y becomes B. Translate triangle ZAB three units to the right. What are the new coordinates of A?

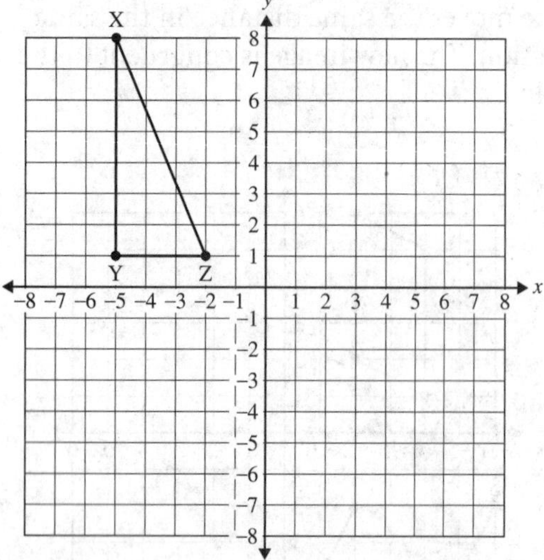

Start by rotating the figure 180 degrees around point Z, and name the points of the new triangle.

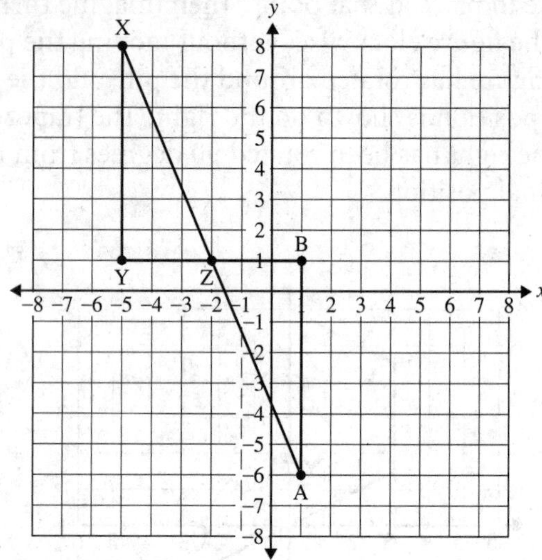

Now translate triangle ZAB three units to the right. That means slide the figure three spaces along the *x*-axis. The *y*-coordinates will remain the same. In other words, the figure will not move up or down along the plane; it will only move to the right.

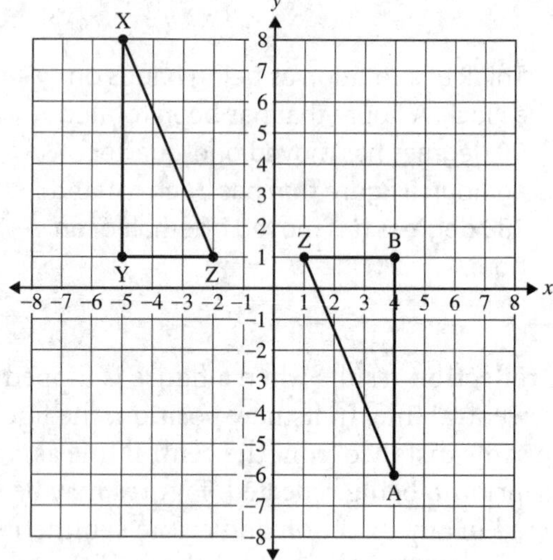

The new coordinates for point A are (4, −6).

You Try It!

In this chapter, you've reviewed the geometry skills you will need to know to do your best on the SHSAT. Use what you have learned to answer the following questions.

1. A decagon has a perimeter of 162 inches. One side has a length of 15 inches, and another has a length of 19 inches. Four sides each measure z inches in length, and the remaining sides each measure $3z$ inches in length. What is the value of z?

A. 8
B. 10
C. 12.25
D. 13.5

Did you select answer choice A? Great! A decagon has 10 sides, so to find the perimeter, we must find the sum of all of the sides. We know that one side measures 15 inches, one measures 19 inches, and four have a length of z inches. So we know the measure of six of the ten sides. That means that four sides remain, and these each have a length of $3z$. Let's list the measures of the sides.

$$15 + 19 + z + z + z + z + 3z + 3z + 3z + 3z$$

That's the same as $15 + 19 + 4z + 4(3z)$.

We know that the sum of these sides is 162 inches. Now we need to find the value of z. To do so, perform the multiplication first, then add to combine like terms. After that, isolate the variable.

$$15 + 19 + 4z + 4(3z) = 162$$
$$15 + 19 + 4z + 12z = 162$$
$$34 + 16z = 162$$
$$34 - 34 + 16z = 162 - 34$$
$$16z = 128$$
$$\frac{16z}{16} = \frac{128}{16}$$
$$z = 8$$

So the value of z is 8.

2. Points J and K are located on the same line and are located at vertices of the hexagon. What is the measure of $\angle M$?

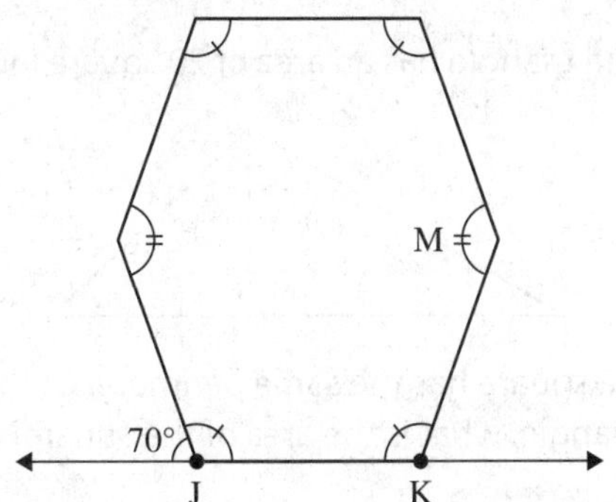

A. 110
B. 120
C. 140
D. 280

In order to determine the measure of angle M, we must first find out the sum of the interior angles of the hexagon. A hexagon has 6 sides, so we'll use this number in the formula for finding the sum of interior angles.

$$(n - 2) \times 180$$
$$(6 - 2) \times 180$$
$$4 \times 180 = 720$$

So the sum of the interior angles of a hexagon is 720 degrees. Now let's figure out the measures of each of the angles. Since the hexagon sits on line JK, the interior angle of the hexagon that is located at point J is supplementary to the 70 degree angle. So it measures 110 degrees $(180 - 70)$. According to the diagram, this angle is equal to three others in the figure. That means the sum of the four equal angles is 440 degrees. Let's subtract this from the total number of degrees in the figure.

$$720 - 440 = 280$$

Now we know that the sum of angle M and the angle whose measure is equal to angle M is 280. We can divide this number by 2 to determine the measure of each of the angles.

$280 \div 2 = 140$

So the measure of angle M is 140 degrees.

3. The triangle has an area of 20 square inches.

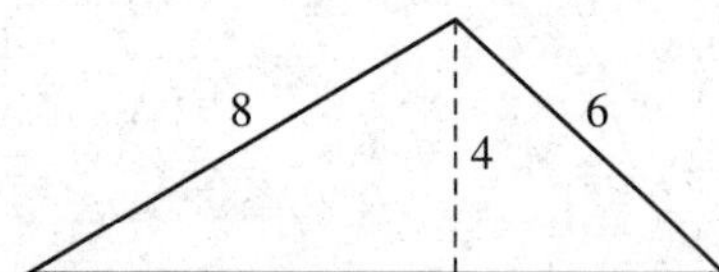

If a square has the same perimeter as the triangle, what is the area of the square?

A. 10 in^2
B. 12 in^2
C. 20 in^2
D. 36 in^2

Let's use the area of the triangle to determine the length of the base. Substitute the known values into the formula for area and determine the missing value, *b*, which is the base.

$$A = \frac{1}{2}bh$$

$$20 = \frac{1}{2}b \times 4$$

$$20 = \left(\frac{1}{2} \times 4\right) \times b$$

$$20 = 2b$$

$$\frac{20}{2} = \frac{2b}{2}$$

$$10 = b$$

Now we know that the base of the triangle is 10 inches, so we can find the sum of the side lengths, which equals the perimeter.

$$10 + 6 + 8 = 24$$

So the perimeter of the triangle is 24. The square has the same perimeter. We know that the lengths of the sides of a square are equal, so we can divide the perimeter by 4 to find the length of each side.

$$24 \div 4 = 6$$

Each side of the square is 6 inches long. The area of a square is length multiplied by width. The length and width are both 6, so we can multiply 6×6 to find the area: $6 \times 6 = 36$. The area of the square is 36 square inches.

Let's Review!

In this chapter, you've reviewed geometry vocabulary, formulas, and skills that will help you be successful on the SHSAT math questions. Let's take a final look at a few of the key points reviewed in this chapter.

- **Lines** continue forever in both directions and are indicated by arrows on both ends. **Line segments** have definite end points and are represented by points on both ends. **Rays** have a specific beginning point but continue forever in one direction. Rays are shown with a point on one end and an arrow on the other.
- **Intersecting** lines or segments cross each other and share a common point. Lines that are **perpendicular** intersect to form a right angle. **Parallel** lines, on the other hand, never meet and remain an equal distance apart at all points on the lines.
- An **angle** is formed by two rays that share an endpoint, called the vertex.
  - **Right angles** measure exactly 90 degrees, and form an L.
  - **Acute angles** measure less than 90 degrees, and are narrower than right angles.
  - **Obtuse angles** measure greater than 90 degrees, and are wider than right angles.
- Angle relationships can be helpful in determining information about geometric figures:
  - Two angles are **complementary** if the sum of their measures is equal to 90 degrees.
  - Two angles are **supplementary** if the sum of their measures is equal to 180 degrees.
  - **Adjacent angles** share a vertex and a common side.
  - **Vertical angles**, which are opposite each other when two lines intersect, have equal measurements.
  - **Alternate interior angles** are created when two parallel lines are cut by a transversal.

The angles are on opposite sides of the transversal, are on the interior of the parallel lines, and have the same measurement.
- **Alternate exterior angles** are on opposite sides of the transversal, are on the outside of the parallel lines, and have the same measurement.

- **Polygons** are two-dimensional figures made from three or more straight sides. These figures are classified by the number of sides they have. The number of angles in a polygon is equal to the number of sides. The sum of the interior angles can be found using the formula shown.
  - Sum of the interior angles of a polygon = $(n - 2) \times 180°$
- **Triangles** are three-sided polygons, and the sum of the interior angles of any triangle equals 180 degrees. Triangles can be classified according to the lengths of their sides.
  - **Equilateral.** Three equal sides.
  - **Isosceles.** Two equal sides.
  - **Scalene.** No equal sides.
- **Triangles** can also be classified according to the measure of their angles.
  - **Acute.** All angles measure less than 90 degrees.
  - **Obtuse.** One angle measures greater than 90 degrees.
  - **Right.** One angle measures exactly 90 degrees.
- The sides of a right triangle that form the 90 degree angle are the **legs**. The longest side, which is opposite from the right angle, is the **hypotenuse**.
- **Quadrilaterals** are four-sided polygons, and the sum of the interior angles of any quadrilateral equals 360 degrees. Quadrilaterals can be classified according to the lengths of the sides and the measures of the angles.
  - **Rectangle.** Four right angles and two pairs of parallel sides.
  - **Square.** Four right angles and four sides of equal length.
  - **Rhombus.** Four sides of equal length and opposite sides are parallel; angles can be any size; opposite angles are equal.
  - **Parallelogram.** Opposite sides are parallel and have equal lengths.
  - **Trapezoid.** Has one pair of parallel sides.
- Figures that are exactly the same shape and size are **congruent**. Figures that are exactly the same shape but different sizes are **similar**.
- **Perimeter** is the distance around a figure. It is the sum of the lengths of all of the sides of a polygon.
- **Area** is the space within a two-dimensional figure and is reported in square units. The formulas below are used to find the area of polygons:
  - Rectangle or square $A = l \times w$
  - Parallelogram $A = b \times h$
  - Trapezoid $A = \frac{1}{2}h(b_1 + b_2)$
  - Triangle $A = \frac{1}{2}b \times h$
- **Circles** are curved figures in which every point is an equal distance from the center. **Radius** is the distance from the center of a circle to any point on its edge. **Diameter** is the distance across the center of a circle, from one edge to the other. **Circumference** is the distance around a circle.
  - Circumference $C = 2\pi r$
  - Area $A = \pi r^2$
- **Three-dimensional figures** have length, width, and height. These figures are classified by their faces and bases.
  - **Cube.** Has six identical faces; the length, width, and height of a cube are equal.
  - **Rectangular solid.** Has six faces, each the shape of a rectangle.
  - **Prism.** Has two parallel bases that are congruent polygons; the number of faces depends on the shape of the bases.
  - **Cylinder.** Has two parallel bases that are congruent circles; the bases are joined by a curved surface.
  - **Cone.** Has one circular base and a curved surface that connects the base to the vertex.
  - **Pyramid.** Has triangle-shaped faces that connect the base and the vertex; the base may be any polygon.
- **Volume** is the capacity of a three-dimensional figure. The formula for finding volume depends on the type of figure.
  - Cube $V = s^3$
  - Rectangular solid $V = l \times w \times h$

- Prism $V = \text{area of base} \times \text{height}$
- Cylinder $V = \pi r^2 h$
- Cone $V = \frac{1}{3}\pi r^2 h$
- Pyramid $V = \frac{1}{3} \times \text{area of base} \times \text{height}$

▶ **Surface area** is the sum of the areas of all of the faces of a three-dimensional figure. While it is possible to determine the surface area of other three-dimensional solids, we just reviewed the formulas for cubes, rectangular solids, and cylinders.

- Cube $6s^2$
- Rectangular solid $SA = 2(lw + wh + lh)$
- Cylinder $2\pi r^2 + 2\pi rh$

▶ On a coordinate plane, the numbers that identify the location of a point are called the **ordered pair**. The first number, or **coordinate**, in the pair is the ***x*-coordinate**, and names the location of the point along the *x*-axis. The second number is the ***y*-coordinate** and names the location of the point along the *y*-axis.

▶ A change that is made to a geometric figure is a **transformation**. Types of transformations include rotation, reflection, translation, and dilation.

- **Rotation.** A figure is turned around a fixed center point; the shape and size of the figure remain constant.
- **Reflection.** A figure is flipped over a central line; the resulting figure is a mirror image of the original, maintaining the same shape and size.
- **Translation.** A shape is moved to another position without being turned; this slide does not change the size or shape of the figure.
- **Dilation.** Changes the size of the figure; the resulting figure is similar to the original, meaning the measurements of the interior angles remain the same and the corresponding sides increase and decrease proportionally.

CHAPTER 10

Probability and Statistics

Have you ever flipped a coin to make a decision? Maybe if it was heads, you would do the dishes, and tails your brother would wash them? A coin toss is a simple example of probability. **Probability** is the likelihood that an event will occur. Suppose that following the coin toss, you pointed out that you have washed the dishes 5 out of 7 nights this week, or that 84 percent of students do not like to wash dishes. Now you're talking statistics. **Statistics** are facts and figures that relate to a given topic.

Some of the questions on the SHSAT will assess your knowledge of these two areas of math. As is true with many of the SHSAT questions, there will be times when you will need to apply your knowledge of arithmetic and algebra to answer probability and statistics questions. In this chapter, we'll review some of the skills that will help you do your best when solving these types of problems.

Central Tendency

One of the basic elements of statistics is central tendency. Whether you realize it or not, measures of central tendency are part of your everyday life. Your report card grades are an average of the scores you've earned on a set of tests and assignments. The batting average of your school's star baseball player is based on central tendency. Even surveys conducted by your local newspaper rely on measures of central tendency.

Measures of **central tendency** are ways to report what information is in the middle of a set of numerical data. There are three ways to measure central tendency.

- Mean
- Median
- Mode

Let's take a closer look at each of these.

Mean

The **mean** is the average of a set of data. To find the mean, add all of the values in a set, then divide the sum by the number of items. For example, suppose your scores on five math quizzes were 88, 100, 90, 95, and 87. To find the mean, or average, of the set of scores, find the sum, then divide by 5, since there were 5 quizzes.

$$88 + 100 + 90 + 95 + 87 = 460$$

$$460 \div 5 = 92$$

So the mean of the set of data is 92. Notice that 92 is not one of the scores on the list. Mean may or may not be a value that is included in the set of data. Also there is only one mean for any set of data. As you will learn later in this chapter, a set of data may have more than one mode; however, it will only have one mean.

As you know, the mean of a set of data is the average of all of the values in the set. If you determine that the mean is greater than the highest value in the set, or is less than the lowest value, double-check your work. Common mistakes when determining central tendency are leaving out one or more of the values or dividing by the incorrect number. Make sure that your answer makes sense.

At times you may be asked to simply find the mean of a given set of data. At other times, you may need to use what you know about mean to solve a problem involving more steps. Let's use what we've reviewed about mean to solve a problem similar to one you might see on the SHSAT.

The table shows the number of car wash tickets sold by 10 members of the cheerleading squad.

Tickets Sold	Number of Cheerleaders
12	2
15	4
18	3
20	1

What is the mean number of tickets sold?

Look carefully at what the question is requiring you to do. At first, it may be tempting to simply find the mean of 12, 15, 18, and 20. But that is not what the question is asking. Notice that two cheerleaders each sold 12 tickets. That means that when we find the sum of the number of tickets sold, we actually have added 12 twice. According to the table, we'll need to add 15 four times, and so on. As you know, the first step in determining the mean is to find the sum of the set of data, so let's do that.

$12 + 12 + 15 + 15 + 15 + 15 + 18 + 18 + 18 + 20 = 158$

So the total number of tickets sold is 158. Next, divide this sum by 10 since there were 10 cheerleaders selling tickets.

$158 \div 10 = 15.8$

So the mean number of tickets sold is 15.8.

Median

Have you ever been on a car trip and noticed the grassy or concrete area in the middle of the street, dividing your lanes from oncoming traffic? That area in the middle is called the *median*. This same word is also used to name a measure of central tendency. The **median** in a set of data is the middle value in the set. Just like the median in the street, the median in math is in the middle. In order to find the median of a set of data, you must first arrange the values in order from least to greatest.

Suppose there are seven homeroom classes at your grade level, and you want to find the median number of students in the homerooms. The number of students in each homeroom is shown below.

21, 25, 17, 19, 23, 20, 26

First, arrange the values from least to greatest.

17, 19, 20, 21, 23, 25, 26

Now find the number in the middle of the set.

17, 19, 20, <u>21</u>, 23, 25, 26

The number in the middle of the set is 21, so 21 is the median number of students in the homeroom classes. Like the mean, a set of data has only one median. In this case, the median was a number included in the set. However, that is not always the case. When a set of data has an even number of values, there is not a single number in the set that is exactly in the middle. Suppose you take six classes each day. The number of students in each of your classes is shown below.

22, 25, 18, 24, 32, 27

To find the median, arrange the values from least to greatest.

18, 22, 24, 25, 27, 32

Now find the numbers in the middle of the set.

18, 22, 24, 25, 27, 32

Since 24 and 25 are in the middle of the set, we must add these together, then divide the sum by 2. In other words, find the average of the two middle numbers.

$24 + 25 = 49$

$49 \div 2 = 24.5$

So the median number of students in the classes is 24.5, a number that is not included in the set of values.

When a set of values is evenly spaced, the mean equals the median.

Mode

Mode is the value that appears most frequently in a set of data. That means mode is always a number that is included in the set. Suppose the friends in your study group earned the following scores on a math exam.

92, 100, 97, 89, 91, 92, 97, 99, 90, 97, 96

The mode is the score that is included in the list the most times. To find which is the mode, let's arrange the scores in order from least to greatest.

89, 90, 91, 92, 92, 96, 97, 97, 97, 99, 100

Notice that the following values each appear in the list a single time: 89, 90, 91, 96, 99, and 100. The number 92 appears twice; 97 appears three times. Since 97 appears the greatest number of times, the mode of the set of data is 97.

As you read previously, a set of data can have more than one mode. When this happens, two or more values must occur in the set an equal number of times, and the number of times these numbers appear must be greater than the occurrences of any other value.

So far this season, the Titusville Tigers football team is undefeated. The scores of their games are listed below.

16, 17, 15, 28, 15, 34, 22, 28, 21, 17, 23

What is the mode of the team's scores?

First, arrange the data in order from least to greatest so you can easily see which values occur more than once.

15, 15, 16, 17, 17, 21, 22, 23, 28, 28, 34

As you can see, 15, 17, and 28 each appear twice in the list. No other number appears more than twice. So this set of data has three modes: 15, 17, and 28.

Did you notice that *mode* sounds a little bit like *most*? That could be helpful in remembering that the mode is the value that occurs most often in a set of data.

Now you try it! Use what you have learned about central tendency to solve the following problem.

A book store had 251 customers on Friday and 384 customers on Saturday. How many customers were there on Sunday if the mean number of daily customers for the three days was 319?

A. 285
B. 318
C. 322
D. 351

Did you select answer choice C? Awesome! Let's review why this answer choice is correct.

In order to find the mean, or average, number of customers per day, we must find the sum of the visitors for each day, then divide by the number of days.

Mean = (sum of the customers for Friday, Saturday, and Sunday) ÷ (number of days)

We know the number of customers for Friday and Saturday but not for Sunday. We also already know that the mean number of customers is 319. Let's substitute this information into the formula, using the variable *c* for the number of customers on Sunday. Then solve the equation to find the value of the variable.

$$319 = (251 + 384 + c) \div 3$$

$$319 \times 3 = (251 + 384 + c) \div 3 \times 3$$

$$319 \times 3 = (251 + 384 + c)$$

$$957 = (251 + 384 + c)$$

$$957 = 635 + c$$

$$957 - 635 = 635 - 635 + c$$

$$322 = c$$

So the number of customers on Sunday was 322.

Determining Probability

Have you ever watched a football game? Before the game begins, a coin is tossed to determine which team will get the ball first. What are the chances that the coin will land on heads? The chances of the coin landing heads up is 1 in 2, or one-half. The chances of the coin landing tails up is also 1 in 2, or one-half.

This is an example of **probability**, or the statistical chance that a given event will occur. Before we go any further discussing probability, let's review a few important key words.

- **Experiment.** A controlled, repeatable situation involving chance or probability.
- **Outcome.** A single possible result of performing an experiment one time.
- **Event.** The set of possible outcomes of an experiment.

In the example of the football game, the coin toss is the experiment. Tossing the coin is a situation of chance; there is a chance it will land on heads, and there is a chance it will land on tails. Other experiments could include rolling a number cube, spinning a spinner, or pulling a marble from a bag.

There are two possible outcomes, or results, of tossing a coin: heads or tails. When rolling a number cube, there are six possible outcomes: rolling the number 1, 2, 3, 4, 5, or 6.

The event is a single coin toss with a single outcome, such as landing on heads. If you were spinning a colored spinner and wanted to find the probability of landing on a blue section, the event would be landing on blue. If you were rolling a number cube and wanted to land on 5, the event would be landing on 5.

In order to measure the probability of an event occurring, we can use the formula shown below, where P represents probability and A represents a given event.

$$P(A) = \frac{\text{the number of ways event A can occur}}{\text{the total number of possible outcomes}}$$

Let's use this formula to prove that the probability of a coin toss resulting in heads is one-half. When a coin is tossed, there is only one way for the result to be heads. That is, it lands heads up. So the top number in the formula will be 1, because there is only one way the event (the coin landing on heads) can occur. There are a total of two possible outcomes: heads up or tails up. So the number on the bottom of the formula will be 2.

$$P(\text{heads}) = \frac{1}{2}$$

This proves that the probability of a coin toss resulting in heads is one-half.

But what about an event that can occur in more than one way? Let's consider rolling a six-sided number cube. Suppose we want to find the probability of rolling an even number. How many ways can the event occur? We could roll a 2, 4, or 6. So there are three possible ways for the event, rolling an even number, to occur. How many possible outcomes are there when rolling the cube? The possible outcomes are rolling 1, 2, 3, 4, 5, or 6. So there are six possible outcomes.

$$P(\text{rolling an even number}) = \frac{3}{6}$$

$$P(\text{rolling an even number}) = \frac{1}{2}$$

So the probability of rolling an even number on a number cube is $\frac{1}{2}$.

Let's try another one.

What is the probability of rolling a number greater than 4 on a six-sided number cube?

First, determine the number of ways the event can occur. The event is rolling a number greater than 4. That would mean rolling either a 5 or a 6, so there are two ways for the event to occur. We know that there are six possible outcomes when rolling a single number cube. Use the formula to determine the probability.

$$\text{P(rolling a number greater than 4)} = \frac{2}{6}$$

$$\text{P(rolling a number greater than 4)} = \frac{1}{3}$$

So there is a one-third chance of rolling a number greater than 4 on a single roll of the cube.

Now you try it. Use the formula for determining probability to solve the problem below.

A jar contains a total of 18 marbles. There are 5 red marbles, 3 yellow marbles, 4 blue marbles, 1 green marble, and 5 black marbles. What is the probability of randomly selecting a marble that is a primary color?

A. $\frac{1}{18}$

B. $\frac{5}{18}$

C. $\frac{1}{3}$

D. $\frac{2}{3}$

To solve this, we must first determine how many ways the event can occur. The event is selecting a marble that is a primary color. Since there are 5 red, 3 yellow, and 4 blue marbles, there are a total of 12 ways to select a primary color, because $5 + 3 + 4 = 12$. We know that there are a total of 18 marbles, so there are 18 possible outcomes to selecting a single marble.

$$\text{P(A)} = \frac{\text{the number of ways event A can occur}}{\text{the total number of possible outcomes}}$$

$$\text{P(primary color)} = \frac{12}{18}$$

$$\text{P(primary color)} = \frac{2}{3}$$

So answer choice D is correct.

Expressing Probability

Probability can be reported in different ways, including as a:

- Fraction
- Decimal
- Percent

When discussing the probability of tossing a coin, the probability of it landing heads up is $\frac{1}{2}$. This is the same as 0.5 or 50%.

> Remember, to convert a fraction to a decimal, divide the numerator by the denominator. To convert a decimal to a percent, move the decimal point two places to the right and add the percent sign.

Probability is never less than zero, nor is it ever greater than 1. An event with a probability of zero is said to be an **impossible** event. For example, the probability of the sun rising in the west tomorrow morning is 0 because it is impossible for that to occur.

On the other hand, an event is **certain** when it will definitely occur. The probability of a certain event is 1. Since the sun will definitely rise in the east tomorrow, the event is certain and has a probability of 1.

Events that have a good chance of happening are considered to be **likely**. Likely events generally have a probability that is between 0.5 and 1. Think about the weather in New York during the winter. It is likely that there will be snow at some point during that season.

An event is considered **unlikely** when there is a small chance of the event happening. Generally, unlikely events have a probability that is less than 0.5. Now think about the weather in September. It is unlikely, but not impossible, that there will be snow at that time of the year.

Suppose you are playing a game that requires you to roll two regular number cubes. What events would be likely, unlikely, certain, or impossible?

- It is *likely* that you will roll a number less than 10.
- It is *unlikely* that you will roll 11 on three consecutive turns.
- It is *certain* that you will roll a number between 2 and 12.
- It is *impossible* that you will roll a 13.

What about the probability of rolling an even number? When the chances of two or more events have the same probability of occurring, they are considered to be **equally likely**. The probability of rolling an even number on a single number cube and the probability of rolling an odd number would be equally likely. When tossing a coin, the chances of it landing on heads are equally likely to the chances of it landing on tails because the chances of both outcomes are equal.

Take a look at the spinner shown below.

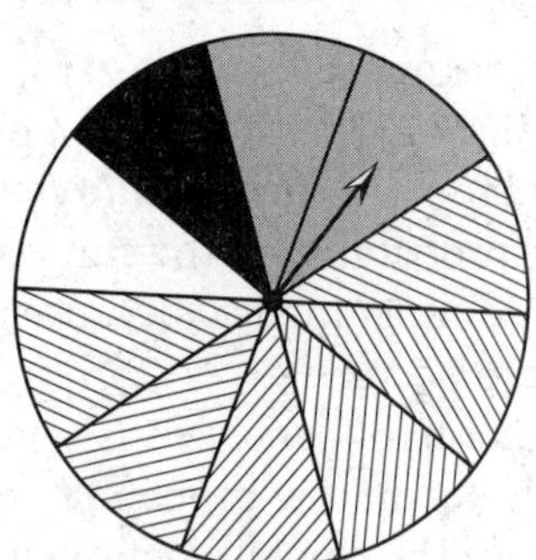

Based on the spinner, which event is likely?

A. landing on white
B. landing on gray
C. landing on black
D. landing on striped

An event that is likely is the one that will probably happen. Since more than half of the sections are striped, landing on one of the striped sections is likely. So the correct answer choice is D.

Let's take a look at the other answer choices. Since one section is white and one section is black, these outcomes are equally likely. The probability of landing on white is $\frac{1}{10}$, and the probability of landing on black is also $\frac{1}{10}$.

Two of the sections are gray. Since the probability of landing on one of these sections is $\frac{2}{10}$, or $\frac{1}{5}$, it is unlikely that this will be the outcome.

Based on the spinner, what is the probability of landing on a striped section?

A. $\frac{1}{6}$
B. 0.6
C. 6%
D. 6

There are six striped sections, so there are 6 possible ways for the event to occur. There are a total of 10 sections, so there are 10 possible outcomes. The probability of landing on a striped section of the spinner is $\frac{6}{10}$.

$$P(\text{striped}) = \frac{6}{10}$$

To express this probability as a decimal, divide the numerator by the denominator.

$$\frac{6}{10} = 6 \div 10 = 0.6$$

This makes answer choice B correct. Let's find out how the correct answer would be expressed as a percent as well. Remember, to change a decimal to a percent, move the decimal point two places to the right and add a percent sign.

$$0.6 = 60\%$$

So, the probability of landing on a striped section is $\frac{6}{10}$, which is the same as 0.6 or 60%.

Solving Problems Involving Probability

Now that we've gone over the basics of probability, let's apply these skills to solve problems. On the SHSAT, you are likely to find questions that require you to do more than simply find the probability of a given outcome. You will need to be comfortable working with the concepts and thinking through the strategies needed to answer the questions.

Let's start by going over a few terms that you may find in the word problems. An experiment is considered to be **fair** when all of the outcomes are equally probable. Take a look at the spinner below.

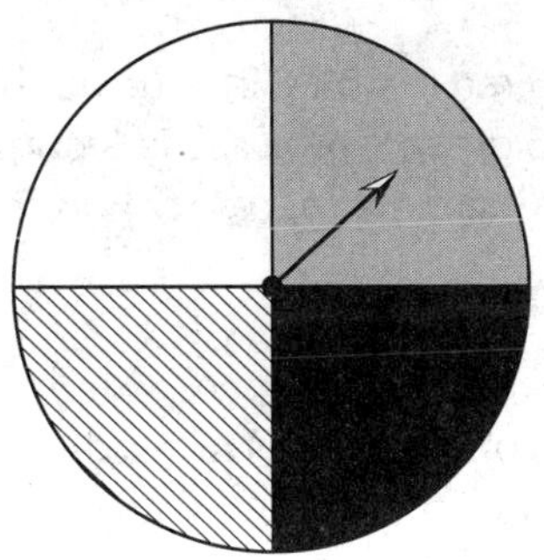

Each of the sections of the spinner is the same size, making the possibility of landing on any given color or pattern equally likely. This is considered to be a fair spinner. If you were conducting a survey, you would want to include a random sample of the population in order to ensure that the results are fair and that everyone is equally represented. Let's suppose you want to survey a sample of the students in your school regarding the best way to spend fund-raising money. The choices are to purchase new football equipment, additional laptops for the computer lab, or instruments for the band. In order for the results of the survey to be fair, you would need to ask students representing all grade levels who are involved in a variety of clubs and activities.

Biased, on the other hand, is the opposite of fair and can impact the outcome of an experiment. Suppose you only ask the football players how they would like for the fund-raising money to be spent. You would probably find that they would prefer the new football equipment. So are the results fair? No, because the outcomes were not equally probable when only the football team was asked to weigh in. The results were biased since one outcome was given a better chance of success.

Sometimes an experiment may involve more than one event, such as spinning a spinner *and* rolling a number cube. These are considered to be **independent events** when they do not affect each other in any way. A few examples of independent events are shown below.

- A spinner landing on yellow *and* a coin toss landing on tails
- Selecting a red marble from a jar *and* rolling a 3 on a number cube
- A coin toss landing on tails *and* tossing the coin again and landing on heads

As you can see, the result of any one of these experiments has absolutely no effect on the outcome of the other experiment. Another way to ensure that events are independent is with **replacement**, which is exactly what it sounds like. When an object is removed, then put back, and a second object is chosen, the events do not affect each other. Consider the following example.

Rosa had a jar containing 15 red marbles and 7 blue marbles. She selected 1 red marble, then returned it to the jar. What is the probability that she will select a blue marble next?

Since Rosa put the first red marble back, this event has no effect on the outcome of the second event. By replacing the red marble back into the jar, the probability of choosing a blue marble is $\frac{7}{22}$.

What if Rosa had *not* replaced the marble? Then the events would have been **dependent**, because the outcome of the first event affected the outcome of the second. At first, the probability of selecting a blue marble was $\frac{7}{22}$, since there were 7 blue marbles and a total of 22 marbles in all. But Rosa removing one of the red marbles affected the outcome of the second event. Now there are only 21 marbles. So, the probability of selecting blue becomes $\frac{7}{21}$, or $\frac{1}{3}$. The events were dependent because the outcome of the first event changed the probability of the outcome of the second.

Not only can events be considered independent or dependent, they can also be mutually exclusive. **Mutually exclusive** events cannot occur at the same time. For example, when tossing a coin, the result cannot be both heads and tails. Landing on heads and landing on tails are mutually exclusive events.

What is the probability of rolling a 2 and an even number on a number cube?

The probability of rolling a 2 is $\frac{1}{6}$. The probability of rolling an even number is $\frac{3}{6}$. Since 2 is an even number, both events can occur at the same time, so these are *not* mutually exclusive.

What is the probability of rolling a 4 and an odd number?

The probability of rolling a 4 is $\frac{1}{6}$. The probability of rolling an odd number is $\frac{3}{6}$. However, since 4 is not an odd number, these events cannot occur at the same time. So, the events are mutually exclusive. The two events have no favorable outcomes in common.

In the previous example, there was only one favorable outcome for rolling a 4 on the number cube: landing on 4. There were three favorable outcomes for rolling an odd number: 1, 3, and 5. The set of all of the possible results or outcomes of an experiment is called the **sample space**. The sample space is listed within braces. For example, the sample space of tossing a coin is {head, tail}.

What is the sample space for the spinner shown?

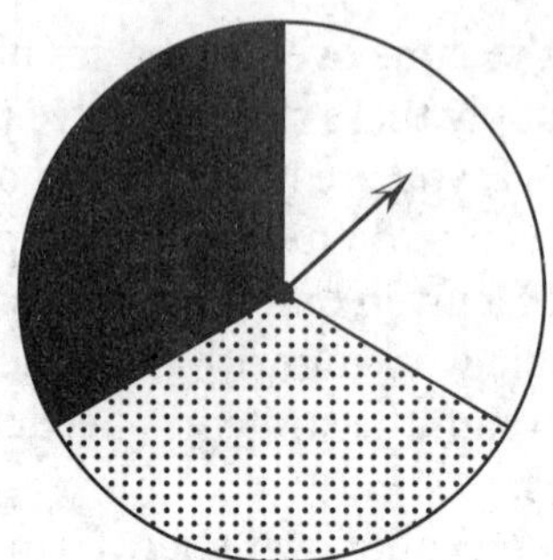

There are three possible outcomes for this spinner. It could land on black, it could land on white, or it could land on spotted. So the sample space for the spinner is {black, white, spotted}.

A jar has 5 red marbles, 25 blue marbles, 7 yellow marbles, 8 green marbles, and 3 purple marbles. What is the sample space for choosing a marble from the jar?

Remember, a sample space simply lists the possible outcomes. It does not indicate the probability of any particular outcome.

{red, blue, yellow, green, purple}

Notice that the sample space includes all of the colors of marbles in the jar. It does not show that selecting blue is likely or that selecting purple is unlikely.

Now that you're familiar with the vocabulary, let's try solving a few probability word problems. As with any word problem:

- Read everything carefully.
- Think about what information you have.
- Determine what you need to find out.

A glass jar contains 28 square tiles. The probability of randomly selecting an orange tile is $\frac{2}{7}$. How many green tiles should be added to the jar in order to change the probability of selecting orange to $\frac{1}{4}$?

First, let's figure out what information is given.

- There are 28 tiles.
- The probability of selecting orange is $\frac{2}{7}$.

There are 28 tiles, and the probability of selecting orange is $\frac{2}{7}$. Since the numerator in the probability tells the total number of possible outcomes, we know that this probability has been reduced. Let's find an equivalent fraction that shows the total number of tiles in the numerator.

$$P(\text{orange}) = \frac{\text{number of orange}}{\text{number of tiles}} = \frac{2}{7} \times \frac{4}{4} = \frac{8}{28}$$

Multiplying the probability $\frac{2}{7}$ by $\frac{4}{4}$ tells that the number of orange tiles is 8.

Now we need to find out how many green tiles should be added to change the probability of orange to $\frac{1}{4}$. By adding green tiles, we are not changing the number of orange tiles in the jar. We will still have 8 orange tiles, but we need for 8 to be $\frac{1}{4}$ of the total number. We can use a proportion to determine what the total number of tiles will need to be in order for the probability of orange to be $\frac{1}{4}$. Use a variable to represent the total number of tiles that are needed in the jar.

$$\frac{8}{t} = \frac{1}{4}$$

Cross multiply to solve the proportion.

$$\frac{8}{t} \times 4 = 1 \times t$$

$$32 = t$$

So the total number of tiles should be 32. We started with 28. Subtract to find how many more tiles are needed.

$$32 - 28 = 4$$

We know that 4 green tiles should be added to the jar.

Now try another one. Remember to read carefully, look for given information, and determine what it is you need to find out to solve the problem.

A gumball machine contains 8 grape flavor gumballs, 12 cherry flavor, 4 watermelon, and 6 mint. Elliot buys 5 gumballs, one of which is mint. If he buys one more gumball, what is the probability that it will be mint?

Start by determining what you know:

- There were 8 grape, 12 cherry, 4 watermelon, and 6 mint gumballs.
- Elliot removed 5 gumballs.
- One of the gumballs Elliot bought was mint.

Based on this information, we can determine that there were 30 gumballs in the machine before Elliot bought any because $8 + 12 + 4 + 6 = 30$.

Now determine what it is we need to find out to solve the problem: What is the probability that Elliot will buy a mint gumball next?

To determine the probability of selecting mint, we need to find how many of the remaining gumballs are mint and how many gumballs remain in all.

We know that there were 6 mint gumballs in the machine, and that Elliot bought 1 of them. That means there are now 5 mint gumballs remaining because $6 - 1 = 5$.

We also know that there were a total of 30 gumballs and Elliot bought 5 of them. That means that now the total number of gumballs is 25 because $30 - 5 = 25$.

Let's use this to find the probability of selecting mint next.

$$P(\text{mint}) = \frac{\text{number of mint gumballs}}{\text{total number of gumballs}} = \frac{5}{25}$$

So the probability of selecting mint is $\frac{5}{25}$, or $\frac{1}{5}$. This can also be expressed as 0.2 or 20%.

Let's work through one more word problem.

A bag contains exactly 7 marbles. Of those, 6 are green and 1 is yellow. Madison randomly selects 6 marbles from the bag without replacement. What is the probability that all of the marbles she chose are green?

As always, begin by thinking about what information was given.

- There are 7 marbles.
- Six of the marbles are green.
- One of the marbles is yellow.
- Madison chose 6 marbles.

Now determine what information you need to find: What is the probability that all of the marbles she chose are green?

To solve this problem, we need to find all of the possible results of selecting 6 marbles. Let's use G to represent a green marble, and Y to represent the yellow.

YGGGGG
GYGGGG
GGYGGG
GGGYGG
GGGGYG
GGGGGY
GGGGGG

Take a look at the list of possibilities. The first shows that she drew the yellow marble first, followed by all greens. The second shows that she chose a green, then the yellow, followed by 4 more greens. This pattern continues to the final possibility listed, in which she chose only greens.

By looking at the list, we can determine that there were 7 possibilities for how Madison selected the marbles. We want to know the possibility of selecting all green.

$$\text{P(all green)} = \frac{\text{outcomes including green only}}{\text{total possible outcomes}} = \frac{1}{7}$$

So the probability of selecting all green is $\frac{1}{7}$.

You Try It!

In this chapter, you've reviewed skills and definitions that will be important in answering the probability and statistics questions on the SHSAT. Now use what we have reviewed to solve the problems below.

1. The mean age of the 12 guests invited to Abby's birthday party was 23. Her cousin was unable to attend, so his age was dropped. This changed the mean of the ages to 24. What age was dropped?

A. 1
B. 11
C. 12
D. 22

The original mean of the ages, 23, is the result of dividing the sum of the ages by 12, the total number of guests. Let's start by finding the original sum of the ages. Let *a* represent this sum.

$$\frac{a}{12} = 23$$

$$12 \times \frac{a}{12} = 23 \times 12$$

$$a = 276$$

So original sum of the ages was 276. If one of the ages was dropped, 11 ages remain. The mean of these 11 ages is 24. Let's find the sum of the 11 remaining ages.

$$\frac{a}{11} = 24$$

$$11 \times \frac{a}{11} = 24 \times 11$$

$$a = 264$$

The age that was dropped is the difference between the original sum of the ages and the sum of the remaining ages.

$$276 - 264 = 12$$

So the age that was dropped from the list is 12.

2. The number of library books checked out by each student in Ms. Callahan's literature class is shown in the table.

Number of Books	Students
0	3
1	4
2	5
3	6
4	2
5	1
6	0
7	2
8	1

What is the median number of books the students checked out?

A. 1
B. 2.5
C. 2.8
D. 3

The median is the middle number in the set. So, begin by listing the number of books checked out, in order from least to greatest. Remember to include each number as many times as it appears. For example, since three students checked out zero books, 0 will be included three times.

0, 0, 0, 1, 1, 1, 1, 2, 2, 2, 2, 2, 3, 3, 3, 3, 3, 3, 4, 4, 5, 7, 7, 8

Now find the number in the middle of the set. Since there are a total of 24 numbers in the set, we need to find the twelfth and thirteenth numbers, since these are the values in the middle.

0, 0, 0, 1, 1, 1, 1, 2, 2, 2, 2, <u>2, 3,</u> 3, 3, 3, 3, 3, 4, 4, 5, 7, 7, 8

Next, average the two values in the middle of the set.

$2 + 3 = 5$

$\frac{5}{2} = 2.5$

So the median number of books checked out by the students is 2.5.

3. Each month, Ivan records the total number of miles he has hiked with his family. The miles for each month this year are shown below.

25, 28, 26, 46, 30, 28, 52, 43, 26, 32, 34, 26

What is the mode of the miles hiked each month?

A. 26
B. 28
C. 29
D. 33

To find the mode, or the number appearing most often in the set, arrange the values from least to greatest. Then look for any value(s) that appear more than once.

25, 26, 26, 26, 28, 28, 30, 32, 24, 43, 46, 52

As you can see, 26 appears three times and 28 appears twice. All other values only appear once. Since 26 appears most often in the set, it is the mode of the data.

4. Lamar had 41 coins in a can. Of those, 16 were quarters, 3 were nickels, 5 were dimes, and the rest were pennies. He took 7 quarters and one additional coin from the can, at random. What is the probability that the coin he removed was a penny?

A. $\frac{17}{41}$
B. $\frac{17}{33}$
C. $\frac{12}{17}$
D. $\frac{1}{2}$

The first step in solving this problem is to determine what information is given.

- Lamar began with a total of 41 coins.
- He had 16 quarters, 3 nickels, and 5 dimes.
- The remaining coins in the can were pennies.
- He removed 7 quarters and one other coin.

Now determine what you need to find out: What is the probability that the additional coin he removed was a penny?

To determine the probability that he removed a penny, we must figure out how many pennies there were in the jar originally. We know how many quarters, nickels, and dimes were in the can, and we know that the total number of coins was 41. So the sum of all of the coins equals 41. Let p represent the number of pennies.

$$16 + 3 + 5 + p = 41$$
$$24 + p = 41$$
$$24 - 24 + p = 41 - 24$$
$$p = 17$$

There were 17 pennies in the can. To find the probability that he removed a penny, we need to determine how many coins were in the can after removing the 7 quarters.

$$41 - 7 = 34$$

When he removed the final coin, there were a total of 34 coins remaining in the can. The probability that he removed a penny can be determined using the following formula.

$$\text{P(penny)} = \frac{\text{number of pennies}}{\text{total number of coins remaining}} = \frac{17}{34} = \frac{1}{2}$$

The probability that the final coin Lamar removed was a penny is $\frac{1}{2}$.

5. Amy, Jason, Hannah, Emma, and Katie all want to be on the student council; however, there is only enough room for four of the students. The principal places each of the students' names in a jar and randomly draws four names to determine who will be on the council. What is the probability that all of the students chosen are girls?

A. $\frac{1}{5}$

B. $\frac{4}{5}$

C. $\frac{1}{4}$

D. $\frac{5}{4}$

To solve this problem, list all of the possible outcomes of randomly drawing four names. Let G represent the girls' names, and B represent the boy's name.

BGGG
GBGG
GGBG
GGGB
GGGG

There are five possible outcomes. Only one of the outcomes is all girls.

$$\text{P(all girls)} = \frac{1}{5}$$

The probability that all of the students chosen will be girls is $\frac{1}{5}$.

Let's Review!

In this chapter, you've reviewed the probability and statistics skills and vocabulary that will help you correctly answer these questions on the SHSAT. Let's take one more look at some of the information discussed in this chapter.

- **Statistics** are facts and figures that relate to a given topic.
- Measures of **central tendency** are often used to report statistical information. These are ways of indicating what information is in the middle of a set of numerical data, and they include mean, median, and mode.
- **Mean** is the average of a set of data and is found by adding the values in a set, then dividing the sum by the number of items. Any set of data will have only one mean, which may or may not be one of the values included in the set.
- The **median** of a set of data is the value in the middle of the set. If the set includes an even number of items, the median is determined by finding the average of the two numbers in the middle. A set of data will have a single median, which may or may not be one of the values that is included in the set.
- The **mode** is the value that appears most frequently in the set of data. Therefore, the mode must always be a number that is included in the set. There may be more than one mode.
- **Probability** is the statistical chance, or likelihood, that an event will occur. It can be expressed in the form of a fraction, decimal, or percent.

$$P(A) = \frac{\text{the number of ways event A can occur}}{\text{the total number of possible outcomes}}$$

The probability of any event is always between 0 and 1.

The following terms are often included in discussions of probability.

- **Experiment.** A controlled, repeatable situation involving chance or probability.
- **Outcome.** A single possible result of performing an experiment one time.
- **Event.** The set of possible outcomes of an experiment.

- The probability of an event can be classified as being likely, unlikely, certain, or impossible.
  - A **likely** event has a good chance of occurring and generally has a probability that is between 0.5 and 1.
  - An **unlikely** event has a small chance of occurring and generally has a probability that is between 0 and 0.5.
  - A **certain** event will definitely occur and has a probability of 1.
  - An **impossible** event cannot occur and has a probability of 0.
  - Two events that have the same probability of occurring are **equally likely**.
- An event is **fair** when all outcomes are equally probable. An event that is **biased** is the opposite of fair.
- Two or more events that do not affect each other in any way are **independent** events. When the first of two events involves **replacement**, in which an object is put back before the second event occurs, the events are independent. Events are **dependent** when the outcome of the first affects the outcome of the second.
- Events that are **mutually exclusive** cannot occur at the same time.
- A **sample space** is the set of all possible results or outcomes of an experiment.

PART 4

SHSAT Practice Tests

CHAPTER 11

SHSAT Practice Test 1

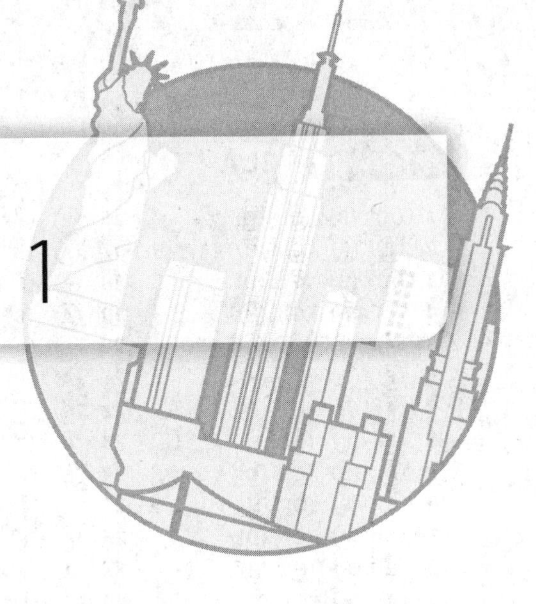

On the following page you'll find a form similar to that of the actual SHSAT. Carefully tear it out of the book and use it as you take the diagnostic test, for both the ELA and Mathematics sections.

PART 1 ELA

1 Ⓐ Ⓑ Ⓒ Ⓓ
2 Ⓔ Ⓕ Ⓖ Ⓗ
3 Ⓐ Ⓑ Ⓒ Ⓓ
4 Ⓔ Ⓕ Ⓖ Ⓗ
5 Ⓐ Ⓑ Ⓒ Ⓓ
6 Ⓔ Ⓕ Ⓖ Ⓗ
7 Ⓐ Ⓑ Ⓒ Ⓓ
8 Ⓔ Ⓕ Ⓖ Ⓗ
9 Ⓐ Ⓑ Ⓒ Ⓓ
10 Ⓔ Ⓕ Ⓖ Ⓗ
11 Ⓐ Ⓑ Ⓒ Ⓓ
12 Ⓔ Ⓕ Ⓖ Ⓗ
13 Ⓐ Ⓑ Ⓒ Ⓓ
14 Ⓔ Ⓕ Ⓖ Ⓗ
15 Ⓐ Ⓑ Ⓒ Ⓓ
16 Ⓔ Ⓕ Ⓖ Ⓗ
17 Ⓐ Ⓑ Ⓒ Ⓓ
18 Ⓔ Ⓕ Ⓖ Ⓗ
19 Ⓐ Ⓑ Ⓒ Ⓓ
20 Ⓔ Ⓕ Ⓖ Ⓗ
21 Ⓐ Ⓑ Ⓒ Ⓓ
22 Ⓔ Ⓕ Ⓖ Ⓗ
23 Ⓐ Ⓑ Ⓒ Ⓓ
24 Ⓔ Ⓕ Ⓖ Ⓗ
25 Ⓐ Ⓑ Ⓒ Ⓓ
26 Ⓔ Ⓕ Ⓖ Ⓗ
27 Ⓐ Ⓑ Ⓒ Ⓓ
28 Ⓔ Ⓕ Ⓖ Ⓗ
29 Ⓐ Ⓑ Ⓒ Ⓓ
30 Ⓔ Ⓕ Ⓖ Ⓗ
31 Ⓐ Ⓑ Ⓒ Ⓓ
32 Ⓔ Ⓕ Ⓖ Ⓗ
33 Ⓐ Ⓑ Ⓒ Ⓓ
34 Ⓔ Ⓕ Ⓖ Ⓗ
35 Ⓐ Ⓑ Ⓒ Ⓓ
36 Ⓔ Ⓕ Ⓖ Ⓗ
37 Ⓐ Ⓑ Ⓒ Ⓓ
38 Ⓔ Ⓕ Ⓖ Ⓗ
39 Ⓐ Ⓑ Ⓒ Ⓓ
40 Ⓔ Ⓕ Ⓖ Ⓗ
41 Ⓐ Ⓑ Ⓒ Ⓓ
42 Ⓔ Ⓕ Ⓖ Ⓗ
43 Ⓐ Ⓑ Ⓒ Ⓓ
44 Ⓔ Ⓕ Ⓖ Ⓗ
45 Ⓐ Ⓑ Ⓒ Ⓓ
46 Ⓔ Ⓕ Ⓖ Ⓗ
47 Ⓐ Ⓑ Ⓒ Ⓓ
48 Ⓔ Ⓕ Ⓖ Ⓗ
49 Ⓐ Ⓑ Ⓒ Ⓓ
50 Ⓔ Ⓕ Ⓖ Ⓗ
51 Ⓐ Ⓑ Ⓒ Ⓓ
52 Ⓔ Ⓕ Ⓖ Ⓗ
53 Ⓐ Ⓑ Ⓒ Ⓓ
54 Ⓔ Ⓕ Ⓖ Ⓗ
55 Ⓐ Ⓑ Ⓒ Ⓓ
56 Ⓔ Ⓕ Ⓖ Ⓗ
57 Ⓐ Ⓑ Ⓒ Ⓓ

PART 2 MATHEMATICS

58

⊖	⊙	⊙	⊙	⊙
	⓪	⓪	⓪	⓪
	①	①	①	①
	②	②	②	②
	③	③	③	③
	④	④	④	④
	⑤	⑤	⑤	⑤
	⑥	⑥	⑥	⑥
	⑦	⑦	⑦	⑦
	⑧	⑧	⑧	⑧
	⑨	⑨	⑨	⑨

59

⊖	⊙	⊙	⊙	⊙
	⓪	⓪	⓪	⓪
	①	①	①	①
	②	②	②	②
	③	③	③	③
	④	④	④	④
	⑤	⑤	⑤	⑤
	⑥	⑥	⑥	⑥
	⑦	⑦	⑦	⑦
	⑧	⑧	⑧	⑧
	⑨	⑨	⑨	⑨

60

⊖	⊙	⊙	⊙	⊙
	⓪	⓪	⓪	⓪
	①	①	①	①
	②	②	②	②
	③	③	③	③
	④	④	④	④
	⑤	⑤	⑤	⑤
	⑥	⑥	⑥	⑥
	⑦	⑦	⑦	⑦
	⑧	⑧	⑧	⑧
	⑨	⑨	⑨	⑨

61

⊖	⊙	⊙	⊙	⊙
	⓪	⓪	⓪	⓪
	①	①	①	①
	②	②	②	②
	③	③	③	③
	④	④	④	④
	⑤	⑤	⑤	⑤
	⑥	⑥	⑥	⑥
	⑦	⑦	⑦	⑦
	⑧	⑧	⑧	⑧
	⑨	⑨	⑨	⑨

62

⊖	⊙	⊙	⊙	⊙
	⓪	⓪	⓪	⓪
	①	①	①	①
	②	②	②	②
	③	③	③	③
	④	④	④	④
	⑤	⑤	⑤	⑤
	⑥	⑥	⑥	⑥
	⑦	⑦	⑦	⑦
	⑧	⑧	⑧	⑧
	⑨	⑨	⑨	⑨

63 Ⓐ Ⓑ Ⓒ Ⓓ
64 Ⓔ Ⓕ Ⓖ Ⓗ
65 Ⓐ Ⓑ Ⓒ Ⓓ
66 Ⓔ Ⓕ Ⓖ Ⓗ
67 Ⓐ Ⓑ Ⓒ Ⓓ
68 Ⓔ Ⓕ Ⓖ Ⓗ
69 Ⓐ Ⓑ Ⓒ Ⓓ
70 Ⓔ Ⓕ Ⓖ Ⓗ
71 Ⓐ Ⓑ Ⓒ Ⓓ
72 Ⓔ Ⓕ Ⓖ Ⓗ
73 Ⓐ Ⓑ Ⓒ Ⓓ
74 Ⓔ Ⓕ Ⓖ Ⓗ
75 Ⓐ Ⓑ Ⓒ Ⓓ
76 Ⓔ Ⓕ Ⓖ Ⓗ
77 Ⓐ Ⓑ Ⓒ Ⓓ
78 Ⓔ Ⓕ Ⓖ Ⓗ
79 Ⓐ Ⓑ Ⓒ Ⓓ
80 Ⓔ Ⓕ Ⓖ Ⓗ
81 Ⓐ Ⓑ Ⓒ Ⓓ
82 Ⓔ Ⓕ Ⓖ Ⓗ
83 Ⓐ Ⓑ Ⓒ Ⓓ
84 Ⓔ Ⓕ Ⓖ Ⓗ
85 Ⓐ Ⓑ Ⓒ Ⓓ
86 Ⓔ Ⓕ Ⓖ Ⓗ
87 Ⓐ Ⓑ Ⓒ Ⓓ
88 Ⓔ Ⓕ Ⓖ Ⓗ
89 Ⓐ Ⓑ Ⓒ Ⓓ
90 Ⓔ Ⓕ Ⓖ Ⓗ
91 Ⓐ Ⓑ Ⓒ Ⓓ
92 Ⓔ Ⓕ Ⓖ Ⓗ
93 Ⓐ Ⓑ Ⓒ Ⓓ
94 Ⓔ Ⓕ Ⓖ Ⓗ
95 Ⓐ Ⓑ Ⓒ Ⓓ
96 Ⓔ Ⓕ Ⓖ Ⓗ
97 Ⓐ Ⓑ Ⓒ Ⓓ
98 Ⓔ Ⓕ Ⓖ Ⓗ
99 Ⓐ Ⓑ Ⓒ Ⓓ
100 Ⓔ Ⓕ Ⓖ Ⓗ
101 Ⓐ Ⓑ Ⓒ Ⓓ
102 Ⓔ Ⓕ Ⓖ Ⓗ
103 Ⓐ Ⓑ Ⓒ Ⓓ
104 Ⓔ Ⓕ Ⓖ Ⓗ
105 Ⓐ Ⓑ Ⓒ Ⓓ
106 Ⓔ Ⓕ Ⓖ Ⓗ
107 Ⓐ Ⓑ Ⓒ Ⓓ
108 Ⓔ Ⓕ Ⓖ Ⓗ
109 Ⓐ Ⓑ Ⓒ Ⓓ
110 Ⓔ Ⓕ Ⓖ Ⓗ
111 Ⓐ Ⓑ Ⓒ Ⓓ
112 Ⓔ Ⓕ Ⓖ Ⓗ
113 Ⓐ Ⓑ Ⓒ Ⓓ
114 Ⓔ Ⓕ Ⓖ Ⓗ

PART 1

ENGLISH LANGUAGE ARTS

90 Minutes ■ 57 Questions

Revising/Editing

QUESTIONS 1–20

Revising/Editing Part A

DIRECTIONS: Read and answer each of the following questions. You will be asked to recognize and correct errors in sentences or short paragraphs. Mark the best answer for each question.

Journeying from salt water to freshwater in order to breed, the wonder of nature is seen in salmon.

1. Which sentence best corrects the dangling modifier in the sentence?

A. Journeying from salt water to freshwater in order to breed, we see the wonder of nature in salmon.
B. While journeying from salt water to freshwater in order to breed, the wonder of nature is seen in salmon.
C. The wonder of nature, journeying from salt water to freshwater in order to breed, is seen in salmon.
D. The wonder of nature is seen in salmon as they journey from salt water to freshwater in order to breed.

A salmons' life cycle begins in freshwater lakes and streams and then, in the first or second year of its life, it is carried along by rivers or mountain streams to the ocean.

2. Which edit is needed for the above sentence?

E. Change "salmons'" to "salmon's."
F. Change "lakes" to "lakes'."
G. Remove the comma after "then."
H. Insert a comma after "along."

CONTINUE ON TO THE NEXT PAGE ▶

(1) For several years, perhaps as many as nine, salmon remain in the ocean. (2) They spend their time eating and growing until they are adult fish. (3) When it is time for it to breed, an extremely strong instinct causes the salmon to leave the ocean. (4) They head back to the freshwater streams where they were born.

3. Which sentence contains an error in pronoun usage?

A. Sentence 1
B. Sentence 2
C. Sentence 3
D. Sentence 4

(1) This journey, called the salmon run, is extremely difficult because the fish must swim upriver against the current, and past strong rapids. (2) Some even leap up waterfalls as they make their way back to their original breeding grounds to fulfill their innate instinct. (3) This may be hundreds of miles away.

4. Which edit is needed in the above paragraph?

E. Insert a comma after "upriver."
F. Insert a comma after "waterfalls."
G. Insert a comma after "grounds."
H. Insert a comma after "this."

(1) It takes a salmon a lot of effort to travel back upstream to it's hatching grounds. (2) Because of this, it will die shortly after spawning. (3) When the embryos hatch, they will eat their own yolk. (4) Once their yolk is gone, they begin searching for other food.

5. Which sentence contains a mechanics error that should be corrected?

A. Sentence 1
B. Sentence 2
C. Sentence 3
D. Sentence 4

As young salmon get older they feed on things such as insects small invertebrates small fish and other sea organisms.

6. Which is the correct way to punctuate the above sentence?

E. As young salmon get older they feed on things such as insects, small invertebrates, small fish, and other sea organisms.
F. As young salmon get older, they feed on things such as insects, small invertebrates, small fish, and other sea organisms.
G. As young salmon get older, they feed on things such as insects small invertebrates small fish and other sea organisms.
H. As young salmon get older, they feed on things, such as insects small invertebrates small fish and other sea organisms.

CONTINUE ON TO THE NEXT PAGE ▶

Revising/Editing Part B

DIRECTIONS: Read the passage below and answer the questions following it. You will be asked to improve the writing quality of the passage and to correct errors so that the passage follows the conventions of standard written English. You may reread the passage if you need to. Mark the best answer for each question.

Passage 1

Operations of the Underground Railroad

(1) From 1830 until the end of the American Civil War, the Underground Railroad played a significant part in American history. (2) There was no actual railroad, but that name has been given to a secret network of people who helped slaves escape from the South throughout that period. (3) These people help escaping African Americans by providing them with a route to travel to the North, means and money for travel, and safe houses to hide in. (4) The safe houses on the Underground Railroad often would put out some sign for the fugitive—perhaps a certain color quilt on the clothesline. (5) After a slave spent the night, he or she would be directed to the next safe house along the route. (6) One of the most famous routes ran from Maryland and Pennsylvania to New York State and across Lake Ontario to Ontario, Canada, but there were other networks in other states also.

(7) The Underground Railroad activities had to be carried out in secret, and its participants used railway terms to refer to their activities. (8) The escaping slaves were referred to as "packages" or "freight," and those who helped them were called "conductors." (9) These conductors were a diverse mix, including free blacks and escaped slaves, philanthropists, church leaders, and Northern abolitionists. (10) They worked together to help slaves to freedom. (11) The routes extended through 14 northern states and ended in Canada, where slave hunters had no authority.

(12) The most famous of the Underground Railroad conductors was a woman named Harriet Tubman. (13) An escaped slave herself, she reportedly made nineteen trips back into the South to help other slaves escape. (14) This was very dangerous because, in addition to being a fugitive, a bounty had been placed on her head. (15) Placing a bounty on someone was often an effective way for the government to apprehend a criminal.

(16) As a result of these people's efforts, somewhere between 30,000 and 100,000 enslaved people of all ages, some in family groups, managed to find safety after traveling that route to Canada. (17) Although this seems like a large number of people, it was only a small fraction of the slaves in the South. (18) Most of them remained in bondage until Abraham Lincoln's Emancipation Proclamation.

7. Which edit is the correct one for sentence 3?
   - **A.** Change "providing" to "having provided."
   - **B.** Change "escaping" to "escaped."
   - **C.** Change "help" to "helped."
   - **D.** Change "help" to "had helped."

CONTINUE ON TO THE NEXT PAGE ▶

8. Where is the best place in the passage for sentence 11?

E. Where it is now
F. After sentence 3
G. After sentence 9
H. After sentence 6

9. Which sentence is irrelevant to the main idea of the passage?

A. Sentence 4
B. Sentence 9
C. Sentence 15
D. Sentence 16

10. Which of these sentences would best follow sentence 7 and reinforce the main message of the passage?

E. Anyone caught helping a runaway slave could be fined or imprisoned.
F. Many people did not want to get involved in the struggle.
G. Some people would change their mind and send the fugitive slaves away.
H. Inquisitive neighbors had to be avoided.

11. Which of the following is the best choice as a concluding sentence for the passage?

A. Most of them remained in bondage until Abraham Lincoln's Emancipation Proclamation.
B. Nevertheless, for the people who found freedom, this railroad was a lifeline.
C. The Underground Railroad is an important part of American history.
D. Harriet Tubman was an integral part of this railway system.

12. Which would be the best transition to put at the beginning of sentence 2?

E. Of course,
F. Although
G. Because
H. In addition,

13. Which is the best way to join sentence 9 and sentence 10 in order to show their relationship?

A. These conductors were a diverse mix including free blacks and escaped slaves, philanthropists, church leaders, and Northern abolitionists; moreover, they worked together to help slaves to freedom.
B. Although these conductors were a diverse mix, including free blacks and escaped slaves, philanthropists, church leaders, and Northern abolitionists, they worked together to help slaves to freedom.
C. Because these conductors were a diverse mix including free blacks and escaped slaves, philanthropists, church leaders, and Northern abolitionists, they worked together to help slaves to freedom.
D. These conductors were a diverse mix including free blacks and escaped slaves, philanthropists, church leaders, and Northern abolitionists because they worked together to help slaves to freedom.

CONTINUE ON TO THE NEXT PAGE ▶

Passage 2

The History of Curing Meat

(1) Prior to the invention of commercially satisfactory methods of refrigeration, the preservation of fresh meat was a difficult task. (2) Fresh meat spoiled quickly, and its weight made it unwieldy for nomadic people to carry while traveling. (3) The lack of a way to preserve meat meant a lot of waste at times and scarcity of food at others. (4) One early solution to the problem of how to preserve meat was to season it with salt and spices. (5) This type of treatment removed the moisture from the meat, which made it easier to transport, and prevented bacteria from growing, which made it last longer. (6) This method worked very well, and was widely used even in ancient times.

(7) Meat preservation developed. (8) Different regions became known for their methods. (9) Salamis was a city that became famous for its specialty meat. (10) In the Middle Ages, meat was mixed with different combinations of seasoning, with each city using its own special blend of additives. (11) Cities were famous for the particular blend of spices that they used to preserve the meat they made into sausages. (12) There are many examples of European cities known for their meat blends. (13) A different type of salted, preserved meat was produced in Ireland during the Middle Ages. (14) This was the forerunner of what is known as Irish corned beef today. (15) Ireland is also known for its production of beer and whiskey.

(16) Over time, preserving meat became an art. (17) The different methods used included salting, poaching, curing, and smoking. (18) In modern times, cured meat remains popular, more for its flavor than for convenience. (19) In fact, most cured meat was kept refrigerated for added safety. (20) In the twenty-first century there was a resurgence in the popularity of artisanal cured meats, with small specialty shops popping up throughout the United States. (21) Each shop boasts its own blend of spices and methods of curing.

14. Which is the best way to combine sentences 7 and 8 to show their relationship?

- **E.** Meat preservation developed because different regions became known for their methods.
- **F.** As meat preservation developed, different regions became known for their methods.
- **G.** Although meat preservation developed, different regions became known for their methods.
- **H.** Meat preservation developed when different regions became known for their methods.

15. Which sentence contains a comma error?

- **A.** Sentence 6
- **B.** Sentence 10
- **C.** Sentence 13
- **D.** Sentence 19

CONTINUE ON TO THE NEXT PAGE ▶

16. Which sentence is irrelevant to the main idea of the passage and should be eliminated?

E. Sentence 4
F. Sentence 10
G. Sentence 12
H. Sentence 15

17. Which revision of sentence 12 would best support sentence 11?

A. The frankfurter, named after the great German city of Frankfurt, and the bologna sausage, from the Italian city of that name, are the most famous examples of these preserved sausages.
B. Quite a few cities in Europe are known for their different types of meat sausages.
C. Germany and Italy both had towns that were known for their special curing methods.
D. Frankfurters and bologna sausages are both named for towns in Europe.

18. Pick the revision of sentence 9 that uses the most precise language.

E. Some ancient cities were known for the spices they used to cure meat; some types of meat were even named after the cities they were made in.
F. Many years ago, as cured meats developed, different regions became known for the types of cured meats that they produced.
G. One city, Salamis, was well known for the spices it used, and the meat named for that city has been famous for a long time.
H. The ancient city of Salamis was well known for the spices it used, and the meat named for that city, the salami sausage, has been famous for more than 2,000 years.

19. Which of these sentences would best replace sentence 21 as a concluding sentence for the entire passage?

A. Over the years, chefs have discovered that certain spices change not just the taste but also the texture of meat.
B. Although these meats are popular in the United States, many people consider the best cured meats to come from Europe.
C. Although it was a method born out of necessity, the evolution of specialty meats has made them a favorite of meat lovers everywhere.
D. Some people will drive a hundred miles just to get products from a specialty meat shop.

20. Which edit needs to be made in sentence 19?

E. Remove the comma after "fact."
F. Insert a comma after "meat."
G. Change "was" to "is."
H. Change "was" to "will be."

CONTINUE ON TO THE NEXT PAGE ▶

Reading Comprehension

QUESTIONS 21–57

DIRECTIONS: Read the passages below, then answer the questions that appear after each passage. Select the best answer for each question. Reread the passages if necessary. You must base your response **only on information contained in the passage.**

One of the greatest discoveries of all time took place in the People's Republic of China. It happened in March 1974 when a farmer who was digging a well stumbled across a clay soldier buried in the dirt. The site of the discovery was in a field 18 miles east of Xi'an, the capital of Shaanxi province. After the farmer's discovery, archaeologists continued to dig. They were amazed to discover what are now called the Qin Terra-cotta Warriors and Horses.

Xi'an is one of the oldest cities in China. It dates back more than 3,000 years. The clay figures were crafted over 2,200 years ago during the reign of the Emperor Qin Shihuang (259–210 BCE). They were found adjacent to Emperor Qin's tomb. Qin is considered by historians to be the first emperor of China. He is credited as the person who unified China. His reign began the Qin Dynasty. He was also responsible for starting construction on the Great Wall of China.

The clay figures are remarkable! They are life-sized but vary in height. The warriors all have different facial expressions and hairstyles. Their uniforms differ according to rank. Their gestures are all different as well. It is as though they were alive. There are horsemen, longbow bearers, archers, officers, and generals. There are even officials, acrobats, and musicians. Included with the soldiers are chariots and horses. And these amazing warriors are all positioned in battle formation as dictated by the *Art of War*. This treatise was written by Sun Tzu some 500 to 200 years earlier.

Altogether, 6,000 figures were discovered. According to historians, it took 720,000 workers 37 years to craft the terra-cotta warriors, chariots, and horses.

The terra-cotta warriors and horses were originally painted with a colored lacquer. This made them look even more realistic and lifelike. Over the years, the paint wore off. The warriors carried iron swords and spears that were coated with chromium oxide. This kept them from rusting over that many years. Remarkably, this preservation technique was not known in the West until the eighteenth century.

Some believe this terra-cotta army was meant to defend the tomb of Qin Shihuang from thieves and marauders. Others think the warriors and horses were there to allow Qin to rule another empire in the afterlife. Whatever the reason, the terra-cotta army is a magnificent spectacle to view. It is a testament to the power the emperor possessed to commission such a monumental undertaking.

21. Which of the following best tells what this passage is about?

A. how archaeologists dug up the terra-cotta army
B. why the terra-cotta army was created
C. what Emperor Qin achieved
D. what the terra-cotta army was like

CONTINUE ON TO THE NEXT PAGE ▶

22. The passage suggests that Emperor Qin
    E. had a problem getting the terra-cotta soldiers made.
    F. was a man of many accomplishments.
    G. believed in an afterlife.
    H. died when he was rather young.

23. Which of these statements is true about the Qin Terra-cotta Warriors and Horses?
    A. They were made by famous artists of the time.
    B. They were the only terra-cotta statues made in China.
    C. They were the only items that Qin wanted buried with him.
    D. They show what an army was like during Qin's reign.

24. Which of the following best describes what is suggested by the statement that "this preservation technique was not known in the West until the eighteenth century" (lines 49–51)?
    E. At that time, the Chinese were more advanced technologically than the Western world was.
    F. At that time, the Chinese were better educated than the people in the Western world.
    G. During this period, the Chinese were in touch with many other cultures in order to learn how to preserve items.
    H. During this period, the Chinese were intent upon being more capable than people in the Western world.

25. What does the existence of the terra-cotta army suggest about this period in China?
    A. It was a time when science flourished.
    B. It was a time when the country was unified.
    C. It was a time when armies had been disbanded.
    D. It was a time when armies were needed.

26. What was **not** a concern of the archaeologists who studied the terra-cotta army?
    E. why the terra-cotta army was created
    F. how the terra-cotta army was discovered
    G. how many soldiers there were in the terra-cotta army
    H. the cost of creating the terra-cotta army

CONTINUE ON TO THE NEXT PAGE ▶

Three hundred feet beneath the surface of the Earth, below rolling hills of farmland and picturesque villages near Geneva, Switzerland, physicists are looking for the building blocks of the universe. What they are seeking are subatomic particles that are not possible to find in a normal laboratory setting. The scientists are using a device called an atom smasher to simulate the conditions that existed when the universe started. The beginning of the universe is called the big bang by scientists. The big bang theory postulates that around 15 billion years ago the universe suddenly expanded. It acted like a balloon that has been popped. And as it expanded, it cooled. It continues to expand and cool to this day.

The Large Hadron Collider (LHC) is the world's largest atom smasher. It started operating in 2009. It is a large ring that is 17 miles in circumference. There are 9,300 magnets in the ring. The collider shoots two beams of proton particles in opposite directions. The beams are guided by the magnets. The more protons are accelerated, the greater the chance that two protons will smash into each other. The bigger the smasher, the more force at collision. The particles travel around the ring 11,245 times a second at 99.99 percent of the speed of light (about 186,282 miles per second). They produce 600 million collisions every second. When they collide, they produce debris that very quickly disintegrates. Computers analyze the results.

The scientists are smashing particles together to see what results. Atoms can be broken down into other, smaller particles. The physicists are looking for rare particles that can't be broken down any further. They are called fundamental or elementary particles and include quarks, leptons, and bosons. So far, 57 elementary particles have been found. Some have an electrical charge and a spin. Scientists believe that other hypothetical particles exist, but their presence has never been proven. One such particle is the Higgs boson. It is proposed by the physicist Peter Higgs as an answer to why some particles possess mass and others don't. It is often referred to as the "God particle." Researchers are also looking to prove the existence of what is called dark matter. This is invisible matter that is thought to be most the prevalent material in the universe. It is theorized that it was what was left over after the big bang. The Large Hadron Collider was created with the hope that it would provide answers to scientists' questions. It will probably revolutionize particle physics. And it may also lead to more questions.

27. Which of the following best tells what this passage is about?

A. why scientists believe in the big bang theory
B. which fundamental particles have been identified
C. that dark matter is invisible
D. what scientists are trying to achieve with the Large Hadron Collider

28. The author implies that some fundamental particles

E. can be shot from the Large Hadron Collider.
F. have been improperly identified.
G. may never be identified positively.
H. are easily tested.

CONTINUE ON TO THE NEXT PAGE ▶

29. Which of these statements is true about the Large Hadron Collider?
   A. It is the first atom smasher ever used.
   B. It can work continuously for 24 hours.
   C. It was designed by astronomers.
   D. It provides new information for physicists.

30. Which best describes the relationship between an atom and a quark?
   E. A quark is a part of an atom.
   F. A quark lasts longer than an atom.
   G. They are the same thing.
   H. They both are fundamental particles.

31. Which is **not** true of the Higgs boson?
   A. It would explain why some particles possess mass and others do not.
   B. It may be found by using the Large Hadron Collider.
   C. It is also called the "God particle."
   D. It has been verified.

32. What might be inferred about dark matter?
   E. It is part of an atom.
   F. It is a very small particle.
   G. It exists only in smaller galaxies.
   H. There is very little known about it.

CONTINUE ON TO THE NEXT PAGE ▶

Haller Park, also known as the Bamburi Nature Trail, located along the Indian Ocean in Mombasa, Kenya, is a lush paradise of forests, ponds, savannahs, and wetlands. Animals thrive in this wildlife sanctuary. Visitors flock to this nature preserve today, but they find it hard to believe that Haller Park is, indeed, an ecological experiment.

When Rene Haller, a Swiss agronomist, a person who studies soil and crop management, first visited the area in 1971, it was an uninhabitable wasteland. The Bamburi Cement Company had mined fossil coral limestone there for years. The exhausted quarry that Dr. Haller first observed had no trees or plants. There were pools of brackish water everywhere, but no living creatures. With the backing of the cement plant, he set out to transform this industrial scar.

At first Haller found that every tree he planted withered and died. Then one day he discovered casuarina trees. Native to Australia, the casuarina tree is an evergreen that can survive in barren, arid locations. He began planting young trees. Conocarpus, a tree native to Somalia that can also withstand harsh environments, were also planted. As the trees began to thrive and grow, the trees dropped needles to the ground. Millipedes fed on the needles. Their droppings contained bacteria that fertilized the soil.

Termites ate the dead vegetation. Their droppings also enriched the ground. Mushrooms began to grow. Slowly the land began to transform. Haller dug out ponds with a bulldozer. He stocked the ponds with guppies, tilapia, and black mollies. Bulrushes were planted along the shores to provide shelter for birds. Ferns were planted. Eucalyptus, coconut palm, banana, and mango trees were all introduced. The baobab tree, native to Kenya, and the neem tree, native to India, which provide excellent shade, also thrived.

Today, there are miles of nature trails where storks, cranes, and weaver birds abound. Antelopes, buffalo, giraffes, and crocodiles also live there. Most of the animals were rescued, such as the hippos, Sally and Potty. The sanctuary is interactive. Each afternoon, visitors can hand-feed the giraffes. There is a 100-year-old tortoise name Mzee that likes to have his throat tickled. In addition, oryx antelopes and elands are domesticated for meat at the Nguuni Wildlife Sanctuary. There is a crocodile farm and an aquaculture fish farm as well. Visitors to the park can even try a taste of crocodile steak, antelope meat, or tilapia filet at a restaurant in the park.

In 1987, Rene Haller was presented with the United Nations Environment Programme "Global 500 Roll of Honor for Environmental Achievement" Award. It is a fitting tribute to a man who had a vision and persevered to see it come true.

33. Which of the following best tells what this passage is about?

A. why Haller Park was a wasteland
B. what kinds of animals are living at Haller Park
C. which trees were used to change Haller Park into a wildlife sanctuary
D. how a wasteland was changed into a wildlife sanctuary

34. What is **not** mentioned as being present at Haller Park?

E. rescued animals
F. ponds with fish
G. crocodiles
H. sheep

CONTINUE ON TO THE NEXT PAGE ▶

35. According to the passage, which of the following statements about Haller Park is accurate?

    A. Haller Park is the only nature sanctuary that was once a wasteland.
    B. Haller Park has acted as a model for other ecologically devoid areas.
    C. Only rescued animals are permitted at Haller Park.
    D. Haller Park was supported by the company that caused it to be a wasteland.

36. The information about the crocodile farm was included in order to illustrate

    E. that crocodile meat is a popular food.
    F. that Haller Park is an experiment.
    G. that Rene Haller enjoys entertaining people.
    H. that Haller Park produces its own food.

37. Which of the following is Rene Haller most likely to choose for another project?

    A. starting fish farms in areas where there is a lot of unemployment
    B. creating a cooperative garden
    C. organizing a community park
    D. changing a desert into a lush area where many fruit trees grow

38. What is probably true of Rene Haller?

    E. He is an animal lover.
    F. He is a humble person.
    G. He enjoys publicity.
    H. He has great determination.

CONTINUE ON TO THE NEXT PAGE ▶

Dolphins are well known to many people. They entertain children and adults in venues like Sea World. There are facilities where people can swim with dolphins, an experience that many call unforgettable. Dolphins are also used in research labs. And they are kept by the U.S. Navy in San Diego for military studies. In all of these circumstances, the dolphins are kept in captivity.

Do animals have rights? The question is a difficult one, with animal rights activists on one side and animal research proponents on the other. As scientists learn more about the mental life of animals, a number of astounding facts have begun to emerge. Scientists and researchers now conclude that dolphins are the second most intelligent creatures after humans. What is important is brain size in relation to overall size.

Dr. Lori Marino, a zoologist with Emory University in Atlanta, Georgia, has conducted extensive MRI (magnetic resonance imaging) scans on the brains of dolphins. She has concluded that the mind of a dolphin works in a manner very similar to the brain of a human. "The tests suggest a psychological continuity between humans and dolphins," said Marino.

In another experiment, researchers marked two dolphins with triangles and circles on their foreheads, backs, and flippers, places they could not see. They then placed a mirror in the tank. Both dolphins immediately swam to the mirror and examined themselves. They exhibited a level of self-awareness only seen in humans and chimpanzees. This showed that dolphins have a concept of themselves.

In Australia, a rescued dolphin was taught by trainers to tail-walk, the feat of moving backward through the water on its tail. After recuperating, the dolphin was released back into the wild. Amazingly, that dolphin taught dozens of other wild dolphins how to tail-walk. Learned behavior in a community of animals is mainly for getting food. Tail-walking has no practical function; it is only done for fun.

The question then becomes, can the same quality of research be done in the wild as in captivity? Pro-captivity supporters contend that the dolphins are better off and reproduce well in captivity. They point out that more than 50 percent of dolphins in the wild have scars from shark attacks. Naval researchers claim that even though their dolphins are penned in San Diego Bay, they could easily jump out and swim away, but they don't. Those who advocate releasing dolphins into the wild feel that dolphins are so much like people that they shouldn't be kept in captivity. They believe that dolphins should be granted a special ethical status and should be treated as nonhuman persons. The debate will no doubt continue for many years.

39. Which of the following best tells what this passage is about?

- **A.** how dolphins are taught to tail-walk
- **B.** why sharks attack dolphins
- **C.** whether or not dolphins should be kept in captivity
- **D.** what research has discovered about dolphins' brains

CONTINUE ON TO THE NEXT PAGE ▶

40. The best reason that the author began the passage by describing how people can swim with dolphins was to

E. remind the readers that dolphins are in captivity.
F. impress the reader with how gentle dolphins are.
G. suggest that dolphins are able to learn tricks easily.
H. show how easy it is to keep dolphins in captivity.

41. Which reason is **not** given for letting dolphins go free?

A. They are extremely intelligent.
B. They have a concept of themselves.
C. Their brains work in the same way as human brains.
D. They are often attacked by predators.

42. Which is true of dolphins?

E. They like to be alone.
F. They try to protect people.
G. They are emotional beings.
H. They do not try to escape when in captivity.

43. The author includes information about Dr. Marino to

A. lend the passage greater authority.
B. show that the author is knowledgeable about the subject.
C. suggest that some research is more accurate than other research.
D. emphasize how much research has been done on dolphins.

44. What is likely to happen if dolphins are no longer kept in captivity?

E. People will swim with them in the ocean.
F. Dolphins will grow in number.
G. People will not bother with them.
H. More dolphins are likely to die.

CONTINUE ON TO THE NEXT PAGE ▶

Beryl Markham was a unique and brave woman. Born Beryl Clutterback in Leicester, England, in 1902, she moved with her family to Kenya when she was three. Her father, Charles, bought a coffee plantation. After a short time, Charles discovered that he had a knack for training horses, and he used the land to breed and train horses for racing. Beryl grew up on the farm. She learned the native language, and she also learned to ride and train horses. Her horses won many races. That was quite unusual because at that time horse racing was a sport dominated by men.

Then one day something happened that would change her life. She met Tom Campbell Black, a world-famous aviator. Once she had experienced flying, Beryl became obsessed with the idea of being a pilot. She learned to fly and received her commercial pilot's license. She was the first woman pilot in Kenya, becoming a "bush pilot," transporting passengers, supplies, and mail to remote parts of Kenya. There were no airports; she landed and took off on fields or clearings in the forest. At that time, in the infancy of the aviation age, air racing was popular, and Tom tried to convince her to enter a race from Nairobi to Johannesburg, South Africa. Instead Beryl determined to fly from Kenya to England. Hindered by persistent engine problems and consistent bad weather, it took her 23 days, but she became the first person to fly solo from Nairobi to London.

In 1936 Beryl decided she wanted to be the first woman to fly alone across the Atlantic. Charles Lindbergh had already soloed across the ocean in 1927 from the United States to England. Beryl wanted to go the opposite way, from east to west. That was much more difficult because of the prevailing winds that would blow against her. On September 4, 1936, Beryl left London in a Vera Gull airplane, a single-engine monoplane crafted from wood and fabric. The plane was outfitted with extra fuel tanks, but Beryl had no radio and no navigational equipment when she took off into the darkness.

Twenty hours later, her fuel line froze, and the plane crash-landed in a peat bog on Cape Breton Island, Nova Scotia. She emerged from the plane unharmed. Two fishermen approached her, and she said calmly, "I'm Mrs. Markham. I've just flown from England." Beryl was taken to New York City and honored with a ticker tape parade. Her feat was reported in newspapers around the world. In 1942 she wrote *West with the Night* about her life and accomplishments. After living in America for a number of years, Beryl returned to Kenya to be with her beloved horses. She won many more races. She died in 1986.

45. Which of the following best tells what this passage is about?

A. why flying to the United States was difficult
B. what Beryl Markham did as a young person
C. how Beryl Markham became a pilot
D. how Beryl Markham made her mark on history

46. How did the experience of meeting Tom Campbell Black affect Beryl Markham?

E. She became a better person.
F. She decided to write a book.
G. She realized what she wanted to do with her life.
H. She left Kenya for the United States.

CONTINUE ON TO THE NEXT PAGE ▶

47. Why does the author call Beryl Markham "a unique and brave woman" (lines 1–2)?
   - A. She was good at training horses.
   - B. She did something that was dangerous and hard to do.
   - C. She returned to Kenya after many years had passed.
   - D. She learned to fly a plane.

48. How did what Charles Lindbergh achieved differ from what Beryl Markham did in her flight across the Atlantic Ocean?
   - E. Her plane was lighter than his.
   - F. She was newer to aviation than he was.
   - G. Her flight lasted a long time.
   - H. The winds were against her.

49. Why do you suppose Beryl Markham returned to Kenya?
   - A. She always considered it her home.
   - B. She could not get an American visa.
   - C. She had run out of money.
   - D. She was asked to by the Kenyan government.

50. What can be inferred about Beryl Markham?
   - E. She was concerned about how she was perceived by the public.
   - F. She was difficult to get along with.
   - G. She was not practical.
   - H. She did not let obstacles stand in her way.

CONTINUE ON TO THE NEXT PAGE ▶

Army Ants: Fact Versus Fiction

Many people have been told that one of the most feared creatures in the jungles of Africa and South America is the army ant, of which there are over 200 species. There are stories of hordes of ants consuming large mammals or even humans when they unwittingly stumble into the path of army ants on the march. However, much of what you have been told about army ants is probably exaggeration.

Army ants are carnivores, and they do march together. For this reason, when a horde of army ants approach, everything gets out of their way. Some species of army ants march in columns, while others create a fan shape. During the march, some of the worker ants carry the immature ants. Other ants gather all the food they can find. As they march, they kill every insect, lizard, or snake in their path. These ants have been known to march right through houses. When this happens, the people leave, taking their livestock with them. When the homeowners return, they find a house that is completely free of roaches or any other insects. These ants have eaten everything that doesn't fly or run.

Each colony of army ants moves through the jungle only two weeks out of every month since the remaining two weeks are spent in one spot, raising a new generation of young ants. After the new generation is grown and the ants are on the move, they travel through the jungle in huge masses that can number as many as 20 million ants, marching in a close-packed line that can stretch for meters.

Contrary to what you may have heard, the main diet of these ants is other insects. They can only catch things that aren't fast enough to get out of the way, which means most creatures don't have to worry. These ants also provide food to many other species. As the ants march, they flush out insects and spiders from the underbrush. Some birds, including ant-birds, get their food by following an ant swarm and eating the insects that are fleeing. In addition, this insect is barely a quarter of an inch long, lives out in the open, is so vulnerable that bright sunlight can kill it in a few minutes, and is not able to see well. Hypothetically, it may be possible for army ants to eat the carcass of a large dead mammal, like a deer, but that would take days. Furthermore, any animal or human would have to be immobilized in order for the ants to consume it. Although a fascinating study, the army ant you have heard about in stories is probably more myth than reality.

51. Which of the following best describes what this passage is about?

A. How army ants march
B. What army ants eat
C. The truth about army ants
D. The physical characteristics of the army ant

CONTINUE ON TO THE NEXT PAGE ▶

52. The author implies that stories about army ants
    E. have likely been embellished.
    F. are interesting and factual.
    G. can't be proved or disproved.
    H. can be teaching tools.

53. From reading the passage, which of these statements do you know to be true about army ants?
    A. They are very dangerous creatures.
    B. Like all other ants, they have a queen.
    C. They march in formations.
    D. They abandon their young.

54. Which is **not** true of army ants?
    E. They eat snakes.
    F. They stop their march to raise their young.
    G. They don't see well.
    H. They like to bask in the bright sun.

55. Which might be inferred about why people leave when they see army ants approaching?
    A. Army ants are stronger than people.
    B. Army ants have a peculiar smell.
    C. Army ants bite, and people are fearful of them.
    D. They want their house to be free of bugs.

56. Which best describes the relationship between army ants and ant-birds?
    E. Ant-birds eat army ants.
    F. Army ants eat ant-birds.
    G. The relationship between the army ants and the ant-birds is hostile.
    H. Army ants help the ant-birds to locate food.

57. From the tone of the passage, which can you infer?
    A. The author thinks that army ants are a dangerous species.
    B. The author thinks that army ants are relatively harmless.
    C. The author thinks that army ants are an important pest control.
    D. The author thinks that army ants are cruel to their young.

CONTINUE ON TO THE NEXT PAGE ▶

PART 2

MATHEMATICS

90 Minutes ■ 57 Questions

Important Notes

(1) No formulas or definitions of mathematical terms and symbols are provided.
(2) Diagrams are not necessarily drawn to scale. Be careful not to make assumptions about relationships in diagrams.
(3) Diagrams can be assumed to be in one plane unless otherwise stated.
(4) Graphs are drawn to scale. Therefore, you may assume relationships according to appearance. This means lines that look parallel can be assumed to be parallel, angles that look like right angles can be assumed to be right angles, and so forth.
(5) All fractions must be reduced to lowest terms.

Grid-In Problems

QUESTIONS 58–62

DIRECTIONS FOR GRID-IN QUESTIONS: In the Mathematics section of the new SHSAT, in addition to the multiple choice questions, there will be five grid-in questions. For these questions, you need to solve a computational question and provide the numerical answer. Once you have found the answer, you must enter it at the top of the grid and then fill in the appropriate circles below to match your answer.

Each grid consists of five columns. Enter your answer beginning at the left. The first column is reserved for the "–" symbol. It only gets used if the answer is a negative number. If your answer is positive, leave that column blank and begin your answer in the second column. For example, if your answer is 28, write 2 in the second column and 8 in the third column. Fill in the circle that contains a 2 below the 2 and the circle that contains an 8 below the 8.

If the answer contains a decimal, enter a "." in the appropriate column. There is a circle that contains a "." that can be filled in. It is important that you do not skip a column in the middle of your answer. For example, if your answer is 203, don't skip the 0 and just leave the column blank! Take time to check your answers carefully. If you forget to write in a digit or fail to fill out the corresponding circle, your answer will be marked wrong even if you calculated the correct answer.

58. Solve and give answer in decimal form:
$(\frac{5}{8} - \frac{1}{4}) \div \frac{1}{6} =$

59. The product of two consecutive integers is 156. What is their sum?

60. For what positive value of x does $\frac{3x}{18} = \frac{3}{2}$?

61. A circle has a circumference of x feet and an area of y square feet. If $x = 2y$, what is the radius of the circle?

62. For what value of x is $3(6 + x) = x(8 - 3)$?

CONTINUE ON TO THE NEXT PAGE ▶

Multiple Choice Problems

QUESTIONS 63–114

DIRECTIONS: Find the solution to each problem; then choose the best answer from the options given. Mark the letter of your answer choice on the answer sheet. You may use your test booklet or paper provided by the proctor as scrap paper for your calculations. However, DO NOT make calculations or put any stray marks on your answer sheet.

---

63. X is 30% of Y and Y is 45% of 600. What is the value of X?

A. 54
B. 81
C. 99
D. 180

64. M O

−14 −12 −10 −8 −6 −4 −2 0 2 4 6 8 10

N (not shown) is a point on the number line such that $\overline{MN}$ is $\frac{2}{5}$ the length of $\overline{MO}$. What is the location of point N?

E. −15
F. −6
G. 6
H. 9

65. Let $X = \frac{3}{5}$, $Y = 0.6$, and $Z = 0.59$. Compare the values of each number.

A. $X = Y = Z$
B. $X > Y > Z$
C. $X = Y > Z$
D. $X < Y < Z$

66. If s is positive and $s^2 = 75$, between which two numbers does s lie?

E. 4 and 5
F. 5 and 6
G. 6 and 7
H. 8 and 9

67. NUMBER OF BOOKS READ DURING THE SUMMER

Books Read	15	20	12	18
Number of Students	4	3	3	5

The table above shows the number of books read by 15 students during the summer. What is the mean number of books read per student?

A. 10.4
B. 12.4
C. 15.5
D. 16.4

68. What is the greatest prime number less than 23?

E. 17
F. 19
G. 20
H. 21

69. $7p(3 - 5q) =$

A. $21 - 5q$
B. $21 - 35q$
C. $21p - 35q$
D. $21p - 35pq$

CONTINUE ON TO THE NEXT PAGE ▶

70. What is the least integer greater than $\frac{31}{3}$?

E. 10
F. 11
G. 12
H. 13

71. W is a point that is not on line *n*. How many lines can be drawn through W that are perpendicular to line *n*?

A. 1
B. 2
C. 3
D. 4

72. At 6:00 a.m., the temperature was 7 degrees below zero Fahrenheit. At noon, the temperature was 10 degrees higher. At 6:00 p.m., the temperature was 5 degrees cooler than it was at noon. What was the temperature at 6:00 p.m.?

E. −2°
F. −1°
G. 3°
H. 5°

73.

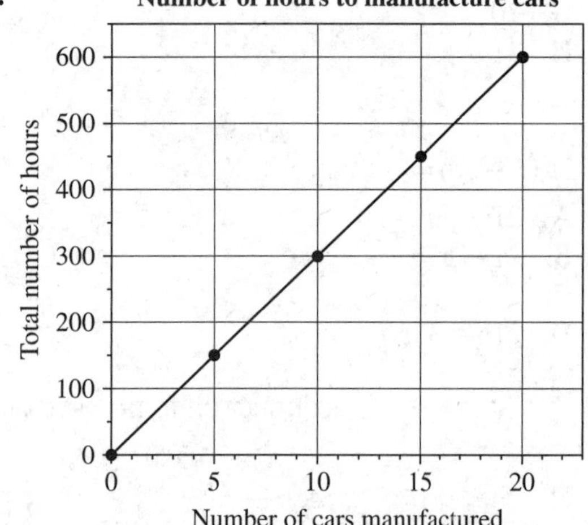

The graph above shows the relationship between the number of cars manufactured and the number of hours it took to manufacture them. How many hours did it take to manufacture one car?

A. 20 hours
B. 30 hours
C. 40 hours
D. 50 hours

74. The product of a nonzero integer and 12 has the same value as the product of 3 and the square of the integer. What is the integer?

E. 2
F. 3
G. 4
H. 6

75.

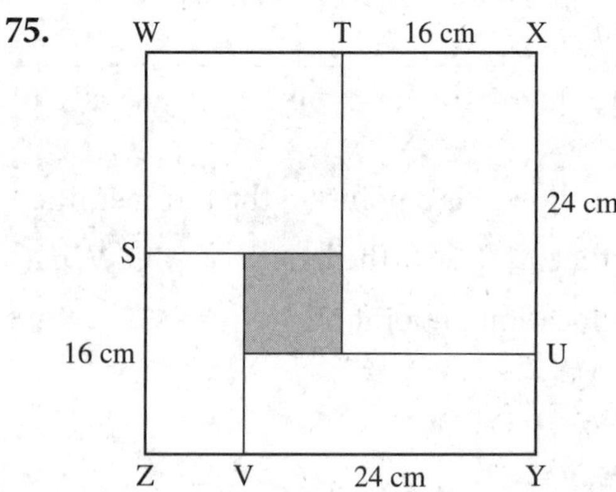

WXYZ is a square that is made up of rectangles and squares. The side length of WXYZ is 32 centimeters. SZ and TX are each 16 cm. UX and VY are 24 cm. What is the area of the shaded region?

A. 16 sq cm
B. 24 sq cm
C. 36 sq cm
D. 64 sq cm

76. Which of the following is equivalent to the inequality $17 > x + 3$?

E. $x < 14$
F. $x > 14$
G. $x < -14$
H. $x < 20$

CONTINUE ON TO THE NEXT PAGE ▶

77. $(-5x+8)-(2+x)=$

A. $-6x+6$
B. $-6x+10$
C. $-4x+10$
D. $4x+6$

78. What is the sum of 30% of 3 and 3% of 30?

E. 0.6
F. 0.9
G. 1.2
H. 1.8

79. If $42{,}592 = 2^x \times 11^y$, what is xy?

A. 8
B. 9
C. 15
D. 22

80. Stuart and Brandy live 5 miles apart on the same street. Stuart starts jogging at 3 miles per hour from his house to Brandy's house. At the same time, Brandy rides her bicycle at 12 miles per hour from her house to Stuart's house. How far from Stuart's house will they meet?

E. 1 mile
F. 2.5 miles
G. 3 miles
H. 4 miles

81. What is the smallest possible integer value of x in order for the product of 720 and x to result in a perfect square?

A. 2
B. 3
C. 5
D. 10

82. One-fourth the product of two numbers is 4. If one of the numbers is 8, what is the sum of the two numbers?

E. 2
F. 8
G. 9
H. 10

83. There were 5,000 beads in a container. Out of 25 beads, 13 were gold and 12 were silver. Which is the best estimate of the total number of gold beads in the container?

A. 400
B. 600
C. 650
D. 2,600

84. The area of a rectangle is 165 square feet. If the width is 11 feet, what is the perimeter?

E. 15 feet
F. 26 feet
G. 37 feet
H. 52 feet

85. The bakery sells 7 different types of bagels. Melissa orders one type of bagel. Then Julio orders a different type of bagel. How many different ways can Melissa and Julio order?

A. 13
B. 14
C. 27
D. 42

86. The operation $x\Delta$ is defined as follows: $x\Delta = x - 2$. What is the value of $\frac{6\Delta}{3\Delta}$?

E. 1
F. 2
G. 3
H. 4

CONTINUE ON TO THE NEXT PAGE ▶

87. What is the value of $xy+\frac{x}{y}$ when $x=-1.5$ and $y=-0.3$?

A. -4.55
B. -3.20
C. 0.95
D. 5.45

88. Jerri was x years old 5 years ago. Serena is half as old as Jerri is now. In terms of x, how old is Serena?

E. $\frac{1}{2}(5x)$
F. $\frac{1}{2}(x-5)$
G. $\frac{1}{2}(x+5)$
H. $\frac{1}{2}x-5$

89.

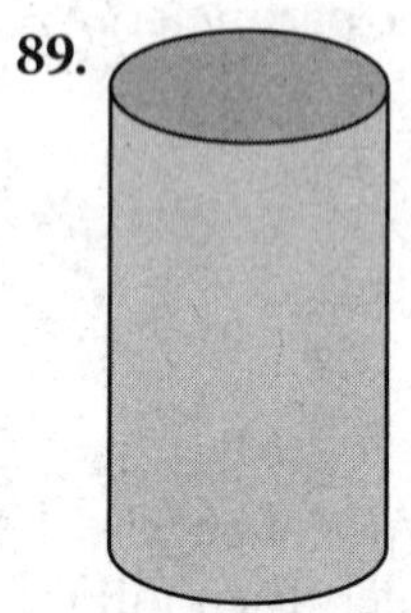

The diagram above shows a cylindrical pipe that is painted gray on the side. The pipe is 9 cm tall and has a diameter of 10 cm. What is the area of the painted portion of the pipe?

A. 20π sq cm
B. 60π sq cm
C. 90π sq cm
D. 140π sq cm

90. What is the least common multiple of X and Y?

$X=2\times2\times2\times2$
$Y=2\times2\times2\times3$

E. 2×3
F. $2^3\times3$
G. $2^4\times3$
H. $2^6\times3$

91. In a scale drawing, 1 centimeter represents 200 meters. How many square centimeters on the drawing represent 10,000 square meters?

A. 0.0025 sq cm
B. 0.025 sq cm
C. 0.25 sq cm
D. 2.50 sq cm

92. Matthew has 16 coins. Together, the coins have a value of $2.19. He spends 7 quarters, 3 dimes, and 1 nickel on a bottle of water. What coins does he have left?

E. 1 quarter and 1 penny
F. 2 dimes and 1 penny
G. 1 nickel and 2 dimes
H. 1 nickel and 4 pennies

93. x, y, and z are consecutive multiples of 4, counting from smallest to largest. What is $x+z$ in terms of y?

A. $2y$
B. $4y$
C. $2y+8$
D. $2y-8$

CONTINUE ON TO THE NEXT PAGE ▶

94. A rectangle has a width of 24 inches and a length of 72 inches. It is made up of squares of the same size. What is the largest possible size of the squares?

E. 6 in. by 6 in.
F. 8 in. by 8 in.
G. 9 in. by 9 in.
H. 24 in. by 24 in.

95. The surface area of the rectangular prism in the picture is 220 cm². The square base has a dimension of 4 cm by 5 cm. What is the height of the prism?

A. 4 cm
B. 5 cm
C. 10 cm
D. 20 cm

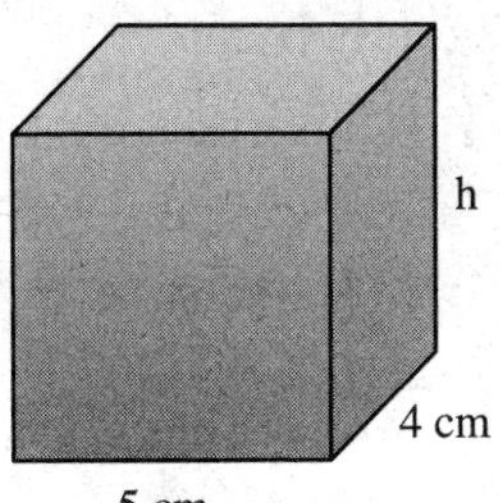

96. What fraction, reduced to its lowest terms, is halfway between $\frac{2}{3}$ and 0.2?

E. $\frac{2}{13}$

F. $\frac{2}{30}$

G. $\frac{7}{15}$

H. $\frac{13}{30}$

97. Which of the following indicates that x is greater than 12 and that x is less than or equal to 3 times the value of y?

A. $4 \leq x < y$

B. $4 < 3x \leq y$

C. $4 < x \leq \frac{y}{3}$

D. $4 < \frac{x}{3} \leq y$

98. If $x = 1$ and $y = 2$, what is the value of $\frac{2x^y}{y^{2x}}$?

E. $\frac{1}{4}$

F. $\frac{1}{2}$

G. 1

H. 4

99. The following table shows the amount of trash put into landfills in the United States. What is the median weight of trash for the years shown?

AMOUNT OF TRASH PUT INTO LANDFILLS (IN MILLIONS OF TONS)

Year	1960	1970	1980	1990	2000	2003	2005	2007	2009
Amount of Trash	83	113	134	142	136	134	139	138	135

A. 83
B. 113
C. 134
D. 135

CONTINUE ON TO THE NEXT PAGE ▶

100. Selena collected six times as many signatures as Liza on a petition. Clare collected 5 times as many signatures as Liza. If Clare collected 150 signatures, how many signatures did Selena collect?

E. 25
F. 30
G. 125
H. 180

101.

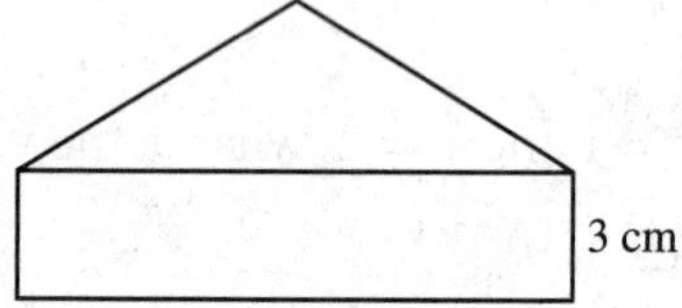

The base of the triangle has the same measure as the length of the rectangle. The width of the rectangle is 3 cm. The area of the triangle is twice the area of the rectangle. What is the height of the triangle?

A. 4 cm
B. 6 cm
C. 8 cm
D. 12 cm

102. Merle has 500 eggs that he needs to pack into egg cartons. Each egg carton can hold 12 eggs. How many more eggs does Merle need to completely fill the last egg carton?

E. 4
F. 5
G. 6
H. 7

103.

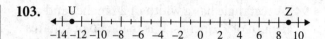

U Z
−14 −12 −10 −8 −6 −4 −2 0 2 4 6 8 10

If $\overline{UZ}$ is divided into 4 equal parts by points W, X, and Y (not shown), what position will point X fall on? (Assume $W < X < Y$.)

A. −7.5
B. −5.5
C. −2
D. 2

104. Marylou bought a used car that has been driven 95,200 miles. Saundra bought a used car that has been driven 88,000 miles. If Marylou drives 3,600 miles a year and Saundra drives 5,400 miles a year, after how many years will Marylou and Saundra have the same miles on their car?

E. 1
F. 2
G. 3
H. 4

105. When n is divided by 7, the remainder is 4. What is the remainder when $n + 3$ is divided by 7?

A. 0
B. 2
C. 4
D. 5

CONTINUE ON TO THE NEXT PAGE ▶

106. Julio has a bag containing 7 red marbles, 8 blue marbles, 3 green marbles, and 9 yellow marbles. He randomly draws 3 red marbles, 1 blue marble, and 2 yellow marbles from the bag. What is the probability that the next marble he draws will be green?

E. $\frac{1}{5}$

F. $\frac{1}{6}$

G. $\frac{1}{7}$

H. $\frac{1}{8}$

107. For how many integer values of x is $\frac{2x}{3x} < 0$? (Assume $x \neq 0$)

A. 0
B. 1
C. 2
D. 3

108. _____, 5, 7, _____, _____, _____, _____

In the list above, each number is one-third the sum of the number that comes before it and the number that comes after it. What is the first number in the list?

E. 1
F. 3
G. 4
H. 8

109. A rectangle is drawn on a coordinate plane. The coordinates of one corner of the rectangle are (0, 0). The coordinates of the opposite corner are (6, 5). Which of the following is a possible set of coordinates for one of the other corners?

A. (0, 6)
B. (0, −6)
C. (6, 0)
D. (−6, 6)

110. Jerry needs $\frac{3}{4}$ cup of oil and 1 cup of vinegar to make salad dressing. If he only has $\frac{2}{3}$ cup of vinegar, how much oil should he use?

E. $\frac{1}{2}$ cup

F. $\frac{1}{3}$ cup

G. $\frac{1}{4}$ cup

H. $\frac{1}{6}$ cup

CONTINUE ON TO THE NEXT PAGE ▶

111. This week, Roxie exercised $\frac{5}{8}$ as many hours as she did last week. If she exercised $6\frac{2}{3}$ hours this week, how many hours did she exercise last week?

A. $3\frac{3}{4}$

B. $4\frac{1}{6}$

C. $9\frac{3}{5}$

D. $10\frac{2}{3}$

112. Allie buys 8 DVDs. The mean price of all 8 DVDs was $9.25. If Allie returns one of the DVDs, the mean price of the remaining DVDs drops to $8. What was the price of the DVD Allie returned?

E. $10.00
F. $10.25
G. $18.00
H. $18.50

113. Paul earns $8.42 an hour. He worked $1\frac{1}{2}$ hours on Monday, Wednesday, and Friday. He worked $3\frac{3}{4}$ hours on Saturday. How much did Paul earn that week?

A. $37.50
B. $78.45
C. $69.47
D. $34.51

114. At a certain college, 225 of its 300 graduates received a business degree. What percentage of the students did not receive a business degree?

E. 25%
F. 30%
G. 35%
H. 15%

THIS IS THE END OF THE TEST. IF TIME REMAINS, YOU MAY CHECK YOUR ANSWERS. BE SURE THAT THERE ARE NO STRAY MARKS, PARTIALLY FILLED ANSWER CIRCLES, OR INCOMPLETE ERASURES ON YOUR ANSWER SHEET.

Test 1 Answer Key

1. D
2. E
3. C
4. E
5. A
6. F
7. C
8. H
9. C
10. E
11. B
12. E
13. B
14. F
15. A
16. H
17. A
18. H
19. C
20. G
21. D
22. F
23. D
24. E
25. D
26. H
27. D
28. G
29. D
30. E
31. D
32. H
33. D
34. H
35. D
36. H
37. D
38. H
39. C
40. F
41. D
42. H
43. A
44. H
45. D
46. G
47. B
48. H
49. A
50. H
51. C
52. E
53. C
54. H
55. C
56. H
57. B

58. 2.25

59. 25

60. 9

61. 1

62. 9

63. B
64. F
65. C
66. H
67. D
68. F
69. D
70. F
71. A
72. E
73. B
74. G
75. D
76. E
77. A
78. H
79. C
80. E
81. C
82. H
83. D
84. H
85. D
86. H
87. D
88. G
89. C
90. G
91. C
92. H
93. A
94. H
95. C
96. H
97. D
98. F
99. D
100. H
101. D
102. E
103. C
104. H
105. A
106. G
107. A
108. H
109. C
110. E
111. D
112. G
113. C
114. E

Explanation of Answers—ELA Section

Revising/Editing

1. **(D)** The question asks you to correct the dangling modifier. The dangling modifier is "journeying from salt water to freshwater in order to breed." This comes right before "the wonder of nature." Yet "the wonder of nature" is not journeying. Options A, B, and C are all incorrect. None of them makes the correction that is needed, which is placing "salmon" near the modifying phrase. Salmon is what is making the journey. Option D indicates this because the modifying clause follows the word "salmon." Therefore, Option D is the answer.

2. **(E)** The question asks you to make another edit, and your choices are between apostrophes and commas. Option E asks you to add an apostrophe to "lakes," but "lakes" is not showing possession, so it doesn't need an apostrophe. Option G asks you to remove a comma, but that comma is necessary, as it is helping to separate a nonessential phrase from the rest of the sentence. Option H asks you to insert a comma where one is not necessary. The correct answer is Option E. That change needs to be made. "Salmon," singular or plural, does not end in "s," so the apostrophe that shows possession needs to be before the "s."

3. **(C)** This question asks you to look for a pronoun that is used incorrectly. There is no pronoun in sentence 1, so Option A can't be right. Sentences 2 and 4 have pronouns, but they are used correctly. It is sentence 3 that contains the problem. Throughout this paragraph "salmon" has been used as a plural noun, and the pronouns used to refer to it are "they" or "them." Sentence 3, however, uses "it": "When it is time for it to breed." The second "it" should be "them"; therefore, Option C is the correct answer.

4. **(E)** The question asks you to make an edit to the paragraph. All your choices have to do with commas. Option F and Option G ask you to insert a comma before a prepositional phrase, but there is no reason to do that. Those phrases are essential to the sentence. Option H asks you to insert a comma between a subject and its verb; that is always wrong. Option E asks you to insert a comma where it is needed because "upriver" is part of a list of items. Three or more items in a list should always be separated by commas; therefore, Option E is correct.

5. **(A)** This question asks you to look for a mechanics error. The error can be found in sentence 1. The word "it's" has an unnecessary apostrophe. Adding an apostrophe to a personal pronoun creates a contraction; it does not help it show possession. So, sentence 1 could be read: "to it is hatching ground." That is wrong. Therefore, Option A is the answer.

6. **(F)** This question asks you to pick the sentence that is punctuated correctly, so you need to pay special attention to any punctuation. What varies in these choices is the comma placement. The sentence needs commas for two different things. It needs a comma after the introductory clause and commas after items in the list. Option E provides commas for the items in the list, but it does not provide one after the introductory clause. Option G and Option H offer a comma after the introductory clause, but there are no commas separating the items in the list; Option H also inserts an unnecessary comma after the word "things." Option F offers both a comma after the introductory clause and commas after the items in the list, so it is the correct choice.

7. **(C)** Sentence 3, as well as the rest of the passage, is written in the past tense. Option A and Option D are in the past perfect tense, which is not needed here. Option B is a participle describing African Americans as they were escaping, so it needs to stay in the progressive tense, not the past. Option A is the correct answer because it changes the present tense "help" into the past tense so that it matches the rest of the passage.

8. **(H)** The best place for sentence 11, which tells about other routes, would be right after the last part of sentence 6, which reads "but there were other networks in other states also." This introduces sentence 11, which tells about other routes. Placing the sentence there would also keep the information about the routes in the same place in the passage. Any of the other options separates the topic and makes the passage disjointed.

9. **(C)** The question asks which sentence is irrelevant to the main idea of the passage. Option A is important because it gives a detail about how the Underground Railroad operated. Option B gives details about who made up the Underground Railroad, and Option D tells what the effect of the Underground Railroad was. Option C explains why a bounty would be placed on someone's head and could be removed from the passage without hindering the reader's understanding of the operations of the Underground Railroad in any way. Therefore, Option C is the correct answer.

10. **(E)** The question asks which sentence would best support sentence 7, which is about the secretive nature of the business. Options F and G give general facts related to the topic but do not support sentence 7. Option H explains what being secretive is (avoiding nosy neighbors), but option E is specific about penalties for being found out, so it is the best option.

11. **(B)** The question asks about a concluding sentence for the entire paragraph. Option A sums up the paragraph it follows but not the whole passage. Option C is too vague. Option D focuses on Harriet Tubman, not the entire passage. Option B is the one that restates the general premise of the passage and gives a reason for people risking their lives.

12. **(E)** Options F and G are both subordinating conjunctions. They can't be used because they turn the first clause into a dependent clause joined to the second clause by a coordinating conjunction. Although they are good choices, the sentence would have to be revised in order to use either of those transitions. Option H does not work at all because it doesn't make sense with the sentence. Option E is the only transition that makes sense and can be added to the beginning of the sentence without causing grammatical errors.

13. **(B)** Option A joins the sentences with "moreover," which indicates that a second fact will be given, but it does not suggest that the two sentences affect each other. Option C indicates that being a diverse mix caused these people to work together. Option D suggests that working together caused them to be a diverse mix. Option B tells us that, in spite of being a diverse mix, these people worked together. That is the correct relationship.

14. (F) The question asks you to show the relationship between sentence 7 and sentence 8. Option E uses "because," which indicates that meat preservation was the result of regions becoming known for their methods. That doesn't make sense. Option G uses "although" to make it seem that regions became known for their methods in spite of the fact that meat preservation developed. That also doesn't make sense. Option H tells us meat preservation developed "when" regions became known. That seems backward also. The only option that makes sense is Option F, "as" meat preservation developed. This shows the proper relationship. As sentence 7 happened, sentence 8 was able to happen. Option F is the correct answer.

15. (A) The question asks about comma errors; therefore, you should look at how the commas are used in each of the sentences listed. There are commas in all the sentence choices, but only one is misused. That is in sentence 6: "This method worked very well, and was widely used even in ancient times." This comma is not needed. It is not helping the conjunction to join two independent clauses because the second part of the sentence, "was widely used even in ancient times," can't stand alone. Therefore, that comma should be removed, and Option A is the correct answer.

16. (H) This question asks you to find a sentence that is irrelevant to the main idea of the passage. The passage is about the history of cured meat. Sentence 4 is about an early method of curing. Sentences 10 and 12 are about the development of cured meat in the Middle Ages. Sentence 5, however, veers off to talk about other things that Ireland is known for. That is irrelevant, so Option H is the answer.

17. (A) This question asks you to pick the choice that best supports sentence 11. Sentence 11 tells us that cities were famous for their particular cured meat. Option B simply restates that thought. Option C and Option D are a little more specific, but clearly the best support comes from Option A. Option A gives specific examples that support the statement that sentence 11 makes. Therefore, Option A is the best choice.

18. (H) Again, it is important to pay attention to what the question asks. Here, you are instructed to look for **precise** language. The first three options include phrases like "types of meat," "many years ago," and "a long time." If you study the options carefully, you will note that Option H uses precise words, while the other options are more vague. Instead of "a long time," Option H says "more than 2,000 years." Instead of "types of cured meat," Option H says "salami sausage." Instead of "ancient cities," Option H says "the ancient city of Salamis." Option H is definitely the most precisely worded option.

19. (C) The question asks you to find the best concluding sentence for the entire passage. The passage is telling about the evolution of cured meats. Option A, Option B, and Option D are details about cured meat that could be included in the passage, but they don't sum up the passage, so they don't make good concluding sentences. Option C is the only sentence given that brings closure to the passage by restating the main idea. That is the correct answer.

20. (G) Option E is not correct because the comma is needed after the introductory phrase "in fact." Option F is incorrect because a comma after "meat" would separate the subject from the verb, which is an error. So, the problem is with the verb. The verb "was" is past tense. Option G offers the present tense ("is"), while Option H offers the future tense ("will be"). The sentence is talking about what is happening right now, so the verb should be in the present tense. Therefore, Option G is the correct answer.

Reading Comprehension

21. **(D)** This question asks you to determine the general theme of the passage. Option A is mentioned but not in any detail. Option B, though this topic is discussed, is not the theme of the passage. Option C is a detail that is mentioned but not the focus of the entire passage. Thus, the best answer is Option D.

22. **(F)** This question asks you to make an inference based on the information in the passage. Option E may be true, but there is not enough information in the passage to draw this conclusion. Option G may or may not be true, but there is little in the passage to support this idea. There is no information on when Emperor Qin died, so Option H can be eliminated. Option F is the best answer.

23. **(D)** The question asks specifically about the Qin Terra-cotta Warriors and Horses. In order to answer the question, you must look at the information in the passage and use it to infer the answer. Option A may be true, but there is nothing to support this idea in the passage. Option C could be true or false, but the passage does not discuss this possibility. Option D is supported by the passage, which tells in great detail what the soldiers looked like and how they were dressed. So Option D is correct.

24. **(E)** The phrase that "this preservation technique was not known in the West until the eighteenth century" implies that the Chinese were more advanced technologically than the Western world was. There is no evidence for Option F. The concept of being well educated probably did not exist at that time. There is no evidence to support either Option G or H.

25. **(D)** This is an inference question. It is necessary to look for information that supports one of the options. Option A could be true, but that is not the suggestion of the terra-cotta army. While Option B is somewhat supported by the fact that it is believed that Emperor Qin unified China, this is not what the existence of the terra-cotta army suggests. There is nothing to suggest that Option C is supported by the passage. There is no evidence in the passage that China was at peace, although it could be true. Choice D is the most logical suggestion.

26. **(H)** To answer this question, you have to go through the passage and try to find the one topic that is not discussed. Options E and F are discussed in the paragraph. So is Option G. That leaves Option H. There is no mention of the cost of creating the terra-cotta army.

27. **(D)** This question asks you to determine the general theme of the passage. While Option A is mentioned, it is not in the context of why scientists believe in the big bang theory. It is also not the main focus of the passage. Options B and C are mentioned, but they are details, not the theme of the passage. The passage describes what scientists are trying to achieve with the Large Hadron Collider. Thus, the correct answer is Option D.

28. **(G)** This is an inference question. You need to make an inference based on the information in the passage. Option E is not supported by the passage, which says that the fundamental particles are created when proton particles smash into each other. Option F is not suggested by the passage; some of the fundamental particles have been identified, but there is no mention of some being improperly identified. Option H seems to be refuted by the passage since it seems difficult to test for them. Option G is the one that is implied by the passage; some fundamental particles may never be identified positively.

29. **(D)** To answer this question, you need to read the passage carefully to see which option is correct. It is impossible to tell whether or not Option A is correct, since this subject is not mentioned. The same holds true for Option B. No discussion of how long the collider can work is included in the passage. Option C is very unlikely since astronomy and physics are two very distinct sciences. This leaves Option D as the best choice.

30. **(E)** To answer this question, you need to concentrate on information about atoms and quarks that is present in the passage. Option F is not mentioned in the passage, so it cannot be the correct choice. Option G is clearly incorrect since a careful reading of the passage will reveal they are different from one another. Option H is not correct either; a careful reading will show that an atom is not a fundamental particle. Thus E is the correct choice.

31. **(D)** To answer this question, you need to review the passage and find what is true of the Higgs boson. You will also need to use the information to figure out the correct answer. Based on the information in the passage, Option A seems to be true, so that cannot be the answer. Option B is something that the passage says indirectly, so it can be eliminated. Option C is stated in the passage. This leaves Option D. The passage says that it was not verified.

32. **(H)** To make an inference, you need to weigh all the information in a passage and come to the most logical conclusion. Option E doesn't seem to be correct. The way the passage talks about dark matter, it would seem to be a separate entity from an atom. Option F seems incorrect for the very same reason. There is nothing in the passage to suggest that Option G is correct. This leaves Option H. This is the best answer.

33. **(D)** This question asks you to determine the main idea or general theme of the passage. Option A is mentioned in the passage, but it is only a detail, not a general theme. Options B and C are details in the passage as well, not the main focus of it. The passage describes how a wasteland was changed into a wildlife sanctuary. Therefore, the correct answer is Option D.

34. **(H)** Check back through the passage to answer this question. Review what is mentioned as being at Haller Park. Options E and G can be eliminated. They are all directly mentioned. The passage also names fish that are in the ponds, so Option F is not correct either. This leaves Option H. There is no mention of there being sheep in Haller Park.

35. **(D)** Option A cannot be verified; it could be true, but this is not discussed in the passage. The same is true of Option B. The passage says that most animals are rescued, not that all animals must be rescued animals, so Option C is not correct. This leaves Option D; the passage says that the cement company that created the wasteland backed Haller's efforts.

36. **(H)** You have to figure out why the author used this information in the passage. Option E doesn't seem to be the reason that the crocodile farm was mentioned, even though it is true in some areas. Haller Park is an experiment, but that is not the reason for the crocodile farm being mentioned. There is no evidence that Option G is correct. Option H is the best answer. This is the most likely reason the crocodile farm was mentioned.

37. **(D)** You need to use your best judgment to answer this question. Option A is appealing, but what Haller did was not so much about creating jobs as transforming a wasteland. Option B and C are possibilities, but again there is nothing that would be transformed. Option D, however, is very similar to what he achieved. This is the best answer.

38. **(H)** To answer this question, you have to examine each option carefully. Many of the options are appealing, but it is important to pick the one option that seems most likely based on the information at hand. Option E is probably true, but other than the fact that the park has animals, there is no specific evidence that Haller was an animal lover. Again, Options F or G may be true, but this side of Haller's personality is not mentioned. Option H is the best answer. It is clear that Haller had great determination based on how he strove to create the park, so this is the best answer.

39. **(C)** This question asks you to determine the main idea or general theme of the passage. Option A is mentioned in the passage, but it is only a detail, not a general theme. Option B is discussed in passing, but it is clearly not the theme. Option D is also only a detail from the passage. The passage talks about whether or not dolphins should be free. This is the main idea. Therefore, the correct answer is Option C.

40. **(F)** The example of how people can swim with dolphins suggests that they are gentle. Options E and H are not the reasons for starting with this example, since many animals kept in captivity do not interact directly with humans because they are dangerous. Polar bears, for example, are successfully kept in captivity, but people do not enter polar bear enclosures for an "unforgettable" experience. Option G focuses on dolphins learning tricks, but this also does not have much to do with why the author stresses that people find it "unforgettable" to swim with them.

41. **(D)** You will need to review the passage to answer this question. Scan through the passage to find what reasons are mentioned for allowing dolphins to go free. Options A, B, and C are definitely mentioned. Option D is mentioned as a reason for keeping dolphins in captivity, so Option D is the correct answer.

42. **(H)** Options E and F are not included in the passage, so it is impossible to know if either one is true or not. Option G is also not mentioned. Option H is the correct answer.

43. **(A)** You will need to analyze the author's intent from what the passage says. It talks about how some people think that dolphins should not be in captivity. The information about Dr. Marino helps to back up those who argue that dolphins are very much like humans, but the intent probably was to lend the passage more authority. That is why the author cites Dr. Marino's credentials. Option A is the correct one. Options B and C are not supported by the passage, nor is Option D.

44. **(H)** Option E is possible, but not the most likely probability based on the information in the passage. Option F seems unlikely. The passage says that dolphins reproduce well in captivity. Option G seems very remote. This leaves Option H. It is likely more dolphins will be attacked by sharks and more will probably die.

45. **(D)** This question asks you to determine the main idea or general theme of the passage. Option A is mentioned in the passage, but it is only a detail, not a general theme. Options B and C are details in the passage, not the main focus of it. The passage describes how Beryl Markham made her mark on history; that is the main theme. Thus, the correct answer is Option D.

46. (G) Use the information in the passage to find the answer to this question. The passage doesn't say whether Beryl became a better person after meeting Tom Campbell Black, so Option E can be eliminated. She did write a book, but that was much later on, so Option F cannot be the effect that Tom Campbell Black had on Beryl Markham. She did not leave Kenya after meeting him; she became a bush pilot there. Consequently, Option G is the correct answer.

47. (B) Option C can be eliminated; it wasn't particularly brave for her to return to Kenya. And while Options A and D are both achievements, the most impressive action that Beryl Markham took was to do something dangerous and hard to do. Option B is the correct answer.

48. (H) Option E cannot be the answer. We are not told whether Beryl Markham's plane was lighter than Charles Lindbergh's. Nor do we learn whether or not she was newer to aviation. Option G is true, but it's likely that Charles Lindbergh's flight was also long. We are left with Option H. This information is in the passage. It is the correct answer.

49. (A) You have to use the information and your own prior knowledge to answer this question. Option A is appealing. She grew up there and probably considered it her home. Option B and C are not mentioned in the passage, so we cannot determine if either is correct. Option D is also not mentioned in the passage, so we need to turn back to Option A. This is the best answer.

50. (H) You need to use the information in the passage to make an inference about Beryl Markham. She certainly had a mind of her own, but there is no sign that Option E was true. Option F is another trait that doesn't seem to apply to Beryl Markham. Option G is a possibility, but in fact, she was practical in that she knew the dangers she faced. Option H is the best answer.

51. (C) This question asks you to determine the general theme of the passage. Options A and B are discussed in the passage, but they are details, not the theme. Option D is not discussed in the passage. The passage contrasts myths about army ants with facts about what they are really like. Thus, the correct answer is Option C.

52. (E) This is an inference question. You need to make an inference based on the information in the passage. Option F is not supported by the passage. While the author does imply that the stories are interesting, she actually also implies that they are not factual. Neither Option G nor H is suggested by the passage either. Although they could be true, the author has not implied anything on those subjects. Option E is supported by the passage, which states, "much of what you have been told about army ants is probably exaggeration."

53. (C) To answer this question, you need to read the passage carefully to see which option is correct. The opposite of Option A is implied in the passage, which states that the ants are tiny, vulnerable to the sun, and almost blind. Option B could very well be true, but the subject of queens is not addressed in the passage, so it can't be the answer. Option D is a misstatement, since the passage tells the reader that worker army ants carry the young. That leaves Option C, which is correct, as the passage states: "Some species of army ants march in columns, while others create a fan shape."

54. (H) To answer this question, you need to look carefully at the passage. Options E, F, and G are all mentioned in the text: "they kill every insect, lizard, or snake in their path"; "the remaining two weeks are spent in one spot, raising a new generation of young ants"; and "is not able to see well." The only option left is H. That is correct. In fact, the passage states that "bright sunlight can kill it in a few minutes," so they definitely can't bask in the sun; Option H is correct.

55. (C) This is an inference question. You need to make an inference based on the information in the passage. The passage tells us that the ants are tiny; they are definitely not stronger than people, Option A. The passage never mentions that the ants have any smell, so the answer is not Option B. Although the ants do eat the bugs in the house, it would be unlikely that the people would leave in order to let the ants get the bugs out of their houses, which rules out Option D. The only option left is C, that the ants could bite people, and they are fearful of them. This idea is implied by the passage, so Option C is correct.

56. (H) The question asks you to examine the relationship between ant-birds and army ants. Although you might assume that ant-birds would eat army ants [Option E], the passage doesn't mention that, so it can't be your choice. To answer this question, you need to reread the section of the passage that talks about ant-birds. If you do this, you will find that only Option H is an accurate description of the relationship between army ants and ant-birds. Army ants help ant-birds to find food because they flush insects out of the underbrush. There is no mention of any of the other three options. Option H is the only correct answer.

57. (B) To make an inference, you need to weigh all the information in a passage and come to the most logical conclusion. The general theme of the passage is that stories of army ants make them seem more dangerous than they actually are. Therefore, Option A is the opposite of what the author is expressing. Although the idea that army ants eat pests is introduced, it does not seem to be important to the author, as it is simply mentioned in passing. Option D is also wrong, because the author pointed out two different instances where army ants took care of their young. The correct answer is Option B, as the author continually downplays the danger that army ants present.

Explanation of Answers—Mathematics Section

58. $(\frac{5}{8}-\frac{1}{4})\div\frac{1}{6}=(\frac{5}{8}-\frac{2}{8})\div\frac{1}{6}$

$\frac{3}{8}\div\frac{1}{6}$

$\frac{3}{8}\times\frac{1}{5}$

$\frac{18}{8}$

$\frac{9}{4}$

Next, convert your answer to a decimal:
$\frac{9}{4}=2.25$

59. The first step is to estimate. Knowing that 12×12 is 144, try 12×13 (156). Add these integers together to find the answer: $12+13=25$.

60. Cross-multiply and then solve for x:

$\frac{3x}{18}=\frac{3}{2}$

$2(3x)=3(18)$

$6x=54$

$\frac{6x}{6}=\frac{54}{6}$

$x=9$

61. The formula for the circumference of a circle is $C=2\pi r$. The formula for the area of a circle is $A=\pi r^2$.

Substitute the formulas into the equation $x=2y$ to solve for the radius of the circle:

$x=2y$

$2\pi r=2(\pi r^2)$

$\frac{2}{2}\pi r=\pi r^2$

$\frac{2}{2}r=r^2$

$\frac{2}{2}=r$

$1=r$

62. $3(6+x)=x(8-3)$

$18+3x=8x-3x$

$18=2x$

$9=x$

63. (B) Translate the verbal descriptions into algebraic equations:

X is 30% of Y means $X=0.30Y$

Y is 45% of 600 means $Y=(0.45)(600)$

Solve for Y:

$Y=(0.45)(600)=270$

Substitute the value of Y into the first equation. Then solve for X:

$X=0.30Y$

$=(0.30)(270)$

$=81$

64. (F) The formula for the distance between two points on a number line is $\underline{b-a}$. Use the formula to find the length of MO.

$MO=O-M$

$=3-(-12)$

$=3+12$

$=15$

$\overline{MN}$ is $\frac{2}{5}$ the length of $\overline{MO}$, so its measure is $\frac{2}{5}\times15=6$ units.

To find the location of point N, start at point M (−12) and count 6 units to the right to −6.

65. (C) To order numbers, it's easiest to write them as decimals to the same place value: $X = \frac{3}{5} = \frac{6}{10} = 0.60$, $Y = 0.60$, and $Z = 0.59$. Thus $X = Y > Z$.

66. (H) Since 75 is not a perfect square, find the two perfect squares that lie on either side of 75: $64 < 75 < 81$.

Since $64 = 8^2$ and $81 = 9^2$:

$8^2 < 75 < 9^2$

$8^2 < s^2 < 9^2$

$8 < s < 9$

67. (D) The mean is the total number of books read divided by the number of students. The table shows that 4 students each read 15 books, 3 students each read 20 books, 3 students each read 12 books, and 5 students each read 18 books. Therefore, the total number of books read is the sum of $(4\times15)+(3\times20)+(3\times12)+(5\times18)$. The mean number of books read per student is:

$$\frac{(4\times15)+(3\times20)+(3\times12)+(5\times18)}{15} = \frac{60+60+36+90}{15}$$
$$= \frac{246}{15}$$
$$= 16.4$$

68. (F) A prime number has only two factors, 1 and itself. Count backward from 23 to find the greatest prime number that is less than 23:

23, 22, 21, 20, 19, . . .

The factors of 22 are 1, 2, 11, and 22, so 22 is not a prime number.

The factors of 21 are 1, 3, 7, and 21, so 21 is not a prime number.

The factors of 20 are 1, 2, 4, 5, 10, and 20, so 20 is not a prime number.

The factors of 19 are 1 and 19, so 19 is a prime number, and it is the greatest prime number that is less than 23.

69. (D) Use the distributive property to write $7p(3-5q)$ as an equivalent expression. The distributive property states that for all numbers a, b, and c, $a(b+c) = a(b) + a(c)$.

$$7p(3-5q) = (7p)(3) - (7p)(5q)$$
$$= 21p - 35pq$$

70. (F) $\frac{31}{3} = 10\frac{1}{3}$, so the least integer that is greater than $10\frac{1}{3}$ is 11.

71. (A) A perpendicular line forms a 90° angle with line n. You can only draw one perpendicular line through point W.

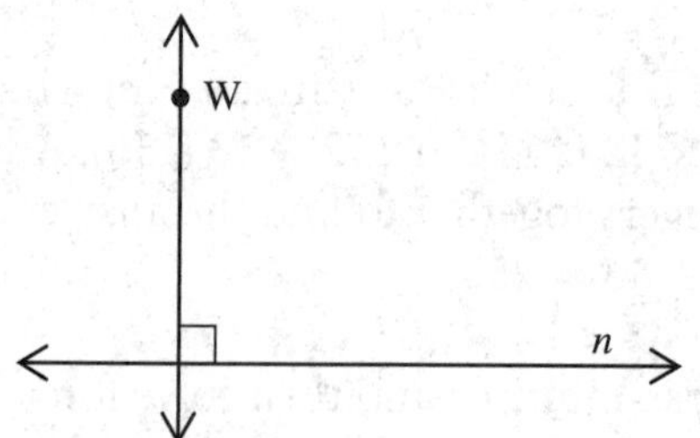

72. (E) At 6:00 a.m., the temperature was $-7°$. The temperature at noon was $-7° + 10° = 3°$. The temperature at 6:00 p.m. was $3° - 5° = -2°$.

73. (B) According to the graph, it took 150 hours to manufacture 5 cars, 300 hours to manufacture 10 cars, and so on. The graph is a straight line, so the rate of change is constant.

Let x represent the number of hours to manufacture one car:

$\frac{x}{1} = \frac{150}{5}$

$5x = 150$

$x = 30$

74. (G) Let x represent the nonzero integer. Translate the verbal description into an algebraic equation:

$$12x = 3x^2$$
$$4x = x^2$$
$$4 = x$$

75. (D) Since the side length of square WXYZ is 32 cm, WT = 16 cm, UY = 8 cm, VZ = 8 cm, and SW = 16 cm. The side lengths of the shaded region can be calculated by subtracting $WT - VZ = 16 - 8 = 8$ and $XU - SW = 24 - 16 = 8$. The shaded region is a square with side lengths of 8 cm. Therefore, the area of the shaded region is 64 sq cm.

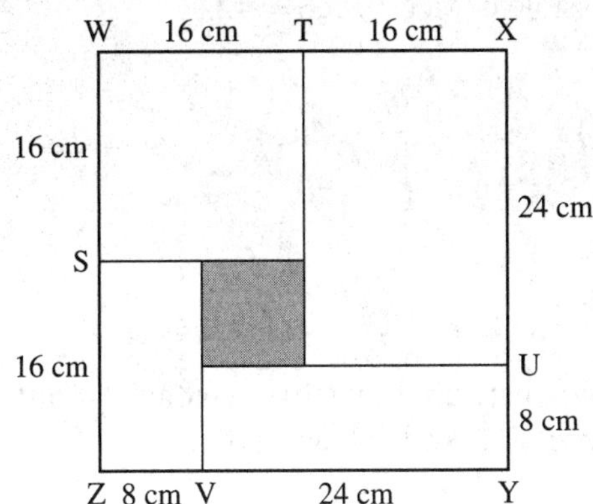

76. (E)

$$17 > x + 3$$
$$17 - 3 > x + 3 - 3$$
$$14 > x$$

That is the same as x < 14.

77. (A)

$$(-5x + 8) - (2 + x) = -5x + 8 - 2 - x$$
$$= -5x - x + 8 - 2$$
$$= -6x + 6$$

78. (H)

30% of $3 = (0.30)(3) = 0.90$

3% of $30 = (0.03)(30) = 0.90$

$0.90 + 0.90 = 1.80$

That is the same as 1.8.

79. (C) $42{,}592 = 2^x \times 11^y$

The equation tells us that 42,592 can be factored into powers of 2 and 11:

$42{,}592 =$

$2 \times 21{,}296 =$

$2 \times 2 \times 10{,}648 =$

$2 \times 2 \times 2 \times 5{,}324 =$

$2 \times 2 \times 2 \times 2 \times 2{,}662 =$

$2 \times 2 \times 2 \times 2 \times 2 \times 1{,}331 =$

$2 \times 2 \times 2 \times 2 \times 2 \times 2 \times 11 \times 121 =$

$2 \times 2 \times 2 \times 2 \times 2 \times 2 \times 11 \times 121 =$

$2 \times 2 \times 2 \times 2 \times 2 \times 2 \times 11 \times 11 \times 11 =$

$2^5 \times 11^3$

Therefore, $x = 5$ and $y = 3$, so $xy = 5 \times 3 = 15$.

80. (E) First, use the formula *distance* = *rate* × *time* to find the time when Stuart and Brandy will meet. The distance that Stuart travels is $3t$ (3 miles per hour times "time"). The distance that Brandy travels is $12t$ (12 miles per hour times "time"). The total distance they travel is 5 miles, the distance between the two houses:

$$3t + 12t = 5$$
$$15t = 5$$
$$t = \frac{1}{3}$$

Stuart and Brandy will meet at $t = \frac{1}{3}$. At $t = \frac{1}{3}$, the distance from Stuart's house is $3t = 3 \times \frac{1}{3} = 1$.

81. (C) First, break down 720 into its prime factorization:

$720 = 2 \times 2 \times 2 \times 2 \times 3 \times 3 \times 5 = 2^4 \times 3^2 \times 5^1$

Since the factor 5 is the only odd exponent, multiplying 720 by 5 would make the product a perfect square. $720 \times 5 = 3600 = 60^2$. Therefore, 5 is the smallest integer value for x which makes the product a perfect square.

82. (H) Let x and y represent the two numbers. Translate the verbal description into an algebraic equation:

$$\frac{1}{4}xy = 4$$

$$\frac{1}{4}(8y) = 4$$

$$8y = 16$$

$$y = 2$$

The sum of x and y is $8 + 2 = 10$.

83. (D) Let x represent the total number of gold beads in the container. We know 13 out of every 25 beads are gold. Set up a proportion to solve for x:

$$\frac{13}{25} = \frac{x}{5{,}000}$$

$$13(5{,}000) = 25x$$

$$\frac{13(5{,}000)}{25} = x$$

$$2{,}600 = x$$

84. (H) Let x represent the length of the rectangle:

$$11x = 165$$

$$x = 15$$

The width is 11 feet and the length is 15 feet, so the perimeter of the rectangle is $2(11) + 2(15) = 52$.

85. (D) Melissa has 7 types of bagels to choose from. Since Julio orders a different type of bagel, there are 6 different ways he can choose. Use the Fundamental Counting Principle to find the number of different ways Melissa and Julio can order. The Fundamental Counting Principle is likely already familiar to you, but—put simply—it is a way of accounting for the number of possible outcomes, given a variety of choices. For example, if you have two skirts and three shirts, what are the number of possible outfits you could make? Using the Fundamental Counting Principle, you would simply multiply 2 by 3 and find that 6 is the answer. In this problem, we must find out how many possible order combinations there are, so we take the number of Melissa's possible choices and multiply them with the number of Julio's possible choices: $7 \times 6 = 42$.

86. (H)

$$\frac{6'}{3'} = \frac{6-2}{3-2} = \frac{4}{1} = 4$$

87. (D) Substitute the values of x and y into the expression and solve:

$$xy + \frac{x}{y} = (-1.5)(-0.3) + \frac{-1.5}{-0.3}$$

$$= 0.45 + (5)$$

$$= 5.45$$

88. (G) Since Jerri was x years old 5 years ago, her current age is $x + 5$. This means Serena's age is $\frac{1}{2}(x + 5)$.

89. (C) The area of the painted portion of the pipe is called the lateral area. The formula for the lateral area L of a cylinder is $L = 2\pi rh$, where r is the radius and h is the height. Substitute the values of r and h into the formula to find the lateral area:

$$\begin{aligned} L &= 2\pi rh \\ &= 2\pi(5)(9) \\ &= 90\pi \end{aligned}$$

90. (G) The least common multiple (LCM) of X and Y is the product of the greatest power of each of its prime factors:

$$X = 2\times2\times2\times2 = 2^4$$

$$Y = 2\times2\times2\times3 = 2^3\times3$$

The LCM is $2^4\times3$.

91. (C) If one centimeter is equivalent to 200 meters, then 1 square centimeter is equivalent to 40,000 square meters:

$$(1\text{ cm})^2 = (200\text{ m})^2$$
$$1\text{ sq cm} = 40{,}000\text{ sq m}$$

Set up a proportion to find how many square centimeters is equivalent to 10 square meters:

$$\begin{aligned} \frac{1}{40{,}000} &= \frac{x}{10{,}000} \\ 40{,}000x &= 10{,}000 \\ x &= \frac{10{,}000}{40{,}000} \\ x &= 0.25\text{ sq cm} \end{aligned}$$

92. (H) The value of 7 quarters, 3 dimes, and 1 nickel is $\$1.75 + \$0.30 + \$0.05 = \$2.10$. If he spends \$2.10 on a bottle of water, he has 5 coins left that have a total value of \$0.09. The only possible combination for the 5 coins is 1 nickel and 4 pennies.

93. (A) If x is the smallest of the 3 consecutive multiples of 4, then $y = x + 4$ and $z = y + 4$. In terms of y, $x = y - 4$. Therefore, $x + z = (y - 4) + (y + 4) = 2y$.

94. (H) Since the rectangle is made up of squares of the same size, the side length of the square must be a factor of both 24 and 72. The largest possible size square will have a side length that is the greatest common factor (GCF) of 24 and 72. The GCF of 24 and 72 is 24. Therefore, the largest possible size is 24 in. by 24 in.

95. (C) The surface area of a prism is the sum of the area of the 6 faces, and each opposite pair of faces has the same rectangular area.

$$\text{Surface Area} = 2\times\text{Area}_{\text{base}} + 2\times\text{Area}_{\text{side}} + 2\times\text{Area}_{\text{front}}$$

$$\begin{aligned} 220\text{ cm}^2 &= 2\times(4\text{ cm}\times5\text{ cm}) + 2\times(4\text{ cm}\times\text{h}) + 2\times(5\text{ cm}\times\text{h}) \\ 220\text{ cm}^2 &= (40\text{ cm}^2) + (8\text{ cm})\text{h} + (10\text{ cm})\text{h} \\ 180\text{ cm}^2 &= (8\text{ cm})\text{h} + (10\text{ cm})\text{h} \\ 180\text{ cm}^2 &= (18\text{ cm})\text{h} \\ \text{Height} &= \frac{180\text{ cm}^2}{18\text{ cm}} \\ \text{Height} &= 10\text{ cm} \end{aligned}$$

96. (H) To find the value that is halfway between $\frac{2}{3}$ and 0.2, add and divide by 2:

$$\frac{\frac{2}{3}+0.2}{2}=\frac{\frac{2}{3}+\frac{2}{10}}{2}$$
$$=\frac{\frac{20}{30}+\frac{6}{30}}{2}$$
$$=\frac{\frac{26}{30}}{2}$$
$$=\frac{26}{30}\div 2$$
$$=\frac{26}{30}\times\frac{1}{2}$$
$$=\frac{13}{30}$$

97. (D) Translate the verbal description into algebraic inequalities:

$12<x\leq 3y$

Divide the equation by three. Of the answer choices, only option D is equivalent to $12<x\leq 3y$:

$$4<\frac{x}{3}\leq y$$
$$4(3)<\frac{x}{3}(3)\leq y(3)$$
$$12<x\leq 3y$$

98. (F) Substitute the values of x and y into the expression and simplify:

$$\frac{2x^y}{y^{2x}}=\frac{2\times 1^2}{2^{2\times 1}}=\frac{2\times 1}{2^2}=\frac{2}{4}=\frac{1}{2}$$

99. (D) List the numbers in order from least to greatest. The median is the middle value.

83 113 134 134 [135]
136 138 139 142

100. (H) Let C represent the number of signatures Clare collected. Let L represent the number of signatures Liza collected. Let S represent the number of signatures Selena collected.

First, solve for L:

$$C=5L$$
$$150=5L$$
$$30=L$$

Next, solve for S:

$$S=6L$$
$$=6\times 30$$
$$=180$$

101. (D) The formula for the area of a triangle is $A=\frac{1}{2}bh$, where b is the base of the triangle and h is the height. The formula for the area of a rectangle is $A=lw$, where l is the length of the rectangle and w is the width. Since the base of the triangle has the same measure as the length of the rectangle, we can write the area of the rectangle as $A=bw$.

The area of the triangle is twice the area of the rectangle, so $\frac{1}{2}bh=2bw$:

$$\frac{1}{2}bh=2bw$$
$$bh=4bw$$
$$h=4w$$
$$=4\times 3$$
$$=12$$

102. **(E)** Divide 12 into 500 to find the number of egg cartons Merle can completely fill and the number of eggs that will be left over:

$500 \div 12 = 41$ R8

Merle can completely fill 41 egg cartons. The last egg carton will have only 8 eggs. Therefore, Merle needs 4 more eggs to completely fill it.

103. **(C)** The distance between points U and Z on the number line is $|U - Z| = |-13 - 9| = 22$.

If $\overline{UZ}$ is divided into 4 equal parts, each part is $5\frac{1}{2}$ units long:

$UW = WX = XY = YZ = 5\frac{1}{2}$

Point X is $5\frac{1}{2} + 5\frac{1}{2} = 11$ units to the right of U, so point X will fall at -2.

104. **(H)** Let x represent number of years:

$$95{,}200 + 3{,}600x = 88{,}000 + 5{,}400x$$
$$7{,}200 = 1{,}800x$$
$$4 = x$$

105. **(A)** Let q represent the quotient when n is divided by 7:

$$n = 7q + 4$$
$$n + 3 = 7q + 4 + 3$$
$$= 7q + 7$$
$$= 7(q + 1) + 0$$

106. **(G)** Julio had $7 + 8 + 3 + 9 = 27$ marbles in the bag. He randomly drew $3 + 1 + 2 = 6$ marbles, none of which were green. He has $27 - 6 = 21$ marbles left in the bag. He still has 3 green marbles. So the probability that the next marble will be green is $\frac{3}{21} = \frac{1}{7}$.

107. **(A)** In order for $\frac{2x}{3x}$ to be less than 0, the denominator and numerator must have different signs. Either the numerator is positive and the denominator is negative, or the numerator is negative and the denominator is positive. There is no single number that can satisfy this condition.

108. **(H)** Let x represent the first number in the list:

$$\frac{1}{3}(x + 7) = 5$$
$$x + 7 = 15$$
$$x = 8$$

109. **(C)**

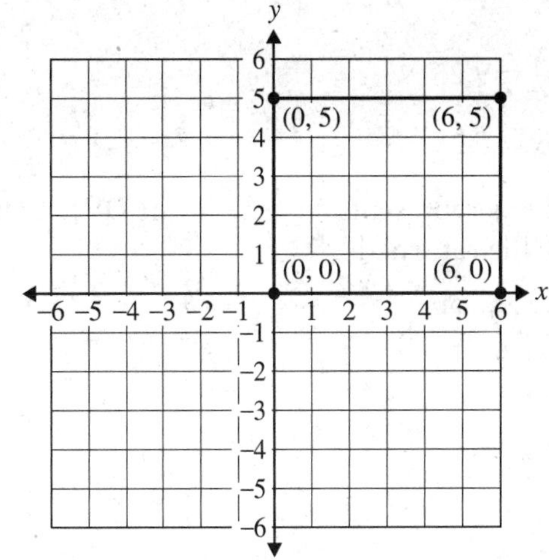

110. **(E)** Let x represent the amount of oil Jerry should use. Set up a proportion to solve for x:

$$\frac{x}{\frac{2}{3}\text{ cup of vinegar}} = \frac{\frac{3}{4}\text{ cup of oil}}{1\text{ cup of vinegar}}$$

$$x = \frac{3}{4} \times \frac{2}{3}$$
$$= \frac{1}{2}$$

111. **(D)** Let x represent the number of hours Roxie exercised last week:

$$\frac{5}{8}x = 6\frac{2}{3}$$
$$\frac{5}{8}x = \frac{20}{3}$$
$$x = \frac{20}{3} \div \frac{5}{8}$$
$$= \frac{20}{3} \times \frac{8}{5}$$
$$= \frac{32}{3}$$
$$= 10\frac{2}{3}$$

112. **(G)** Let x represent the total price of the 8 DVDs:

$$\frac{x}{8} = 9.25$$
$$x = 74$$

Let y represent the price of the DVD that Allie returned:

$$\frac{74 - y}{7} = 8$$
$$74 - y = 56$$
$$74 - 56 = y$$
$$18 = y$$

113. **(C)** First, add the hours that were worked:

$$1\frac{1}{2} \times 3 + 3\frac{3}{4} = 8\frac{1}{4}$$

Then, change the fraction to a decimal:

$$8\frac{1}{4} = 8.25$$

Next, multiply the number of hours worked by the amount of money paid:

$8.25 \times \$8.42 = \$69.47$

114. **(E)** First, decide what number of students did not get a business degree:

$300 - 225 = 75$

Then, use this formula:

$75 \div 300 = .25$

Finally, convert the decimal to a percentage:

$.25 = 25\%$

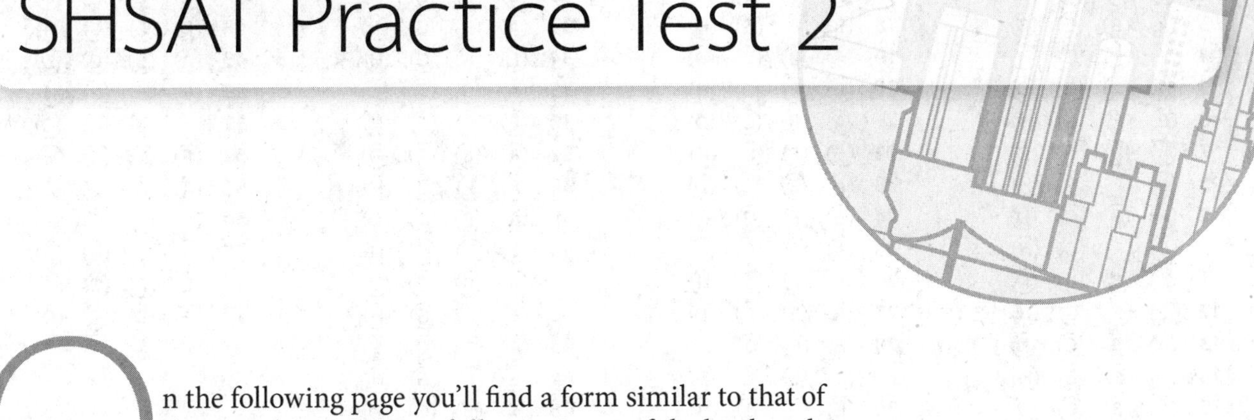

CHAPTER 12

SHSAT Practice Test 2

On the following page you'll find a form similar to that of the actual SHSAT. Carefully tear it out of the book and use it as you take the diagnostic test, for both the ELA and mathematics sections.

PART 1 ELA

1 A B C D
2 E F G H
3 A B C D
4 E F G H
5 A B C D
6 E F G H
7 A B C D
8 E F G H
9 A B C D
10 E F G H
11 A B C D
12 E F G H
13 A B C D
14 E F G H
15 A B C D
16 E F G H
17 A B C D
18 E F G H
19 A B C D
20 E F G H
21 A B C D
22 E F G H
23 A B C D
24 E F G H
25 A B C D
26 E F G H
27 A B C D
28 E F G H
29 A B C D
30 E F G H
31 A B C D
32 E F G H
33 A B C D
34 E F G H
35 A B C D
36 E F G H
37 A B C D
38 E F G H
39 A B C D
40 E F G H
41 A B C D
42 E F G H
43 A B C D
44 E F G H
45 A B C D
46 E F G H
47 A B C D
48 E F G H
49 A B C D
50 E F G H
51 A B C D
52 E F G H
53 A B C D
54 E F G H
55 A B C D
56 E F G H
57 A B C D

PART 2 MATHEMATICS

58

59

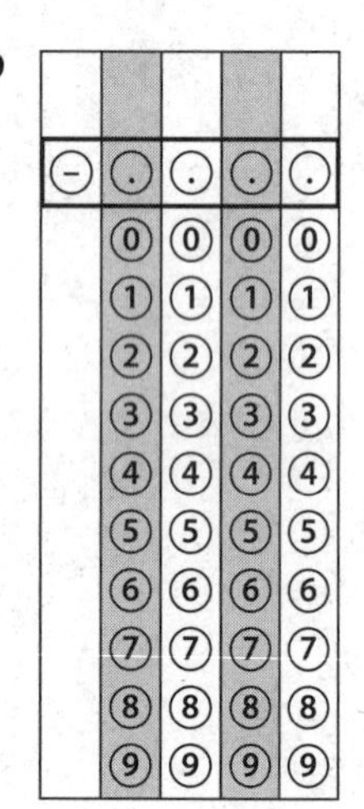

60

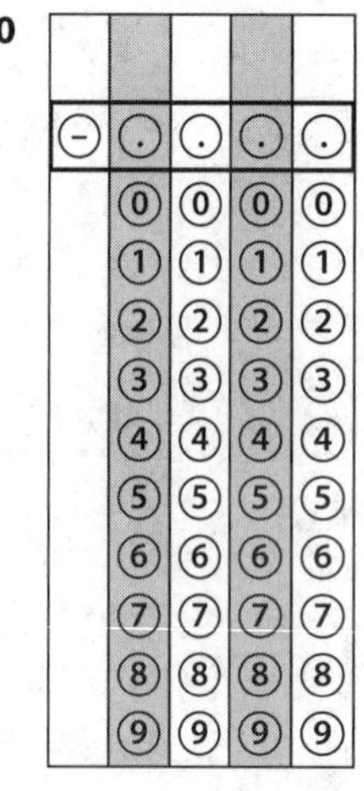

61

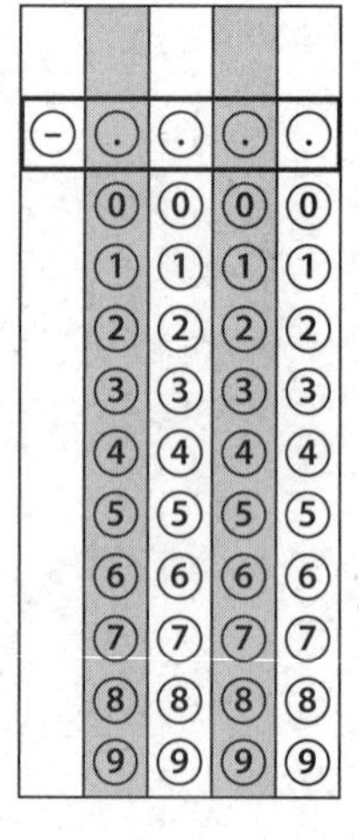

62

63 A B C D
64 E F G H
65 A B C D
66 E F G H
67 A B C D
68 E F G H
69 A B C D
70 E F G H
71 A B C D
72 E F G H
73 A B C D
74 E F G H
75 A B C D
76 E F G H
77 A B C D
78 E F G H
79 A B C D
80 E F G H
81 A B C D
82 E F G H
83 A B C D
84 E F G H
85 A B C D
86 E F G H
87 A B C D
88 E F G H
89 A B C D
90 E F G H
91 A B C D
92 E F G H
93 A B C D
94 E F G H
95 A B C D
96 E F G H
97 A B C D
98 E F G H
99 A B C D
100 E F G H
101 A B C D
102 E F G H
103 A B C D
104 E F G H
105 A B C D
106 E F G H
107 A B C D
108 E F G H
109 A B C D
110 E F G H
111 A B C D
112 E F G H
113 A B C D
114 E F G H

PART 1

ENGLISH LANGUAGE ARTS

90 Minutes ■ 57 Questions

Revising/Editing

QUESTIONS 1–20

Revising/Editing Part A

DIRECTIONS: Read and answer each of the following questions. You will be asked to recognize and correct errors in sentences or short paragraphs. Mark the best answer for each question.

Many people have the misconception that chess is complicated, they think it can only be played by older people.

1. Which edit needs to be made to the above sentence?

   A. Insert a comma after "misconception."
   B. Change the comma after "complicated" to a semicolon.
   C. Insert a semicolon after "think."
   D. Insert a comma after "played."

The truth is that most of the world's great chess players show signs of their greatness when they were in their teens and usually reached the peak of their prowess when they were in their twenties.

2. Which edit needs to be made in the above sentence?

   E. Change "is" to "was."
   F. Put the apostrophe after the "s" in "worlds."
   G. Change "show" to "showed."
   H. Insert a comma after "teens."

CONTINUE ON TO THE NEXT PAGE ▸

(1) José Raoul Capablanca of Cuba started to play chess after watching his father and his uncle when he was only nine. (2) He figured out the rules by himself. (3) Within a few years he was considered the best player in the world. (4) This fact prompted chess experts to conclude that a 13-year-old boy who is learning the game today may be as good as the recognized experts in a year and better than any of them in two years.

3. Which sentence from the paragraph above contains a misplaced modifier?

A. Sentence 1
B. Sentence 2
C. Sentence 3
D. Sentence 4

Bobby Fischer, which was the strongest player in America and possibly the strongest in the world, also revealed his special genius at an early age. He won the United States chess championship at the age of 13.

4. Which edit needs to be made to the above sentences?

E. Remove the comma after "Fischer."
F. Change "which" to "who."
G. Insert a comma after "America."
H. Change "revealed" to "reveals."

Chess, which rely on a player's ability to strategize, is one of the oldest and most respected games in Western culture.

5. Choose the edit needed for the above sentence:

A. Change "rely" to "relies."
B. Change "is" to "was."
C. Change "most" to "more."
D. Change "respected" to "respectable."

(1) The challenging complicated game of chess traces its origins to northern India and the sixth century A.D. (2) From India, it was carried to Persia. (3) In Persia, it was adopted by the Muslims and taken with them to Spain during the Moorish conquest. (4) From Spain, it spread throughout the rest of Europe.

6. Which sentence needs a comma inserted?

E. Sentence 1
F. Sentence 2
G. Sentence 3
H. Sentence 4

CONTINUE ON TO THE NEXT PAGE ▶

Revising/Editing Part B

DIRECTIONS: Read the passage below and answer the questions following it. You will be asked to improve the writing quality of the passage and to correct errors so that the passage follows the conventions of standard written English. You may reread the passage if you need to. Mark the best answer for each question.

Passage 1

Adventures of Henry M. Stanley

(1) Few people know that Henry M. Stanley, the African explorer who found the missing Dr. David Livingstone in Zanzibar, was a runaway from Wales who grew to manhood in America. (2) His real name was John Rowlands. (3) His parents were not married, and at first, he was raised by his grandfather, who died when John was about five. (4) Rowlands lived in a workhouse where he suffered numerous abuses.

(5) At eighteen, he left Wales for New Orleans. (6) It was there that he met and was befriended by a wealthy trader, Henry Hope Stanley, and his wife. (7) They offered him a job, and over time, they became very close. (8) Young Rowlands so loved his benefactor that he took the man's name as his own prior to joining the Confederate army, an act that was meant to honor his adopted father's memory.

(9) After the Civil War, he became a renowned journalist for the *New York Herald*. (10) In 1869, Stanley was commissioned by that newspaper to go to Africa to search for Dr. Livingstone. (11) Enduring nightmarish conditions, the route Stanley's search party took was through the tropics of Africa. (12) They faced harsh climates and deadly diseases. (13) When Stanley's group finally found Livingstone he was weak and ill. (14) Stanley uttered the line he is most famous for: "Dr. Livingstone, I presume?" upon finally finding Livingstone, the only white man in a village in the heart of Africa. (15) Once Livingstone was recovered, he joined the Stanley group, and they continued to explore the African region around Lake Tanganyika. (16) This lake is the longest freshwater lake in the world.

(17) After returning home to write a book about his adventures, he went back to Africa to explore other regions. (18) He was the first European to map the area along the Congo to the Atlantic. (19) He also led a successful rescue mission for the governor of Equitoria, Eman Pasha. (20) Stanley wrote numerous articles and a book about his adventures.

7. Which of these sentences would best follow sentence 7 and provide support and a smooth connection to sentence 8?

- **A.** The childless Stanleys treated Rowlands like a son.
- **B.** Rowlands had never known a mother's love.
- **C.** Rowlands enjoyed a lifestyle he had never experienced before.
- **D.** Rowlands was able to build a better life.

8. Which transition is the best choice to begin sentence 4?

- **E.** Moreover,
- **F.** After that,
- **G.** In other words,
- **H.** Nevertheless,

CONTINUE ON TO THE NEXT PAGE ▶

9. Which sentence should be revised to correct a misplaced modifier?
   A. Sentence 5
   B. Sentence 7
   C. Sentence 9
   D. Sentence 11

10. Which edit should be made to sentence 13?
   E. Remove the apostrophe from the word "Stanley's."
   F. Insert a comma after the word "Livingstone."
   G. Insert a comma after the word "weak."
   H. Insert a comma after the word "group."

11. Which concluding sentence provides the best summation for the passage?
   A. From very humble beginnings, Stanley rose to fame.
   B. Stanley led a long and interesting life.
   C. Stanley must have really loved Africa!
   D. During Stanley's time, much of Africa was explored by Europeans.

12. Which sentence would best follow and support sentence 10 by providing important information?
   E. Livingstone, famous for his African explorations, had disappeared during an expedition and was presumed dead by some.
   F. This was a dangerous and exciting mission.
   G. Much of Africa had not been explored by Europeans, and it was a dangerous task.
   H. Stanley was an interesting writer and documented his journey.

13. Which sentence strays from the main idea presented in the passage and should be deleted?
   A. Sentence 3
   B. Sentence 9
   C. Sentence 16
   D. Sentence 18

CONTINUE ON TO THE NEXT PAGE ▶

Passage 2

Saving *Star Trek*

(1) As most Trekkies know, the cultural phenomenon, *Star Trek*, did not seem destined for greatness when it was first developed. (2) In fact, it almost did not survive past season two. (3) Created by Gene Roddenberry, it was marketed as a Western set that was set in outer space.
(4) Roddenberry wants each episode to have both an adventure story and a moral lesson. (5) *Star Trek* was first aired in 1966, but despite Roddenberry's high hopes, by the end of the first season ratings had fallen. (6) During the second season, NBC decided to cancel the show.

(7) This is when Betty Jo ("Bjo") and John Trimble stepped in. (8) The Trimbles had met Roddenberry at a convention and become friends. (9) They often visited the set of *Star Trek* during its filming. (10) Both Bjo and John were big fans of the show. (11) The Trimbles witnessed the somber mood when the actors were informed that the show was to be canceled on the set.

(12) As the Trimbles drove home, John remarked that it seemed like something should be done to save the show. (13) Bjo agreed wholeheartedly. (14) They decided to launch a letter-writing campaign. (15) In a newsletter, they explained the situation and asked for help. (16) The newsletter asked each participant to recruit 10 more participants to join. (17) Everyone was asked to write a letter to the network requesting that *Star Trek* not be canceled.

(18) The response was tremendous. (19) In a voice-over during prime time, NBC announced that *Star Trek* would be extended for another season and asked everyone to please stop writing letters!
(20) This letter-writing campaign did not extend the show's life indefinitely. (21) It still only aired for one more season.
(22) This third season was crucial to the series becoming the cultural phenomenon that it is today. (23) In the 1960s, the rule was that a show had to have three seasons in order to be syndicated. (24) This was just one of many strange rules that governed television during that time.

14. Which edit is needed in sentence 4?

E. Change "wants" to "wanted."
F. Change "wants" to "is wanting."
G. Insert a comma after "episode."
H. Insert a comma after "story."

15. Which sentence contains a misplaced modifier?

A. Sentence 8
B. Sentence 9
C. Sentence 10
D. Sentence 11

CONTINUE ON TO THE NEXT PAGE ▶

16. Which would be the best way to combine sentences 9 and 10 to clarify their relationship?

E. Although they often visited the set of *Star Trek* during its filming, both Bjo and John were big fans of the show.
F. They often visited the set of *Star Trek* during its filming because both Bjo and John were big fans of the show.
G. Nevertheless, they often visited the set of *Star Trek* during its filming, as both Bjo and John were big fans of the show.
H. Because they often visited the set of *Star Trek* during its filming, both Bjo and John were big fans of the show.

17. Which would be the best transition to put at the beginning of sentence 22 to show the relationship between sentences 21 and 22?

A. In contrast,
B. Nevertheless,
C. Furthermore,
D. Moreover,

18. Which choice would best follow and support sentence 10?

E. They were also activists who loved to champion a great cause.
F. They had been interested in science fiction for many years, and that is actually what had brought them together.
G. They loved its underlying message of peace and equality, and they appreciated its multidimensional characters.
H. They had been aficionados of science fiction for many years and understood its hidden depths.

19. Which sentence strays from the topic of the passage and needs to be eliminated?

A. Sentence 12
B. Sentence 16
C. Sentence 20
D. Sentence 24

20. Which sentence should go at the end of the passage to best sum up its argument?

E. *Star Trek* has embedded itself into the American culture with recognizable quotes including "Live long and prosper" and "Beam me up, Scotty."
F. Without the action of the Trimbles, the legend of the *Enterprise* and its crew might have faded quietly into oblivion.
G. More than 50 years later, *Star Trek*'s fan base continues to multiply.
H. The original series spawned a half-dozen series spin-offs as well as more than a dozen movies.

CONTINUE ON TO THE NEXT PAGE ▶

Reading Comprehension

QUESTIONS 21–57

DIRECTIONS: Read the passages below; then answer the questions that appear after each passage. Select the best answer for each question. Reread the passages if necessary. You must base your response **only on information contained in the passage.**

For centuries explorers and traders looked for a way to travel from Europe to Asia without making the long and dangerous trip around the continent of Africa or South America. Before the Suez Canal and the Panama Canal were in existence, that route was the Northwest Passage through the Arctic Ocean. The first recorded attempt to traverse the Northwest Passage was in 1497. At that time John Cabot became the first European to discover the mainland of North America. Cabot could go no farther, however. The Arctic was completely frozen and impassable. Consequently, he returned to Italy. Over the years others tried and failed. Some disappeared, never to be heard from again. In 1854 the British explorer John Rae arrived. He mapped the Canadian Arctic coastline and learned how to survive the brutal winter with the help of the Cree Indians. But he too found the waters locked with thick ice.

Finally, in 1903, Norwegian Roald Amundsen departed Norway in a small fishing trawler, the *Gjoa*. It was only 70 feet long and had a crew of just six. His expedition did successfully navigate the Northwest Passage. The trip from the Atlantic to the Pacific took three years. The ship was stuck frozen in two-foot-thick ice for two winters. But everyone survived. He too learned survival skills from the Inuit Eskimos including how to hunt for food. Then in 1906 he sailed through the Bering Strait and on to Nome, Alaska. If he had taken a larger ship, he would never have made it through because the water in some parts was only three feet deep.

The Northwest Passage on the eastern side starts with the Davis Strait between Greenland and Canada. It continues into Baffin Bay and then through the Canadian Arctic Archipelago, a collection of more than 36,000 islands, most of them small and uninhabited. There are seven possible routes through the Archipelago, but some of them are too shallow for anything but a small ship. From there one passes into the Beaufort Sea, the Chukchi Sea, through the Bering Strait, and into the Pacific Ocean.

Today, because of global warming, the Northwest Passage is becoming an option for shipping. At the beginning of the twenty-first century, it was recorded that parts of the route were ice free for a short time in the summer months. For 36 days in August and September 2007, the entire route was ice free and navigable. Continuing record sea ice melting may indicate that the route will be used by commercial carriers, instead of going through the Panama Canal. It is about 2,500 miles less in distance, which would save both time and money. As a result, the Canadian government is experiencing new challenges from other governments about international travel through the Northwest Passage.

CONTINUE ON TO THE NEXT PAGE ▶

21. Which of the following best tells what this passage is about?

A. how the Canadian government is dealing with use of the Northwest Passage
B. what waterways the Northwest Passage runs through
C. how the Northwest Passage was discovered and its future potential
D. how explorers discovered the North American mainland

22. The passage suggests that the search for the Northwest Passage

E. caused tension between the various explorers.
F. was undertaken by the Canadian government.
G. was paid for by European royalty.
H. caused the death of many explorers.

23. Which of these statements is true about Roald Amundsen?

A. He became a rich man because of the discovery.
B. He realized that a big ship would never get through the Northwest Passage.
C. He had great determination in the face of significant hardships.
D. He was the only explorer to learn how to deal with the cold from natives.

24. Which of the following best describes what is suggested by the statement that "Continuing record sea ice melting may indicate that the route will be used by commercial carriers . . ." (lines 60–62)?

E. Global warming is impacting which routes commercial carriers may take.
F. Fewer small ships will transverse the Northwest Passage because of global warming.
G. Commercial carriers are forced to carry heavier cargoes because of global warming.
H. Global warming will make the Northwest Passage more difficult to use.

25. Which of these is most likely what the Canadian government will do in the future?

A. The government will declare the Northwest Passage an international zone.
B. The government will allow only European countries to use the route without interference.
C. The government will develop rules about traveling through the Northwest Passage.
D. The government will create a series of canals in the Northwest Passage.

26. What is **not** mentioned as a difficulty in traversing the Northwest Passage?

E. ice floes
F. cold weather
G. shallow waters
H. hostile natives

CONTINUE ON TO THE NEXT PAGE ▸

The Netherlands has spent much effort managing and controlling the sea and the many rivers that run through it using a system of barriers. Dike construction goes back to the tenth century in this European country along the North Sea. One-quarter of the country is at or below sea level, and the country is very densely populated. There are over 3,000 polders, low-lying tracts of land reclaimed from fens and marshes that are protected by dikes. Every Dutch child knows the fable of Hans Brinker, the boy who put his finger in a hole in the dike and saved his town from flooding.

In January 1953, a cataclysmic windstorm accompanied by an abnormally high spring tide pushed an 18-foot-high storm surge toward the province of Zeeland, a popular summer resort area in southwestern Holland. Dikes were destroyed, and nearly 600 square miles of land were flooded. Over 1,800 people died. The government immediately formed a commission to study how to increase safety in the delta areas. The problem was how to improve safety but still leave the economically important seaways to the Dutch ports open for shipping.

After years of studies and testimony by engineers, fishermen, farmers, and environmentalists, a plan was agreed upon. It was called Delta Works (*Deltawerken* in Dutch). Work began on the ambitious plan at once. By 1958 the first phase of Delta Works was completed. A storm surge barrier was built across the river Hollandse IJssel, a branch of the Rhine delta. The barrier is almost 300 feet wide and over 40 feet high. Over the next four decades, a system of storm surge barriers, sluices, dams, and dikes was constructed all across the Netherlands. They manage everything from the North Sea to the runoff from the spring snow melt in the Alps that cascades down the Rhine and its tributaries. They total more than 6,000 miles in length with 300 structures. Many of the Delta Works have visitor centers where one can learn about the history of the area and the construction of the dams. There are many miles of walking and bicycle paths as well.

Delta Works is an undertaking that many consider to be one of the Seven Wonders of the Modern World. They rate it in the same category as the Panama Canal and the Empire State Building. The project is far from over. It is constantly ongoing. Managing saltwater levels and freshwater levels, and balancing the needs of fishing and agriculture, are continually being reassessed. Planners are currently researching rising sea levels because of global warming. Delta Works is an example of what can happen when people work together to ensure that something like the Great Flood of 1953 will never occur again.

27. Which of the following best tells what this passage is about?

- **A.** why Delta Works is known as one of the Seven Wonders of the Modern World
- **B.** why the snow runoff from the Alps affects the Netherlands
- **C.** how the Netherlands is the only country that has a plan to manage sea and river water
- **D.** how the Netherlands developed and built its sea and river water management program

CONTINUE ON TO THE NEXT PAGE ▶

28. The author implies that without Delta Works
   E. the Netherlands would have been absorbed by another European country.
   F. the lives of the people of the Netherlands would be unchanged.
   G. the Netherlands would have been less popular as a tourist destination.
   H. the Netherlands might have lost land to the water.

29. Why did the author include the information about Hans Brinker at the beginning of the article?
   A. to explain how leaks are stopped in dikes
   B. to show that everyone can help when flooding is imminent
   C. to show that the Netherlands has many stories written about it
   D. to emphasize that the Netherlands has always had a problem with flooding

30. Which best describes the way in which the plan for Delta Works was developed?
   E. It was a cooperative effort by many different people.
   F. It was the work of advanced engineers.
   G. It was modeled after a similar program in Germany.
   H. It came about somewhat by accident.

31. Which of the following is **not** true of Delta Works?
   A. It is an engineering masterpiece.
   B. It was built because of the Great Flood of 1953.
   C. Many people are interested in seeing it.
   D. It is completely finished.

32. With which of the statements would the author most agree?
   E. More countries should follow the example of the Netherlands in solving their problems.
   F. Delta Works will soon be the most popular stop for people traveling to Europe.
   G. More time should have been taken in developing the plan to contain storm surges.
   H. Delta Works did not have to be as large a project as it was.

CONTINUE ON TO THE NEXT PAGE ▶

The traditional Mehndi Celebration that takes place as part of an Indian wedding has roots that go back over 9,000 years. This was when the henna plant was first used for a variety of purposes in Africa, the Middle East, and India. The origin for using henna was its cooling and astringent effect when applied to the skin. But the custom was also tied into the cultural belief that henna would bring love and good fortune.

Henna, or *mehndi* in Hindi, was brought to India in the twelfth century by the Mongols who traded for centuries with Arabs. It grows best in desert-like conditions; hence, when the desert people of Rajasthan, Punjab, and Gujarat states became aware of the cooling aspect of the plant, they dipped their hands and feet in a paste made from the plant's crushed leaves. While the plant did cool, it also left a red stain. After a while, some women grew tired of having bright red palms all the time. They found that one large dot in the center of the palm still provided a cooling effect. It was also pleasing to the eye. Other, smaller dots were placed around the center dot. This gradually gave way to the idea of creating artistic designs on the palms.

Over time this process evolved into the Mehndi Celebration for the bride. Indian weddings are elaborate affairs, with many festivities before, during, and after the wedding. A Mehndi Celebration is held at the bride's house before the wedding. Her palms and feet are painted, usually by a henna professional. The stronger the paste, the longer the designs will last. This is desirable since the designs are a symbol of a long-lasting marriage. Popular images of mehndi art are conch shells, flowers, and peacocks. Hidden in the detailed designs of the bridal henna design is the bride's future husband's name. The groom must find his name in the mehndi to show his future wife that he has sharp eyes and an alert mind.

While henna has long been used to dye hair in the United States, it is only in recent years that henna tattoo body painting has become popular as a painless, fashionable, and nonpermanent tattoo alternative. Henna body art kits and traditional mehndi stencils are even available for do-it-yourselfers online. Henna art studios are popping up across the United States offering traditional Indian bridal designs as well as decorative body painting. Some artists will come to parties or events and decorate everyone there. The tradition of henna body painting has definitely evolved with the times.

33. Which of the following best tells what this passage is about?

A. what needs to be done to apply henna
B. how henna designs are made
C. how henna is used to dye hair
D. the use of henna to create body designs

34. What reason is **not** mentioned for using henna?

E. enables a change of hair color
F. ease of using
G. not a permanent design
H. symbol of love

35. According to the passage, which of the following statements about the Mehndi Celebration is probably true?

A. The participants of the celebration are all women.
B. The celebration lasts for several days.
C. Many Indian brides do not participate in such a celebration.
D. Indian weddings in the United States do not have this tradition.

CONTINUE ON TO THE NEXT PAGE ▶

36. The information about a bride's mehndi containing the name of her future husband was included in order to illustrate

E. how the designs are attractive to the future husband.
F. why the designs take so long to do.
G. how beautiful the designs are.
H. how complex the designs can be.

37. Which of the following is the most likely reason that Indian brides choose to have mehndi designs on their palms?

A. They are attractive to look at.
B. They cool the skin.
C. They leave a red stain.
D. They promise good luck.

38. Why does the author say that the "tradition of henna body painting has definitely evolved with the times"?

E. to make readers aware that henna body painting is used more now than in the past
F. to show that people use mehndi for wedding celebrations
G. to show that henna uses have changed over the years
H. to make light of people who use henna

CONTINUE ON TO THE NEXT PAGE ▶

Learning how to swim is very important for people of all ages. It's never too late to learn how to swim. Accidents can happen around water of any kind, from a swimming pool to a lake or river to the ocean, even a water park. Knowing how to react if you fall into the water can save your life, especially if you are young. In fact, according to the Centers for Disease Control (CDC), drowning is the second most likely cause of death in children under the age of 14. Learning how to swim is something you can't do online or learn by yourself. You need a teacher, either with a group or privately. YMCAs, community centers, and gyms all offer swimming lessons.

Certain groups of people, like African Americans and Hispanics, statistically face greater dangers near water. A survey conducted by USA Swimmers, an organization that governs competitive swimming in the United States at all age levels, polled nearly 1,800 people in 16 cities. They found that 60 percent of black children under 14 cannot swim. That is twice the rate for white children. Most of the black children who could not swim were inner city residents. Black children drown at three times the rate of white children. Several conclusions emerged. The children didn't learn to swim because their parents didn't learn to swim and were afraid of the water. Also, many parents and grandparents grew up when pools were segregated, and few pools were available to African Americans. USA Swimmers is expanding its learn-to-swim programs, especially in inner cities, to reach more African American children.

The best place to learn how to swim is in a swimming pool. It is possible to start out where a person can stand with his or her head above water. All professional teachers of swimming will tell you that the first step is to get rid of the fear of water. Whether a child or an adult, the individual needs to get used to being in the water. Beginners need to realize that when swimming, the body is more buoyant, the muscles loosen up, and the spine becomes more relaxed. That is why water is used extensively for rehabilitation from accident or injury.

Beginners will learn to develop confidence in the water as well as the motor skills necessary for swimming. They will learn about safety and what to do if somebody accidentally falls into the water. Discipline is necessary. A beginning swimmer needs to obey rules, do what the lifeguard says to do, and most important, never swim alone. Ultimately, the student will discover, as USA Swimmers states on its website, that "swimming is a technical and specialized activity involving extensive skill development."

39. Which of the following best tells what this passage is about?

A. the reasons for people drowning
B. how people learn to swim in a pool
C. the reasons why people should learn to swim
D. the kind of motor skills that are used when swimming

40. The best reason why the author included the information that drowning is the second most likely cause of death in children under the age of 14 was to

E. remind the reader that many people drown every year.
F. stress to the reader how important knowing how to swim is.
G. suggest that swimming can help improve a child's life experience.
H. show how difficult it is for children to get swimming classes.

CONTINUE ON TO THE NEXT PAGE ▶

41. Which reason is **not** given for learning to swim?

A. to feel confident in the water
B. to know what to do if you fall into the water
C. to improve new motor skills
D. to be able to become a life guard

42. Why should beginning swimmers swim with someone else?

E. It will help them improve their swimming.
F. They will learn to compete with others.
G. They will enjoy the company.
H. It will keep them safer.

43. The author includes information about African American children to demonstrate

A. the difficulty of making this group aware of the water's dangers.
B. his knowledge of the African American population's history.
C. why African Americans are good athletes.
D. how cultural disparities have influenced children in terms of learning to swim.

44. Why do you suppose that USA Swimmers is expanding its programs in inner cities?

E. to create jobs for inner city people
F. to explore the new possibilities that come with expansion
G. to lower the cost of swimming classes in cities
H. to reach more African American and Hispanic children

CONTINUE ON TO THE NEXT PAGE ▶

The great African American explorer Matthew Henson was born in Maryland in 1866 to parents who were sharecroppers. When he was four, the family moved to Washington, DC, to find work, but tragically, when he was 12, both his parents died. Hard work and determination were traits that showed up early in Henson. They were most evident when he walked to Baltimore to get a job as a cabin boy.

The captain of the merchant ship *Katie Hines* was struck by this boy's persistence and hired him. Soon enough Henson learned to be a good seaman. The captain took an interest in him and taught him geography, math, and history. Henson also learned how to navigate and he traveled with the captain to China, Africa, and the Middle East. After the captain suddenly died, Matthew returned to Washington and found a job working for a furrier.

It was at the furrier's that he met Robert E. Peary, a naval officer. Peary, who traded with Eskimos in Greenland, brought furs with him to sell. Peary realized that Henson had a great sense of adventure and offered him a job as his assistant. The two made several trips to Greenland. Henson learned to speak Inuit, and the Eskimos taught him how survive the harsh climate. Peary told Henson about his dream to be the first person to reach the North Pole, and Henson eagerly accepted his invitation to join him. Between 1898 and 1908 the pair made numerous attempts to reach the Pole, each time to turn back in failure.

In 1908 Peary's expedition, including Henson, left on the USS *Roosevelt* from New York for Cape Columbia, the northernmost point of Canada. On March 1, 1909, the team pointed their dog sleds north and set out on the 475-mile journey. Crossing the ice-covered Arctic Ocean was treacherous because the shifting ice would split open without warning. Most of the expedition members turned back. Some were angered that Henson, a black person, had better skills than they did. Finally, on April 6, Peary, Henson, and four Eskimos reached their goal: 90 degrees north.

On their return, Peary was given many honors. Because of the prevailing prejudice against blacks at that time, Henson was ignored. But in 1937 Henson was made an honorary member of the famous Explorers Club of New York. Henson died in 1955 and was buried in New York. In 1987 there was a movement to have the remains of both Henson and his wife moved to lie next to Robert Peary in Arlington National Cemetery. President Reagan granted permission, and on the seventy-ninth anniversary of the discovery of the North Pole, Henson was laid to rest near his fellow explorer. On Henson's tomb there is a quote from his autobiography: "The lure of the Arctic is tugging at my heart. To me the trail is calling. The old trail. The trail that is always new."

45. Which of the following best tells what this passage is about?

- **A.** the relationship between Matthew Henson and Robert Peary
- **B.** why Matthew Henson became a cabin boy
- **C.** how Matthew Henson learned Inuit
- **D.** how Matthew Henson made his mark on history

46. How did the experience of being a cabin boy affect Matthew Henson?

- **E.** He was protected from dangers.
- **F.** He started to read a lot.
- **G.** He learned many new things.
- **H.** He met many people who helped him.

CONTINUE ON TO THE NEXT PAGE ▶

47. Which of the following was **not** something that Matthew Henson did?

A. traveled all around the globe
B. learned to trade for furs
C. learned to speak Inuit
D. traveled to the North Pole

48. Why did some members of the expedition not like Matthew Henson?

E. They were trained explorers.
F. They did not like him telling them what to do.
G. They were jealous of Peary's friendship with him.
H. They were prejudiced against black people.

49. Why do you suppose Matthew Henson was made an honorary member of the famous Explorers Club of New York?

A. to give him the respect he deserved for reaching the North Pole
B. to show that he had the same skills as other explorers
C. to inspire other African Americans to become explorers
D. to show that the group was not prejudiced against black people

50. What can be inferred about Matthew Henson from the quotation from his autobiography?

E. He enjoyed writing.
F. He thought he would die in the Arctic.
G. He was a kind and thoughtful man.
H. He was a born explorer.

CONTINUE ON TO THE NEXT PAGE ▶

The forerunner to the United Nations was a little-remembered coalition called the League of Nations. Founded on what is referred to as Wilsonian idealism, the League of Nations called for a coming together of the nations of the world to create a forum where nations could air their grievances and a general consensus could be reached. President Wilson wanted this council to be viewed as a place where the nations of the world could debate and find agreement, not as a force of retribution.

Because during that time period many people espoused isolationism, the League of Nations was born into a world that was not entirely welcoming. In fact, although President Wilson had sponsored the formation of the organization, the United States Congress voted against becoming a member. The only two Great Powers that were steadfast members of this organization were Great Britain and France. The League of Nations was beset with problems from the start, yet it persevered, mainly on the dreams of libertarians who believed in the innate goodness of the people who make up the nations of the world. These dreams were dashed with the rise of Hitler and Nazi Germany.

The formation of the United Nations at the end of World War II was in a completely different political environment. Very few believed that mankind was innately good or that isolationism was a valid solution. The world was finally ready for a global solution. The United Nations really wasn't a new concept. It was a restructuring of the League of Nations. Some of the same internal bodies were kept; some of the same goals remained (like world peace). It was not, however, restructured with the same Wilsonian idealism with which the League of Nations had been formed. In contrast, it was reformed from a realist's perspective. Its founders expected controversies and wars and built the UN charter to accommodate these eventualities. The delegates that met in 1945 to structure the United Nations charter knew that the threat of force would be necessary. They were looking for a way that would allow diplomacy to guide and control that force.

The United Nations was founded with the knowledge that the world needed a policeman. It would use force, if necessary, to impose its will on member and nonmember nations. However, unlike the League of Nations, it was not viewed as a threat to nationalism. On the contrary, for the beleaguered nations emerging from World War II, it was viewed as a lifeline. Each country became willing to give up some things in order to be a part of a global system where diplomacy went first and force was a last resort.

51. Which of the following best tells what the passage is about?

A. how the League of Nations worked
B. how President Wilson was a progressive thinker
C. the foundation on which the United Nations was created
D. what the United Nations has accomplished since its founding

52. The passage suggests that the League of Nations failed because

E. Congress would not cooperate with President Wilson.
F. Great Britain and France couldn't cooperate.
G. the world's nations were not ready to cooperate.
H. President Wilson was not equipped to spearhead the project.

CONTINUE ON TO THE NEXT PAGE ▶

53. Which of these statements is true about the United Nations?

A. It was formed shortly after the First World War.
B. It was built on an idealistic platform.
C. It was built on a realistic platform.
D. It was structured on the premise that the nations could resolve differences with words and would not have to use force.

54. This passage suggests that in order to be a member of the United Nations, a nation would have to

E. give up some of its sovereignty.
F. pay an annual fee.
G. commit to sending delegates to the meetings.
H. embrace the doctrines of the UN Charter.

55. Which is not mentioned as a difficulty that the League of Nations encountered?

A. A strong isolationist sentiment
B. Lack of member nations
C. The United States' refusal to join
D. Lack of funding

56. Which best describes what is suggested by this statement: "President Wilson wanted this council to be viewed as a place where the nations of the world could debate and find agreement, not as a force of retribution"?

E. The League of Nations was a forum for nations to air their grievances.
F. There would be a lot of disagreement when the council met.
G. The League of Nations was not supposed to punish nations.
H. President Wilson was intricately involved in the formation of the League of Nations.

57. Which of the following might be inferred about the United Nations?

A. It did not have trouble finding member nations.
B. Its members believe in the innate goodness of mankind.
C. Only certain nations are allowed to join.
D. Only certain countries make up its Security Council.

CONTINUE ON TO THE NEXT PAGE ▶

PART 2

MATHEMATICS

90 Minutes ■ 57 Questions

Important Notes

(1) No formulas or definitions of mathematical terms and symbols are provided.
(2) Diagrams are not necessarily drawn to scale. Be careful not to make assumptions about relationships in diagrams.
(3) Diagrams can be assumed to be in one plane unless otherwise stated.
(4) Graphs are drawn to scale. Therefore, you may assume relationships according to appearance. This means lines that look parallel can be assumed to be parallel, angles that look like right angles can be assumed to be right angles, and so forth.
(5) All fractions must be reduced to lowest terms.

Grid-In Problems

QUESTIONS 58–62

DIRECTIONS FOR GRID-IN QUESTIONS: In the Mathematics section of the new SHSAT, in addition to the multiple choice questions, there will be five grid-in questions. For these questions, you need to solve a computational question and provide the numerical answer. Once you have found the answer, you must enter it at the top of the grid and then fill in the appropriate circles below to match your answer.

Each grid consists of five columns. Enter your answer beginning at the left. The first column is reserved for the "–" symbol. It only gets used if the answer is a negative number. If your answer is positive, leave that column blank and begin your answer in the second column. For example, if your answer is 28, write 2 in the second column and 8 in the third column. Fill in the circle that contains a 2 below the 2 and the circle that contains an 8 below the 8.

If the answer contains a decimal, enter a "." in the appropriate column. There is a circle that contains a "." that can be filled in. It is important that you do not skip a column in the middle of your answer. For example, if your answer is 203, don't skip the 0 and just leave the column blank! Take time to check your answers carefully. If you forget to write in a digit or fail to fill out the corresponding circle, your answer will be marked wrong even if you calculated the correct answer.

58. Lisa has a bag of jelly beans. There are 8 red jelly beans in the bag, and the probability of drawing a red jelly bean out is $\frac{1}{6}$. When she adds more red jelly beans to her bag, the probability becomes $\frac{1}{5}$. How many red jelly beans did she add to the bag?

59. The museum had x visitors on Friday. On Saturday, it had 150 more visitors than it did on Friday. The total number of visitors on Friday and Saturday was twice the number on Sunday. Compared to Friday, how many more visitors did the museum have on Sunday?

60. There were 8.5 million people living in New York City. That was approximately 43% of the population of the entire state. In millions, about how many people lived in New York but not in New York City?

61. Material x has a mass of 9 grams. The ratio of the masses of material x to material y is 2:3. The ratio of the masses of material y to material m is 3:4. What is the sum of the mass of material y and the mass of material m?

62. For what value of x does $3x + 2.62 = 7x - 8.3$?

Multiple Choice Problems

QUESTIONS 63–114

DIRECTIONS: Find the solution to each problem; then choose the best answer from the options given. Mark the letter of your answer choice on the answer sheet. You may use your test booklet or paper provided by the proctor as scrap paper for your calculations. However, DO NOT make calculations or put any stray marks on your answer sheet.

63. A farmer needs to plant 135 yellow pepper plants and 210 red pepper plants. He wants to plant them in rows that have the same number of peppers, and each row is to have only one color of pepper. What is the greatest number of plants he can have in each row?

A. 3 plants
B. 5 plants
C. 9 plants
D. 15 plants

64.

R S

−12 −10 −8 −6 −4 −2 0 2 4 6 8 10 12

If $\overline{RS}$ is divided into 3 equal parts by points P and Q (not shown), what position will point Q fall on? (Assume P < Q.)

E. −2
F. −1
G. 1
H. 3

65. If $Q = \frac{8}{25}$, $R = \frac{3}{10}$, and $S = \frac{1}{\sqrt{16}}$, which of the following shows the correct comparison between the numbers?

A. $S > R > Q$
B. $R < S < Q$
C. $S < R < Q$
D. $Q < R = S$

66. Tony bought a computer, a cell phone, and a television. The computer cost 2.5 times as much as the television. The television cost 5 times as much as the cell phone. If Tony spent a total of $925, how much did the cell phone cost?

E. $37
F. $50
G. $68
H. $74

67. The table below shows the number of hours of volunteer work completed by 20 students. What is the mean number of hours per student?

HOURS OF VOLUNTEER WORK COMPLETED

Hours	Number of Students
16	7
12	6
20	4
10	3

A. 10.7
B. 13.2
C. 14.7
D. 16.5

68. A 9-sided polygon has 1 side of length x centimeters, 4 sides each of length $1.25x$, and 4 sides each of length $1.5x$. If the perimeter of the polygon is 156 centimeters, what is the value of x?

E. 11
F. 12
G. 13
H. 14

CONTINUE ON TO THE NEXT PAGE ▶

69. $6x(2y - 9) =$

A. $8xy - 9$

B. $8xy - 3x$

C. $12xy - 9$

D. $12xy - 54x$

70. $(\sqrt{9})(\sqrt{49}) =$

E. 21
F. 24
G. 27
H. 28

71.

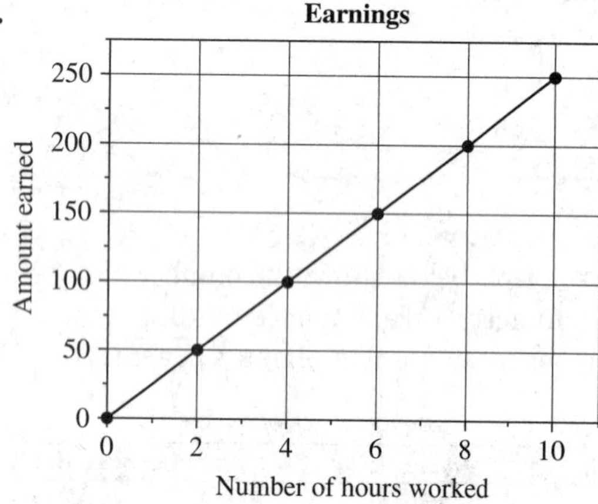

The graph shows the relationship between the number of hours Megan works and the amount she earns. How much does Megan earn per hour?

A. \$10
B. \$15
C. \$20
D. \$25

72. What is the least integer greater than $\frac{43}{7}$?

E. 4
F. 5
G. 6
H. 7

73. What is the value of $|6x| - |-2y|$ if $x = -3$ and $y = 5$?

A. −28
B. −8
C. 2
D. 8

74. At 5:00 a.m., the temperature was 15 degrees below zero Fahrenheit. Then the temperature rose 5 degrees per hour for 8 hours. What was the temperature at 12:00 p.m?

E. 15°
F. 20°
G. 25°
H. 30°

75.

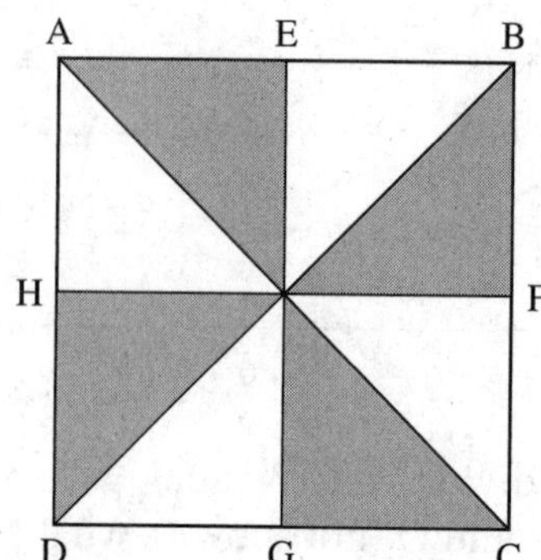

ABCD is a square. Line segments $\overline{EG}$ and $\overline{FH}$ and diagonals $\overline{AC}$ and $\overline{BD}$ pass through the same point. The total area of the shaded triangles is 18 square centimeters. What is the side length of square ABCD?

A. 6
B. 9
C. 12
D. 24

CONTINUE ON TO THE NEXT PAGE ▶

76. Which of the following is equivalent to the inequality $21+x<-7$?

E. $x<-28$
F. $x>-28$
G. $x>-14$
H. $x<14$

77. Brooke worked $3\frac{1}{2}$ hours every day for 5 days. She earned $5.10 per hour. How much did Brooke earn in all?

A. $17.85
B. $40.80
C. $43.35
D. $89.25

78. What is the difference between 15% of 7 and 7% of 7?

E. −0.385
F. −3.85
G. 0.56
H. 1.54

79. Twenty-one out of 70 customers at the restaurant ordered dessert. What percentage of the customers did **not** order dessert?

A. 21%
B. 30%
C. 49%
D. 70%

80. Andy is driving in a straight line on the freeway heading east. Morgan is driving on the same freeway heading west. At 1:00 p.m., they are exactly 60 miles apart. They pass each other at 1:30 p.m. If Andy is driving at 55 miles per hour, at what speed is Morgan driving?

E. 45 miles per hour
F. 50 miles per hour
G. 55 miles per hour
H. 65 miles per hour

81. A circle has a circumference of C inches and an area of A square inches. If $C=\frac{2}{5}A$, what is the diameter of the circle?

A. 0.4 inches
B. 0.8 inches
C. 2.5 inches
D. 10 inches

82. One-third the difference of two numbers is 12. If the larger number is 9, what is the sum of the two numbers?

E. −27
F. −18
G. 36
H. 45

83. For what negative value of x does $\frac{5}{8}=\frac{40}{x^2}$?

A. −8
B. −7
C. −6
D. −5

84. The perimeter of a rectangle is 40 inches. If the width is 9 inches, what is the area of the rectangle?

E. 18 sq in.
F. 27 sq in.
G. 99 sq in.
H. 198 sq in.

85. The sporting goods store sells 6 different brands of tennis rackets and 4 different brands of tennis balls. If Amanda buys one brand of tennis racket and one brand of tennis balls, how many different combinations of brands can she buy?

A. 10
B. 12
C. 16
D. 24

CONTINUE ON TO THE NEXT PAGE ▶

86. If $\dddot{x} = \frac{x}{4}$, what is the value of $\dddot{5}(\dddot{8})$?

E. 1.25
F. 2.5
G. 3.75
H. 5.0

87.

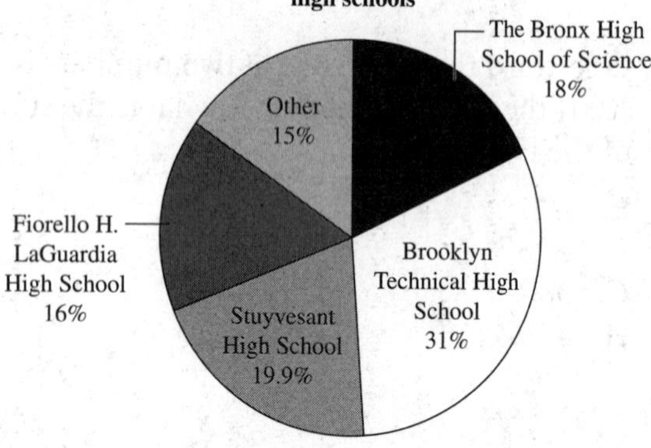

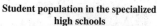

There are 16,405 students enrolled in specialized high schools. The graph shows the approximate percentage of students enrolled in the different schools. Approximately how many students are enrolled at Stuyvesant High School?

A. 2,526
B. 3,002
C. 3,265
D. 4,101

88. Fernando is now x years old. Erika is 7 years older than Fernando. In terms of x, how old was Erika 4 years ago?

E. $7x$
F. $7x-4$
G. $x+11$
H. $x+3$

89. If $x=23$ and $y=15$, what is the value of $\frac{x+y}{x-4}$?

A. 2.00
B. 3.75
C. 6.00
D. 8.00

90. What is the least common multiple of X and Y?

$X = 3 \times 3 \times 5$

$Y = 2 \times 2 \times 3 \times 5$

E. 15
F. 30
G. 65
H. 180

91. In a scale drawing, 1 inch represents 25 feet. How many square inches on the diagram represent 1 square foot?

A. 0.0016
B. 0.009
C. 0.04
D. 0.48

92. Katy has a bag of yellow and red balls. There are a total of 30 balls in the bag. The probability of drawing a yellow ball is $\frac{1}{6}$. How many red balls should be removed from the bag in order to increase the probability to $\frac{1}{3}$?

E. 5
F. 9
G. 10
H. 15

CONTINUE ON TO THE NEXT PAGE ▶

93. Cody has a box of cereal. On Monday, he ate $\frac{1}{7}$ of the cereal. On Tuesday, he ate $\frac{1}{6}$ of the remaining cereal. What fraction of the cereal is left in the box?

A. $\frac{5}{6}$

B. $\frac{2}{7}$

C. $\frac{5}{7}$

D. $\frac{2}{13}$

94.

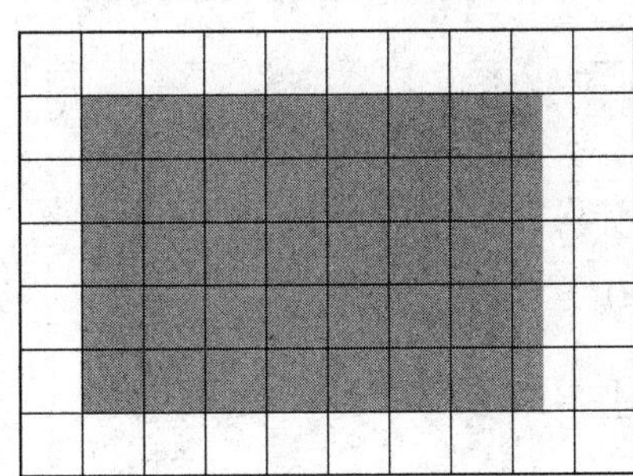

The grid above is made up of 1-inch squares. About how many square yards are in the shaded region?

E. $12\frac{2}{3}$

F. $16\frac{2}{3}$

G. $22\frac{1}{3}$

H. $66\frac{2}{3}$

95. Lines p and q are perpendicular and lines r and s are also perpendicular. Given the value of the angle shown, find the measure of angle x on the figure.

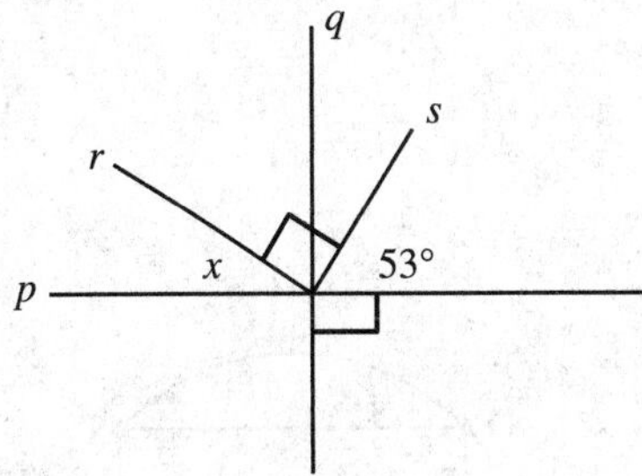

A. 37 degrees
B. 42 degrees
C. 45 degrees
D. 53 degrees

96. What number is halfway between $\frac{1}{2}$ and 0.85?

E. 0.525
F. 0.575
G. 0.625
H. 0.675

97. Julianne is half as old as Benita. If Benita will be 24 years old in 8 years, how old was Julianne 3 years ago?

A. 3
B. 5
C. 7
D. 9

98. There are approximately 13,000 registered voters in Montour County. About 46% of the voters are registered as Republicans. About 38% of the voters are registered as Democrats. About how many more registered voters are Republican than Democrat?

E. 800
F. 900
G. 1,000
H. 2,000

CONTINUE ON TO THE NEXT PAGE ▶

99. Tameka has 220 yards of fabric. She cuts the fabric into equal sized pieces that are each 12 yards long. How many yards of fabric does she have left over?

A. 1
B. 2
C. 3
D. 4

100.

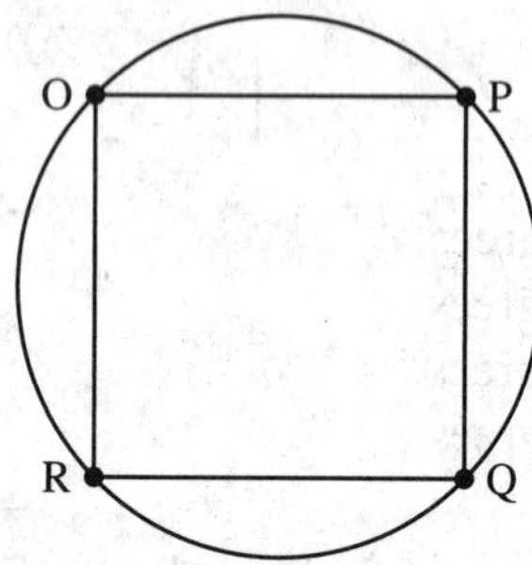

In the figure above, O, P, Q, R are points on a circle and OPQR is a square. If the area of the circle is 36π square centimeters, what is the measure of the diagonal of the square?

E. 6 cm
F. 8 cm
G. 10 cm
H. 12 cm

101.

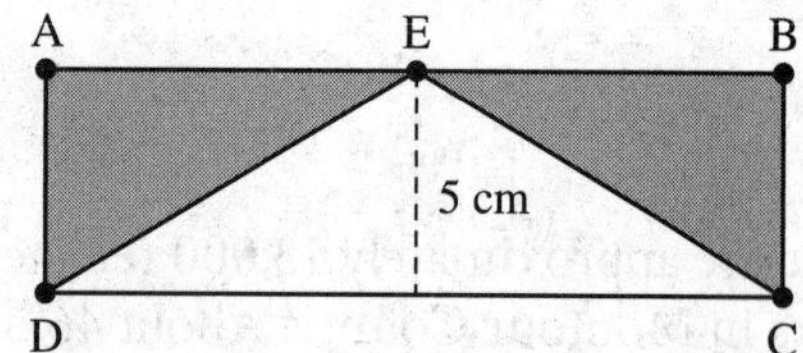

In the diagram above, ABCD is a rectangle and E is a point on $\overline{AB}$. The area of triangle CDE is 25 square centimeters, and its height is 5 centimeters. What is the area of the shaded region?

A. 10 sq cm
B. 15 sq cm
C. 25 sq cm
D. 40 sq cm

102. If $x = 7$ and $(3x - 1)(y - 2x) = 60$, what is the value of y?

E. 11
F. 17
G. 21
H. 30

103.

R T

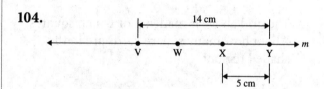

−10 −8 −6 −4 −2 0 2 4 6 8 10 12 14

Point S (not shown) is located on line segment $\overline{RT}$ so that $\overline{RS}$ is $\frac{1}{3}$ the length of $\overline{ST}$. What is the location of point S?

A. −2
B. $-\frac{1}{2}$
C. 0
D. $\frac{1}{2}$

104.

14 cm

V W X Y m

5 cm

On line m, if VW = WX, what is the length of WY?

F. 7.0
G. 7.5
H. 9.0
I. 9.5

CONTINUE ON TO THE NEXT PAGE ▶

105. Julio bought a book for x dollars. The electronic version of the book costs y dollars. The electronic version costs one dollar less than one-fourth the cost of Julio's book. What is the value of y in terms of x?

A. $\frac{1}{4} - x$

B. $\frac{1}{4}x - 1$

C. $1 - \frac{1}{4}x$

D. $1 - 4x$

106. Tia has a box containing 15 blue marbles, 12 green marbles, 7 red marbles, and 1 white marble. Tia removed 8 marbles, 6 of which were blue. If she removes one more marble at random, what is the probability that it will be blue?

E. $\frac{1}{3}$

F. $\frac{2}{5}$

G. $\frac{1}{7}$

H. $\frac{2}{9}$

107. $\left(\frac{2}{6} + \frac{1}{7}\right) \div \frac{2}{5} =$

A. $\frac{6}{65}$

B. $\frac{4}{21}$

C. $\frac{15}{26}$

D. $\frac{25}{21}$

108. Lance is 39 years old. Ted is 22 years old. Rosalinda is 45 years old. How old is Erik if the mean age of the four friends is 33.5?

E. 19
F. 28
G. 33
H. 48

109. One side of a square lies on the x-axis of a coordinate system. The coordinates of one corner of the square are (2, 0) and the coordinates of another corner are (6, 0). What could be the coordinates of the third corner?

A. (−4, 4)
B. (−2, −4)
C. (0, 4)
D. (2, −4)

110. Allan can drive 32 miles on one gallon of gas. How many miles can he drive if he only has $\frac{7}{8}$ of a gallon?

E. 21
F. 23
G. 25
H. 28

111. Melissa uses $\frac{3}{5}$ as much water as Neil to water her plants. If Melissa use $4\frac{1}{3}$ gallons of water, how many gallons does Neil use?

A. $1\frac{3}{5}$

B. $2\frac{3}{5}$

C. $4\frac{4}{9}$

D. $7\frac{2}{9}$

CONTINUE ON TO THE NEXT PAGE ▶

112. Mr. Hirsch teaches 5 classes. The mean number of students per class is 17.4. If he teaches one more class, the mean increases to 18.5. How many students are in the sixth class?

E. 19
F. 21
G. 24
H. 38

113. Nancy is working to pay down her debt. She paid $\frac{1}{3}$ of her total debt in May. In June, she paid $\frac{3}{5}$ of the debt she had left. What fraction of her debt does Nancy have left to pay?

A. $\frac{4}{15}$

B. $\frac{3}{4}$

C. $\frac{11}{15}$

D. $\frac{5}{6}$

114. There are 5 blue, 3 yellow, and 4 red chips in a bag. You draw two chips out of the bag without replacement. Given the first chip is blue, what is the probability the second chip will be red?

E. $\frac{4}{11}$

F. $\frac{9}{12}$

G. 20%

H. $\frac{5}{12}$

THIS IS THE END OF THE TEST. IF TIME REMAINS, YOU MAY CHECK YOUR ANSWERS. BE SURE THAT THERE ARE NO STRAY MARKS, PARTIALLY FILLED ANSWER CIRCLES, OR INCOMPLETE ERASURES ON YOUR ANSWER SHEET.

Test 2 Answer Key

1. B
2. G
3. A
4. F
5. A
6. E
7. A
8. F
9. D
10. F
11. A
12. E
13. C
14. E
15. D
16. F
17. B
18. G
19. D
20. F
21. C
22. H
23. C
24. E
25. C
26. H
27. D
28. H
29. D
30. E
31. D
32. E
33. D
34. F
35. A
36. H
37. D
38. G
39. C
40. F
41. D
42. H
43. D
44. H
45. D
46. G
47. B
48. H
49. A
50. H
51. C
52. G
53. C
54. E
55. D
56. G
57. A
58. 2
59. 75
60. 11
61. 31.5
62. 2.73

63. D
64. H
65. C
66. F
67. C
68. G
69. D
70. E
71. D
72. H
73. D
74. F
75. A
76. E
77. D
78. G
79. D
80. H
81. D
82. F
83. A
84. G
85. D
86. F
87. C
88. H
89. A
90. H
91. A
92. H
93. C
94. H
95. A
96. H
97. B
98. G
99. D
100. H
101. C
102. F
103. D
104. I
105. B
106. E
107. D
108. F
109. D
110. H
111. D
112. G
113. A
114. E

Explanation of Answers—ELA Section

Revising/Editing

1. **(B)** The question asks you to make the correct edit in the sentence. Options A, C, and D all ask you to insert unnecessary punctuation. Option B, however, asks you to turn the comma into a semicolon. That is correct. The error in the sentence is that a comma is joining two independent clauses. That can be fixed by replacing the comma with a semicolon. Therefore, Option B is the correct choice.

2. (G) The question asks you to edit a problem in the sentence. The problem is not Option E; there is no reason to change the tense of "is." The problem isn't corrected by Option F or H either. The apostrophe is correct as it is, and there is no need for a comma with the conjunction following "teens," because it is not joining two independent clauses. The problem in the sentence is with the verb "show." It should not be in the present tense. The sentence goes on to say "when they were teens," so we know it was sometime in the past. "Show" needs to be changed to "showed," so Option G is your answer.

3. **(A)** The question asks you to look for a misplaced modifier. There is only one modifier in the wrong place, and that is in sentence 1. "When he was only nine" comes right after "his uncle." This is confusing because it could be that his uncle was nine. That is not what the sentence means to say. "When he was only nine" should come right after "started to play chess." Then it is clear that it was José who was nine. Therefore, Option A is the correct answer.

4. **(F)** The question asks you to find the error in the sentences. Option E is incorrect because the comma after "Fischer" introduces a nonessential clause and needs to be there. Option G is incorrect because the conjunction following "America" is not linking two independent clauses and so doesn't need a comma. Option H is incorrect because this happened in the past, not the present. Option F is your answer because the pronoun is referring to Fischer. When referring to a person, you should always use "who," not "which."

5. **(A)** Again, the question asks you to look for the mistake that needs to be fixed in the sentence. This time, the mistake is in subject/verb agreement. Option B puts the verb into the past tense, which is not correct for this sentence. Options C and D ask you to make corrections that aren't necessary. Option A, however, is necessary. It changes "rely" to the singular "relies" so that it matches the subject, "chess," which is also singular.

6. **(E)** The question asks you to find the sentence that needs a comma inserted. The only missing comma is in sentence 1. In sentence 1 there are two coordinating adjectives describing "game." Those adjectives should be separated by a comma: "challenging, complicated game." Therefore, your answer is Option E.

7. **(A)** The question asks you to look for a sentence that provides support and joins sentences 7 and 8. Although all the options are true, only Option A continues the idea of the couple and Rowlands becoming very close and provides a reason for Rowlands to take Stanley's name. This provides a bridge from one sentence to the next.

8. **(F)** Option G erroneously indicates that the previous sentence is being restated. Option H suggests that sentence 4 happens in spite of sentence 3, which is also false. Option E could work, as another fact is being stated, but option F is the better choice because it shows a time progression that is important to the passage.

9. **(D)** The question asks you to find the misplaced modifier. Options A, B, and C all contain some modifying phrases, but they are positioned appropriately. Only option D contains a dangling modifier. It is "Enduring nightmarish conditions." This modifying phrase comes right before "the route." However, a route can't endure. This sentence should have been worded so that "Stanley's party" came right after the modifying phrase. That is who endured nightmarish conditions.

10. **(F)** The question asks you to make the correct edit. Option E removes an apostrophe that is important. It shows that the group belonged to Stanley. Options G and H would insert unnecessary commas that would break up the sentence. Option F inserts a comma after an introductory clause. That is a necessary comma and, therefore, the correct answer.

11. **(A)** The question asks for a concluding sentence that sums up the passage. Options C and D refer to some of the passage but not all of it. Option B is a very general summation of the topic, Henry Stanley, but Option A is much better. It sums up the main idea of the passage.

12. **(E)** The question asks for a sentence that supports and adds important information. All the options would provide some support for the sentence, and they supply some information, but Option E is the only one that supplies important information regarding who Dr. Livingstone was. Without this, the reader is left wondering why the *New York Herald* is chasing down Dr. Livingstone. This makes Option E the best choice.

13. **(C)** The question asks you to pick a sentence that strays from the main topic of the passage. The passage is about Henry Stanley's life. Options A, B, and D all deal with things that happened in his life. Only Option C strays from the topic to give a fact about Lake Tanganyika. That sentence should be eliminated.

14. **(E)** The question asks you to make the edit that is needed in sentence 4. This passage is written in the past tense. The present tense "wants" needs to be changed to "wanted" so that this sentence can match the rest of the passage [Option E]. Option F is still in the present tense. Options G and H ask you to insert commas where they are not needed, so they are not correct either. Option E is your only correct choice.

15. **(D)** The question is asking you to locate a misplaced modifier. All the modifiers in sentences 8, 9, and 10 are correct. However, at the end of sentence 11 is the modifying phrase "on the set." Because it comes right after the word "canceled," it seems as if the show was "canceled on the set." That most likely was not the case. More likely, "the mood on the set was somber." "On the set" should be put right after "mood." Placing the phrase next to the word it modifies gives it much more clarity. Option D is your answer.

16. **(F)** The question asks you to find the best way to combine sentences 9 and 10 to show their relationship. Option E indicates that they visited the set in spite of the fact that they were fans of the show. That doesn't make sense. Option G adds "nevertheless" to the beginning of the combined sentences, which creates a confusing relationship with the previous sentence. Option H suggests that they were fans **because** they visited the set, which is probably not true. Option F tells us they visited the set **because** they were fans. That is much more likely, so Option F is the correct answer.

17. **(B)** The question asks you to pick the transition that best shows the relationship between the two sentences. After reading the sentences carefully, you will see that they are almost opposite. Sentence 21 talks about it just having one more season, and sentence 22 talks about how important that season was. This means that Options C and D can't be right. "Furthermore" and "moreover" suggest that another fact is being added to reinforce the previous sentence. Option A is not correct either. Even though there are two sides to the story, they do not contradict one another. The correct answer is Option B, which tells us that, in spite of the first thing, the second thing was also true.

18. **(G)** All these options could follow sentence 10, but pay attention to what the question asks. It wants you to identify the choice that would best follow and **support** sentence 10. Sentence 10 states that the Trimbles were big fans of the show. Option E doesn't support that. Options F and H do, but those choices are only vaguely related. Option G, on the other hand, gives specific reasons why they were fans of the show. It is the best choice.

19. **(D)** Options A, B, and C all help to further the story in the passage. Only Option D strays from the topic to give unrelated information about the television.

20. **(F)** The question asks you to sum up the passage's argument in a concluding sentence. Options E, G, and H all give relevant information, and some of them could be used as a concluding sentence. However, the argument in the passage is that the Trimbles saved the show through their activism. Therefore, Option F is the correct answer.

Reading Comprehension

21. (C) This question asks you to determine the general theme of the passage. Option A is mentioned in passing; it is a detail. Option B is discussed in detail, but it is not the theme of the passage. Option D is a detail that is mentioned, but not the focus of the entire passage. The passage describes how the Northwest Passage was discovered and its future potential. Thus, the best answer is Option C.

22. (H) This question asks you to make an inference based on the information in the passage. Option E may be true, but there is not enough information in the passage to draw this conclusion. Option F does not agree with the information in the passage about the nationality of the explorers. Option G might be true, but there is nothing to suggest this was so. A close reading of the text will show that Option H is the correct answer since the sentence "Some disappeared, never to be heard from again" (lines 16–17) strongly suggests this was the case.

23. (C) The question asks specifically about Roald Amundsen. In order to answer the question, you must look at the information in the passage and use it to infer the answer. Option A may be true, but there is nothing to support this idea in the passage. Option B could be true or false, but the passage does not discuss this possibility. Option C is supported by the passage, which states, "The ship was stuck frozen in two-foot-thick ice for two winters. But everyone survived." (lines 30–32). Only someone with great determination would endure this. Option D is contrary to the information in the passage.

24. (E) The statement "Continuing record sea ice melting may indicate that the route will be used by commercial carriers . . ." implies that global warming is the reason the ice is melting, therefore allowing commercial carriers to traverse the Northwest Passage, so there is support for Option E. It does not imply that Option F is correct; there is no suggestion that fewer small ships will use the Northwest Passage. There is also no evidence for Option G or H.

25. (C) This is an inference question. It is necessary to look for information that supports one of the options. Neither Option A nor B is supported by the passage. There is no evidence of the Canadian government creating canals in the Northwest Passage, so Option D is not correct. The best answer is Option C.

26. (H) To answer this question, you have to go through the passage and try to find the one topic that is not discussed. Options E and F are discussed in the paragraph. So is Option G. That leaves Option H. There is no mention of hostile natives.

27. (D) This question asks you to determine the general theme of the passage. Option A is not discussed in the passage. Option B is just a detail, not a main theme. Option C is not mentioned in the passage at all. Option D is the best answer.

28. **(H)** This is an inference question. You need to make an inference based on the information in the passage. Option E is not supported by the passage. There is nothing to suggest this. Option F is probably not true; without Delta Works the lives of some of the people of the Netherlands would have been affected. Option G might be true, but there is nothing to directly support this idea. Option H is supported by the passage, which talks about "low-lying tracts of land reclaimed from fens and marshes that are protected by dikes" (lines 10–12), and it can be inferred that without Delta Works much of this land might revert to the sea.

29. **(D)** To answer this question, you need to read the passage carefully to see which option is correct. Option A might appeal, except the rest of the passage shows that fixing dikes is much more complicated than that. Option B really has no bearing on the passage, so it cannot be the correct answer. While it is true that the Netherlands has had many stories written about it, this is not the reason the author included the story of Hans Brinker at the beginning of the article. Thus, Option D is the correct answer. This can be inferred from the passage.

30. **(E)** To answer this question, you need to reread the section of the passage that talks about how Delta Works was developed. If you do this, you will find that only Option E is an accurate description of how many people contributed to the plan. Option F might appeal, but there is nothing in the passage to indicate that only engineers worked on the plan. There is nothing to suggest that Option G or H is correct.

31. **(D)** To answer this question, you need to review the passage and find what is true of Delta Works. Option A is not likely because the author calls Delta Works "one of the Seven Wonders of the Modern World" (lines 53–54). Option B is something that is directly stated in the passage, so it can be eliminated. Option C is also correct according to the passage. However, Option D is not true; the project is ongoing. So Option D is the correct answer.

32. **(E)** To make an inference, you need to weigh all the information in a passage and come to the most logical conclusion. Options F and G don't seem to be likely. Nothing that the author says would indicate that Option H is correct. Option E seems to be the only logical reason. Therefore, it is the correct answer.

33. **(D)** This question asks you to determine the main idea or general theme of the passage. Option A is mentioned in the passage, but it is only a detail, and not a general theme. Options B and C are details in the passage, but not the main focus of it. Therefore, the correct answer is Option D.

34. **(F)** Check back through the passage to answer this question. Review the reasons that are mentioned for using henna. Although the word *dye* is not mentioned in Option E, this means the same thing. Only Option F is not given as a reason for using henna.

35. **(A)** This question requires you to take the information in the passage and make an inference. Based on the information in the passage, which only talks about women putting henna designs on their palms before weddings, Option A seems to be a logical conclusion. There is no suggestion that Option B is correct, although it could be true. Option C does not seem likely; there is nothing to suggest this is so. Option D is probably not true either.

36. (H) You have to figure out why the author used this information in the passage. Option E might be a possibility, although this is not mentioned in the passage. Option F is not correct. There is no reference to how long the designs take to be done. Option G is probably true, but that is not why the information about the name of the bride's future husband is included. Option H is the best answer.

37. (D) You need to use your best judgment to answer this question. While all of the options are true, Option D seems to be the best answer. Option A is tempting. A bride wants to be attractive. But you need to weigh all the answers before choosing one. Options B and C are possible, but not as likely as D.

38. (G) To answer this question, you have to examine each option carefully. Option E is appealing, but that is not stated in the passage. Option F might be true, but this is not what the phrase states. Option G seems to be correct. This seems to be a good reason. Option H does not seem likely. Option G is the best answer.

39. (C) This question asks you to determine the main idea or general theme of the passage. Option A is mentioned in the passage, but it is only a detail, not a general theme. Option B is also mentioned but is only a detail, not what the passage is mostly about. Option D is only discussed in passing. Most of the article is about why people should learn to swim. Therefore, the correct answer is Option C.

40. (F) The statistic offers a strong motivation for the author's premise that learning to swim is important. The other options are incorrect.

41. (D) You will need to review the passage to answer this question. Scan through the passage to find what reasons were mentioned for learning to swim. Options A, B, and C are definitely mentioned. Hence Option D is the correct answer.

42. (H) A clue to the answer is the sentence "A beginning swimmer needs to obey rules . . ." Rules are meant to keep new swimmers safe; not swimming alone is one of the rules.

43. (D) You will need to analyze the author's intent from what the passage says. It talks about how many parents or grandparents of African American children were not allowed to swim in pools reserved for use only by white people; there were not many pools where blacks could swim. Showing how cultural disparities have influenced children in terms of swimming is the reason for including this information. Option A is not the reason, nor is Option B: you must keep in mind the general subject and purpose of the passage, which is water safety. Option C has no bearing on the importance of learning to swim.

44. (H) While some of the options may occur as a result of USA Swimmers expanding its program in inner cities, such as Options E and F, the most important reason is Option H. Option G would probably not be a reason.

45. (D) This question asks you to determine the main idea or general theme of the passage. Option A is definitely a possibility, but while this is important, it is not the main focus of the passage. Options B and C are details in the passage, not the main focus of it. The passage describes how Matthew Henson made his mark on history, so Option D is the correct answer.

46. (G) Use the information in the passage to help find the answer to this question. The passage says that Matthew Henson traveled all over the world as a cabin boy; from that information it could be inferred that there were many dangers. Option F could be a possibility; perhaps he did read a lot. But that is not the best answer. Option G is something that the passage supports. Therefore it is the correct answer. Option H is probably true, but it was not the main effect.

47. (B) A careful review of the passage will help you answer this question. Option A is something that Matthew Henson did, as are Options C and D. There is no mention in the passage that he learned to trade furs, so Option B is correct.

48. (H) The passage talks about how many on the expedition did not like Matthew Henson because he had better skills; but the main point is that he was a black man. Later in the passage it talks about how prejudiced people were against African Americans at that time, so it is possible to infer that Option H was the reason they did not like him. Option E is probably true of these members of the expedition, but that was not the underlying reason for their dislike of him. There is nothing in the passage to suggest Option F or G is correct. Therefore Option H is the best answer.

49. (A) You have to use the information and your own prior knowledge to answer this question. Option A is appealing. The fact that Matthew Henson helped Peary get to the North Pole was originally ignored; having him become an honorary member of the Explorers Club was one way to rectify what had happened earlier. While he did have the same, or better, skills as other explorers, this was not the reason for the honor, so Option B is not correct. While the honor might inspire other African Americans, this was not the main reason he received this honor, so Option C is not correct either. Option D is not the reason even if it is true. The best answer is Option A.

50. (H) You need to use the information in the passage to make an inference about Matthew Henson. Options E and F do not seem to be the correct choices; he may have enjoyed writing, but that is not what the quote suggests, nor does it suggest he thought he would die in the Arctic. Option G might be true, but this is not what is suggested by the quote. Option H is what is suggested by the quotation from his autobiography.

51. (C) This question asks you to determine the general theme of the passage. Option A is discussed in detail, but it is not the theme. Option B is implied in passing, but it is not the theme of the passage. Option D is not ever discussed and so can't be the theme. The passage describes the circumstances that led to the creation of the United Nations. Thus, the best answer is Option C.

52. (G) This question asks you to make an inference based on the information in the passage. Although Option E was one of the problems that the League of Nations faced, the passage does not present enough evidence to infer that this is why it failed. Option F may be true, but there is not enough information in the passage to draw this conclusion. Option H is not addressed in the passage and so can't be the right answer either. A close reading of the text will show that Option G is the correct answer. This is shown in the sentence "Because during that time period many people espoused isolationism, the League of Nations was born into a world that was not entirely welcoming," followed later in the passage by "The world was finally ready for a global solution" (the UN).

53. (C) The question asks specifically about the United Nations. In order to answer the question, you must look at the information in the passage and use it to infer the answer. Option A is not true. The League of Nations was formed after the First World War; the United Nations was formed after the Second World War. Similarly, Options B and D are true of the League of Nations, not the United Nations. Option C is supported by the passage, which states, "In contrast, it [the UN] was reformed from a realist's perspective."

54. (E) This is an inference question. It is necessary to look for information that supports one of the options. Neither Option F, G, nor H is supported by the passage. Although one might assume that all these options are necessary to becoming a UN member, the passage doesn't mention them. The best answer is Option E. This is supported by the sentence "It [the UN] would use force, if necessary, to impose its will on member and nonmember nations."

55. (D) To answer this question, you have to go through the passage and try to find the one topic that is not discussed. Options A and C are discussed in the second paragraph. So is Option B. The passage says that "The only two Great Powers that were steadfast members of this organization were Great Britain and France," which implies that there was a lack of member nations. That leaves Option D. There is no mention of funding issues.

56. (G) The statement "President Wilson wanted this council to be viewed as a place where the nations of the world could come together to debate and find agreement, not as a force of retribution" implies that retribution (the punishment of nations) was not supposed to be a part of the League's mission, so option G is the answer. We can assume that nations would air grievances [option E], but that is not really implied by "debate and find agreement." Also, although this passage implies that President Wilson was involved in the formation of the League of Nations, we can't assume by this statement that he was intricately involved. Similarly, "debate and find agreement" might imply that there would be disagreement, but is doesn't necessarily imply that there would be a lot of disagreement, so options F and H do not fit as well as option G.

57. (A) This is another inference question. Option B was true of the League of Nations, but the passage implies that the opposite was true of the United Nations. The passage never mentions the rules for UN membership or the Security Council, so options C and D can't be correct. Option A is implied by the sentences "The world was finally ready for a global solution" and "it was viewed as a lifeline [by nations]." These sentences suggest that the United Nations was widely accepted, so Option A is correct.

Explanation of Answers—Mathematics Section

58. Let x represent the original number of jelly beans in the bag. There are 8 red jelly beans, and the probability of randomly drawing one of them is $\frac{1}{6}$. Set up a proportion to solve for x:

$$\frac{8}{x} = \frac{1}{6}$$

so, using cross-multiplication, $x = 48$.

Let y represent the number of red jelly beans Lisa added to the bag. When Lisa adds the red jelly beans, the probability becomes $\frac{1}{5}$. Use another proportion to solve for y:

$$\frac{8+y}{48+y} = \frac{1}{5}$$

$$5(8 + y) = 48 + y$$

$$40 + 5y = 48 + y$$

$$4y = 8$$

$$y = 2$$

59. If x represents the number of visitors on Friday, then the number of visitors on Saturday is expressed as $x + 150$. The total number of visitors on Friday and Saturday is $x + x + 150 = 2x + 150$.

The total number of visitors on Friday and Saturday is twice the number on Sunday, so that number of visitors on Sunday is expressed as $\frac{2x + 150}{2} = x + 75$. There were 75 more visitors on Sunday than on Friday, so grid in 75.

60. First, find the total population of New York State. If 8.5 million is 43%, then solve:

$$.43 \times x = 8{,}500{,}000$$

$$x = 19{,}767{,}442$$

Next, subtract the population of New York City:

$$19{,}767{,}442 - 8{,}500{,}000 = 11{,}267{,}442$$

The question asks about how many millions, so grid in "11".

61. Substitute the mass of material x into this ratio and solve for the mass of material y:

$$\frac{x}{y} = \frac{2}{3}$$

$$\frac{9}{y} = \frac{2}{3}$$

$$2(y) = 3(9)$$

$$y = 13.5 \text{ grams}$$

Now, substitute the mass of material y into this ratio and solve for the mass of material m:

$$\frac{y}{m} = \frac{3}{4}$$

$$\frac{13.5}{m} = \frac{3}{4}$$

$$3(m) = 4(13.5)$$

$$m = 18 \text{ grams}$$

Now add the two masses together:

$$13.5 + 18 = 31.5 \text{ grams}$$

62. Solve:

$$3x + 2.62 = 7x - 8.3$$

$$3x = 7x - 10.92$$

$$-4x = -10.92$$

$$x = 2.73$$

63. (D) This is a greatest common factor problem because he's looking for the greatest number of plants that can factor into both numbers. Factor each number into its prime factors:

$135 = 3 \cdot 3 \cdot 3 \cdot 5$

$210 = 2 \cdot 3 \cdot 5 \cdot 7$

The common prime factors are 3 and 5:

$135 = \boxed{3} \cdot 3 \cdot 3 \cdot \boxed{5}$

$210 = 2 \cdot \boxed{3} \cdot \boxed{5} \cdot 7$

The greatest common factor (GCF) is the product of the common prime factors:

$\text{GCF} = 3 \times 5 = 15$

64. (H) The formula for the distance between two points a and b on a number line is $b - a$. Use the formula to find the length of $\overline{RS}$:

$$\begin{aligned} RS &= S - R \\ &= 7 - (-5) \\ &= 7 + 5 \\ &= 12 \end{aligned}$$

$\overline{RS}$ is divided into 3 equal parts, so each part is $12 \div 3 = 4$ units long. Start at point R and count 4 units to the right to point P. Then count another 4 units to point Q.

65. (C) Convert the fractions to a common denominator for easy ordering:

$$Q = \frac{8}{25} = \frac{32}{100}$$

$$R = \frac{3}{10} = \frac{30}{100}$$

$$S = \frac{1}{\sqrt{16}} = \frac{1}{4} = \frac{25}{100}$$

Thus, $S < R < Q$.

66. (F) Let x represent the cost of the cell phone. The television cost 5 times as much as the cell phone, so the cost of the television is $5x$. The computer cost 2.5 times as much as the television, so the cost of the computer is $2.5(5x)$. Together, they cost \$925, so $2.5(5x) + 5x + x = \$925$. Solve for x:

$$\begin{aligned} 2.5(5x) + 5x + x &= \$925 \\ 12.5x + 6x &= \$925 \\ 18.5x &= \$925 \\ x &= \$50 \end{aligned}$$

67. (C) The mean is the total number of hours divided by the number of students. The table shows that 7 students completed 16 hours, 6 students completed 12 hours, 4 students completed 20 hours, and 3 students completed 10 hours. The mean number of hours completed per student is:

$$\begin{aligned} \frac{(7\times16)+(6\times12)+(4\times20)+(3\times10)}{20} &= \frac{112+72+80+30}{20} \\ &= \frac{294}{20} \\ &= 14.7 \end{aligned}$$

68. (G) The sum of all nine sides of the polygon is 156, so $x + 4(1.25x) + 4(1.5x) = 156$. Solve for x:

$$\begin{aligned} x + 4(1.25x) + 4(1.5x) &= 156 \\ x + 5x + 6x &= 156 \\ 12x &= 156 \\ x &= 13 \end{aligned}$$

69. (D) Use the distributive property to write $6x(2y - 9)$ as an equivalent expression.

$$\begin{aligned} 6x(2y - 9) &= 6x(2y) - 6x(9) \\ &= 12xy - 54x \end{aligned}$$

70. (E) $(\sqrt{9})(\sqrt{49}) = (3)(7) = 21$

71. **(D)** According to the graph, Megan earns \$50 if she works 2 hours, \$100 if she works 4 hours, and so on. The graph is a straight line, so the rate of change is constant.

The amount Megan earns per hour is:

$$\frac{\$50}{2} = \$25$$

72. **(H)** $\frac{43}{7} = 6\frac{1}{7}$, so the least integer that is greater than $6\frac{1}{7}$ is 7.

73. **(D)** Substitute the values of x and y into the expression:

$$\begin{aligned} |6x| - |-2y| &= |6(-3)| - |-2(5)| \\ &= |-18| - |-10| \\ &= 18 - 10 \\ &= 8 \end{aligned}$$

74. **(F)** At 5:00 a.m., the temperature was $-15°$. At 12:00 p.m., the temperature had risen 5 degrees per hour for 7 hours, for a total rise of $5° \times 7 = 35°$. The temperature at 12:00 p.m. was $-15° + 35° = 20°$.

75. **(A)** Diagonals $\overline{AC}$ and $\overline{BD}$ intersect at the center of the square. Therefore, they divide square ABCD into four large triangles of the same size. Line segments $\overline{EG}$ and $\overline{FH}$ also pass through the center of the square, so they divide each of the large triangles into 2 smaller triangles of the same size. Four of the smaller triangles are shaded, and their total area is 18 sq cm. Therefore, the total area of all 8 triangles is $18 \times 2 = 36$ sq cm. This is also the area of the square. If the area of the square is 36 sq cm, then the side length is $\sqrt{36} = 6$ cm.

76. **(E)**

$$\begin{aligned} 21 + x &< -7 \\ 21 - 21 + x &< -7 - 21 \\ x &< -28 \end{aligned}$$

77. **(D)** Brooke worked a total of $3\frac{1}{2} \times 5 = 17.5$ hours. Therefore, she earned $17.5 \times \$5.10 =$ \$89.25.

78. **(G)**

15% of $7 = (0.15)(7) = 1.05$

7% of $7 = (0.07)(7) = 0.49$

$1.05 - 0.49 = 0.56$

79. **(D)** The number of customers who did not order dessert is $70 - 21 = 49$, so the fraction who did not order dessert is $\frac{49}{70}$. Reduce the fraction to lowest terms and then multiply by 100 to find the percentage who did not order dessert:

$$\frac{49}{70} = \frac{7}{10}$$

$$\frac{7}{10} \times 100 = 70\%$$

80. **(H)** Let M represent Morgan's speed. Use the formula distance = rate × time to find the distance Morgan traveled in 0.5 hours: distance = rate × time = $0.5M$.

In 0.5 hours, Andy traveled $55 \times 0.5 = 27.5$ miles. Together, they traveled a total distance of 60 miles:

$$\begin{aligned} 27.5 + 0.5M &= 60 \\ 0.5M &= 32.5 \\ M &= 65 \end{aligned}$$

81. (D) The formula for the circumference of a circle is $C = 2\pi r$. The formula for the area of a circle is $A = \pi r^2$. Substitute the formulas into the equation $C = \frac{2}{5}A$ to solve for the radius of the circle:

$$C = \frac{2}{5}A$$
$$2\pi r = \frac{2}{5}(\pi r^2)$$
$$\frac{5}{2}(2\pi r) = \pi r^2$$
$$5r = r^2$$
$$5 = r$$

The diameter is $5 \times 2 = 10$ inches.

82. (F) Let x and y represent the two numbers. Translate the verbal description into an algebraic equation:

$$\frac{1}{3}(x - y) = 12$$
$$x - y = 36$$
$$9 - y = 36$$
$$-y = 27$$
$$y = -27$$

To solve for x, plug -27 for y in the second equation above:

$$x - y = 36$$
$$x - (-27) = 36$$
$$x + 27 = 36$$
$$x = 9$$

The sum of x and y is $9 + (-27) = -18$.

83. (A) Cross-multiply and then solve for x:

$$\frac{5}{8} = \frac{40}{x^2}$$
$$5x^2 = 8(40)$$
$$x^2 = \frac{320}{5}$$
$$x^2 = 64$$
$$x = 8 \text{ or } -8$$

84. (G) Let x represent the length of the rectangle:

$$9 + 9 + x + x = 40$$
$$18 + 2x = 40$$
$$2x = 22$$
$$x = 11$$

The width is 9 inches and the length is 11 inches, so the area of the rectangle is $9 \times 11 = 99$ square inches.

85. (D) Amanda can choose among 6 brands of tennis rackets and 4 brands of tennis balls. Use the Fundamental Counting Principle to find the different combinations of brands that she can buy:

$6 \times 4 = 24$

86. (F)

$$\dddot{5}(\ddot{8}) = \frac{5}{4}\left(\frac{8}{4}\right) = \frac{40}{16} = \frac{5}{2} = 2.5$$

87. (C) According to the circle graph, approximately 19.9% of the students are enrolled at Stuyvesant High School:

$16{,}405 \times 0.199 = 3{,}264.595$

3,264.595 rounded to the nearest whole number is 3,265.

88. (H) Erika is 7 years older than Fernando, so she is now $x+7$. Four years ago, her age was $x+7-4=x+3$.

89. (A) Substitute the values of x and y into the expression:

$$\frac{x+y}{x-4}=\frac{23+15}{23-4}=\frac{38}{19}=2$$

90. (H) The least common multiple (LCM) of X and Y is the product of the greatest power of each of its prime factors:

$$X=3\times3\times5=3^2\times5$$
$$Y=2\times2\times3\times5=2^2\times3\times5$$

The LCM is $2^2\times3^2\times5=4\times9\times5=180$.

91. (A) If 1 inch is equivalent to 25 feet, then 1 square inch is equivalent to 625 square feet:

$$(1\text{ in.})^2=(25\text{ ft})^2$$
$$1\text{ sq in.}=625\text{ sq ft}$$

Set up a proportion to find how many square inches is equivalent to 1 square foot:

$$\frac{1\text{ sq in.}}{625\text{ sq ft}}=\frac{x}{1}$$
$$625x=1$$
$$x=\frac{1}{625}$$
$$=0.0016$$

92. (H) Let x represent the number of yellow balls in the bag. There are 30 balls in the bag, and the probability of randomly drawing a yellow one is $\frac{1}{6}$. Set up a proportion to solve for x:

$$\frac{x}{30}=\frac{1}{6}$$
$$6x=30$$
$$x=5$$

Let y represent the number of red balls to be removed in order to increase the probability to $\frac{1}{3}$. Set up another proportion to solve for y:

$$\frac{5}{30-y}=\frac{1}{3}$$
$$30-y=15$$
$$-y=-15$$
$$y=15$$

93. (C) Cody ate $\frac{1}{7}$ of the cereal on Monday, so the fraction left in the box is $1-\frac{1}{7}=\frac{6}{7}$. On Tuesday, he ate $\frac{1}{6}\times\frac{6}{7}=\frac{1}{7}$ of the cereal. Therefore, Cody has eaten a total of $\frac{1}{7}+\frac{1}{7}=\frac{2}{7}$ of the cereal. The fraction that is left in the box after Tuesday is $1-\frac{2}{7}=\frac{5}{7}$.

94. (H) On the grid, the shaded region has a width of 5 inches and a length of about 7.5 inches. The scale is 1 in. $=4$ feet, so the actual width is $5\times4=20$ feet and the actual length is $7.5\times4=30$ feet. One yard is equal to 3 feet, so the width is $\frac{20}{3}$ yd and the length is $\frac{30}{3}$ yd. Therefore, the area of the shaded region is $\frac{20}{3}\times\frac{30}{3}=66\frac{2}{3}$ square yards.

95. **(A)** Angle x, the 90° angle formed by lines r and s, and the 53° angle all add up to 180 degrees because they share the common line p. Therefore:

$$x° + 90° + 53° = 180°$$
$$x = 180° - 90° - 53°$$
$$x = 37°$$

96. **(H)** To find the value that is halfway between $\frac{1}{2}$ and 0.85, add and then divide by 2:

$$\frac{\frac{1}{2} + 0.85}{2} = \frac{0.5 + 0.85}{2}$$
$$= \frac{1.35}{2}$$
$$= 0.675$$

97. **(B)** Benita will be 24 years old in 8 years, so her age now is $24 - 8 = 16$. Julianne is half as old as Benita, so Julianne is now $16 \div 2 = 8$ years old. Three years ago, Julianne was $8 - 3 = 5$ years old.

98. **(G)** The number of registered Republicans is about $13{,}000 \times 0.46 = 5{,}980$. The number of registered Democrats is about $13{,}000 \times 0.38 = 4{,}940$. There are about $5{,}980 - 4{,}940 = 1{,}040$ more Republicans than Democrats. The number 1,040 rounded to the nearest thousand is 1,000.

99. **(D)** Divide 220 by 12. The remainder represents the amount of fabric Tameka has left over:

$220 \div 12 = 18\,\text{R}4$

100. **(H)** Since points O, P, Q, and R are points on the circle, the diagonal of the square is equal to the diameter of the circle. Use the formula for the area of a circle, $A = \pi r^2$, to find the radius:

$$A = \pi r^2$$
$$36\pi = \pi r^2$$
$$36 = r^2$$
$$6 = r$$

Diameter is $2r$, so the answer is 12.

101. **(C)** Use the formula for the area of a triangle, $A = \frac{1}{2}bh$, to find the measure of the base:

$$A = \frac{1}{2}bh$$
$$25 = \frac{1}{2}b(5)$$
$$50 = 5b$$
$$10 = b$$

The base of the triangle is equal to the length of the rectangle, and the height of the triangle is equal to the width of the rectangle, so the area of the rectangle is $10 \times 5 = 50$ sq cm. The area of the shaded region is $50 - 25 = 25$ sq cm.

102. **(F)** Substitute the value of x into the expression and solve for y:

$$(3x - 1)(y - 2x) = 60$$
$$(21 - 1)(y - 14) = 60$$
$$20(y - 14) = 60$$
$$y - 14 = 3$$
$$y = 17$$

103. **(D)** Let s represent the location of point S. The distance between points R and S on the number line is $s-(-4)=s+4$. The distance between points S and T on the number line is $14-s$. We know that RS $=\frac{1}{3}$ ST. So:

$$s+4=\frac{1}{3}(14-s)$$
$$3s+12=14-s$$
$$4s=2$$
$$s=\frac{1}{2}$$

104. **(I)** It is given that VY = 14 cm and that XY = 5 cm. We can use this information to find the length of $\overline{VX}$:

VX = VY − XY = 14 − 5 = 9 cm

If VW = WX, then they are each $9 \div 2 = 4.5$ cm. Therefore, WY = 4.5 + 5 = 9.5 cm.

105. **(B)** Translate the verbal description into an algebraic equation: if the electronic version costs one dollar less than one-fourth the cost of Julio's book, then:

$$y=\frac{1}{4}x-1$$

106. **(E)** Tia had a total of 35 marbles in the box. Before she removed any marbles, the probability of randomly drawing a blue marble was $\frac{15}{35}$. After she removed the 8 marbles, the probability of drawing a blue marble is:

$$\frac{15-6}{35-8}=\frac{9}{27}=\frac{1}{3}$$

107. **(D)**

$$\left(\frac{2}{6}+\frac{1}{7}\right)\div\frac{2}{5}=\left(\frac{14}{42}+\frac{6}{42}\right)\div\frac{2}{5}$$
$$=\left(\frac{20}{42}\right)\div\frac{2}{5}$$
$$=\frac{20}{42}\times\frac{5}{2}$$
$$=\frac{100}{84}$$
$$=\frac{25}{21}$$

108. **(F)** Let x represent Erik's age:

$$\frac{39+22+45+x}{4}=33.5$$
$$\frac{106+x}{4}=33.5$$
$$106+x=134$$
$$x=28$$

109. (D)

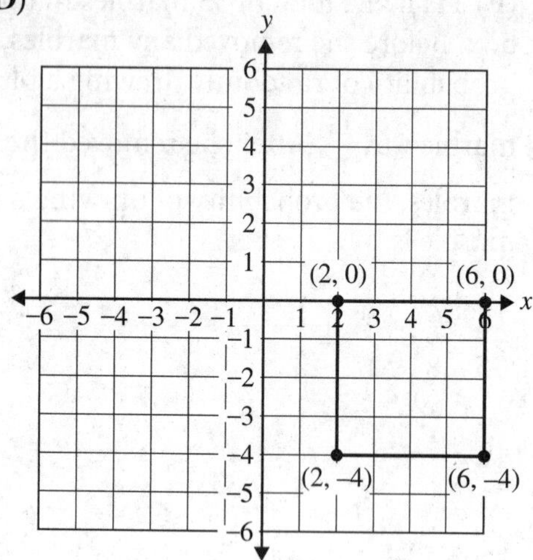

110. (H) Let x represent the number of miles Allan can drive. Set up a proportion to solve for x:

$$\frac{x}{\frac{7}{8}\text{ gallon of gas}} = \frac{32\text{ miles}}{1\text{ gallon of gas}}$$

$$x = 32 \times \frac{7}{8}$$

$$= 28$$

111. (D) Let x represent the number of gallons of water Neil uses to water his plants:

$$\frac{3}{5}x = 4\frac{1}{3}$$

$$\frac{3}{5}x = \frac{13}{3}$$

$$x = \frac{13}{3} \div \frac{3}{5}$$

$$= \frac{13}{3} \times \frac{5}{3}$$

$$= \frac{65}{9}$$

$$= 7\frac{2}{9}$$

112. (G) Let x represent the total number of students in the 5 classes:

$$\frac{x}{5} = 17.4$$

$$x = 87$$

Let y represent the number of students in the sixth class:

$$\frac{87 + y}{6} = 18.5$$

$$87 + y = 111$$

$$y = 24$$

113. (A) Nancy pays $\frac{1}{3}$ of the debt in May, so she has $\frac{2}{3}$ left.

In June, she pays $\frac{3}{5}$ of $\frac{2}{3}$ of her debt:

$$\frac{3}{5} \times \frac{2}{3} = \frac{6}{15}$$

So, she has paid $\frac{1}{3} + \frac{6}{15}$.

Find a common denominator:

$$\frac{5}{15} + \frac{6}{15} = \frac{11}{15}$$

Nancy has paid $\frac{11}{15}$ of her total debt. Therefore, she has $\frac{4}{15}$ left to pay.

114. (E) Altogether there are 12 chips. If one of the two withdrawn is blue, you are choosing from 11 for the second chip. There are 4 chances it could be red out of the 11 options in the bag.

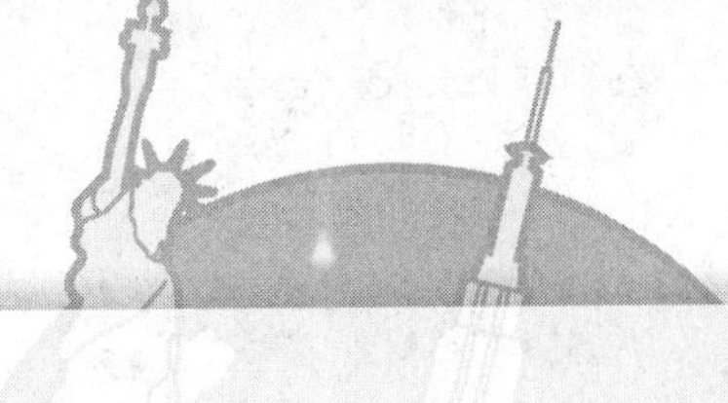

CHAPTER 13

Grade 9 SHSAT Mathematics Practice Problems

Students taking the Grade 9 SHSAT are responsible for mathematics material covered through the eighth grade New York City Mathematics Curriculum. This chapter has 30 questions that test your understanding of the *additional* mathematics content that is covered in the eighth grade year. Make sure you also practice the problems on the other practice tests, because all students are responsible for the content covered prior to the eighth grade year. There is no sample answer sheet for this section, so write your answers directly in this book or on a separate piece of paper and check them against the answer key.

1.

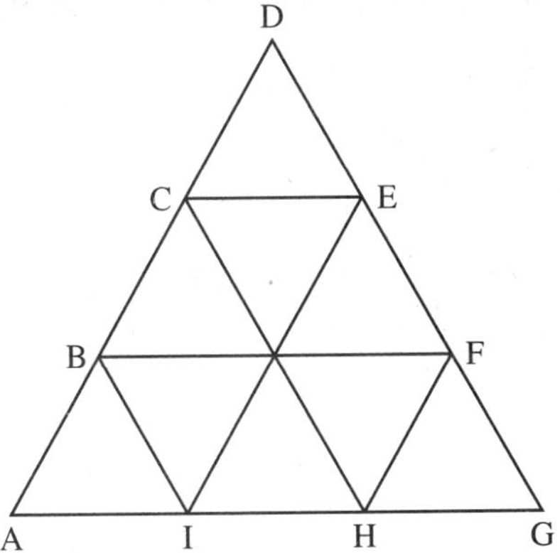

The figure above is made up of 9 equilateral triangles. How many triangles in the figure are similar to triangle ABI? (Do not include ABI itself.)

A. 1
B. 3
C. 8
D. 12

2.

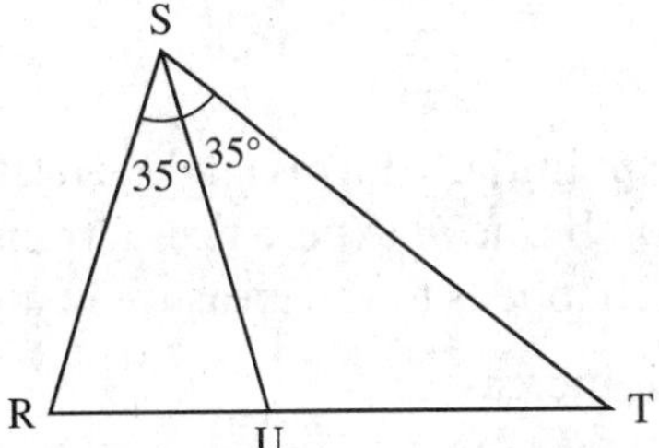

Triangles RSU and TSU are similar triangles. What is the measure of ∠SUR?

E. 55°
F. 70°
G. 90°
H. 110°

3.

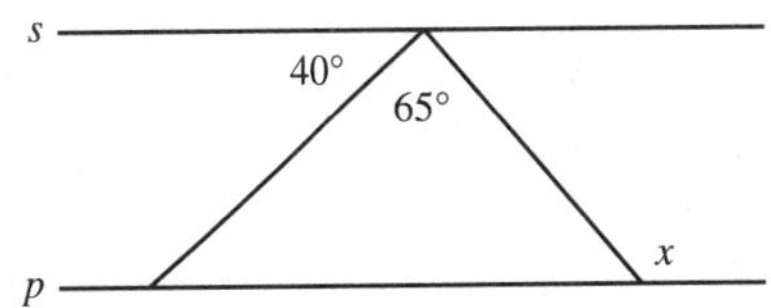

Lines s and p in the figure are parallel. Given the values of the angles shown, find the measure of angle x.

A. 65°
B. 75°
C. 95°
D. 105°

4.

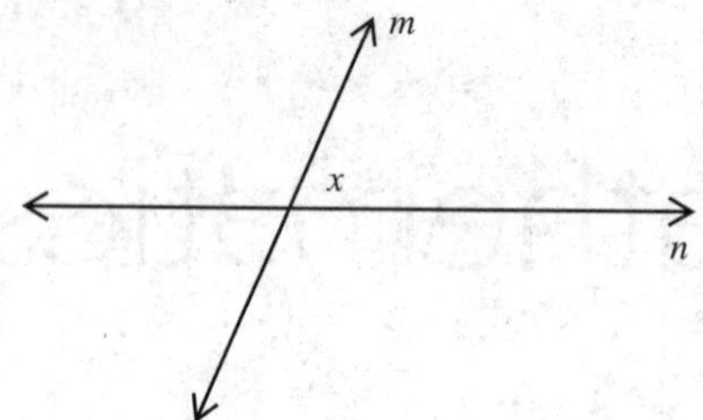

Determine the value of x in the following expression: $(4^6)(2^{-6}) = 2^x$.

E. −6
F. 0
G. 6
H. 36

5. Line *m* initially forms angle *x* relative to line *n*. If line *m* experiences a translation, what happens to the measure of angle *x*?

A. It increases.
B. It decreases.
C. It initially increases and then decreases.
D. It stays the same.

6.

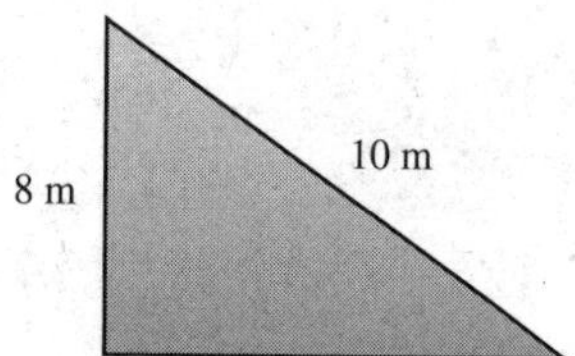

Find the length of the missing side in the right triangle in the figure.

E. 4 m
F. 6 m
G. 8 m
H. 13 m

7. Determine the value of *y* in the following expression:

$(25 \times 10^2) + (5 \times 10^4) = (y \times 10^3)$

A. 52.5
B. 125
C. 525
D. 3,000

8. An empty right circular oil drum has a base with a diameter of 6 dm and a height of 9 dm. A solid lead sphere has a radius of 3 dm. If the sphere is placed inside the drum, how much water will the drum hold?

E. 9π dm^3
F. 27π dm^3
G. 36π dm^3
H. 45π dm^3

9.

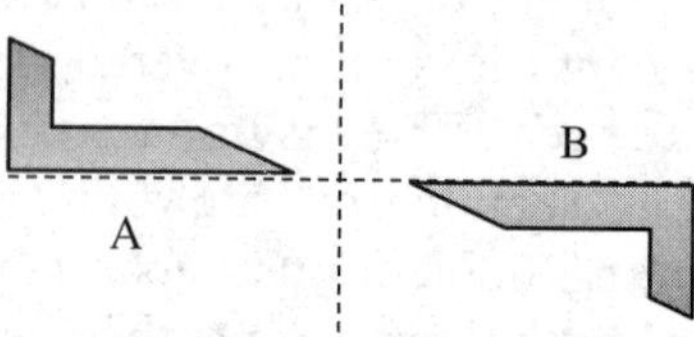

Which of the following will transform figure A into figure B?

A. translation
B. reflection
C. dilation
D. rotation

10. Consider the equations for two lines:

$y = 2x$
$y = -x + 3$

These lines will intersect at which points on the coordinate system?

E. (0, 0)
F. (0, 3)
G. (1, 2)
H. (2, 1)

11.

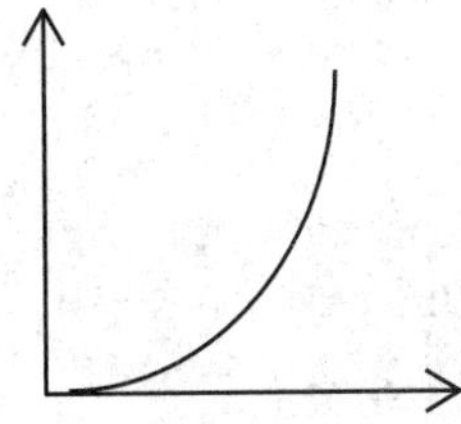

Which of the following equations shows a relationship similar to that displayed on the given graph?

A. $y = 3x + 5$
B. $y = \frac{5}{x}$
C. $y = 4x^2$
D. $y = -2x + 3$

12. What value of x will satisfy this expression: $5^x = 625$?

E. 2
F. 4
G. 5
H. 10

13. The value of the square root of 43 is between the values of which two integers?

A. 5 and 6
B. 6 and 7
C. 7 and 8
D. 42 and 44

14. Which of the following is an irrational number?

E. $\sqrt{17}$
F. $\frac{1}{8}$
G. 0.320
H. 150

15.

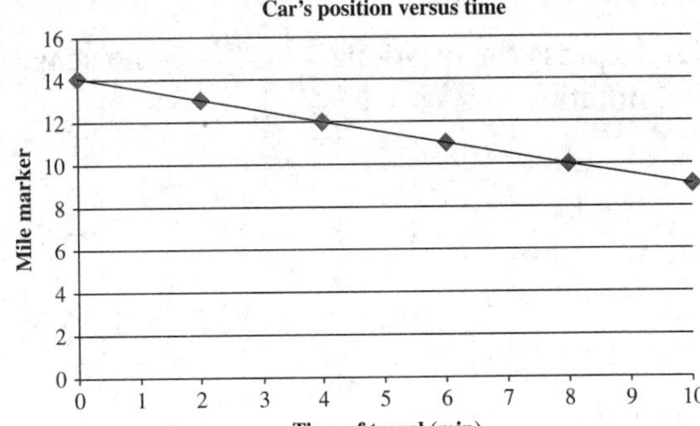

A car moves along the highway mile markers according to the graph. What is the speed of the car in miles per hour?

A. 0.5 mph
B. 2 mph
C. 8 mph
D. 30 mph

16.

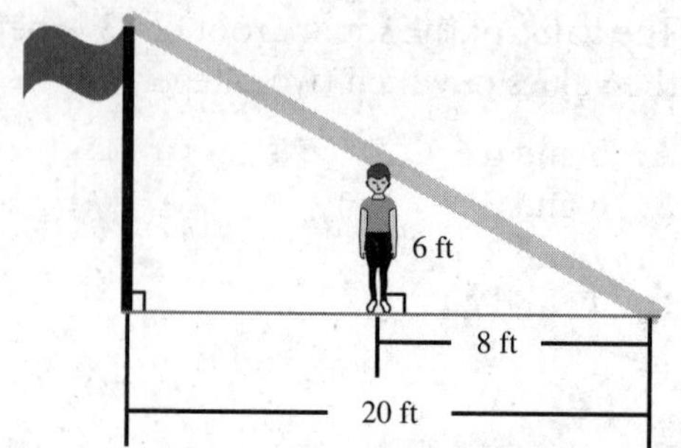

A 6-ft-tall person casts an 8-ft shadow that ends at the same location as the 20-ft shadow cast by a flagpole. What is the height of the flagpole?

E. 12 ft
F. 15 ft
G. 20 ft
H. 25 ft

17. Express the quotient $\frac{2.4 \times 10^6}{2.0 \times 10^{-4}}$ using scientific notation.

A. 1.2×10^2
B. 1.2×10^{10}
C. 4.8×10^2
D. 4.8×10^{10}

18. A line has a y-intercept of -5 and goes through the point (2, 11). Which of the following is the equation of the line?

E. $y = -8x - 5$
F. $y = -5x - 11$
G. $y = 5.5x - 5$
H. $y = 8x - 5$

19. The value of $\sqrt[3]{450}$ lies between which two integers?

A. 4 and 5
B. 5 and 6
C. 6 and 7
D. 7 and 8

20.

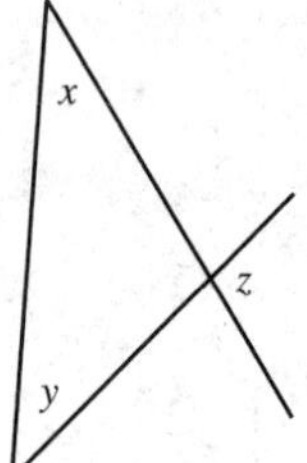

Find an expression for angle z in terms of angles x and y.

E. $z = 90° - x + y$
F. $z = 90° - (x + y)$
G. $z = 180° - (x + y)$
H. $z = 180° + x + y$

21. At what point does the function $y = -6x + 12$ cross the x-axis?

A. $(-6, 12)$
B. $(-2, 0)$
C. $(0, 0)$
D. $(2, 0)$

22. A square has a side of length $\sqrt{14}$. What is the area of the square?

E. $2\sqrt{14}$
F. $4\sqrt{14}$
G. 7
H. 14

23. Using $(x, y) \rightarrow (x + 2, y - 3)$ as the translation rule, find (r, s) if $(r, s) \rightarrow (15, 12)$.

A. (17, 12)
B. (2, −3)
C. (30, −36)
D. (13, 15)

24.

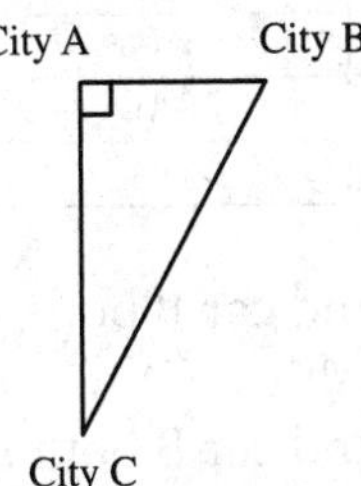

The arrangement of three cities forms a right triangle as shown in the diagram. If cities B and C are 13 mi apart and cities A and C are 12 mi apart, find the distance between city A and city B.

E. 1 mi
F. 5 mi
G. 8 mi
H. 10 mi

25. A large ice cream cone has a volume of 30 cm³. If the cone has a circular top surface with a diameter of 6 cm, what is the height of the cone?

A. 3.3 cm
B. 6 cm
C. 5 cm
D. 10 cm

26. If $a = \frac{1}{\sqrt{3}}$ and $b = \sqrt{2}$, find the value of $\frac{b^3}{a^2}$.

E. $\frac{2\sqrt{2}}{3}$
F. $\frac{8}{3}$
G. $6\sqrt{2}$
H. 24

27. A cube has a volume of 64 cm³. What is the length of one side of the cube?

A. 2 cm
B. 3 cm
C. 4 cm
D. 6 cm

28.

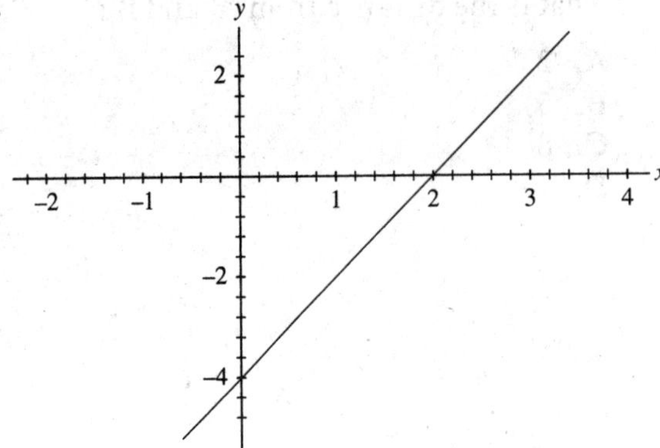

Identify the equation of the line on the graph.

E. $y = 0.5x + 2$
F. $y = -2x + -4$
G. $y = 0.5x - 4$
H. $y = 2x - 4$

29.

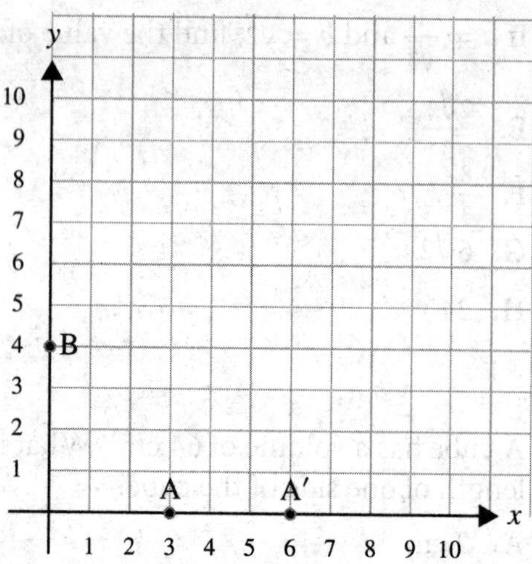

Point A experiences a dilation about the origin of the coordinate system such that dilation(A) = A′. If point B experiences the same dilation such that dilation(B) = B′, what is the distance from A′ and B′?

A. 2
B. 5
C. 8
D. 10

30. Which statement best describes the relationship between distance and time for car A and car B?

Time (s)	Distance Car A (m)	Distance Car B (m)
0	0	0
1	1	6
2	3	12
3	7	18
4	15	24
5	31	30
6	63	36

E. Car A and car B both show linear relationships.
F. Car A and car B both show nonlinear relationships.
G. Car A shows a linear relationship, and car B shows a nonlinear relationship.
H. Car A shows a nonlinear relationship, and car B shows a linear relationship.

Grade 9 Mathematics Answer Key

1. D
2. G
3. D
4. G
5. D
6. F
7. A
8. H
9. D
10. G
11. C
12. F
13. B
14. E
15. D
16. F
17. B
18. H
19. D
20. G
21. D
22. H
23. D
24. F
25. D
26. G
27. C
28. H
29. D
30. H

Explanation of Answers—Grade 9 Mathematics

1. **(D)** There are 8 triangles that are congruent to triangle ABI.

   Triangles ACH, EGI, and BDF are similar to triangle ABI. Triangle ADG is also similar to triangle ABI.

   The number of triangles that are similar to triangle ABI is $8 + 3 + 1 = 12$.

2. **(G)** Corresponding angles of similar triangles have the same measure. Since triangles RSU and TSU are similar, angles R and T have the same measure.

   Let x represent the measure of angle R and angle T. The sum of the angles of triangle RST is 180°, so $35+35+x+x=180$. Solve for x:

   $$35+35+x+x=180$$
   $$70+2x=180$$
   $$2x=110$$
   $$x=55$$

   Let y represent the measure of $\angle SUR$. The sum of the angles of triangle RSU is 180°, so $55 + 35 + y = 180$. Solve for y:

   $$55+35+y=180$$
   $$90+y=180$$
   $$y=90$$

3. **(D)** Line s forms a straight angle; therefore, the two angles given and angle y must add up to 180°. Thus:

   $$y = 180° - 40° - 65°$$
   $$y = 75°$$

   Angle z is alternate interior to angle y and thus has the same value of 75°. Angle x is supplementary to angle z; therefore:

   $$x = 180° - 75° = 105°$$

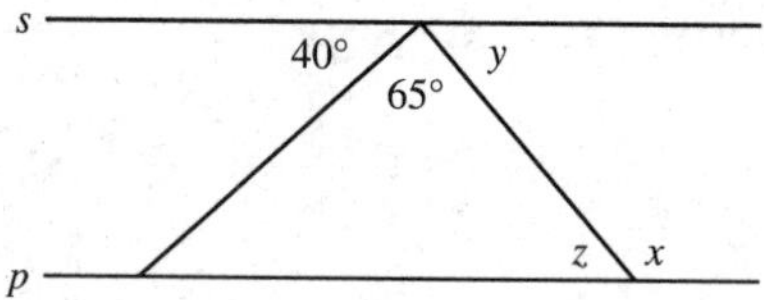

4. **(G)** $4^6 \times 2^{-6} = (2^2)^6 \times 2^{-6} = (2^{12}) \times (2)^{-6} = 2^{12-6} = 2^6$

   Therefore, since x is the value of the exponent, $x = 6$.

5. **(D)** During a translation, line m will always form the same angle with line n because there is no rotation or reflection involved.

6. **(F)** Because we have a right triangle, the Pythagorean theorem may be used to solve for the length of the unknown leg.

   $$a^2 + b^2 = c^2$$
   $$8^2 + b^2 = 10^2$$
   $$64 + b^2 = 100$$
   $$b^2 = 100 - 64$$
   $$b^2 = 36$$
   $$b = 6 \text{ m}$$

7. **(A)**

$$(25 \times 10^2) + (5 \times 10^4) = (y \times 10^3)$$
$$(2{,}500) + (50{,}000) = (y \times 10^3)$$
$$52{,}500 = (y \times 10^3)$$
$$(52.5 \times 10^3) = (y \times 10^3)$$

Thus, $y = 52.5$

8. **(H)** The water capacity of the drum will be the difference between its volume and the volume of the solid sphere:

$$\text{Water capacity} = \text{volume}_{\text{cylinder}} - \text{volume}_{\text{sphere}}$$
$$= \pi r^2 h - \frac{4}{3}\pi r^3$$
$$= \pi 3^2(9) - \frac{4}{3}\pi 3^3$$
$$= 81\pi - 36\pi$$
$$= 45\pi$$

9. **(D)** A 180° rotation about the origin will transform figure A into figure B.

10. **(G)** There are many methods for finding the point of intersection between the lines. One method is to graph both the lines to find the intersection point. Another method is to set the functions equal and solve for x:

$$2x = -x + 3$$
$$3x = 3$$
$$x = 1$$

Plugging back into the original functions gives $y = 2$. Another method is to plug the x-coordinate of each answer choice into the equations and see which one yields the same answer for y.

11. **(C)** Choices A and D are both linear relationships. Choices B and E are inverse relationships. Only choice C is a quadratic relationship like that shown on the graph.

12. **(F)** $625 = (25)(25) = (5^2)(5^2) = 5^4$. Thus, $x = 4$.

13. **(B)** 6^2 is 36 and 7^2 is 49. Thus, $\sqrt{43}$ is between 6 and 7.

14. **(E)** To qualify as rational, the number must be able to be calculated by the ratio between whole numbers. The numbers $\frac{1}{8}$ and 150 clearly satisfy this condition. $0.032 = \frac{32}{1000}$ and $\sqrt{49} = 7$ also satisfy the requirement. The square root of 17 is irrational because it cannot be expressed as the ratio of whole numbers. The square root of all prime numbers produces an irrational number.

15. **(D)** The graph shows that in 10 min the car travels from mile marker 14 to mile marker 9. Thus the car traveled 5 mi in 10 min. Since 10 min is $\frac{10}{60}$ of an hour, you can calculate the speed as follows:

$$v = \frac{d}{t} = \frac{5\text{ mi}}{10\text{ min}} = \frac{5\text{ mi}}{\frac{10}{60}\text{ h}} = 30\text{ mph}$$

16. (F) The smaller triangle is similar to the larger triangle, so the ratios between the legs are the same.

$$\frac{\text{Height of person}}{\text{Length of person's shadow}} = \frac{\text{Height of flagpole}(H)}{\text{Length of pole's shadow}}$$

$$\frac{6\text{ ft}}{8\text{ ft}} = \frac{H}{20\text{ ft}}$$

$$H(8\text{ ft}) = (6\text{ ft})(20\text{ ft})$$

$$H(8\text{ ft}) = (120\text{ ft}^2)$$

$$H = \frac{120\text{ ft}^2}{8\text{ ft}}$$

$$H = 15\text{ ft}$$

17. (B)

$$\frac{2.4\times10^6}{2.0\times10^{-4}} = \left(\frac{2.4}{2.0}\right)\left(\frac{10^6}{10^{-4}}\right) = (1.2)(10^6)(10^4)$$
$$= 1.2\times10^{10}$$

18. (H) Starting with the slope-intercept equation, substitute the y-intercept in for "b," plug in the value of x and y giving the point (2, 11), and then solve for the slope, m:

$$y = mx + b$$

$$y = mx - 5$$

$$11 = m(2) - 5$$

$$11 + 5 = m(2)$$

$$16 = m(2)$$

$$m = 8$$

Finally, substitute the slope value back into the slope-intercept equation to get:

$$y = 8x - 5$$

19. (D) To solve for $\sqrt[3]{450}$, one must solve this equation for x:

$$x = \sqrt[3]{450}$$

$$x^3 = 450$$

$$(x)(x)(x) = 450$$

Probably the simplest method to solve this without a calculator is to try a guess-and-check method. Since $7^3 = 343$ and $8^3 = 512$, the cube root of 450 must be between 7 and 8.

20. (G) The angle z' has been added to the figure. Since all angles in a triangle add up to 180°:

$$x + y + z' = 180°$$

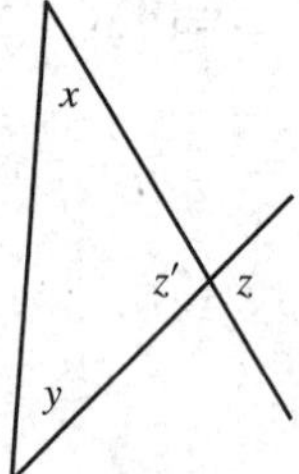

Since opposite angles of intersecting lines (vertical angles) are congruent, then angle z' marked on the figure is equal to z:

$$x + y + z = 180°$$

Solving for z gives:

$$z = 180° - (x + y)$$

21. (D) A function crosses the x-axis at points on the function where $y = 0$.

$$y = -6x + 12$$
$$0 = -6x + 12$$
$$6x = 12$$
$$x = \frac{12}{6} = 2$$
$$(x, y) = (2, 0)$$

22. (H) A square has four equal sides with length given as $\sqrt{14}$. The area of a square, just like the area of any rectangle, is length times width. Thus, the area is $(\sqrt{14})(\sqrt{14}) = 14$.

23. (D) Given $(x, y) \rightarrow (x + 2, y - 3)$ as the translation rule, one can write the rule in terms of (r, s) as follows:

$$(r, s) \rightarrow (r + 2, s - 3)$$

Since $(r, s) \rightarrow (15, 12)$, one can solve for the variables as follows:

$$r + 2 = 15$$
$$r = 13$$
$$s - 3 = 12$$
$$s = 15$$

Thus point $(r, s) = (13, 15)$.

24. (F) The distances between the cities form a right triangle and are constrained by the Pythagorean theorem:

$$a^2 + b^2 = c^2$$
$$12^2 + b^2 = 13^2$$
$$b^2 = 13^2 - 12^2$$
$$b^2 = 25$$
$$b = 5$$

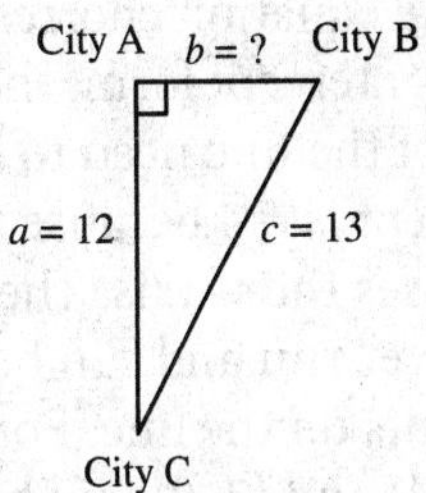

25. (D) The volume of a cone is:

$$\text{Volume} = \frac{1}{3}\pi r^2 h$$

The volume is given as 30π cm³. Since the radius is half the diameter, the radius is 3 cm. Plug these values in and solve for h:

$$30\pi = \frac{1}{3}\pi 3^2 h$$
$$30\pi = 3\pi h$$
$$h = (30\pi)/(3\pi)$$
$$h = 10 \text{ cm}$$

26. (G) Substitute the values for a and b into the equation and simplify as follows:

$$\frac{b^3}{a^2} = \frac{\left(\sqrt{2}\right)^3}{\left(\frac{1}{\sqrt{3}}\right)^2} = \frac{\sqrt{2}\sqrt{2}\sqrt{2}}{\left(\frac{1}{\sqrt{3}}\right)\left(\frac{1}{\sqrt{3}}\right)} = \frac{2\sqrt{2}}{\left(\frac{1}{3}\right)} = \left(2\sqrt{2}\right)\left(\frac{3}{1}\right) = 6\sqrt{2}$$

27. **(C)** A cube is a rectangular prism with equal width, length, and height. The volume is the product of the three equal sides, s:

$$\text{Volume} = s^3$$
$$64 = s^3$$
$$s = \sqrt[3]{64}$$
$$s = 4 \text{ cm}$$

28. **(H)** Since the equation choices are written in the slope-intercept form, the slope and the y-intercept of the line need to be found. The y-intercept is -4 because this is where the line crosses the y-axis. The slope of the line is rise over run and can be found using any two points on the line. For convenience, points $(0, -4)$ and $(2, 0)$ will be used:

$$\text{Slope} = \frac{y_2 - y_1}{x_2 - x_1} = \frac{0-(-4)}{2-0} = 2$$
$$y = mx + b$$
$$y = 2x - 4$$

29. **(D)** In the dilation about the origin, point A moves from (3, 0) to (6, 0). This corresponds to a dilation about the origin with scale factor $r = 2$. Applying this same scale factor to point B at (0, 4), the coordinates of B′ are (0, 8) as show in the figure. To find the distance from A′ to B′, apply the Pythagorean theorem as follows:

$$a^2 + b^2 = c^2$$
$$6^2 + 8^2 = c^2$$
$$c^2 = 100$$
$$c = 10$$

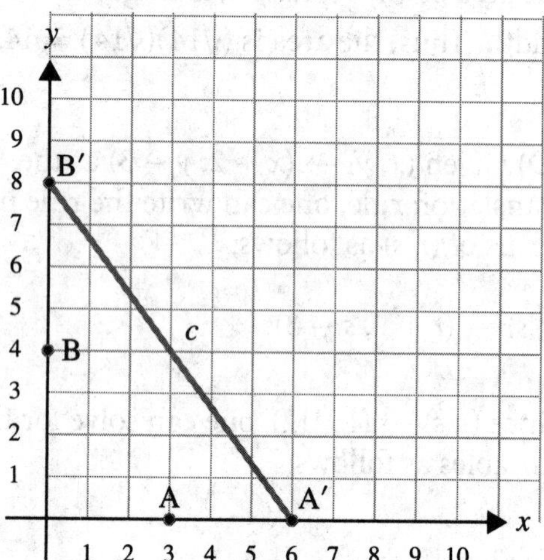

30. **(H)** Car B's distance increases linearly with time because in the 1st second it moves 6 m, in the 2nd second it moves 6 m, in the 3rd second it moves 6 m, etc. Car A's distance does *not* increase linearly with time because in the 1st second it moves 1 m, in the 2nd second it moves 2 m, in the 3rd second it moves 3 m. Thus Car A shows a nonlinear relationship, and Car B shows a linear relationship.

Notes

Notes

Notes

Notes

Notes

Notes